D1615718

The Socialness of Things

Approaches to Semiotics
115

Mouton de Gruyter
Berlin · New York

The Socialness of Things

Essays on the Socio-Semiotics of Objects

Edited by
Stephen Harold Riggins

Mouton de Gruyter
Berlin · New York 1994

Mouton de Gruyter (formerly Mouton, The Hague)
is a Division of Walter de Gruyter & Co., Berlin.

♾ Printed on acid-free paper which falls within the guidelines of the
ANSI to ensure permanence and durability.

Library of Congress Cataloging-in-Publication Data

The socialness of things : essays on the socio-semiotics of objects /
    edited by Stephen Harold Riggins.
            p.   cm. — (Approaches to semiotics ; 115)
    Includes bibliographical references and index.
    ISBN 3-11-014133-7 (cloth : acid-free paper) :
    1. Material culture. 2. Culture — Semiotic models. 3. Symbolic
interactionism. I. Riggins, Stephen Harold. II. Series.
GN406.S63 1994
306 — dc20   94-11988
                                                         CIP

Die Deutsche Bibliothek — Cataloging-in-Publication Data

The **socialness of things** : essays on the socio-semiotics of objects / ed.
by Stephen Harold Riggins. — Berlin ; New York : Mouton de
Gruyter, 1994
    (Approaches to semiotics ; 115)
    ISBN 3-11-014133-7
NE: Riggins, Stephen Harold [Hrsg.]; GT

Disk conversion and printing: Arthur Collignon GmbH, Berlin.
Binding: Lüderitz & Bauer GmbH, Berlin.
Printed in Germany.

Dedicated to

Paul Bouissac

who saw the theoretical potential
of the socialness of things

Contents

Introduction

Stephen Harold Riggins

The term "socialness" is a neologism that is used in this volume to call attention to the integration of objects in the social fabric of everyday life. Specialists in material culture studies have understood for some time — unlike many sociologists — that societies consist of both people and artifacts. It is not only with people and animals that we interact but also with objects. Objects are a cause, a medium, and a consequence of social relationships. Truly the only context in which artifacts can be observed is in their relation to humans. We practically always perceive other people in situations in which they interact with objects and are surrounded by them. Even during our most socially isolated experiences we are never alone in that sense. Hence the quality of socialness which is legitimately imputed to things by the contributors to this volume.

Recent research in material culture studies (Appadurai 1986; Bronner 1986; Csikszentmihalyi — Rochberg-Halton 1981; Douglas — Isherwood 1979; Hodder 1989; McCracken 1988; Miller 1987; Pocius 1991; Riggins 1990a; Schlereth 1982; Stocking 1985) tends to contradict two of the basic assumptions about objects that characterize commonsense thought in North America. First, in commonsense thought objects are generally conceptualized in opposition to people, a perception which imputes a strong semantic contrast to the differences between things and organisms, matter and life. From this perspective people are assumed to be active agents who determine the physical configurations and meanings of objects; objects are apparently nothing but the passive embodiment of human intentions. It is characteristic of this rigid distinction between matter and life that the term "objectivity" is used to represent knowledge endowed with unquestionable and universal validity irrespective of an observer, while the term "subjectivity" is used to represent attitudes or judgments characterized by changeability, relativity, and unreliability. Material stability thus seems to guarantee a certain invariability to artifacts while social structures are seen as being in constant flux. The second feature of commonsense knowledge about artifacts is the relative insensitivity to the complexities of deciphering the rich symbolic meanings inherent in or imposed upon objects. Consequently, interpreted meanings appear to be relatively simple and straightforward, essentially timeless, and largely identical for any observer within the same culture.

In material culture studies the consideration of objects as features of social transactions has resulted in a conceptualization of artifacts as agencies or quasi-agencies. Thus, the vocabulary which would normally be reserved for humans is applied to objects. Researchers are writing about the "cultural biography" of artifacts (Kopytoff 1986), artifacts as "agents of socialization" (Csikszentmihalyi — Rochberg-Halton 1981: 50 – 52), "socially entangled objects" (Thomas 1991), and about the way people "interact intellectually" with objects (Prown 1991: 148). Consistent with this perspective, the first collection of articles in this volume has been titled the "dialogic object." One might speak of people being in dialogue with objects in the sense that it is difficult to construct one's self, and to present that self to others, in the absence of objects which symbolize achieved and desired statuses. Artifacts are consequently powerful in their own right and not just in the sense of physically constraining human action. Through objects we keep alive the collective memory of societies and families which would otherwise be forgotten.

This blurring of the human-object boundary is most obvious, on the one hand, in the concept of fetish and, on the other hand, in the literature about the way people are treated as if they were things. A fetish is an object endowed with exceptional power, a level of social influence greater than that possessed by ordinary people. In assuming that spiritual forces animate objects, the concept of fetish humanizes artifacts and negates the traditional notion of people as controllers of objects (Ellen 1988; 1990). The concept of fetish has been derived from the study of West African religions, but is seen as a characteristic of both traditional and modern societies, although not necessarily expressed in the same manner. One sees in the chapter by Danet and Katriel in this volume the extent to which goods take on fetishistic aspects for collectors who daydream about objects, talk to them, and exert exorbitant amounts of energy towards maintaining objects that may be as humble as used beer cans. Research in material culture studies which makes little or no explicit use of the concept of fetish nonetheless imputes a high degree of power to artifacts in defining social situations and in constraining social interaction (Gagliardi 1990; Vastokas, this volume). Conversely, Erving Goffman, among others, has written about the vulnerability of "non-persons," as he referred to people determined by powerful social structures, and compares their inconsiderate treatment to that accorded objects. In mental asylums "there is always a danger that an inmate will appear human," according to Goffman (1961: 81).

Just as language is polysemic, open to multiple interpretations, so are material artifacts. This reversal of commonsense is due to a thorough consideration of the complexities of the mental process through which artifacts are interpreted. Meanings read into artifacts are now thought to derive from at least four sources of information, only one of which is an artifacts's actual physical characteristics. The other three include: the information conveyed by objects (and space) which surround an artifact; the observer's life-long experience with similar types of artifacts, few of which will be present in a given situation; and texts about artifacts (museum labels, advertisements, newspaper articles, etc.). Objects are "intertextual" in the sense that the meanings imputed to them are influenced by printed and broadcast statements (Hebdige 1988: 80-84). They are caught in a semiotic web with which they become consubstantial. These features of the interpretative process vastly expand — chronologically and synchronically — the range of potential meanings which can be read into artifacts. Imputed meanings may be as varied as the social positions of observers because this gives them different kinds of personal experience with objects and with texts about objects. Daniel Miller (1987: 108) thus refers to the "extreme visibility and invisibility" of objects. The materiality of objects gives the false impression of rendering their meanings more visible than those of linguistic statements. In fact, there may be no difference in the level of polysemy between language and artifacts or one might claim that language functions to limit potential interpretations (and consequently social confusion) more effectively than do the physical characteristics of objects.

This book is based on the proceedings of an international conference which took place at the University of Toronto in 1990[1]. It comprises a selection of revised papers chosen in view of their diversity with respect to methodology and domains of application. The chapters in the first part of the volume deal with artifacts such as furniture, mementoes, and knickknacks, which can be manipulated as social "others" — acquired or adopted, desired or mourned — entities with which one can socialize or make a part in socialization processes such as establishing a bond, conveying a message, etc. The second section of articles concerns artifacts whose dimensions take such proportions that humans become dwarfed with respect to them, such as tourists travelling to visit them or shoppers being herded through their artifactual geography as though flowing within an oversized organism. In the concluding section, the artifacts examined are by contrast so adjusted to the proportion of the human body, so close to it that they become an indissociable part of the social persona sticking to the skin, expressing better than any other means the socialness of people, their class, ethnicity, gender, age status, etc. and even betraying the secrets of the psyche that psychoanalysts tackle. The three parts of the book form a dialogic relationship in an almost dramaturgical sense.

Confronted with the richness and complexity of human-object interaction, it could be expected that all of the contributors would attempt to identify a methodology which is best adopted to their object of study. Not unexpectedly there is a certain unavoidable methodological eclecticism which characterizes this book as a whole. For instance, some authors look to linguistics for inspiration; others see linguistics as simply a distraction. Some authors extol a focus on the object itself; others prefer to give an equal amount of attention to texts. Some authors hypothesize an intimate link between self and objects; others, believing that artifactual messages are evocative and elusive, hypothesize no close link with the self.

The socio-semiotics of objects which has been slowly emerging since the 1980s from anthropology and material culture studies is still in a developing stage. Some academic specialties that in theory are highly relevant to an understanding of the social information of artifacts, most obviously the sociological perspectives known as symbolic interactionism (Blumer 1969) and dramaturgical analysis (Brissett — Edgley 1990), have yet to make an impact (however, see, Davis 1992). Thus, the purpose of this book is to adumbrate the mapping of this immense field of research, surveying its main territories, and trying methods of analysis as they seem fit.

Note

1. Several papers in this volume were first presented at the conference "The Socio-semiotics of Objects: The Role of Artifacts in Social Symbolic Processes." Grateful acknowledgement is made to the Social Sciences and Humanities Research Council of Canada (Program of Aid to Occasional Scholarly Conferences in Canada, Program 443, Grant no. 443-90-0069) for its financial support for this conference.

References

Appadurai, Arjun (ed.)
   1986   *The social life of things: Commodities in cultural perspective.* Cambridge: Cambridge University Press.
Blumer, Herbert
   1969   *Symbolic interactionism: Perspective and method.* Englewood Cliffs, NJ: Prentice-Hall.
Brissett, Dennis — Charles Edgley (eds.)
   1990   *Life as theater: A dramaturgical source book.* New York: Aldine de Gruyter.
Bronner, Simon J.
   1986   *Grasping things: Folk material culture and mass society in America.* Lexington: University Press of Kentucky.
Csikszentmihalyi, Mihaly — Eugene Rochberg-Halton
   1981   *The meaning of things: Domestic symbols and the self.* Cambridge: Cambridge University Press.
Davis, Fred
   1992   *Fashion, culture, and identity.* Chicago: University of Chicago Press.
Douglas, Mary — Baron Isherwood
   1979   *The world of goods.* New York: Basic Books.
Ellen, Roy
   1988   "Fetishism," *Man* 23: 213—235.
   1990   "Nuaulu sacred shields: The reproduction of things or the reproduction of images?," *Etnofoor* III: 5—25.
Gagliardi, Pasquale (ed.)
   1990   *Symbols and artifacts: Views of the corporate landscape.* New York: Aldine de Gruyter.
Goffman, Erving
   1961   *Asylums: Essays on the social situation of mental patients and other inmates.* New York: Doubleday.
Hebdige, Dick
   1988   *Hiding in the light.* London: Routledge.
Hodder, Ian (ed.)
   1989   *The meanings of things: Material culture and symbolic expression.* London: Unwin Hyman.
Kopytoff, Igor
   1986   "The cultural biography of things: Commoditization as process," in: Arjun Appadurai (ed.), 64—91.
McCracken, Grant
   1988   *Culture and consumption: New approaches to the symbolic character of consumer goods and activities.* Bloomington: Indiana University Press.

Miller, Daniel
1987   *Material culture and mass consumption.* Oxford: Basil Blackwell.
Pocius, Gerald L. (ed.)
1991   *Living in a material world: Canadian and American approaches to material culture.* St. John's, Newfoundland: Institute of Social and Economic Research.
Prown, Jules David
1991   "On the 'art' in artifacts," in: Gerald Pocius, (ed.), 144 – 155.
Riggins, Stephen Harold
1985   "The semiotics of things: Towards a sociology of human-object interaction," *Recherches Sémiotiques/Semiotic Inquiry* 5: 69 – 77.
1990a   "The power of things: The role of domestic objects in the presentation of self," in: Stephen Harold Riggins (ed.), 341 – 367.
1993   "Life as a metaphor: Current issues in dramaturgical analysis," *Semiotica* 93(3/4): 229 – 239.
Riggins, Stephen Harold (ed.)
1990b   *Beyond Goffman: Studies on communication, institution, and social interaction.* Berlin: Mouton de Gruyter.
Schlereth, Thomas J. (ed.)
1982   *Material culture studies in America: An anthology.* Nashville, TN: American Association for State and Local History.
Stocking, George
1985   *Objects and others: Essays on museums and material culture.* Madison: University of Wisconsin Press.
Thomas, Nicholas
1991   *Entangled objects: Exchange, material culture, and colonialism in the Pacific.* Cambridge, MA: Harvard.

Part I
The dialogic object: Artifacts as agents and processes

The genuine article

Mary Douglas

Introduction

Roland Barthes once suggested that there should be a science of grades. The context was his discussion of Anthelme Brillat-Savarin and the question was whether metal or wooden coffee mills were better, and whether wood was the more noble material (Barthes 1984: 290 – 291).[1] He was calling for more attention to the grading of objects in everyday life. Standardized grading is associated with centralization and expanding political and market networks across ancient boundaries. More universalistic measures of space and time are achieved in every decade. Whereas an inch was the length of a thumb, and a yard the length of an arm, the foot of a foot, a metric system detached from the human body has superseded most local systems of measurement. Time used to be measured by the movements of shadows recording the place of the sun in the sky. Cooking instructions used to measure time by the length of prayers, telling the cook to stir for the length of two *aves* or to boil for the length of time it takes to recite the *pater noster* five times. But now, industrialism and the factory system have given us clocks. Europe is looking for a single monetary system. All these shifts to universal measures give us new vocabulary, and though one may have a folklorist's regret for the hourglass and the sun dial, there are now possibilities of co-ordination one would not wish to be without. By implication, Barthes was suggesting that to deepen our understanding of types and grades of objects we need to go beyond anecdote and description and to supersede local provincial vocabularies. In being gathered here we are taking up his challenge to think about the semiotics of objects.

Context

As the first speaker, I have the privilege of being the first to ask the obvious questions. For example, some of the time we are going to be setting objects back into context, and some of the time taking them out of context for theoretical purposes. But what puzzles me is how are we to know what is object and what is context? For example, does the teapot provide the context of a teapot lid? Should we treat the set of silver teapot and milk jug as one object? If so, are the tray and the sugar bowl context or object? How does one define an automobile? Is it a wheeled vehicle? In which case, are the wheels an intrinsic part of the object? Or are they four parts related by complementarity in use to the chassis? The antiques auctioneer would say that a teapot and its lid are one object, since he cannot sell one without the other. But a friend of mine who lives in a dangerous district of London used to park his car in the road outside his house. Naturally the car was insured against theft. One day, to his consternation, he came out and found the car there, but all four wheels removed. He checked his insurance which covered theft of the car but not accessories and, since there is no way that the wheels can be thought of as accessories on a par with the radio and cigarette lighter, he put in his claim. It was rejected. The reply from the insurance company directed his attention to the small print which said that accessories are movable parts, and since his wheels had been moved, there was no arguing with them. So on this accounting the wheels are one kind of object, and the car has to be the context of the wheels. I cannot help wondering what the insurance company would have said if the wheels had been left in the road, and the car removed. The moral is that the idea of context is adapted to the needs of the inquiry and we will need to make our own technical decisions about how we use the idea of context for the semiotics of objects.

The question is far from trivial. We do not want to impose arbitrary classifications upon the streams of objects that flow around us. All the problems that we can have with metaphor (Davidson 1979) raise their heads in new guise when we identify objects. We do not escape from the predicaments that language prepares for us by turning away from the semiotics of words to the semiotics of objects. It would be illusory to hope that objects present us with a more solid, unambiguous world. There is no end to finding metaphors and there is no end to finding objects. The problem is how to control our imagination, how not to be arbitrary in the connections we make. Or to put it another way, how to secure our categories by theoretical schemes that work. In given contexts some protection against arbitrariness may be sought in human usage, but not very much, for the social usages change. For example, I am glad to notice that Arum Lilies have come into fashion as garden plants. As a child, I once asked my father why he did not grow Arum Lilies in our garden. He replied that they were so closely associated with the graveyard and death and mourning that they were unsuitable for gardens. Something has changed. How to explain it? A semiotician from Mars might conclude that our culture has narrowed the distance between life and death, and that we have reached a kind of civilization which does not mind about dying. Discarding this suggestion at once, we could ask if it is due to our tendency to send cheques for charity instead of wreaths or to our tendency not to attend funerals as assiduously as our parents did? If lilies and roses are no longer linked as opposites in a contrast set of dying and living, the explanation has to be traced back to the system of formal presentations between persons at lifecycle events. Some events have become more prominent since the eighteenth century, such as weddings which were casual, family occasions if novelists are to be relied on. Other events have receded into the background, such as deaths of very old persons who have not been credited with enough personality to warrant attendance at their funeral. In a small community everybody's and anybody's death might have been significant; in our present culture the significance depends on whose death. The context for the meanings of the flowers is the context of persons. Reflection on objects leads us back to persons.

The fact is that there are many objects which we never see in context. I once stayed in an elegant apartment in Toronto filled with exquisite objects each of which created a context for the others, and which filled me with delight. One morning, wanting a change from Twinings' tea bags, and perhaps wanting my life to be a little more in tune with the furnishings, I raided my hostess's tea caddy and helped myself to her China tea. When I emptied the pot after breakfast I found a whole tea leaf in the sink. Whole leaves! Macrobiotic tea! In London the tea comes chopped or even minced into fine dust which we call "tea leaves." Never having beheld an unmutilated tea leaf I was unexpectedly moved to find in my hand a sample of the original context of the tea dust. I mention these incidents out of respect for our subject. As we shall see, there are reasons why the topic calls forth humor, irony and pathos.

Autographic/allographic

The concept of the genuine article has the advantage that a major philosopher has paid attention to it. According to Nelson Goodman, one would not ask "is this the genuine, authentic thing?," if you knew and could be sure of its history. You would start to ask that question if it turned out that some part of the history of the object were missing. If you are asking such questions, it will be about a kind of object whose identity is anchored only by its history. Is it authentic? The answer has to provide the missing information, and to dispel doubt by giving evidence. The question calls for a unique history, continuously vouched for. There is another kind of object which may pose the question of authenticity, but requires a quite different answer. Confronted by the police and charged with speeding, you may doubt that they are testing your state of sobriety with the right apparatus. So you might be rash enough to ask, "is this a genuine breathalyser? It looks like a vacuum cleaner to me." In this case the authenticity of the instrument does not require uniqueness, nor guaranteed continuity from the time it issued from its maker's hands. The answer can rely entirely on stylistic and material criteria. If you want information about the origin and history of objects of this kind, you can get it from the design, the kind of materials, and also from the signs of manufacturing methods. Nelson Goodman uses the word "autographic" for production whose value depends on historical continuity. The idea of possible forgery applies to autographic objects such as paintings and sculptures, because the idea of authenticity is somehow central to their value. Goodman uses "allographic" for the object whose value does not depend on its historic uniqueness. It will be better to give his own example which compares paintings with photographs:

> Paintings belong to what I may call a *singular* symbol system. Each painting is unique; in the technical sense of replica, there are no replicas of pictures as there are of words... A photograph on the other hand is not unique. Photographic picturing is a multiple symbol system. The relation among several prints from a negative is to some extent comparable to the relation among several replicas of a word; but the two relations are not the same. In the first case, we have an autographic and in the second an allographic symbol system. That is, the relation among the prints consists in their having been produced from the same negative while the relation among the inscriptions consists in their being spelled the same way... (Goodman 1978: 48).

This example is a coda to his much fuller discussion of fakes and legitimate replicas in *Languages of Art* (Goodman 1976). Considering how much value is attached to the fact of some kinds of objects (paintings) being unique and so little to the uniqueness of other kinds of objects, he clearly has an important distinction. And a puzzle:

> ... we may be faced with the protest that the vast aesthetic difference thought to obtain between the Rembrandt and the forgery cannot be accounted for in terms of the search for, or even the discovery of, perceptual differences so slight that they can be made out, if at all, only after much experience and long practice (Goodman 1976: 108).

This objection, he says, can be dismissed at once, because "the slightest perceptual differences sometimes matter the most aesthetically; gross physical damage to a fresco may be less consequential than slight but smug retouching" (Goodman 1976: 108). He claims that, by contrast with painting, in music there is no such thing as a forgery of a known work. In the world of music the idea of the genuine object is quite different. Music produces objects whose authenticity is of another kind:

> Hayden's manuscript is no more genuine an instance of the score than is a printed copy off the press this morning, and last night's performance no less genuine than the premiere. Copies of the score may vary in accuracy, but all accurate copies, even if forgeries of Hayden's manuscript, are equally genuine instances of the score. Performances may vary in correctness and quality and even in "authenticity" of a more esoteric kind; but all correct performances are equally genuine instances of the work. In contrast, even the most exact copies of the Rembrandt painting are simply imitations or forgeries, not new instances of the work. Why this difference between the two arts? (Goodman 1976: 112−113).

Here he introduces his distinction between allographic and autographic, and uses it to develop his full aesthetic theory. I hope it does not do too much violence to the theory to say that some art is produced for reproduction, as music, which makes notation systems important. Other art not being produced for replication can display the subtle and complex symptoms of the aesthetic which defy notationality. Sometimes the method of production of the object is susceptible to notationality (in which case it is more apt for allographic production); sometimes it is not (in which case there is a presumption in favor of autographic recognition if only because a dispute about the authenticity cannot be settled by reference to something like a score or other notation system). Beyond recognizing an aptness for notationality, the anthropologist would be doubtful that there is anything intrinsic in the nature of painting or music that swings it to one or other of the two kinds. We can think of contrary instances, such as peoples among whom the unique history of a painting is not treated in the same way as among ourselves, or among whom the option of identifying a piece of music by the score is not available, or where no one but the composer has a right to utter his own composition and could be expected to challenge a player who used it to a duel. Though we can recognize the two categories of object, something more like a collective decision about the kind of prestige and the amount of originality allowed to the various stages of production assigns art forms in these cases to the class of allographic or of autographic objects. I have tried to explain the distinction because in what follows I will pay attention to another aspect of it.

Allographic production can be anonymous, or at least the credit can go to a group of people, not to one person and the actual assigning of origins may not be important in evaluating it. Whether there is a score or not, something about the organization of our music world and the arrangements for paying royalties to the composer and fees to the musicians make it more important to know who composed the music than who performed it at all stages of its history. This is even more true for the organization of the world of painting and sculpture. The makers of canvas stretchers and the paint manufacturers and the other industries which service the painters get hardly any recognition beyond the discriminating choice of professionals who buy their products. On the other hand, Stradivarius is a great name in the making of violins: the violin itself is very much an autographic object. Are we to assume that because of the nature of painting there is nothing equivalent to a violin signed by a master instrument maker in the world of painting? Is the autographic possibility determined by the art form, or by the intentions of the artists and their public to elevate some parts of the process to a special distinction? We can go further by noting that the authentic signature on the violin carries authority. The readiness of the public to confer authority has to be considered. In short, we can recognize two different classes of objects, and also recognize that their difference rests on decision taking in the community of users about the distribution of prestige and reward. Sometimes the community wants authenticity, sometimes it wants inspiration.

Israel Scheffler (1986) has worked out an application of the distinction to religious ritual. He assimilates to Goodman's terms the distinction that separates efficacious ritual from simple ceremonial. In Catholic doctrine if the officiant is a priest in valid orders, his act and words transform bread and wine into the saving body and blood of Christ; their efficacy depends on the history of his ordination, and the unbroken continuity of the bishops conferring priesthood on him. That is an autographic ritual and there is much to be said about its implications for authority and control. The same applies to rival practioners in healing cults: in some cults, every one and anyone can get up and lay on hands and it might work if there is enough faith; in others the gift of healing has to be vouched for and the laying on of hands will not work unless they are the authentic hands of an accredited healer whose initiation or unique vision are part of the autograph. Control is at issue in both cases. Likewise, objects which have autographic quality are the locus of stronger claims on the part of their owners than allographic objects.

Genuine antiques

In our days the idea of the genuine and the fraudulent article belong in the context of the auction room. So the idea of the genuine article comes into our common speech with some irony. Entering a modern house and penetrating to the bathroom, we notice that the plumbing seems not to have changed since it was first installed. Admiring the huge porcelain bath with the clawed feet each grasping a ball, and hearing the rattling croak as the taps are turned on, we may exclaim: "Ah! Here is the genuine article!" But unless we are in the antiques business we are not likely to bother to look for the signature of the maker. The idea of its being a fake does not apply. If the host explained that he had commissioned it in exact replica of the bathroom in Buckingham Palace, that would neither add to nor take away its value in our eyes. The issue of forgery is irrelevant.

Two things sever an object decisively from its context, one is being thrown on the rubbish heap, and the other, turning up on the auctioneer's table. When he holds a genuine something or other, the auctioneer tries to give it a context by recalling bits of its pedigree: "This is a bronze casting of Princess Alexandria's foot when she was one year old. It was made by ... it weights ... and was given as a present to Queen Victoria ... and inherited on her death by... It remained in the X family until last year..." And he contrives to make a joke or two. To hear his artificial contextualizing of a sentimental object that has been so thoroughly decontextualized is a sad business. The saleroom has a voyeurist titillation. The antique shop is like a cocktail party in which no one knows anyone else except the host — and he does not even like them very much — an alienating, anonymizing evening for all. There is something faintly indecent about rummaging in the detritus of other people's lives. There is more to boast of in having inherited or having been given an ancient object of autographic value than to have paid cash for it. This is not just because inheritance implies the legitimacy of ancient lineage, or because the valuable gift implies good friends. It is because you have not only got the thing, but you are its context. On seeing what looks like a genuine pot of blue woad among the knickknacks in a friend's house, you, being a connoisseur of Celtic antiquities, might say: "Hullo! This looks like a pot of blue woad! How did you get it?" If your friend explains that he dug it up in his garden or bought it for a song in the flea market, or paid a crazy price at Sotheby's, there is always the missing context, which no money can buy. But if he says that his maternal great-grandfather was descended from a long line of druids, and that it has been in his family every since, that his aunt used it for potpourri, the known pedigree supplies the continuous context. Of course it is still decontextualized, even if it were kept among other cosmetic jars in the bathroom. But its guaranteed history rescues it from the anonymous miscellany of the antique shop. The guaranteed continuous history turns it into an auto-graphic product.

The contrast between allographic and autographic does not quite coincide with the well-known line between market commodities and other kinds of objects. That in itself makes it interesting. Objects which are not produced for sale are not necessarily allographic nor does being auto-graphic mean that the object is not for sale. The guaranteed authentic painting can certainly be sold. But the distinction between gift and commodity comes under the same umbrella. The direction to which this distinction leads us is not to different kinds of objects, but to different kinds of relations between persons. For the essential distinction between allographic and autographic even applies to people as well as to objects. For example, in the days of domestic service, a hostess might be asked: "How did you get that wonderful cook?" She might say that she bought her services for a huge price, or for a song. Either way the cook would be without a context and likely to be cast as a sinister, unaccounted figure in an Agatha Christie mystery. It would have been better to be able to say that she cooked for Mrs. Jones for twenty years and was looking for a job when Mrs. Jones died. Or even better if she is an aunt and has always lived here, then she and her services are uniquely autographed, and every thing that she does is by way of gift exchange.

Distance

Talking about objects will inevitably lead us to prize them out of their context. We will try to recontextualize them, like the auctioneer. We will find ourselves trying to annul the pervasive "rubbish effect" (Thompson 1978) which lingers around an object which has been in low esteem, relegated to the attic, and now refurbished for a new context, the Chippendale sofa on the wall-to-wall carpet, the Limoges chamber pot displaying an elaborate flower arrangement. Making a new kind of curiosity shop, we will surely engage pathos and humor to meet the occasion. But to neutralize the rubbish effect we need to do more than identify the contexts of the objects and describe the meanings they have in those contexts, though that is very necessary. The problem is to get theoretical distance.

To neutralize the rubbish effect there are several remedies: (a) We do not want to lose the association of objects with their contexts, yet we do not want context to suffocate us. We can get theoretical distance by a typification of contexts. (b) The other remedy is to accept the full challenge of semiotics. That means disengaging our talk from the authority of linguistics which too much dominates the analysis of the meaning of objects. (c) A third solution would be to take seriously the editor's idea that objects and persons have to be studied together.

You may well ask how the allographic/autographic distinction is going to help. The examples I have given sound trivial. I suggest that it will help a lot in several ways. For one, it has already made a new theoretical distinction among contexts of objects. The autographic object cannot be separated entirely from people as can the other kind. A gift is always a gift from someone. A signed painting is always a painting by someone. For another, it will make a contribution to the theory of gift which has become fashionable. If you know that philanthropy has deservedly and at last become an academic subject of study, you may also know that the theory of gift has run out of ideas since Marcel Mauss (1954 [1922–24]). And above all, this approach will free the discussion of objects from the heavy hand of linguistics by providing another vocabulary for talking about meaning without invoking the relation between sign and signified.

Suppose we stop looking at individual objects. See them instead as participating in a long stream of events that unfold through time; chart their flow; then consider persons only as the points where flows of objects originate, congregate and from which they disperse. This long view takes both producers, distributors and recipient-users into account at once. Now think of a society in which all the objects produced are autographic, every one. A good example is David McKnight's (1973) description of the kinship system of the Wik-Mungkan tribe in Australia. Any kinship role is defined by obligations to give to various relations, and even more strictly defined by obligatory gifts are the relations of alliance by marriage. A father-in-law is a person who received from his son-in-law certain big fishes, so if the catch includes one, the man knows at once that it belongs to his father-in-law. The latter is a collection point, a resting place for the flow of these fishes through the community. All the other fishes in the catch are earmarked for specific relatives. The same for the hunter who kills a wallaby or cockatoo. All his products are destined to mark out the lines of his relationships. Ideally there are no free-floating objects in this system, which incidentally implies that here there is no such thing as a free gift in that system either.

The Wik-Mungkan system of distribution puts every object into the category of public goods which cannot be distrained for private or market purposes like London parks (Douglas 1989). It is not quite the socialist ideal of measuring out to everyone according to his needs, but it gives to all according to their role. In its practical effect the system provides a strong buffer of structure to protect against the jealousy which is apt to tear small groups apart. And these reflections would serve to remind sociologists that small communities that seem to run entirely on public spirited solidarity usually survive by implementing a lot of structure: contrary to the view of German and Chicago sociologists, *Gemeinschaft* is not just a warm, cosy feeling. Furthermore, the comparison on these lines would draw our attention to the person in the gift system who is not an assembly point for gift objects. For example, streams of flowers and hothouse grapes flow toward persons in the sick role; for some they pile up and create a nuisance at night when they have to be removed from the sick room; but not all sick persons draw these streams to themselves. The flow of gift objects is a marker for tracing marginality and centrality. Anthropologists routinely make this tracing in their studies (e.g., Marriott 1976), with important results, but the method also has much to tell us about our use of objects in modern industrial society.

You can turn the picture round and say that the roles of kin and affines are assembly points for all the objects that are produced. Because each object has a unique point of origin in the social system, it is autographic in Goodman's terms. Yet, the analogy does not quite work. Each object is doubly autographic since it has a unique destiny as well as a unique point of provenance. In this example there is no contrast with other objects which are allographic, and because the objects are classed as obvious natural kinds, there is no real question of fake or forgery: the fish is the fish, every one can recognize it. Suppose on the way home the successful fisherman was waylaid by another whose big fish got away, and who robbed the first so as to present the fish to his own grandfather. That would be a case of the wrong kind of grandfather, not the wrong kind of object. In extending Goodman's idea to things perhaps very remote from his original concerns we notice that autographic in his sense only means being able to go back to the point of origin. It is a backward link of the object to its maker. A gift also has forward linkage, tracing the object to its point of destination. I have found it very illuminating to think about objects in this way, as streams issuing forth from known points, and arriving at expected points of assembly. In *The World of Goods* (Douglas 1980) I adopted the terminology of Albert Hirschman's (1958) analysis of international trade. He analyzed the forward and backward linkages of occupational sectors in the economy so as to get a measure of economic integration. I borrowed the idea to suggest using the flow of objects as a measure of social integration.

Signifying and exemplifying

Semiotics, trying to transcend its linguistic heritage, could do well to tidy up the language of signification. When anthropologists study a system of objects flowing to various collection points, we learn to read off from the movements of the objects who is who and what day it is and other information. We can rightly say that the flows of objects signify the pattern of roles. But if we want to take a further step back we can adopt another argument of Nelson Goodman's. Seeing objects as representing or standing for something else has an obscuring effect. The objects do end up denoting relationships, but it is instructive to notice how they first exemplify relationships. To be a father-in-law or grandfather or aunt in the Wik-Mungkan system of prescribed transfers is to *be* a recipient of the fishes and cockatoos, etc. Giving the objects *makes* the role; receiving the objects and redistributing them *is* to perform in the role; to fail to give them is likely to *end* the role. The streams of objects exemplify what it is to be that sort of person. They do not first signify the role, they are examples of what the role is. They are also functional for the role, since father-in-law and grandfather and aunt will also be roles defined by required redistributing of what has arrived at their doorstep. To be given a meal does not signify hospitality, it is actually, truly a sample of the hospitality (Douglas 1984). The many rich implications of this for the study of objects are drawn out by Goodman (1976) in his chapters on exemplification and on samples and labels in *Languages of Art*. It is useful for us at this stage to try to remember that objects constitute social systems and would have no recognizability if they did not. We may often be on the wrong track trying to decide what they signify, since that question does not necessarily lead directly to the part the objects play in human transactions.

Conclusion

Along these lines we are ready to answer the question about where objects start and where they blur into their context. We can identify as many classes of objects as we please, to be tried along with the theories that imply them. The insurance agent is entitled to his definitions, so is the antique dealer. The challenge is only to have interesting theories and to make them explicit. The explicit theory protects the categories from the charge of arbitrariness. I have a theory about complexly organized objects. By complexity I mean the entailment of one object by another, a teapot by a teapot lid, four wheels by a car. The theory supposes that a complex system of mutual implication needs time to develop and so is a symptom of stability in social life. Making a complex system also means hard work, and submitting to a lot of constraints. For example, the complex rules of implication in French *cuisine haute bourgeoise* used to interlock the occasion with the persons present, turning the occasion of food and wine into an element in a tight, coherent logical system. To study the amount of coherence in the flows of objects around events would be rewarding for semiology (Douglas 1984). It would be a way of showing up the classes of persons who are not going to be awarded funerals with lilies or chrysanthemums. The person who is not getting the flowers and grapes at the hospital bedside will fall into the marginal niches which tracing the flows of goods can identify for us before their inhabitants become derelicts of the industrial system. The theory is that complexity in the social life of objects is a response to complexity in the social life of persons. A complex cuisine is too much work to be indulged regularly for its own sake. Though some husbands tell me that when their wives are away they rise to an even higher culinary standard than the household regularly achieves, I am still to be convinced that they would keep this up if they were long-term bachelors. The complexity of a meal is a service to others, not a statement about a relationship, but an example of what the relationship is, and that is why it has to be a lot of work if the relationship is important. The amount of work, as well as the quality of objects, is relative to the statuses being created. Therefore a person who regularly has an extremely low level of complexity in use of objects is (other things being equal) likely to have an extremely low level of involvement with other people. In some cases, this isolation will mean vulnerability. The measure of complexity would also be an independent measure of atomization of social life. This line of investigation links semiology directly with social concerns and, I fondly hope, matches Roland Barthes' idea of a science of grades.

Note

1. Anthelme Brillat-Savarin (1755 – 1826) was a French magistrate and famous epicurean who published several books, the most famous of which was the *Physiologie du goût* (1825). He is remembered in particular for his epigraph: "Dis-moi ce que tu manges, je te dirai ce que tu es."

References

Barthes, Roland
　1984　　*La bruissement de la langue*. Paris: Editions du Seuil.
Davidson, Donald
　1979　　"What metaphors mean," in: Sheldon Sacks (ed.), 29 – 45.
Douglas, Mary
　1980　　*The world of goods*. New York: Basic Books.
　1989　　"Culture and collective action," in: Morris Freilich (ed.), 39 – 56.
Douglas, Mary (ed.)
　1984　　*Food in the social order*. New York: Russell Sage Foundation/Basic Books.
Freilich, Morris (ed.)
　1989　　*The relevance of culture*. New York: Bergin and Garvey.
Goodman, Nelson
　1976　　*Languages of art*. Indianapolis, IN: Hackett.
　1978　　*Ways of worldmaking*. Indianapolis, IN: Hackett.
Hirschman, A. O.
　1958　　*The strategy of economic development*. New Haven, CT: Yale University Press.

Kapferer, Bruce (ed.)
  1976   *Transaction and meaning: Directions in anthropology of exchange and symbolic behavior*. Philadelphia: Institute for the Study of Human Issues.
Marriott, Kim
  1976   "Hindu transactions: Diversity without dualism," in: Bruce Kapferer (ed.), 109 – 143.
Mauss, Marcel
  1954 [1922 – 1924]   *The gift*. Glencoe, IL: Free Press.
McKnight, David
  1973   "Sexual symbolism of food among the Wik-Mungkan," *Man* 8(2): 194 – 209.
Sacks, Sheldon (ed.)
  1979   *On metaphor*. Chicago: University of Chicago Press.
Scheffler, Israel
  1986   *Inquiries*. Indianapolis, IN: Hackett.
Thompson, Michael
  1978   *Rubbish theory: The creation and destruction of value*. Oxford: Oxford University Press.

Glorious obsessions, passionate lovers, and hidden treasures: Collecting, metaphor, and the Romantic ethic

Brenda Danet and Tamar Katriel

Introduction

The sociologist Colin Campbell (1987) has developed the provocative thesis that the Romantic movement played a critical role in the birth and development of modern consumerism.[1] In an attempt to extend Max Weber's (1930) well known analysis of the rise of modern capitalism and the attendant drive toward rationalization in modern life, Campbell argues that just as a Puritan ethic promoted the spirit of capitalist production − Weber's famous thesis − so a competing Romantic ethic worked to promote a complementary spirit of consumerism.

While there has been endless debate over the essence of the Romantic movement and how it is to be defined, Campbell calls attention to the central theme of Romanticism as "an impulse toward chaos" (Campbell 1987: 179), and "a way of feeling, a state of mind in which *sensibilité* and imagination predominate over reason; it tends toward the new, towards individualism, revolt, escape, melancholy, and fantasy" (Gaudefroy-Demombynes 1966, cited in Campbell 1987: 181).[2] Campbell adds: "Other typical characteristics of this way of feeling would be: dissatisfaction with the contemporary world, a restless anxiety in the face of life, a preference for the strange and curious, a penchant for reverie and dreaming, a leaning to mysticism, and a *celebration of the irrational*" (Campbell 1987: 181; italics added).

Campbell links Romanticism and consumerism via a distinction between traditional and modern forms of hedonism. Modern and traditional forms alike are "pulled along by desire for the anticipated quality of pleasure which an experience promises to yield" (Campbell 1987: 77). However, in modern hedonism:

pleasure is sought via emotional and not merely sensory stimulation ... the images which fulfil this function are either imaginatively created or modified by the individual for self-consumption... Modern hedonism tends to be covert and self-illusory ... individuals employ their imaginative and creative powers to construct mental images which they consume for the intrinsic pleasure they provide, a practice best described as day-dreaming or fantasizing (Campbell 1987: 77).

Thus, whereas the classical hedonist seeks to repeat experiences known to be pleasurable, the modern hedonist fills the hiatus between desire and consummation with the joys of day-dreaming about new experiences (Campbell 1987: 86). "The essential activity of consumption is thus not the actual selection, purchase or use of products, but the imaginative pleasure-seeking..." (Campbell 1987: 89).

Campbell concludes that the spirit of modern consumerism is, paradoxically, anything but materialistic. The tension between illusion and reality creates a permanent longing in the individual, and an incessant search for novelty. He sees this dynamic of desire − acquisition − use − disillusionment − renewed desire − at work primarily in the arenas of fashion, advertising, Bohemianism, the avant-garde, and romantic love. In this paper we shall argue that collecting is yet another important contemporary cultural form in which the Romantic ethic is given powerful expression.

Our analysis of the phenomenology of collecting reveals it to contain strong tensions between elements associated with the Puritan ethic, on the one hand, and dialectically opposed elements associated with the Romantic ethic, on the other. In a previous paper (Danet − Katriel 1989), we developed the hypothesis that collecting is a means to strive toward a sense of closure, completion, or perfection. In elaborating this hypothesis, we inevitably highlighted the order-making aspects of collecting, and were able to give only passing attention to aspects of collecting which suggest, paradoxically, that collectors also experience, even invite chaos. An over-emphasis on order-making too easily reduces collectors to nothing but custodians of little bureaucracies of objects − of stamps, old milk bottles, or buttons − all neatly classified and displayed in their proper place. Indeed, some interpreters of collecting see it as only this.[3]

In the present paper we shall complement our previous analysis by focusing mainly on the Romantic elements in collecting. We shall demonstrate that contemporary collecting is very much permeated by Romantic conceptualizations of experience. Our evidence will be drawn from an analysis of the metaphors that occur in discourse about collecting − in autobiographies of collectors, in interviews we conducted with informants and in other interviews conducted by journalists, as well as in manuals for collectors and other popular literature on collecting.

While collecting, taken broadly, has probably existed as a distinctive cultural form for something like 3000 years, in important respects the Industrial Revolution has shaped the activities of collectors over the last 150 years.[4] For one thing, it transformed and expanded the range of items treated as collectibles. The phenomenon of aestheticization of the obsolete was made possible by the Industrial Revolution.[5] Second, social changes set off by the Industrial Revolution, notably, the rise of a newly prosperous bourgeoisie, led to a widespread new interest in objects for the home, and to the democratization of collecting, once primarily the province of kings, princes, and the Church.[6]

As a result of processes of industrialization and urbanization, three new social types of collectors came into being in the latter part of the nineteenth century. One was identified by Walter Benjamin (1973) as a *flâneur*. The *flâneur* was a new type of aesthetic observer, a casual lounger who walked the streets and the arcades of Paris, and later of other European cities, in search of people, objects, sensations to arouse his curiosity and to give free play to his imagination. While the *flâneur* did not necessarily buy anything, he was a new kind of collector of experience.[7]

The second new type of collector was the industrialist art collector of plebeian origins. The economic success of the new industrialists was a testament to the efficacy of the Puritan ethic − of industriousness, rationality, and so on. Contrary to the view of Veblen (1979), the creation of great art collections by these industrialists, in the United States and in Europe, was motivated by far more than a desire to display one's status or to make a claim for respectability (Saisselin 1985).

> Art came to be reserved for the private domain, the intimate interior, the private world of the bourgeois, so that it came to be associated with an imaginary universe at variance with and sometimes in conflict with the public world, values, and activities of the bourgeois. Hardheaded in business, the bourgeois might be softheaded in art. The bourgeois interior, in contrast to the spaces in which others worked for him, became the space of private fantasies (Saisselin 1985: 29).[8]

A third new type of collector also came into being in the latter half of the nineteenth century − the person of modest means who collected a specialized category of mundane objects not belonging to the world of fine art. The prototype of this kind of collector is perhaps the stamp collector. Although many mass-produced objects came into their own as popular collectibles only in the twentieth century, especially after World War II, stamps came to be seen as collectibles within only a few years of their introduction in England in 1840.[9]

We suggest that for all these types of collectors, the experience of collecting is fruitfully viewed as an expression of the tension between the Puritan work ethic on the one hand, and the Romantic ethic, on the other. Campbell claims that while the Puritan ethic dominates the world of work, some occupations do give greater expression to the Romantic ethic, notably, the arts and the allied professions of those who teach them. Similarly, while the Romantic ethic probably informs all contemporary leisure more than most work, within this domain some forms are more strongly colored by Romanticism than others. We see collecting as one such form.

We move on now to our analysis of metaphors in collecting. The analysis will take us in three directions. First, we will offer some thoughts as to why metaphor is so common in discourse about collecting. Second, we will consider the inherently paradoxical elements inherent in collecting activities, whose recognition may have prompted one of our informants, a stamp collector and trader in Philadelphia, to define collecting as a "metaphor for life."[10]

Third, having explored the nature of collecting as enacted metaphor, we will turn to the metaphors collectors "live by" (Lakoff − Johnson 1980). We will examine the nature of the second-order metaphors which populate discourse on collecting. As we shall see, the essential tensions articulated in the structuring and texture of the collecting experience are verbally addressed in the metaphors of collecting.

Play, metaphor, and the inexpressible

A play perspective on the study of "serious leisure" activities, such as tourism (Cohen 1985), amateur chamber music (Stebbins 1979, 1980, 1982), or, in the present case, collecting, highlights their phenomenological quality as varieties of what Schutz has termed "finite provinces of meaning," as activities which are set apart from the "paramount reality of everyday life" (Schutz 1962). In this paper we further explore the theoretical and empirical implications of viewing collecting as a form of play. In particular, we respond to Schwartzman's (1982) call to "re-metaphorize play," i. e., to recognize the conceptual affinity between play and metaphor as forms of communication which "are both characterized, in varying degree, by *the production of paradoxical statements or images*" (Schwartzman 1982: 28; italics added).

As Fernandez (1972: 41) put it, "metaphor is one of the few devices we have for leaping beyond the essential privacy of the experiential process." It is especially likely to be mobilized wherever and whenever people struggle to *express the inexpressible*. In a paper titled "Why Metaphors are Necessary and Not Just Nice," Ortony (1975) developed three theses about the functions of metaphor. They are, first of all, a compact way of conveying a great deal of information. Second, they help to convey the inexpressible, or the more dynamic, continuous aspects of experience. Third, metaphor is more vivid than literal expression.[11]

Fernandez (1972, 1974, 1977) distinguishes between metaphors in performance (verbal and non-verbal), and in persuasion. He argues that metaphors are not merely a matter of explicit linguistic use of figures of speech. Substituting the word "play" for "ritual," we can paraphrase a passage from one of his papers with illuminating effect:

> It is proposed here that metaphors provide organizing images which [play] action puts into effect. This [ludicalization] of metaphor enables the pronouns participating in [play] to undergo apt integrations and transformations in their experience. The study of [play] is the study of the structure of associations brought into play by metaphoric predications upon pronouns (Fernandez 1977: 101–102).

For Fernandez, then, metaphors may be enacted through whole sequences of activity, and not just expressed in figurative language.

In short, in play as in ritual, metaphors are mobilized to express the inexpressible at two distinct but complementary levels. Primary enacted metaphors "provide images in relation to which the organization of behavior can take place;" Fernandez also calls them "organizing or performative metaphors" (Fernandez 1972: 42). At another level, within the frame of play activity organized metaphorically, second-order metaphors may be mobilized to convey various ineffable aspects of that activity.

Collecting as metaphor

Collecting is a leisure activity playfully constructed out of a range of existential paradoxes, which ordinarily remain submerged in the ongoing flow of our workaday lives. A closer look at the paradoxical elements and experiential tensions that ground collecting experiences leads to a better understanding of the world of collecting as a distinctive province of meaning which involves a specific form of self-experience, a specific form of sociality, a specific temporal perspective, and a prevalent form of engagement (or "spontaneity" in Schutz's [1962] terms). At least some of these existential paradoxes may be universal, but in our view they are given their particular character in contemporary collecting by the cultural symbiosis of the Puritan and Romantic ethics. We now discuss, in turn, each of eight paradoxes which we have discerned as inherent in contemporary collecting.

Decontextualization/recontextualization

Like many artistic engagements, collecting is a "world-making" activity. Most commonly, it involves the recycling of materials ready-at-hand and their use in the construction of a collection. That is, it involves processes of decontextualization on the one hand and of recontextualization on the other. Objects are removed from their contexts of use and become incorporated into a new context, a world defined by the collection as an orderly system of subtly differentiated objects (Stewart 1984). A major experiential feature of collecting is thus the attitudinal shift from an orientation toward objects as forming a functional part of the paramount reality of everyday life to one involving an accent on their aesthetic, systemic dimensions (cf. Danet – Katriel 1989).

This contextual shift is also associated with a shift in temporal orientation. Removed from their contexts of use, collectible items are often classified with reference to their date of production, but their incorporation into the collection marks a new order of time, with the history of acquisition often overriding the history of production. Objects thus become temporally anchored in the collection rather than in their individual pre-collection histories. Production dates turn into a principle of classification, and temporally marked occasions of acquisition become the point of reference for a new kind of history, the history that tells of the growth of the collection as a whole.

Concrete/imaginary

The collectible item itself is classified and appreciated as a concrete, usually aesthetically pleasing object and as what we might call a springboard to fantasy.[12] In contemplating their collections, collectors often spend much time physically handling the items, and readily state that physical contact with them is inherently satisfying. They come to develop and savor an expert mode of touch that marks their privileged position vis-a-vis the collection. The importance of this aspect of the collecting experience is brought out by a subgenre of collectors' stories which thematize the danger non-experts (most notably, children and pets) pose for collections through their uncontrolled clumsiness. Decontextualization of the objects is an aid to reverie; removed from their original contexts, one can invent one's own stories surrounding them.[13] Collecting, then, brings together a twofold interest in the world of objects — objects viewed in their distinctive concreteness and objects viewed as invitations to reverie and fantasy.

Collectors are often labelled "eccentric" by others because they talk to their objects, treating them like "family" or "children." The attribution of emotions to objects is one of the ways in which the concrete/imaginary dimension of collecting is realized. This tendency to attribute the features of living beings to inanimate objects is sometimes called fetishism.

In a useful overview of the anthropological, Marxist, and psychoanalytic traditions of the use of the term "fetishism," Ellen (1988) pointed to four cognitive processes underlying the concept: concretization, animation, conflation of signifier with signified, and an ambiguous tension between person and object in terms of control. In pre-literate societies:

> Objects from widely separated cultures are frequently represented as if they were human, are involved in processes which are recognisably human, are treated in ways that humans are treated — and in particular are themselves subject to rites of passage, other rituals and attitudes, which are usually reserved for humans... Fetishes are given gifts, are named, massaged and talked to... Social interactions with them are as behaviour between persons, not that of persons toward objects (Ellen 1988: 225).

These phenomena do not disappear in modern societies; indeed, Ellen's comments are strikingly applicable to modern collectors' orientation toward their favored objects. Popular notions of collectors' eccentricity notwithstanding, it is only in rationalized modern societies that the personification of inanimate nature has been partially extinguished.

In Benjamin's (1969, 1973) terms, collectors seek in their objects the "aura" which mass production and commodification incessantly undermine in contemporary cultural products. In a 1939 essay in which he reworked some of his ideas on the notion of the "aura," first developed in the famous 1936 essay "The Work of Art in the Age of Mechanical Reproduction" (Benjamin 1969), he wrote, "experience of the aura thus rests on the transposition of a response common to human relationships to the relationship between the inanimate or natural object and man. To perceive the aura of an object means to invest it with the ability to look at us in return" (Benjamin 1973; cited in Wolin 1982: 237). Thus, it is in keeping with the Romantic ethic to "conceive of inanimate objects *fraternally* rather than manipulatively, to grant them the capacity to project signals and attributes which transcend their simple quality of being-there. ... It bespeaks of an earlier relation of man to nature which modern man has all but repressed from memory" (Wolin 1982: 237–238).[14]

Order/chaos

Collecting also embodies a dialectical movement between order and chaos. As noted earlier, in our previous paper (Danet – Katriel 1989) we emphasized the systemic organization and the striving for closure as order-producing elements of collecting activities. Collections vary in the extent to which they are constructed around ordering devices such as series.[15] Collectors, however, often engage in re-ordering and re-arranging activities as they "take care" of their collections, thereby experiencing the possibility of alternative orders and the potential chaos that lurks behind this possibility. Hunting for collectibles in antique shops, flea markets, and garbage dumps, or chancing upon them in one's basement or attic, are clearly experiences that dramatize and mediate collectors' continuous movement between a disorderly "heap" of disparate objects and a systematically classified and thoughtfully arranged collection. Some collectors come to abandon a collection in which order-making is "too easy," for example, if stamp series are very easily obtained; others may find a particular challenge too great, and abandon the collections.[16]

Open-ended/highly directed

Collecting sets an agenda for collectors. It is a life-project that is at once open-ended and highly directed. On the one hand, collectors recognize that they are not likely to complete their collection (and would probably lose interest if it were easy to do so), but they make tremendous, well-regulated efforts to attain their subgoals within the larger, open-ended project.[17] Paradoxically, then, collectors both cherish the open-ended nature of the collecting enterprise and at the same time, structure and constrain at least some of their life-activities in relation to it. Thus, involvement in collecting may structure individuals' spare time and channel some of their financial resources. It may guide their avocational engagements and constrain their affiliations, and so on. In short, it serves both to articulate and to reconcile competing possibilities for the conceptualization and structuration of human projects, as open-ended and unending on one level, and as carefully circumscribed, finite, on another.

Rationality/irrationality

Many aspects of the commitment to a collecting agenda are "irrational." The fixation on a given category of objects appears quite irrational, to spouses and friends, if not to collectors themselves — particularly when these objects are formerly functional, obsolete items like antique typewriters, collected in the era of computers. Collectors often take up collecting some item or other, purely on impulse. "Falling in love" with objects, treating them as if they were children or pets, spending large amounts of time, money, and energy in their pursuit can all be difficult to justify.

At the same time, many aspects of collectors' activities require even-headed calculation of moves designed to cultivate one's collection. Collectors sometimes make infinitely detailed assessments as to the value of a given item on the current market, and whether buying it would be opportune. In short, there are strong elements of both rationality and irrationality in collecting.

As we shall see, recognition of the boundless passion fuelling collecting activities gives rise to an anxiety with regard to one's ability to control them. The fear of "going overboard," or "overdoing it," is strongly colored by collectors' awareness of the social disrepute attending un-checked, uninhibited involvements and expressions of subjectivity in our society. At the same time, collectors relish the free expression of passion, using the institutionalized context of collecting to celebrate the realm of irrational desire.

Interestingly, for a collector to be considered "serious," he or she must both manifest an appropriate degree of irrational passion and a commit-ment to the enterprise as indicated by an ongoing "object-hunting" agenda.[18] The world of collecting thus enables individuals to play out irrational desire and rational calculation in a well integrated life-project.

Controlling/being controlled

Collecting is imbued with the theme of control, articulated both as striving toward controlling and as the fear of being controlled. A collector gains control over the objects that comprise his or her collection through the power of ownership, which is actualized in the right to handle, rearrange, and even sell items in the collection. As Stewart (1984) suggests, the fact that so many collections involve miniature objects — thimbles, Japanese *netsuke* and sword fittings, antique keys, stamps and coins — further dramatizes the control element in collecting, as does (in a more sinister way) the killing associated with the collecting of live things, e.g., butter-flies.[19]

The drive toward control in collecting activities is accompanied by concern with loss of control, the aforementioned fear of "being carried away," devoting more time and resources to one's collection than one can afford, either materially or psychologically, or both. Thus, collectors often speak of the need to guard against the almost irresistible impulse to purchase new items for their collection, and, as noted, are often explicitly concerned about the rationality (i. e., controllability) of their endeavors. The experience of collecting thus combines a striving for control with a constant fear of losing it — a paradoxical position the metaphors of collecting make particularly clear, as will later be elaborated in greater detail.

The tendency to personalize objects, referred to earlier, in our discus-sion of the concrete/imaginary dimension of collecting, is, in fact, a two-edged sword: to attribute emotions to one's objects is to grant some powers of control to them. "The desire to control increases with the intrinsic powers attributed to objects, but as these powers increase so they may counter the power which people have over them. This paradoxical tension is very characteristic of fetishes" (Ellen 1988: 229).

Isolation/affiliation

As a social activity, collecting institutionalizes and legitimizes the experience of privacy and isolation, creating contexts in which the self-absorbed individual can experience a sense of meditation-like "flow" (Csikszentmihalyi 1977). At the same time, it creates an institutionalized context in which the web of affiliations woven around shared collecting interests is given shape, whether in casual encounters or in various formalized associations, such as collectors' clubs. Both meditative isolation and intense social engagements are inherent possibilities in the world of collecting, and the movement between them articulates an essential tension that grounds collecting as a form of sociality.

Although the most common pattern is probably for collectors to work alone, there are also instances where couples, or even whole families collect together. We know, for example, of a Jerusalem couple who collect Judaica together. And a Jerusalem family with five children has long cultivated a collection of candles of all shapes, colors, and sizes. Joint collections obviously provide a focus for these relationships, encouraging the pursuit of common goals, activities, and sources of satisfaction.

Energizing/relaxing

A final paradox inherent to the world of collecting is that it is both a form of self-regulated energizing activity and, at the same time, a frame within which one can "rest" from, or diffuse, tensions experienced in the paramount reality of one's life. The views of Kreitler and Kreitler (1972) about the role of tension in art experience are equally applicable to the experience of collecting. They hypothesize that:

> A major aspect of the art experience consists in the arousal and the relief of tension in the spectator by the work of art. The work of art is capable of producing tensions, which on the one hand are sufficiently variegated and multidimensional to enable the evoked tensions to absorb and combine

with the more and less diffuse residual tensions in the spectator; on the other hand, these tensions are specific enough to be resolved through some other aspects of the art input. Thus, the resolution of the specific tensions implies relief also for the diffuse tensions with which they have combined. The relief of these tensions is accompanied by pleasure (Kreitler — Kreitler 1972: 22).

It is not simply that accountability for one's actions is lowered in the frame of leisure. The acts of pursuing new acquisitions, working on the collection, e.g., cleaning, dusting, or mending, and most especially, simply contemplating the objects or handling them devotedly, are all often experienced as calming or restful. This dialectical relationship between the energizing and relaxing aspects of collecting may be associated with that of control/fear of being controlled. Perhaps control is equated with a state of calm, with forms of tension one initiates or is relatively capable of regulating, while a sense of lack of control creates negatively valued tension in the collector.

Paradoxes in collecting and the Romantic ethic

A brief review of the paradoxes inherent to collecting, as outlined above, shows that the Romantic elements are strikingly prevalent in at least five of them. Via objects, collectors can pursue the imaginary, allow themselves to experience chaos, take on the challenge of an open-ended agenda with many unknowns, surrender to irrational impulses, enjoy the thrilling risk of being out of control, and luxuriate in a deeply engrossing solo activity whose sensuous components are prominent, and which singularizes them as unique "interesting" individuals. What's more, they can indulge in all of these, while gaining social credit for cultivating good taste (Clifford 1988), for contributing to local history, for carrying on a family tradition, or for any number of other socially meritorious acts! Of course the tendency to emphasize the Romantic aspects of collecting will vary with the individual and with the type of collectible. Still, our analysis of the language of collecting will provide empirical support for the thesis that Romantic elements are indeed prominent in twentieth-century collecting.

Root metaphors collectors live by: An invocation of butterfly-collecting

One of the most evocative portrayals of the experience of collecting which we have encountered is that of the writer Vladimir Nabokov, who devoted an entire chapter of his autobiography, *Speak Memory* (Nabokov 1969), to his lifelong pursuit of butterflies. The invocation of his private world of butterfly-collecting is especially vivid because it is unusually rich in metaphors. Nabokov writes, "from the age of seven, everything I felt in connection with a rectangle of framed sunlight (under the door of his bedroom) was dominated by a single passion. If my first glance of the morning was for the sun, my first thought was for the butterflies it would engender..." (Nabokov 1969: 94). He describes his feelings as he observed the very first butterfly to enter his collection: "As it probed the inclined flower from which it hung, its powdery body slightly bent, it kept restlessly jerking its great wings, and my desire for it was one of the most intense I have ever experienced" (Nabokov 1969: 94).

Hunting is yet another motif threaded throughout the chapter, as in "I have hunted in various climes and disguises: as a pretty boy in knickerbockers and sailor cap; as a lanky cosmopolitan expatriate in flannel bags and beret; as a fat hatless old man in shorts... All my American captures from 1940 to 1960 ... are in [American museums]..." (Nabokov 1969: 99). For Nabokov, nature, like art, offers "a form of magic, ... a game of intricate enchantment and deception" (Nabokov 1969: 98). On moonless nights, he used to lay out a sheet on the ground, with a light shining on it, to attract moths. "Upon that magic sheet, ... I took a beautiful *Plusia*" (Nabokov 1969: 105). Here, he gives expression to the common elements in hunting and in erotic pursuits. To capture a butterfly is to move from desire to fulfilment and possession: full possession of a living creature in this case, paradoxically, also means killing the object of one's delight.

Nabokov writes that he preferred being alone, rather than playing with other children, because "any companion, no matter how quiet, interfered with the concentrated enjoyment of my mania" (Nabokov 1969: 99). Terms like mania indicate, at the least, ambivalence about the activity involved, or an awareness that others might think his pre-occupation strange or excessive. Pursuing this theme of activity potentially out of control, he continues: "Let me look at my demon objectively. With the exception of my parents, no one really understood my obsession, and it was many years before I met a fellow sufferer" (Nabokov 1969: 100).

In partial overlap with the notion of magic, Nabokov also invites the reader to think of his experiences in terms of religious transcendence:

> I confess I do not believe in time. I like to fold my magic carpet, after use, in such a way as to superimpose one part of the pattern upon another... And the highest enjoyment of timelessness ... is when I stand among rare butterflies and their food plants. This is ecstasy, and behind the ecstasy is something else, which is hard to explain. It is like a momentary vacuum into which rushes all that I love. A sense of oneness with the sun and stone. A thrill of gratitude to whom it may concern — to the contrapuntal genius of human fate or to tender ghosts humoring a lucky mortal (Nabokov 1969: 109 – 110).

Five root metaphors

We have identified five sets of root metaphors which are prominent in discourse about collecting, most of which occur in Nabokov's chapter. They are:

(1) collecting is hunting.
(2) collecting is therapy.
(3) collecting is passion, desire.
(4) collecting is a disease.
(5) collecting is supernatural experience.

As we have just seen, the metaphors of hunting, passion and desire are all very prominent in Nabokov's invocation of his experiences. That of disease, however, is not explicitly used, though other associated metaphors, notably obsession, mania, and source of suffering are all mobilized. And collecting is also portrayed as both positive and negative forms of supernatural experience. Positive spiritual transcendence is in evidence in the metaphors of magic, religious worship, and ecstasy. In Nabokov's reference to his demon, there is a hint of the idea that, paradoxically, the collector can also be viewed as controlled by malevolent supernatural forces.

The fifth root metaphor we have identified, collecting as therapy, is the only one absent from Nabokov's chapter. This may be attributed to the fact that he highlights the lived experience of butterfly-collecting as perceived from within. To speak of therapy, or even to imply it, would be to view collecting from a distance, as offering a rest or respite from other activities. Thus, Nabokov has stressed the energizing capacities of collecting, rather than its potential for relaxation. We can now see why his chapter is so powerfully evocative. It is not just because he uses so many metaphors, or uses them with such consummate literary skill, but also because he evokes so many very different types of metaphors, which, as we shall show below, invite associations of very different, partially conflicting kinds.

Structural versus textual metaphors

Of the five root metaphors we have identified, only the first one focuses on the activity or activities of collecting; all the others deal in one way or another with the experience of collecting — how one feels about it. Fernandez (1974: 120) makes a distinction between structural and textual metaphors. As he puts it, structural metaphors "conform ... closely to the shape of experience," while textual ones conform more closely to the feelings of experience.

> In the case of structural or analogic metaphor, a metaphor is assigned to its subject on the basis of some isomorphic similar structure or pattern of relationships. Thus we say the *branch* of the stream...
>
> By textual metaphor one means that metaphor in which the assimilation made is on the basis of similarity in feeling tone-glowering clouds, a brooding landscape, a dyspeptic bureaucracy (Fernandez 1977: 105).

It is evident that the hunting metaphor is primarily structural. It conveys something of how the objective features of the activity look to the observing eye. It points to the fact that some of the objective features of the pursuit of collectibles are isomorphic with the hunting of animals.

In contrast, metaphors of desire and longing, of madness and addiction, of magical enchantment or therapeutic catharsis all primarily convey something of how it feels to be involved in collecting; they attempt to convey subjective reports of subjective states. Thus, one can say, "collecting feels like madness," or "there is a mad quality to collecting," but collecting "looks like, or resembles hunting."[20]

Collecting as hunting

We begin with the metaphor which is most commonly used to characterize the activities associated with collecting. Images of hunting abound in autobiographical accounts and other talk about collecting. A manual for collectors of antiques is titled *The Joys of Hunting Antiques* (Salter 1971). Another is called *Treasure Hunting for All* (Fletcher 1975). [21] Many kinds of texts are chock-full of hunting-related language:

> It has been my fortune in the course of my career as a bibliographical huntsman to bring away spoils of the chase neither few or unimportant (Hazlitt 1897: 117).

> It was Julie [his wife] who found the Swiss "Strad" [music box in the shape of a Stradivarius violin] for me... The box was the prize she bagged after a hunt which would have done credit to any big game expert in Africa. The chase began in a downtown Boston antique shop where she engaged in a little preliminary stalling just to see if she could stir up some interesting game ... the dealer answered [the door]; and, as the door opened, Julie spotted her quarry (Templeton 1958: 74–75).

> I always found London to be the most likely hunting ground ... many [netsuke] still remain in private homes where they accompany other miniature objets d'art in display cabinets. An elusive prey adds zest to the chase, and I was delighted when by chance I ran to earth a fine wood dragon housed in this way. However, although I tried to persuade him, he refused to come home with me (Cohen 1974: 10). [22]

> There are many different reasons for collecting art. One is the thrill of the search — it is like having an Easter egg hunt 365 days of the year... We began to make collecting forays to the New York galleries in the late 1960's (Center for African Art 1988: 6).

> We hunt [beer] cans only when the spirit hits us (Beer Can Collectors of America 1976: 106).

> The longer and harder the chase, the greater the satisfaction (Biddle 1983: 11).

> It's like a day in the hunting field — stalking great works of art. You are up against adversaries who are warding you off the game you are hunting (Balzac 1968[1848]: 52).

It is not surprising that hunting is such a prominent metaphor in discourse about collecting. In our opinion, it gives expression to all of the paradoxes and tensions we identified earlier in this paper. First, phrases like to "bag a prize," or to "capture an elusive prey" embody the physical act of appropriating objects, removing them from their previous context, a precondition for their eventual recontextualization within the collection. Second, this metaphor gives expression to the activity of actual pursuit of concrete entities in the physical world, as discussed in our juxtaposition of the concrete/imaginary dimension. Third, to pursue game, prey, prizes — especially if specific objects are sought, and not just the chance discovery at a flea market — is to attempt to incorporate desired items in the grand plan of one's collection, and thereby to pursue order, yet paradoxically, to expose oneself to the chaotic, unpredictable nature of the physical environment. Fourth, both collecting and hunting contain agonistic elements. Just as there is competition between collectors for the best items at a flea market or auction, so hunters compete for game.

This metaphor also gives clear expression to the tension between the openendedness of the collection, on the one hand, and the directed nature of collecting activities, on the other. One can never know in advance on a given occasion for hunting if one will come home with anything at all. Even if one manages to bring home some trophies, more often than not, the agenda will remain uncompleted, or, as we have shown, if there is a "danger" of completing it, it may be redefined, so that there will always be a next occasion to go hunting.

Thus, this metaphor also embodies the future-oriented nature of collecting; it articulates the essence of a commitment to collecting as propelling one forward, toward future activity. Something of the restlessness of the collector, the tendency to live for what will happen next, are thereby conveyed. As for the close connection between hunting and control, this was clear, already, in the passage from Nabokov's autobiography cited earlier. To capture an object is to control it, most especially, of course, if one kills it! Yet, paradoxically, as has already been pointed out, on any given hunting occasion, the hunter cannot control all the contingencies in the environment, and therefore cannot know how the day will end.

Finally, this metaphor is clearly pertinent to the contrast we drew between energizing and relaxing activity. It obviously highlights the energizing quality of collectors' activities. Since a major source of tension is the inability to predict the outcome of a day's hunting expedition, the hunting metaphor also gives expression to the suspense collectors live with, even relish. In short, hunting is the metaphor which best expresses the quality of collecting as action in the sense discussed by Erving Goffman (1967) in his essay "Where the Action Is."[23] A passage from the conclusion to Goffman's essay nicely sums up this section of the paper:

Looking for where the action is, one arrives at a romantic division of the world. On one side are the safe and silent places, the home, the well-regulated role in business, industry, and the professions; on the other are all those activities that generate expression, requiring the individual to lay himself on the line and place himself in jeopardy during a passing moment. It is from this contrast that we fashion nearly all our commercial fantasies. It is from this contrast that delinquents, criminals, hustlers ... sportsmen [and, we would add, collectors] draw their self-respect (Goffman 1967: 268).[24]

Collecting as therapy

The motif of collecting as therapy is the least likely of the five root metaphors to find expression in discourse about collecting. Collectors are apparently much more likely to dwell on the energizing, even exciting aspects of their activities than the relaxing ones. At the same time, they are occasionally quite articulate about the latter aspects. They come to the forefront mainly in later stages of working on the collection at home — while dusting or mending objects, sorting stamps and placing them in the proper slots in an album, and so on. Most of all, the therapeutic aspects of collecting find expression during moments of quiet contemplation of the collection.

In an interview in a local Jerusalem newspaper, a collector of fountain pens, Miki Bavli, who is an official at the Israel Foreign Ministry, is quoted as saying, "when I am tense I present myself to my psychiatrist [a pen dealer] in Tel Aviv... Moshe Hacohen [the dealer] 'treats' the community of pen collectors there.[25] You don't open his door if you don't have at least an hour or two free" (Mediskar 1990).

In answer to a question as to whether she spends time with her collection in a particular mood, one of our informants, a gallery-owner of about sixty from New York who herself collects both Judaica and jewelry, told us, "Oh sure. I'll be very upset and I'll get into bed with my nightgown and I'll start putting jewelry on — like 30 pieces at a time. Just to play with it. Sure, the same as people have doll houses."

Kenneth Brecher (1988), anthropologist and director of the Children's Museum in Boston, published a charming memoir built around his postcard collection. The collection helped him to cope with grief when two dear friends died prematurely of cancer: "When I couldn't sleep and felt too exhausted to read, I would take out my postcard collection.

Looking through it, I felt a lessening of my grief. The cards bore witness to my own life" (Brecher 1988: 2).

The theme of collecting and collection as therapy is also overtly expressed in some remarks by Tali, a sixteen-year-old girl, a resident of an Israeli kibbutz who has a collection of about 200 key chains. Unlike many collectors, her collection is not displayed; rather, it is kept in a cabinet in her parents' room.[26] As Tali revealed to one of our students, "When I need a moment to myself I open up the cabinet, look, and calm down. It's like nostalgia. When I see the collection, I think 'all this — you collected!' It's mine and nobody else's! I feel consoled and the mood I was in passes — I feel different." Katriel's eighteen-year-old stamp collector daughter expressed much the same idea when she queried, "how can anybody cope without a stamp collection and a guitar?" Apparently, the calming effects of the collection have to do with control: one retreats from a situation in which one has lost control to one in which the collector dominates — if possible, totally.

Collecting as passion

As we have seen, one of the most striking and most common sets of metaphors in discourse about collecting is the cluster surrounding the notion of passion.[27] This cluster includes related motifs of desire, passion, love, possession, giving the beloved attention, and even rivalry. The motif of passion appears explicitly in the titles of two recent trade books about collectors, *Collecting: The Passionate Pastime* (Johnston — Beddow 1986) and *The Passionate Collector* (Land-Webber 1980). As for examples from various texts, we cite here only a sampling from a much longer list we have culled. First, here is a selection from autobiographies:

> Inevitably, if you fall in love with something, you want to possess it... There are many varieties of collectors, but the ones I trust most ... are the ones who just can't help it... They want to handle it ... feel it, if it is touchable. They have to go to bed near it ... and in the end 'marry it' by purchase (Price 1959: 214).

> Drawings are my passion (Price 1959: 220).

> Safely home with the [painting by] Diebenkorn we fell deeply in love with it (Price 1959: 231).

> Books, as they were my father's only, and my uncle's chief paramours, were my first love (Hazlitt 1897: 5).

> [I was] tempted by a milk jug with a silver hinge... (Hazlitt 1897: 204).

> Finally, and above all, I love objects (Rheims 1980: 258).

> I must confess I was actuated chiefly at first by the instinct of possession. I was beside myself with joy ... when for 18 francs I succeeded in purchasing a little china plaque of a girl with a broken pitcher (Vollard 1978: 14).

> Among the irresistible members of the collection are the beautiful Swiss box on its own table (Templeton 1958: 73).

These metaphors are also prominent in other first-person accounts, such as collectors' introductions to catalogs of their collection, as in "since I am an artist who works in woodcuts, it is not surprising that I fell in love with the Japanese woodblock print" (Pins 1980: 9). Similarly, a snuff bottle collector wrote, "while visiting the art show [at his synagogue in Toronto, at the age of 12], I saw and fell in love with these miniature art works" (Silver 1987: 3).

Nineteenth and twentieth-century novels also abound in these metaphors:

> No account whatever had been taken of her relation to her treasures, of the passion with which she had waited for them, worked for them, picked them over, made them worthy of each other and the house, watched them, loved them, lived with them (James 1987[1886]: 43).

> He loved them as a man loves a beautiful mistress ... those who have it in them to admire great works have the sublime capacity of true lovers for feeling as much bliss today as they did yesterday (Balzac 1968[1848]: 27).

> As a young child will reach out to handle the thing it names, so the passionate collector, his eye in harmony with his hand, restores to the object the life-giving touch of its maker (Chatwin 1988: 20).

Collectors may even come to constitute a rival of spouses, who sometimes express their jealousy quite openly. Here are two examples: "I realized that my wife was playing second fiddle to the beer can" (Beer Can Society of America 1976: 106). "He told us that he had sold most of his collection because his wife had declared 'either they go or I go'"(Templeton 1958: 35).

Some expressions carry erotic connotations; others are desexualized. Thus, Chatwin's (1988: 58) character gazes at "his miniature family." Hazlitt also invites the reader to think of his collections as a sort of family:

> The man who possesses a miniature cabinet with a few hundred samples [of coins] is apt to wax tired of surveying his property, even if they are all favorites with little histories of their own... When the collection is very

extensive, and constantly growing, the personal attachment is transferred to the newest comers. It is like the mother with her last child (Hazlitt 1897: 352).

Similarly, in a Mark Twain short story, a collector of Aztec inscriptions and stuffed whales eventually comes to sell his collection: "So my uncle sold out, and saw his darlings go forth" (Twain 1957: 123). The same theme was especially prominent in the interview with the snuff bottle collector: "I like to own things ... it bothers me to see them in museums. When I see them behind glass and no one is fondling them and no one is playing with them and no one is giving them a loving home..." Asked why he does not display his collection at home, but keeps it in boxes instead, he replied: "I've been influenced by my Chinese friends... And they'd never display them. They keep them in the box and then they take them out of the box. It's more personal. You take out the box and you give it personal attention."

Like the root metaphor of hunting, those of desire give expression to most, if not all of the paradoxical elements experienced in the paramount reality of everyday life. First, the motif of passion realizes the state of permanent longing in which collectors find themselves. The lines written by the poet John Keats, "Heard melodies are sweet, but those unheard are sweeter,"[28] could be a collectors' motto: they can take greater pleasure in fantasizing about objects not yet possessed than in contemplating those already in the collection. Thus the motif of passion brings into focus the open-endedness of collecting, the prominence of fantasy, its energizing quality of propelling the collector forward toward the next object, and, perhaps, most of all, the legitimation it gives to the expression of emotion and impulse.

The occurrence of motifs of passion in the context of collecting is one expression of an idea already present at the beginning of the Romantic movement. This movement cultivated the ideal of the "man of feeling," a person of acute emotional sensibility, which raises him or her above their less sensitive brothers (Hugo 1965: 31). As Susan Sontag puts it, "the early Romantic sought superiority by desiring to desire" (Sontag 1979: 44).

Moreover, the celebration of the irrational makes collectors "interesting," different from ordinary people who lead drab lives.

Perhaps the main gift to sensibility made by the Romantics is not the aesthetics of cruelty and the beauty of the morbid ... or even the demand for unlimited personal liberty, but the nihilistic and sentimental idea of "the interesting" (Sontag 1979: 30−31).[29]

Thus, passion singularizes — collectors are proud of being driven by such strong emotions. These metaphors of longing, desire, passion, and so on, then, make a virtue of letting go. At the same time, to let go is to risk going out of control altogether; consequently, in using these metaphors collectors are also acknowledging their awareness that society does not approve of wholesale letting go, and that they themselves may have anxieties about going out of control. Thus, the dialectical tension between control and being controlled is also implicit in these metaphors. Finally, we might add that while celebrating collectors as "more interesting," more "alive" than others, motifs of passion inevitably also connote the ultimate inability to communicate to others who do not share the same passion. As a result, these themes can also connote the existential loneliness of collectors.

Collecting as disease

Like the metaphors of passion, those connoting disease and related associations are remarkably plentiful in discourse about collecting. The term "disease" itself is not very often cited explicitly. An exception was the remark of one of our informants, the artist-collector of Far Eastern art who was mentioned earlier. When we came to interview him, he greeted us at the door with the unexpected exclamation, "it's a disease!"

More commonly, collectors speak of the urge to collect as a bug — adopting the notion from medicine that "bugs" (insects) carry germs, and that germs, in turn "cause" disease, as in:

> ... This bug of collecting... All collectors I've ever known will agree that it is a disease, one from which there is no cure (Price 1959: 214).

> I am now convinced that the collecting bug is a quite common one and most infectious (Cohen 1974: 23).

> Once you've been bitten by the collecting bug, you won't be able to pass a dump, lovers lane, old stage show set, unoccupied building, dilapidated barn, abandoned railroad station, closed brewery or tavern cellar without at least a cursory search for old beer cans (Beer Can Collectors of America 1976: 97).

> There is no such thing as safe collecting! Either you have been bitten by the collecting bug or you are immune (Center for African Art 1988: 58).

> Oil rags, I watch for them all the time. They're in my system (Carmichael 1971: 8). [30]

Mania or madness is clearly one of the most popular metaphors in talk about collecting. It occurs occasionally in book titles, as in *Pop Culture Mania: Collecting 20th-Century Americana for Fun and Profit* (Hughes 1984). The expression *timbromanie* was already in use for the excess of stamp collectors in the early 1860s, twenty-five years after the introduction of postage stamps in Britain (Briggs 1988: 349).[31] And at the turn of the twentieth century, Hazlitt (1897: 2) described himself as "smitten by *bibliomania*." Here are some recent examples.

> Collectors know ... that there are thousands of other people out there just as crazy as they are (Beer Can Collectors of America 1976: 103).

> I think that if someone has a mania to collect, it's a fantastic thing (Informant, collector of Judaica).

> You have to be crazy to be involved in these things! And I am crazy too (Informant, coin collector).

> What? There are other crazies like me? (Informant, gun collector).

Related metaphors are addiction, obsession, carrying a cross, slavery, and prison. Addiction appears, for instance, in the subtitle of Peggy Guggenheim's (1980) autobiography, *Out of this Century: Confessions of an Art Addict*. A beer can collector described himself as "hooked on the hobby" (Beer Can Collectors of America 1976: 89). Maurice Rheims called the English version of his memoirs *The Glorious Obsession* (Rheims 1980). A beer can collector confessed that "we have been to beer can hell many times" (Beer Can Collectors of America 1976: 108). Vincent Price (1959: 213) writes, "I was a collector the day I was born ... this is my cross, and until the greatest auction sale in history cuts me down to the bare essentials, I'm doomed to carry that cross." And here is Hazlitt again: "We are slaves to our passions; and the genuine collector certainly is unto his... The servitude presses very heavily on ... the ... moderately endowed (Hazlitt 1897: 189 – 190); "time was, when the bijou tea-pot held me in bondage" (Hazlitt 1897: 204). Chatwin (1988: 90) writes of Utz that "the collection held him prisoner." It is evident that the family of metaphors clustering around the notion of disease carry connotations which overlap heavily with those carried by metaphors of passion. Like the latter group, they clearly connote the ambiguities surrounding control and being out of control, surrendering to impulse, and so on. At the same time, these metaphors also carry other, unique connotations.

While passions may be ultimately uncontrollable, the notion of disease implies phenomena for which a "cure" may someday become available.

In the present context, it implies that collecting is "caused," that the impetus to collect comes from outside the individual, and that it can be controlled, if the "cause" is found — more and more diseases are controlled, after all, as medicine progresses. The choice of bug as the preferred expression thus concretizes the ineffable, making the urge to collect seem more controllable than it is, yet simultaneously admitting that control is a problem. Since disease as a general phenomenon in the world will probably never disappear, it also, ironically, offers a way of justifying one's activities: if it is a disease for which there is no "cure," then "I can't help it!"

Disease-related metaphors carry meanings which acknowledge, albeit ambivalently, that collecting may be viewed as untoward, deviant activity, which perhaps warrants being labelled as "eccentric," "peculiar," "excessive." Some observers might want to argue that collectors really are obsessive, crazy, sick, and these expressions are not metaphorical at all — that collectors are just admitting that they are crazy, sick, and so on, and perhaps even confessing shame over their excesses. While we do not doubt for a moment that there are pathological forms of collecting, which do deserve the label "sick," and for which people may be in need of psychiatric help, it is our contention that these metaphors connote not shame, but — once again — a celebration of collectors' surrender to their impulses — along with some acknowledgement of the dangers of getting out of control. Here again, as with the metaphors of passion, the Romantic ethic is in evidence.[32]

We return to Susan Sontag's analysis of the metaphors of illness for insights. In nineteenth-century Romantic notions of illness, "health becomes banal, even vulgar" (Sontag 1979: 25), while illness, especially tuberculosis, makes one more passionate, more alive. "Sickness was a way of making people 'interesting'" (Sontag 1979: 30). Thus, paradoxically, disease spiritualized the person — by dissolving the body, it "etherealized the personality, expanded consciousness" (Sontag 1979: 18).

In particular these connotations of illness apply to mania. "In the twentieth century, the repellent, harrowing disease that is made the index of a superior sensitivity, the vehicle of 'spiritual' feelings and 'critical' discontent, is insanity... The romanticizing of madness reflects ... the contemporary prestige of irrational or rude (spontaneous) behavior" (Sontag 1979: 34−35).

The opening comment of our art collector informant, "it's a disease!" now becomes comprehensible. He is neither hanging his head in shame over his activities nor asking us to call in a doctor. On the contrary, it is as if he is saying, "yes, some think this is excessive behavior, and there are perhaps potentially out-of-control aspects to collecting, but it is also wonderful to let yourself go in this way — welcome to my private world. Step in, and let me try to share something of it with you!"

The celebration of madness and excess is fully explicit in the remark of another of our informants, a collector of Judaica — rare books. When asked if he thought collecting is crazy or silly, he exclaimed, *Ze kef shel shigaon!* Loosely translated, this idiomatic expression means something like, "it's a joyful madness!" or "it's a madness full of fun or joy!"

Collecting as supernatural experience

Metaphors connoting supernatural experience are somewhat less common in discourse on collecting than those of passion and disease. Most of them carry positive connotations, but as we shall see, metaphors suggesting the influence of malevolent out-of-control forces also occur occasionally.

One theme is that of worship of the objects; related motifs are revelation, supplication, and idolatry.

> The exaltation of the comic book is typical of the transformation an item undergoes when enough collector interest turns it into a collectible (Hughes 1984: 13).

> If you're proud of your collection, show it and spread the faith (Beer Can Collectors of America 1976: 104).

> [A collector], an aggressive and successful businessman, quietly told me ... that African art was the closest he would ever come to God (Center for African Art 1988: 5).

> It's great to see more and more people "seeing the light" with regard to collecting (Beer Can Collectors of America 1976: 93).

> [Mark Burns] and his partner Louis DiBonis, who in recent years has become as great a supplicant to the collection as Burns himself... (Burns and DiBonis 1988).

> Collecting is idolatry (Chatwin 1988: 19).

Although none of these passages has the eloquence of Nabokov's evocation of the ecstasy he experienced while standing in a field contemplating his beloved butterflies, they all point in the same direction. Even if beer can collectors do not quite intend to claim that contemplating beer cans is spiritually exalting, it is clear that some of them use the same basic metaphor to constitute their experience.

Metaphors invoking malevolent spiritual forces are much rarer. We saw that among the mostly very positive metaphors woven into Nabokov's invocation of butterfly collecting was his passing reference to his demon. In his semi-popular overview of collecting and collectors, Jullian (1967) used this expression too: "If the demon of accumulation wins the day, the gentleman is no longer altogether normal" (Jullian 1967: 112). A rare reference to the devil occurred, once again, in the manual for beer can collectors:

> Finally, I realized that I was neglecting my loved ones and I took a long look at what I was doing. I realized that my wife was playing second fiddle to the beer can and that I was pressing my 14-year-old son into hunting with me, leaving him little time with his friends. I've now regained some of my senses... I have been in a beer can hell, but I proved that I can beat the devil! (Beer Can Collectors of America 1976: 106).

This collector quite evidently contradicts himself in this passage. On the one hand, he takes responsibility for his actions — "I was neglecting my loved ones." Yet his reference to the devil appears to locate responsibility for the actions outside himself. The contradiction nicely epitomizes the dialectical tension between control and lack of control in collecting.

Reference to the devil may also be located within the context of the Romantic movement. The Faustian motif of selling one's soul to the devil, in exchange for the promise of some desired good, although prominent throughout Western history, came into its own during the Romantic period.[33]

Themes of magic and enchantment, and of being transported to another world belong in this section, since they too call up associations of positively toned transformation — of a move outside of the ordinary frame of experience. Here is a sampling:

> Miniature things cast a sort of spell, and not all spells can be explained (Jacobs 1965: 13).

> Of the passions of the human mind, that which directs us to a certain object or aim ... and holds us bound within its range as by a spell, is one of the strongest (Hazlitt 1897: 302–303).

> The most profound enchantment for the collector is the locking of individual items within a magic circle in which they are fixed as the final thrill, the thrill of acquisition, passes over them... The period, the region, the craftsmanship, the former ownership — for a true collector the whole

background of an item adds up to a magic encyclopedia whose quintessence
is the fate of his object (Benjamin 1969: 60).

The collectibles of the 1930's and 1940's constitute a fairyland of wonders
and marvels for the uninitiated (Mebane 1972: 22).

... This precocious child ... found himself bewitched by a figurine of
Harlequin (Chatwin 1988: 18).

The many references in discourse on collecting to objects and whole
collections as treasure also belong here. Reference to conventionally
valuable objects like jewels and other objects made of gold or other
precious materials is, perhaps, more literal than metaphoric, and is,
accordingly, not of particular interest in this chapter.[34] However, calling
beer cans or old lawnmowers treasure is another matter. The aestheticization
of lowly everyday objects is frequently accompanied by this metaphor,
as the following titles of handbooks for collectors attest:

Tavern Treasures: A Book of Pub Collectibles (Tresise 1983).
Hidden Treasure: How and Where to Find It (Horn 1962).
A Thimble Treasury (Lundquist 1975).
Treasure Hunting for All: A Popular Guide to a Profitable Hobby (Fletcher
1975).
A Treasury of American Bottles (Ketchum 1975).

First-person accounts of collecting experiences similarly draw on the
motif of treasure:

I could tell you stories ... that would either get you hysterical or start you
crying about pieces that I have discovered... We don't know why or how;
and every other collector will tell you that by some miracle a piece will
come into their hands that they have been looking for... That's a treasure
(American informant, collector of Judaica and antique jewelry).

I had an erotic dream... I dreamt that I found a treasure: 70 fountain pens
at one time! (Mediskar 1990).

Other popular literature about collecting also makes use of this metaphor:

Diamonds from the dumps (Beer Can Collectors of America 1976; chapter
heading).

Most of what you uncover ... will be in deplorable condition, but you may
find a gem here and there (Beer Can Collectors of America 1976: 98).

For the beer can collector, a supermarket or drugstore ... can prove as
valuable a treasure trove of cans as an old dump (Beer Can Collectors of
America 1976: 153).

An upstairs room above the crowded shop contains Tony Barwick's personal treasure trove [of antique woodworking tools] (Johnson — Beddow 1986: 17).

Whether you are into discovering treasures in the attic or browsing through antique stores and flea markets, this book will help you... (Hughes 1984; book jacket).

Conclusions

Toward the end of the third section of this chapter, we argued that via objects collectors cultivate the imaginary, confront chaos, pursue an open-ended agenda, surrender to irrational impulses, risk being out of control, and luxuriate in a form of sensuous activity which singularizes them as "interesting." We have now demonstrated that at the verbal level, these Romantic elements are given vivid expression through metaphorical usage. Our analysis thus supports Campbell's (1987) thesis that the Romantic ethic has informed the material culture of industrial society in the last 150 years.

There are collectors whose verbal accounts of their activities do not contain the metaphors we have discussed in this paper. Some seem to use little or no metaphor; others mainly create their own, idiosyncratic ones, as is true of Brecher's (1988) memoir. The first chapter of his book is called "A Lock of Hair, a Book of Hours, an Amulet." These metaphors are his way of expressing the idea that his collection helps to structure memories of very personal experiences. For most collectors, then, metaphor is a powerful device for the attempt to communicate the ineffable in collecting, and, in the context of the Romantic ethic, to give form to collectors' search for self-transcendence.

Some cultural analysts might want to argue that collecting is nothing but a glorified form of consumerism, an excess brought on by bureaucratization and late capitalism. While we do not underestimate the power of commercialization to manipulate people, the metaphors used in discourse on collecting indicate that collectors' objects and activities carry a rich set of meanings for them that have little to do with commercialization.

Another question is whether the metaphors discussed in this chapter are unique to a particular period in history, or to collecting. One way the analysis developed here could be extended is to search for first-person accounts by collectors in earlier periods in history.[35] Our hunch is that the metaphors used in earlier eras are significantly different, since different cultural epochs are likely to provide a different vocabulary of motives (Mills 1940; Burke 1965, 1969) for experiences which bear superficial resemblances.

As for the question of whether the metaphors discussed in this paper are unique to collecting, it would be worthwhile to carry out comparative analyses of the discourse of different forms of serious leisure and even of professionalized forms of activities usually thought of as leisure, such as sports. Thus, we could ask, do professional and amateur athletes conceptualize their activities and experiences in similar ways? A related question is whether people use the same or different metaphors when talking about work and leisure. In the world of amateur chamber music, for instance, enthusiasts make very heavy commitments, which may conflict with others taken on within the framework of the paramount reality of the workaday world. Do they too use the metaphors discussed in this chapter? And do the same metaphors occur in their talk about their occupations? Such comparative analyses would, we believe, throw further light on the nature of the collecting experience. It may be that, for the middle classes, at least, the same metaphors are increasingly being used to constitute both work and leisure. This finding would support the view that the borderline between the realms of work and leisure in our postmodern world is experienced as increasingly blurred.

Notes

1. This research was supported in part by the Smart Family Foundation for Communications Research of the Hebrew University of Jerusalem. We also thank the Canada-Israel Foundation for Academic Exchanges and Alain Goldschlager for assistance with travel funds.
2. See, e.g., Halsted (1965); Praz (1933); Peckham (1970); and Campbell (1987: chapter 9).
3. For an extreme statement of this position, in a semi-popular work which contrasts stamp collectors with those who pursue fine art — his own preferred form of collecting — see Jullian (1967). Jullian makes no effort to hide his condescending attitude toward the former type of collector.
4. It is difficult, if not impossible to state just when collecting in the sense we have defined it began. Earlier forms of assemblage of objects which resemble it and may be precursors are coin hoards buried in ancient times, plunder brought home from wars, grave goods buried with the dead, as in the case

of the extraordinary objects buried with King Tutankhamen at Luxor, and the treasuries created by ancient kings and emperors. No comprehensive, analytical, fully annotated history of collecting exists, but see, e.g., Alsop (1982); Bazin (1967); Impey and MacGregor (1985); Rheims (1967); Rigby and Rigby (1944); Taylor (1948); von Holst (1967).

5. Aestheticization of the functional objects of other cultures preceded the Industrial Revolution. So-called "cabinets of curiosities" which proliferated in the Age of Discovery, the sixteenth and seventeenth centuries, included rare and curious objects both from nature and from exotic cultures. See Impey and MacGregor (1985).

6. See, e.g., Lynes (1980); Briggs (1988); Grier (1988); Saisselin (1985).

7. For further elaboration, see Benjamin (1973) and Saisselin (1985: chapter 5).

8. For examples of the new industrialists who became serious art collectors, see, e.g., Lynes (1980); Briggs (1988); and Saisselin (1985), as well as popular biographies and autobiographies, such as Le Vane and Getty (1955); Taylor (1970); and Saarinen (1958). Histories of individual museums also provide much information on businessmen-collectors who helped to create them. See, e.g., Tomkins (1970).

9. See Briggs (1988: chapter 9). Of course princes and kings soon began to collect stamps too.

10. The same idea was expressed in a semi-popular analysis of collecting by Jullian, a French illustrator, writer, and collector. In a chapter on age and collecting, he writes: "The collection has to be fed; its death will be [the collector's] own" (Jullian 1967: 48). The idea of the collection as metaphor for one's life is also central to Tennessee Williams' (1984) play "The Glass Menagerie." The daughter Laura is as delicate, fragile, and ethereally beautiful as her collection of miniature glass animals.

11. See also Fogelin (1988: 79), who writes that "likeness statements [including other types of comparison besides explicit linguistic metaphors] solve (or help to solve) the *ineffability problem*."

12. In some types of collections the collector "needs" items even if they are not individually pleasing. Thus, a record collector we interviewed pursued, say, all available recordings of a Mozart piano concerto. Once acquired, he might listen to a particular recording only once, because he did not like the interpretation, but would still keep it to complete the set.

13. It is possible to contrast the concrete physicality of objects with their nature as a kind of "node" in the system of information which makes up the non-tangible component of each collecting world. Collecting often involves the gathering of rather stunning amounts of detailed information that is directly (or even remotely) relevant to the particular collecting domain. Much of the activity involved in caring for one's collection, or expanding it, requires the ongoing gathering of information concerning the nature, provenance and value of collectible items, the places and prospects for acquisition, and so on.

14. Benjamin was a passionate collector of books. For more on his feelings about his collection, and the aura the various volumes exuded for him, see Benjamin (1969b).

15. We have identified five types of strategies which collectors use to pursue a sense of closure or perfection (Danet − Katriel 1989).

16. Some kinds of collectibles constitute finite worlds; in theory it is possible to ascertain the complete set of all stamps produced by a given country. In contrast, it may be impossible to determine objectively how many or how many different kinds of, e.g., Chinese snuff bottles there are.

17. That collectors are ambivalent about completing a collection is well illustrated by an example from Dannefer's (1980) study of vintage car collectors. Since it is not feasible for most to collect more than one or two cars, many also collect miniatures. One such collector, on the brink of completing his collection of miniatures, "saved himself" by redefining his goal as obtaining an exemplar of each model in each available color.

18. On the relevance of the concept of commitment to serious leisure activities, see Shamir (1980).

19. The fascination of the miniature deserves further attention. See Stewart (1984), as well as, e.g., Lee (1984); Bachelard (1969: chapter 7); Tuan (1984). The jacket to a book for collectors and makers of miniatures − doll houses and their appurtenances − entices its readers with the following passage:
    Welcome to the world of Miniatures. This world of Lilliputian art and artistry is a world of infinite possibilities. When you craft and collect miniatures, you can create whatever world you want, visit any historical period that suits your fancy, or bring a fantasy of your own into reality. The scope and freedom of a child's imagination is happily coupled with an adult's dreams and skills (Editors of Consumer Guide 1979).

20. A related distinction sometimes made in the literature on metaphor is that between internal and external metaphor. See Sapir (1977).

21. Professional collectors of objects − curators and dealers − are not immune to the use of metaphor, as in *The Chase, the Capture: Collecting at the Metropolitan* (Hoving et al. 1975), and *Tracking the Marvelous: A life in the New York Art World* (Myers 1984).

22. Netsuke are miniature carvings, usually of ivory or wood, which Japanese men and women used as toggles and counterweights, to hold small cases for medicine or tobacco tied to their *obi*, or belt. They were in use between the seventeenth and nineteenth centuries, and became obsolete when the Japanese switched to Western dress. See, e.g., Barker and Smith (1976).

23. In the spirit of our discussion of collecting as a master-metaphor for life, we can even paraphrase the opening epigraph of Goffman's essay, changing it from "To be on the wire is life; the rest is waiting" to "To collect is life; the rest is waiting!" This declaration is attributed to the high-wire artist Karl Wallenda, on going back up to the high wire after a fatal accident of his troupe (Goffman 1967: 149).

24. The activities of collectors are also sometimes compared to other types of goal-oriented activity, such as detective work, sports, or gardening. That of detective work appears, for example, in an accolade which Alec Templeton, the pianist and music box collector, proffers to his wife in his autobiography: "When it comes to finding music boxes, she has a talent for detective work that combines all the best attributes of Sherlock Holmes, Nero Wolfe and Sergeant Friday" (Templeton 1958: 35). Here are examples for the metaphors of sport and gardening:

    For the Fehers, collecting in itself represents much pleasure, yet, the contact with other collectors, dealers and experts adds immense enjoyment, as each has a love of the art which enriches the "sport" and the "obsession" (Center for African Art 1988: 16).

    The ... course to take when the collection becomes uncomfortably big for the house, is to weed out the less good pieces... I have weeded out all my life (Eccles 1968: 27).

25. The Hebrew word for "treats," *m'tapel*, is a pun here. It both means "take care of" in a general sense, and "do psychotherapy with."

26. In some kibbutzim, children sleep apart from their parents. In recent years, this arrangement has declined, in favor of a return to the traditional sleeping arrangements of the nuclear family.

27. A related metaphor is that of eating, which shares with passion notions of appetite, consumption, etc. Examples are: "what I have tried to do is to whet the appetite of would-be collectors" (Ackrill 1983: 7); "if we are asked why we bought this porcelain figure or that modern painting, we reply that we simply had to have it. We were hungry and we had to eat" (Eccles 1968: 3).

28. Campbell (1987) uses these lines as an epigraph to one of his chapters.

29. See Praz (1933).

30. The metaphor occurred already at the end of the nineteenth century, as the following lines from the autobiography of W. C. Hazlitt testify: "Reynolds was instrumental in inoculating me with a new weakness − the Postage Stamp" (Hazlitt 1897: 215).

31. "Timbre" is the French word for stamp.

32. This point is illustrated in the titles of the memoirs of Maurice Rheims (1980), the French auctioneer-collector, *The Glorious Obsession*, and of Peggy Guggenheim (1980), celebrity art collector, *Confessions of an Art Addict*. In literal-minded discussions of disease and obsessions, people would not brag about their activities. It is unlikely, for example, that a person addicted to drugs would title his or her autobiography *The Glorious Obsession*.

33. See Praz (1933: chapter 2). References to the devil are clearly culture-bound. As Trachtenberg (1979) has pointed out, preoccupation with the devil has been a theme of Christian folklore in Europe, but is alien to Jewish tradition. Jewish folk tradition, on the other hand, is rich in demons, creatures of a "middle world" between heaven and hell. The only example of a reference

to collecting as demon that we have encountered in our Israeli materials is Katriel's stamp-collecting daughter's passing reference to her *"dybbuk."*

34. Following Lakoff and Johnson (1980), we would argue, more precisely, that the use is metaphorical in both cases, but that in the former, the metaphor has become conventionalized, and so we do not experience it as such.

35. There is, for example, a large body of literature on collecting among the ancient Romans, which apparently includes some first-person accounts (Alsop 1982; Taylor 1948; Rigby — Rigby 1944: chapter 7). Journals of Renaissance collectors could also provide interesting materials.

References

Ackrill, David
    1983   "Preface," in: Biddle, 7–9.
Alsop, Joseph
    1982   *The rare art traditions: A history of collecting and its linked phenomena.* New York: Harper and Row.
Bachelard, Gaston
    1969   *The poetics of space.* Trans. Maria Jolas. Boston: Beacon Press.
Balzac, Honoré
    1968 [1848]   *Cousin Pons.* Trans. H. L. Hunt. Harmondsworth: Penguin.
Barker, Richard — Lawrence Smith
    1976   *Netsuke: The miniature sculpture of Japan.* London: British Museum.
Baudrillard, Jean
    1968   *Le system des objets.* Paris: Gallimard.
Bazin, Germain
    1967   *The museum age.* New York: Universe.
Beer Can Collectors of America
    1976   *The beer can: A complete guide to beer can collecting.* Metteson, IL: Greatlakes Living Press.
Benjamin, Walter
    1969   *Illuminations.* New York: Schocken.
    1973   *Charles Baudelaire: A lyric poet in the era of high capitalism.* Trans. H. Zohn. London: New Left Books.
Biddle, Ernest
    1983   *Collectors' corner.* London: Independent Television Books.
Brecher, Kenneth S.
    1988   *Too sad to sing: A memoir with postcards.* New York: Harcourt Brace Jovanovich.
Briggs, Asa
    1988   *Victorian things.* Chicago: University of Chicago Press.

Burke, Kenneth
    1965   *Permanence and change: An anatomy of purpose.* Indianapolis, IN: Bobbs-Merrill.
    1969   *A rhetoric of motives.* Berkeley: University of California Press.
Campbell, Colin
    1987   *The Romantic ethic and the spirit of modern consumerism.* Oxford: Basil Blackwell.
Carmichael, Bill
    1971   *Incredible collectors, weird antiques and odd hobbies.* Englewood Cliffs, NJ: Prentice-Hall.
Center for African Art
    1988   *The art of collecting African art.* New York: Center for African Art.
Chatwin, Bruce
    1988   *Utz.* New York: Viking.
Clifford, James
    1988   *The predicament of culture: Twentieth-century ethnography, literature, and art.* Cambridge, MA: Harvard University Press.
Cohen, Erik
    1985   "Tourism as play," *Religion* 15: 291–304.
Cohen, George
    1974   *In search of netsuke: An introduction.* London: Jacey.
Csikszentmihalyi, Mihaly
    1975   *Beyond boredom and anxiety.* San Francisco: Jossey-Bass.
Danet, Brenda – Tamar Katriel
    1989   "No two alike: Play and aesthetics in collecting," *Play and Culture* 2(3): 253–277.
Dannefer, Dale
    1980   "Rationality and passion in private experience: Modern consciousness and the social world of old-car collectors," *Social Problems* 27: 392–412.
DiBonis, Louis – Mark Burns
    1988   *Fifties homestyle: Popular ornament of the USA.* New York: Harper and Row.
Eccles, Lord David
    1968   *On collecting.* London: Longmans, Green.
Editors of Consumer Guide
    1979   *Miniatures.* New York: Beekman House.
Ellen, Roy
    1988   "Fetishism," *Man* 23: 213–235.
Fernandez, James W.
    1972   "Persuasions and performance: Of the beast in every body ... and the metaphors of everyman," *Daedelus* 101: 39–60.
    1974   "The mission of metaphor in expressive culture," *Current Anthropology* 15: 119–145.

1977   "The performance of ritual metaphors," in: J. David Sapir —
            J. Christopher Crocker (eds.), 100 – 131.
Fine, Gary
1987   "Community and boundary: Personal experience stories of mush-
            room collectors," *Journal of Folklore Research* 24: 223 – 240.
Fletcher, Edward
1975   *A treasure hunter's guide*. Dorset: Blandford.
Fogelin, Robert J.
1988   *Figuratively speaking*. New Haven: Yale University Press.
Gaudefroy-Demombynes, Jean
1966   "The inner movement of romanticism," in: Anthony Thorlby (ed.),
            138 – 142.
Goffman, Erving
1967   *Interaction ritual: Essays on face-to-face behavior*. Garden City, NY:
            Anchor Books.
Grier, Katherine C.
1988   *Culture and comfort: People, parlors and upholstery, 1850 – 1930*.
            Rochester, NY: The Strong Museum.
Guggenheim, Peggy
1980   *Out of this century: Confessions of an art addict*. Garden City, NY:
            Anchor Books.
Halsted, John B.
1965   *Romanticism: Problems of definition, explanation, and evaluation*. Bos-
            ton: D. C. Heath.
Hazlitt, William Carew
1897   *The confessions of a collector*. London: Ward and Downey.
Horn, Jeanne
1962   *Hidden treasure: How and where to find it*. New York: Bonanza
            Books.
Hoving, Thomas — Dietrich von Bothmer — Richard Ettinghausen — Wen
Fong — Henry Geldzahler — Morrison H. Heckscher — Julie Jones — Christine
Lilyquist — Douglas Newton — Helmut Nickel — Olga Raggio — Margaretta
Salinger — Susan Vogel
1975   *The chase, the capture: Collecting at the Metropolitan*. New York:
            Metropolitan Museum of Art.
Hughes, Stephen
1984   *Pop culture mania: Collecting 20th century Americana for fun and
            profit*. New York: McGraw-Hill.
Hugo, Howard E.
1965   "Components of Romanticism," in: John B. Halsted (ed.), 30 – 36.
Impey, Oliver — Arthur MacGregor
1985   *The origins of the museum: Cabinets of curiosities in the sixteenth and
            seventeenth centuries*. Oxford: Clarendon.

Jacobs, Flora Gill
  1965   *A world of doll houses*. New York: Gramercy.
James, Henry
  1987 [1886] *The spoils of Poynton*. Harmondsworth: Penguin.
Johnston, Susanna — Tim Beddow
  1986   *Collecting: The passionate pastime*. Harmondsworth: Penguin.
Jullian, Philippe
  1967   *The collectors*. Trans. Michael Callum. Rutland, VT: Charles
          E. Tuttle.
Ketchum, W. E.
  1975   *A treasury of American bottles*. Indianapolis: Bobbs-Merrill.
Kreitler, Hans — Shulamith Kreitler
  1972   *Psychology of the arts*. Durham, NC: University of North Carolina
          Press.
Lakoff, George — Mark Johnson
  1980   *Metaphors we live by*. Chicago: University of Chicago Press.
Land-Webber, Rosemarie
  1980   *The passionate collector*. New York: Simon and Schuster.
Lee, O-Young
  1984   *Smaller is better: Japan's mastery of the miniature*. Tokyo: Kodansha.
Le Vane, Ethel — J. Paul Getty
  1955   *Collector's choice: The chronicle of an artistic odyssey through Europe*.
          London: W. H. Allen.
Loy, John W.
  1982   *The paradoxes of play*. West Point, NY: Leisure Press.
Lynes, Russell
  1980 [1949] *The tastemakers: The shaping of American popular taste*. New York:
          Dover.
Malraux, Andre
  1967[1947] *Museum without walls*. New York: Doubleday.
Maquet, Jacques
  1986   *The aesthetic experience: An anthropologist looks at the visual arts*.
          New Haven: Yale University Press.
Mebane, John
  1972   *Collecting nostalgia: The first guide to the antiques of the 30's and the
          40's*. New York: Popular Library.
Mediskar, Ofra
  1990   "Collector's war," *Jerusalem*, January 26.
Mills, C. Wright
  1940   "Situated actions and vocabularies of motive," *American Sociological
          Review* 5: 904–913.
Myers, John Bernard
  1984   *Tracking the marvelous: A life in the New York art world*. London:
          Thames and Hudson.

Nabokov, Vladimir
1969   *Speak, memory*. Harmondsworth: Penguin.
Neider, Charles (ed.)
1957   *The complete short stories of Mark Twain*. Garden City, NY: Dou-
        bleday.
Ortony, Andrew
1975   "Why metaphors are necessary and not just nice," *Educational Theory*
        25: 45 – 53.
Peckham, Morse
1970   *The theory of Romanticism: Collected essays*. Columbia, SC: Univer-
        sity of South Carolina Press.
Pins, Jacob
1980   *The Pins collection: Chinese and Japanese paintings and prints*. Jeru-
        salem: Israel Museum.
Praz, Mario
1933   *The Romantic agony*. Trans. Angus Davidson. London: Oxford Uni-
        versity Press.
Price, Vincent
1959   *I like what I know: A visual autobiography*. Garden City, NY: Dou-
        bleday.
Rheims, Maurice
1967   *Art on the market: Thirty-five centuries of collecting and collectors,
        from Midas to J. Paul Getty*. Trans. D. Pryce-Jones. London: Wei-
        denfeld and Nicholson.
1940   *The glorious obsession*. Trans. P. Evans. London: Souvenir.
Rigby, Douglas — Elizabeth Rigby
1944   *Lock, stock and barrel: The story of collecting*. Philadelphia: Lippin-
        cott.
Saarinen, Aline B.
1958   *The proud possessors: The lives, times, and tastes of some adventurous
        American art collectors*. New York: Random House.
Saisselin, Remy G.
1985   *Bricabracomania: The bourgeois and the bibelot*. London: Thames
        and Hudson.
Salter, Stefan
1971   *The joys of hunting antiques*. New York: Hart.
Sapir, J. David
1977   "The anatomy of metaphor," in: J. David Sapir — J. Christopher
        Crocker (eds.), 3 – 32.
Sapir, J. David — J. Christopher Crocker (eds.)
1977   *The social use of metaphor: Essays on the anthropology of rhetoric*.
        Philadelphia: University of Pennsylvania Press.
Schutz, Alfred
1962   *Collected Papers*, I. The Hague: Martinus Nijhoff.

Schwartzman, Helen B.
1982   "Play and metaphor," in: John W. Loy (ed.), 25 – 32.
Shamir, Boas
1988   "Commitment and leisure," *Sociological Perspectives* 31: 238 – 258.
Silver, Joseph Baruch
1987   *Chinese snuff bottles from the collection of Joseph Baruch Silver.* Jerusalem: Israel Museum.
Sontag, Susan
1979   *Illness as metaphor.* New York: Vintage Books.
Stebbins, Robert A.
1979   *Amateurs: On the margin between work and leisure.* Beverly Hills, CA: Sage.
1980   "'Amateur' and 'hobbyist' as concepts for the study of leisure problems," *Social Problems* 27: 413 – 417.
1982   "Serious leisure: A conceptual statement," *Pacific Sociological Review* 25: 251 – 272.
Stewart, Susan
1984   *On longing: Narratives of the miniature, the gigantic, the souvenir, the collection.* Baltimore, MD: John Hopkins University Press.
Taylor, Francis Henry
1948   *The taste of angels: A history of art collecting from Ramses to Napoleon.* Boston: Little, Brown.
Templeton, Alec
1958   *Alec Templeton's music boxes.* New York: Funk.
Thorlby, Anthony (ed.)
1966   *The Romantic movement.* London: Longmans.
Tomkins, Calvin
1970   *Merchants and masterpieces: The story of the Metropolitan Museum of Art.* New York: Dutton.
Trachtenberg, Joshua
1979   *Jewish magic and superstition: A study in folk religion.* New York: Antheneum.
Tresise, Charles E.
1983   *Tavern treasures: A book of pub collectables.* Poole, Dorset: Blandford House.
Tuan, Yi-fu
1984   *Dominance and affection: The making of pets.* New Haven: Yale University Press.
Twain, Mark
1957   "The canvasser's tale," in: Charles Neider (ed.), 122 – 127.
Veblen, Thorstein
1979 [1899] *The theory of the leisure class.* New York: Viking Penguin.
Vollard, Ambroise
1978   *Recollections of a picture dealer.* Trans. Violet M. MacDonald. New York: Dover.

Von Holst, Niels
   1967   *Creators, collectors, and connoisseurs: The anatomy of artistic taste
                from antiquity to the present day.* Trans. Brian Battershaw. New
                York: Putnam.
Weber, Max
   1930 [1904 – 05]   *The Protestant ethic and the spirit of capitalism.* Trans. Talcott
                Parsons. London: Unwin University Books.
Williams, G. R.
   1976   *The world of model cars:* New York: Putnam.
Williams, Tennessee
   1984   *The glass menagerie.* Harmondsworth: Penguin.
Wolin, Richard
   1982   *Walter Benjamin: An aesthetic of redemption.* New York: Columbia
                University Press.

Objects and their maker: Bricolage of the self

Vera Mark

The central role of objects in social life has long been recognized by students of material culture in disciplines such as art history, archeology, and folklore. Emphasis may focus upon the shifts in values when an object gains commodity status, as in the case of the art and artifacts markets (Stewart 1984; Stocking 1985; Clifford 1988), or upon the traditional knowledge and craftsmanship needed to make the object, as in the case of folklore (Hufford et al. 1987). In recent years attention has been directed to the complex semiotic nature of objects within the symbolic economies of individuals and collectivities. Studies such as those by Douglas and Isherwood (1979), Csikszentmihalyi and Rochberg-Halton (1981), Schlereth (1982), Ward (1984), Appadurai (1986), and more recently, Kirshenblatt-Gimblett (1989), and Riggins (1990) have focused upon the profoundly social lives of objects and artifacts within domestic interiors and as commodities.

This essay traces the semiotic paths between a series of objects, their recipients, and their creator, Pierre Sentat (1894–1984), a cobbler and shoe merchant of Spanish ancestry and native of Lectoure, a small Gascon town in southwestern France. In the last three decades of his life (1950s-1980s), Mr. Sentat fashioned airplane mobiles out of discarded mineral water bottles, religious crosses from cobblers' nails, rope from twine debris, small scenes of animal figures from scrap metal, and scribbled poems on shoe brochures or old ice cream wrappers. He frequently offered these diverse objects as gifts. His most significant motivation for their creation resided in a problematic political past which he reinscribed in the objects and through their offering.

Like many of the other young men of his generation born in the final years of the nineteenth century, Pierre Sentat had volunteered for military service and served a full term of duty as a soldier in World War I. With the onset of World War II, he was too old to serve as a soldier. However, he remained engaged in local politics and aligned himself with the extreme right. In the immediate period after France's liberation, a local tribunal judged him guilty of collaboration and so he served a prison sentence in nearby Toulouse for two years, from 1945 to 1947. Released early for good behavior, upon his return to Lectoure many town residents refused to patronize his formerly successful shoe shop or even to talk with him.

Made for specific individuals thirty years after his problematic, and for him, stigmatizing experience, Mr. Sentat's objects and poems defined the boundaries of a social world constructed to counter intense psychological isolation. These objects and poems repeatedly and insistently encoded several time periods — Mr. Sentat's memories of his military service during World War I, World War II and its aftermath, and, on a larger scale, the long-term shift from a rural society to a modern world of advanced technologies, typified in the French supersonic airplane *Concorde*, which he re-created in mobile form. Mr. Sentat's own life experiences, which included regular farm work during summer vacations between the ages of six and twelve and an apprenticeship between the ages of twelve and sixteen, first with his father and then with another cobbler, involved a transition from the traditional rural world of his childhood to the modern one of his mature adulthood.[1]

Yet Mr. Sentat's identification with peasant and artisanal worlds must also be framed with respect to French politics of the 1930s and 1940s. Among many of its facets, fascism has been seen as a revolt against modernity, the result of the crisis of a society passing from a traditional framework to that of industrialism, a rebellion designed to create a deliberately archaic utopia (Friedländer 1984: 29; Kaplan 1986: 3, 25 – 26). In his study of how this archaic utopia found expression in France from 1940 to 1944, historian Christian Faure focuses upon folklore. Re-imaged and re-written via a nostalgic past, folklore provided a reification of a rural space in which the peasant and artisan became archetypal figures of the new society (Faure 1989: 105).[2] This reimagined rural world attempted to displace the presence of the industrial working classes which had agitated for various social and political reforms, as well as that of the German soldiers in occupied France (Faure: 105). While Faure draws upon a range of domains within French society to make his point, his discussion of imagery provides a particularly dramatic example of how the political was aestheticized (Faure: 175). In an inversion or perversion of pictorial signs, medieval iconography concerning artisanal and rural culture was revived to illustrate principles of "social peace." Thus Mr. Sentat's repeated framing of objects and symbols with respect to peasant and artisanal worlds must be understood both in personal and in larger socio-political terms.

An incident that took place on Veteran's Day during my 1981−82 field stay revealed to me what a powerful hold the memories of World Wars I and II continued to exert on Mr. Sentat and his family. As was my daily habit, I stopped by the shoe store that morning in order to say hello to the cobbler and his daughter. I witnessed a sharp altercation between the two, for Madame Sentat had just discovered that her father had displayed his medals from World War I in the right front window. She retorted that she did not want to think about war, that she had suffered too much, and she demanded that her father remove the medals immediately. For Mr. Sentat, the medals were "collective and esteem objects" (Riggins 1990: 349−350) that positively encoded his experiences in World War I, whereas for his daughter, they could only be charged "stigma objects" (Riggins 1990: 350) which recalled the later World War II. Mr. Sentat grumbled about the fact that he was no longer in charge, but he removed the offending objects and slowly made his way to his back workshop, where he hid them away.

The present study derives from fieldwork first undertaken in 1981−82, continued in the summer of 1987 and part of 1988−89; as well as from on-going correspondence with Mr. Sentat's daughter since her father's death in 1984. In a nostalgic search for twentieth-century survivals of nineteenth-century popular literature, I began the 1981−82 research in order to gather folktales and other related genres. However, I encountered a quite different genre − local poetry − and another tale, that of Mr. Sentat's life, which emerged in the conversations that he and I had on an almost daily basis from August 1981 until May 1982, and in the one hundred and fifty poems that he had written, only some of which I consulted at that time. On several occasions during the year, Mr. Sentat maintained to me that he had been a *Pétainiste*, or merely a follower of his "good" leader from World War I, rather than a collaborator. He insisted that he was not a fascist. Certain of his poems, portions of his personal correspondence, and interviews conducted with him by two local journalists and myself in the last five years of his life indicate that he was engaged in political activity throughout World War II. What kind of political activity and what specifically led to his imprisonment is for me still an unknown, one that I would like to refer to as the "black hole" in my narrative and analysis. As family and state restrictions prevent me from consulting proceedings from his 1945 trial and other relevant documents, I cannot dwell on these issues at this point in time. I plan to do so at a later date, however.

In the course of my contextual analysis of Mr. Sentat's poems,[3] my attention was caught by the visual, represented in the objects which preceded or accompanied the offering of the poems, and sent primarily to individuals residing within the town. The present essay consequently focuses on the material objects which Mr. Sentat created or remade, within the framework of a larger study of symbolic exchange and representations of self. The analysis inscribes my own presence in order to detail the historical evolution in my understanding of Mr. Sentat, a cobbler and shoe merchant whose voice under most circumstances would have remained voiceless. I therefore alternate past and present tense so as to avoid the limitations of the ethnographic present frequently favored by anthropologists, but which effaces historical shifts in the ethnographer's perceptions (Clifford 1988). Initially drawn to this engaging *raconteur* because he appeared to embody the image of a traditional, if eccentric, artisan, my field notes and audiotapes from the 1981–82 fieldwork reveal my sympathy for a clearly traumatized individual. From 1983 to the present my position has become more critical, a result of repeated readings of Mr. Sentat's texts, further fieldwork, more nuanced political contextualizations and a certain distance achieved through historical time. I have purposely left both tones – the sympathetic and the critical – to intermingle in my narrative so as to share my shifting experiences with the reader. The presence of several other outsiders, who saw Mr. Sentat as an eccentric traditional artisan – as initially I did – is also written into the text. These outsiders included local journalists who between 1979 and 1984 interviewed Mr. Sentat for two regional publications; two fellow graduate student friends from the University of Texas who visited me in the course of the 1981–82 fieldwork; and a crew of three young men from a technical *lycée* in the nearby town of Auch, who in April 1982 came to videotape an artisan they had heard about from their work colleague, the husband of Mr. Sentat's elder granddaughter.

Mr. Sentat's workshop

The Sentat's store – to this day – has rows and rows of boxes of shoes, boots and slippers, ranging from the most recent styles to those from the 1940s and 1950s. Work and dressy shoes are available, displayed on side counters and shelves. All ages of society are represented in footwear for babies, children, adolescents, adult men and women. For many customers, curious schoolchildren, passing journalists and summer tourists, the store and the workshop were and remain "old" places. One journalist qualified the main store in the following way: "now the large room decorated with a multitude of airplanes ... resembles a baroque museum" (Gardère 1979: 16). The adjective "baroque," in the sense of odd, singular, or bizarre, can also refer to its artistic meaning of visual excess of decoration achieved through the fantastic and the accumulation of mass, light, and movement. The journalist may have used this adjective to describe the singular, highly personal ambience of the store, marked by several photographs of family members, vases of fresh flowers, and airplane mobiles made by Mr. Sentat that were suspended from the ceiling. Baroque could also qualify the accumulation of boxes and boxes of shoes, piled high from floor to ceiling and which fill every available inch of space in the Sentats' shop.

The sales section of the business is run, as it was for many years, by Mr. Sentat's daughter, Madame Sentat, who kept her maiden name. She sells footwear and shoe care products. The greatest part of the shop's income derives from the sales of factory-made shoes brought in by regional distributors, as has been the case for shoe shops in rural France since the late nineteenth century (Laffontan 1969). Her father remained in the back workshop, where he undertook all of his repairs on shoes, boots, and leather goods. These repairs formed a small but steady percentage of the shop's total revenues.[4] In this engendered division of work space, the Sentats continued the tradition of artisanally-based businesses divided into a back workshop, the man's domain of creation and production, and the front sales portion of the store, the woman's domain for distribution of hand-made goods.

The *atelier* or workshop was perceived as an "old" place for several reasons. First, it was the space of a traditional craftsman. In this respect it embodied an earlier mode of economic production in which shoes were sometimes made by hand. The wooden shoe molds on some of the shelves are a reminder of more prosperous times in the 1930s, when Mr. Sentat's clientele numbered some 1,500 individuals from Lectoure and the surrounding countryside. In a letter sent to me in September 1990 his daughter explained that her father typically had made shoes for special needs, such as orthopedic footwear. He made few shoes to order, and he did not sell them as part of the store stock. Thus the shoes were probably given within a system of barter, or payment in kind, which surfaces in the late twentieth century as tips on top of monetary compensation. At the turn of the century barter was a major basis of economic transactions in this and other rural settings. At present cobblers do not make shoes and so the old shoe forms remain a curiosity, reflecting an earlier mode of production in a predominantly modern world.

Once the yard of the original house, the present workshop was created in the 1920s through the addition of walls and a glass ceiling. Cobwebs and dust line the walls and ceiling, making the room seem unoccupied. In disjunction with modern times, its main occupant appeared to live more in the past than in the present. Like the home of Miss Savidge, a *bricoleuse* from a different place who lived surrounded by her old clock and family portraits from a bygone era, Mr. Sentat's workshop gave the impression of "a personal world which needed to intensify and fall back on itself, becoming more self-sufficient and also more private and occult in its significance in order to survive not just time ... but also the abrupt and sudden traumas of recent history" (Wright 1987: 196). The decay, dislocation and a strangely determined survival which characterize Miss Savidge's home were evident in Mr. Sentat's workshop. Its elements of decay — the dust, cobwebs, and old shoe forms — of dislocation — the deeply personal amidst the work space — and of survival — in the tools and machines which attested to active engagement with the cobbler's profession — situated it in the past.

This sense of past could at times be experienced in positive rather than alienating terms. The links with an earlier mode of production, part of the region's and country's history, found organic expression in a harmonious relation between individual (Mr. Sentat), objects (his machines and tools), and environment (the workshop). Visitors to his workshop could experience a kind of psychological connection as well, as Santa Fe cabinetmaker and furniture builder Bill Harper explained when asked why he was so enthralled with old tools, which are merely the workaday implements of antiquated kinds of manual labor.

> I feel an obligation to use a tool in the manner for which it was designed. You can picture in your mind the shop where they made these tools and the craftsmen who made them; and you can picture how they would want you to use it, keep it clean and sharp. Sometimes you feel as if you are working with the ghosts of your predecessors who worked before you (Neary 1991: 57).

This sense of organic unity between persons and their products, described as typical of precapitalist societies, stands in stark contrast to the split between persons and the things that they produce and exchange in capitalist societies (Taussig 1980: 37).

The workshop amused some people because of its apparent disorder. In the course of the video-taping session with the young men from Auch, Mr. Sentat commented approvingly that things were in their place. To the outsider nothing could seem further from the truth, for the dusty shelves and the mass of objects clustered in the workbench suggested the opposite — "a true adventure into a mysterious disordered shambles where the uninitiated are not at ease" — as a local journalist had described a visit to the workshop three years earlier (Gardère 1979: 16). To the outsider's eye of the journalist, the workshop was a place which could only remain distant and unknowable. Yet it was an ordered space with its own logic. A symbolic environment, overlapping physical structure and emotional space, it formed a world which Mr. Sentat had created to embody what he considered significant (Csikszentmihalyi — Rochberg-Halton 1981: 123).

Mr. Sentat's back workshop was the public space of a cobbler who undertook all kinds of repairs on shoes and leather goods, and a place where he engaged in private conversations with his customers. The workshop was as well Mr. Sentat's creative space, where he worked with materials ranging from rubber to leather, plastic to metal, to create artistic objects. He constructed airplane mobiles from old mineral water bottles and decorated the store, workshop and family back garden with them. In addition to being a creator and transformer of physical objects ranging from shoes to school satchels to airplane mobiles, Mr. Sentat was a creator of literary objects, letter-poems which he wrote in French and Gascon, the regional language. Two satchels located to the side of one of his sewing machines overflowed with his poems and their drafts, typically composed between shoe-repair jobs, as was the case of cobblers and other artisans who composed poems in the mid-nineteenth century (Rancière 1983). One pair of journalists characterized his workshop as "a poem" (Carsalade — Durand 1982: 9), underscoring it as a space of fantasy and of the imagination.

The *atelier* was also Mr. Sentat's personal living space, filled with a range of meaningful objects. Like the inner sanctum of bedrooms, a private area that gives a greater feeling of control over the activities and objects than other rooms, Mr. Sentat's workshop was a place where autonomy could be cultivated through dialogues with the self in the course of conversations or during his writing of poetry. Cherished possessions such as his World War I and fireman's helmets made it into an intensely personal place (Csikszentmihalyi — Rochberg-Halton 1981: 137). In talking to me about this room, Mr. Sentat asserted "*Ici, je suis*

chez moi" [Here, I am at home]. Being at home meant that he was safe
from the eyes of outsiders who might remind him of his problematic
political past. His workshop provided a space for action and interaction
in which he could develop, maintain, and change his identity (Csikszentmihalyi — Rochberg-Halton 1981: 144).

In his final years Mr. Sentat's time spent in the workshop reflected a
turning inward. He spent most of his waking hours in this room, and
only left his home on Sunday afternoons for a short drive in the country
with his daughter and invalid granddaughter. His insistence on remaining
in the *atelier* during work hours stemmed partially from his identification
with his profession. He felt that he needed to uphold his reputation as a
serious merchant, which called for constant availability to serve any
customer. Yet Mr. Sentat felt constrained by his domestic space. On
several occasions during my fieldwork year of 1981 — 82, I offered to go
for a walk with him. He refused, saying that his legs were not strong
enough. With this he articulated his awareness of diminishing physical
abilities. The second part of his answer — that he did not want to risk
hearing people laugh at him behind his back — expressed his continuous
trauma of rejection from the larger social world after his return in 1947
to Lectoure upon his release from prison. He said several times that he
was more a prisoner in his own home than when incarcerated in Toulouse.
Thus his home was both a shelter from a larger hostile world and a *huis
clos.*

Finally, the workshop was a setting for Mr. Sentat to dramatize himself
to others. I witnessed this on two important occasions at the end of my
stay, in the late spring of 1982. The first instance involved a visit in mid
April from my friend Joan Gross. A fellow anthropology student from
the University of Texas, she was conducting her doctoral research on
puppetry in Liège, Belgium, at the time. I brought her along to meet the
Sentats. Much of our conversation took place in the workshop, where
our talk ranged from explaining how to repair a shoe, to a general
discussion of the cobbler's trade, to elements of ethnic identity and local
customs, as Mr. Sentat explained festive traditions in southwestern France
and Spain. He also read and recited portions of a number of his poems
for the two of us.

Two weeks later, on April 28, several work colleagues of the husband
of Mr. Sentat's elder granddaughter came up from Auch to prepare a
videotape of the cobbler in his *atelier* so as to document a "traditional
craftsman" at work. I was present throughout the taping, during which
Mr. Sentat walked around the workshop and pointed out important

objects, as he had two weeks earlier, demonstrated how to use the tools of his trade, and told numerous stories and jokes. He also read from a number of his poems. The young men had already heard about these poems from Mr. Sentat's elder granddaughter. Interspersed throughout the more serious explanations of work tools and machines were humorous anecdotes and narratives, told in male complicity before myself, the sole female onlooker. In the style of folktales, the narratives revealed Mr. Sentat's ability to make the most of a situation and turn it to his advantage, either through his physical strength or his wits. He concluded by highlighting significant events from an outline of his life, which he had drafted especially for the occasion and scribbled on an old envelope. The visits from my friend and the young men motivated him to consciously dramatize himself with respect to me, the ethnographer, a more familiar outsider, and with respect to these other outsiders. A significant element of his self-staging involved display and commentary of personally meaningful objects.

After Mr. Sentat's death in March 1984, his daughter and granddaughter cleaned out much of the scrap paper and metal from the workshop. Although someone offered to buy the cobbler's tools and machines for a local museum documenting traditional life, Madame Sentat refused. Covered with paper, the larger machines stand silently in storage. The workbench still has many of its tools, but its entrance is boarded up. During my field stay in the summer of 1987, Madame Sentat took two of the satchels out from their storage place under one of the sewing machines. She had granted me permission to consult the drafts of poems which her father had written during the last twenty years of his life. As she lifted up the two bags, she trembled "I feel as if I'm opening up his tomb." She added that she never dwelled long in the workshop, even though she crossed it several times daily to get to the front store from her back living quarters. The workshop now (1991) contains flower pots and gardening supplies. During the winter potted plants from the family's back garden occupy every free spot on the shelves and benches. Although its association with Mr. Sentat's artisanal identity — which extended for a period of some fifty years — ended upon his death, his workshop continues to express a critical element of the family's identity, its interest in plants and gardens. The collective sense of family identity is represented in the plants, many of which grew from cuttings given by other friends and neighbors. In this respect, the workshop remains a place of lived relationships.[5]

Mr. Sentat as bricoleur

Mr. Sentat's ability to do repairs was a significant aspect of his work identity, and through it he realized multiple talents as artist and as engineer, as Lévi-Strauss defines the *bricoleur* or resourceful tinkerer (1966: 17). The verb *bricoler* is strongly gender encoded, for it typically refers to the puttering around and fixing things up undertaken by men in their leisure time. The verb *bricoler* also appears in artisanal discourse and refers to how to first learn a trade.[6] Mr. Sentat's identity as *bricoleur* was exemplified in one of his favorite mottoes: "*Je fais tout de rien, et je fais rien du tout*" [I make everything out of nothing, and I do nothing at all]. He indeed could make something out of nothing. Hanging from the store and shop ceilings are the whirligigs and airplane mobiles for which he was famous. His fascination with machines and their functioning enabled him to repair his two sewing machines, both of which he acquired in the 1930s, as well as his 1950s automobile. In his old age, Mr. Sentat continued to work daily, repairing the shoes, boots, and other leather goods that customers brought him. He was well-known for the skill and artistry of his repairs, a quality highly valued in a peasant culture which emphasizes making do with modest means and repairing an item until it literally cannot be used any more.

As *bricoleur*, Mr. Sentat resembled those artists or repairers who use as raw materials what other people discard. He was like Willie, the auto mechanic of rural North County in upstate New York profiled by sociologist Douglas Harper. In describing how he could take hinges from one object and use them for a wood stove which he was building to heat a greenhouse, Willie commented: "To everyone else it looks like junk; to me it looks like stuff I can use. I was looking for something to make the hinges with" (Harper 1987: 54). The sociologist observes:

> to an outsider, a shop like Willie's seems to be filled with junk. Junk, however, is material without value. When you understand how the shop operates, you see how use or exchange value comes out of the most unlikely objects. Willie salvages the value from all the material that comes through the shop; what is left over is junk, by *his* definition (Harper 1987: 154; my emphasis).

The same could be said of Mr. Sentat. The boxes of old shoes, leather scraps, of thread, of metal bits, all could serve to repair something at some undetermined point, but only the repairer knew how and when.

The second part of Mr. Sentat's self-definition as *bricoleur*, "*je fais rien du tout*" is deeply ironic, for "I do nothing at all" contrasts with how Mr. Sentat actually spent his time. Mr. Sentat insisted on working into his old age. In the course of our conversations during the 1981 – 82 year he often proudly observed that he had worked for 75 years without a break. He counted from the year 1906, when at age twelve he began as a cobbler's apprentice to his father. He continued to work until five months before his death at age ninety, on March 9, 1984. His self-depiction as a *bricoleur* appears in the italicized sections of the following exchange during the April 1982 video-taping session:

> Mr. Sentat: Now, that is for doing farrier's work and that's my anvil for my jobs, for my jobs, for when for when I'm free, I'm doing nothing – I do something here, I keep busy there, I do anything, anywhere ... *what the others can't do, they bring to me to fix.*
> Young man: Shoes?
> Mr. Sentat: *Oh anything*, shoes, not pianos, but *anything*!
> Young man: Oh really?
> Mr.Sentat: Oh yes, oh yes. *I do it all.* You don't have anything broken, do you? A watch? ... (T-12, April 28, 1982).

His joke could have also contained a self-judgment which saw his time spent working in the shop as wasted time. His consciousness of the transformations in his profession are evident in these comments:

> ... my tools at arm's reach, for work, I don't have much of it. Oh well, those are things you can't avoid... I do what is necessary, I'm not a cobbler like others, I stopped making shoes because ... twenty years ago ... I'm eighty-eight years old – consequently I content myself with repairing well if I know how, sometimes I think I don't do badly... (T-12, April 28, 1982).

In reality Mr. Sentat stopped making shoes much earlier than twenty years ago, in the late 1960s. Yet his shift to repair work came about not merely due to the transformations in the shoe industry.[7] It also reflected his engineering capabilities which allowed him to fix and even create machines. Furthermore, continuing to work on diverse repairs in his old age gave him a vital link with the larger society, and made him feel still useful.

Mr. Sentat's sense of artisanal knowledge was at times expressed in humorously ironic terms. In the course of a conversation between Mr. Sentat, Joan Gross, and myself, Joan observed that clogs, traditional footwear, were no longer worn. Mr. Sentat disagreed and explained that some farmers still wore clogs because they remained the most effective protection from the hooves of barnyard animals. He distinguished between wooden clogs, which were far more solid and practical for farmers, and the leather clogs that he sold to a general public. He then added

with a chuckle "I really can't tell you very much about shoes, by golly."
In fact this disclaimer communicated the opposite, that he had deep
knowledge about machines and tools, about chemical and physical properties of objects in the natural world, and about shoes. Shoes were objects
of social knowledge, as when Mr. Sentat observed to me on another
occasion "I can tell everything about people just by looking at their feet."
He explained that he could determine an individual's social class and,
more importantly, according to the condition of that person's shoes, "see
through clothes" to judge his or her moral character.

Mr. Sentat's bricolage in the workshop

As one enters the workshop after leaving the front sales room, one sees
to the immediate left Mr. Sentat's workbench surrounded by pockets of
shoe-repairing tools. Here the cobbler sat for long hours as he worked
on his repairs. Mr. Sentat modified his workbench to suit his purposes,
particularly in old age. His cobbler's stool consisted of a chair, on top
of which was first an old automobile inner tube and then a square piece
of foam. Both were attached to the seat with rope. This practical solution
allowed him to sit higher and work more comfortably, in closer reach of
his tools and lamp. The inner tube was a typical example of Mr. Sentat's
recycling of discarded items to prolong their use. Many items found their
way into the workshop through this process.

   In addition to raising the height of his stool, Mr. Sentat moved his
tools close to the bench, at shoulder level, for in his final years it became
difficult for him to bend down. In conversation with the young men who
filmed him in the 1982 session, he explained: "And here I have all I need
at my service, this is ... to make nail holes... I don't need that one ... it
falls down, *so since I'm clever, bon appétit* (said in Gascon[8]), anyway,
that's the way I am − my tools at arm's reach..." (T-2, April 28, 1982).
Mr. Sentat then demonstrated how he used an iron horseshoe as a magnet
to pick up cobbler's nails and metal tools that had fallen to the floor and
that he wished to hold in place. He used a shoe originally intended for
protecting the feet of a horse in another context, that of the workshop,
for an equally functional need − keeping his nails together for repairs
on shoes worn by people. The horseshoes tied him to the rural world of
his youth, when during summer vacation he had worked on farms between
the ages of six and twelve, from 1900 to 1906, as mentioned above. The

horseshoes also tied in with his identity and that of his father during two different wars. His father was a cavalry man in the Franco-Prussian War of 1870, and so was he, some forty years later, in World War I. The horseshoes encoded the rural world and recalled his days of glory through World War I before the fall in World War II. Madame Sentat's description of her father's workshop tools reads as follows:

> ... an electric motor connected to a transmission, in turn connected to three machines — a hammer to work the leather of soles, a Petits Points sewing machine (for small stitches), a Black sewing machine (for large stitches); a finishing bench for grinding, scraping, waxing, polishing. The tools are more or less old, more or less personalized by Papa Pierrot, he made them as he needed them, [they are] not always elegant, but very efficient... There are several sorts of pliers; pinchers for pulling out nails; several types of hammers — for driving in nails, for working leather, for closing rivets; awls, more or less long and big, smooth and with holes for handsewing; shoemaker's knives for cutting leather; nails of different forms and lengths; thread, and *poisse*, a greased thread used for heavy sewing, like they used to make... (Personal communication, September 1990).

In her description, Madame Sentat emphasized the age of her father's tools and his abilities to transform them to suit his needs.

In addition to using the standard machines and tools of his trade, Mr. Sentat remade other objects, such as a hot plate, to suit his cobbling needs:

> ... Oh yes, that, so, that I use, when I put on glue, like that, I put glue, there, fine, I go to the shop, I talk and I go to ... it's too dry. So I have the glue, like that, when it's done. But if it's like that, it can't glue. I glue with infrared rays, and it vulcanizes. See, rubber and glue blend together, it holds and here... (T-8, April 16, 1982).

He explained that sometimes he needed to heat up cobbler's glue which had hardened after being left to dry on a shoe or boot while he tended to a customer in the main store. He accomplished this with the help of the "infrared rays" that came from a hot plate which dangled from a wire above his bench. His knowledge of two substances — rubber and glue — and of their physical qualities allowed him to determine the point at which the glue was just the right texture for his repair. As with the horseshoe magnet, he used the hot plate in a way different from its original and commonly understood function, of heating up liquids or foods for nourishment.

Several notable objects were located close to his workbench. A box marked *Lunettes* contained eyeglasses retrieved by Mr. Sentat from dead soldiers on the battlefield in World War I. His scavenging led him to appropriate the glasses rather than go through the official channels of seeing a doctor and paying for a prescribed pair. Over the bench hung a statue of Jesus. Next to this sacred symbol hung a symbol of the profane. The object in question was a tourist souvenir of the Mannekin-Pis, a miniaturized version of the cherubic statue first created by Duquesnoy in 1619. The original bronze statuette is a famous fountain in Brussels whose water passes through a naked little boy urinating in a wide arc. In name the statue is scatological, as the following discussion makes clear:

> ... and I've got my buddy there. You don't know him, Miss, I haven't shown it to you yet. It's a Manneken-Pis that comes, that comes (laughter) from Belgium, did you see, you know from whom? It's the doctor's young miss who gave it to me as a present, he broke his feet, I fixed him up. Well, it's fine (T-12, April 28, 1982).

Male-female relations were played out in this interchange between Mr. Sentat, the three young men who were filming him, and myself, the single female ethnographer. One half of the statement was serious, as Mr. Sentat explained how he received the statue as a gift from his family doctor's daughter, a young woman in her late twenties. She was living in Brussels at the time, and by offering this symbol of the city she could also affirm her ethnic solidarity with her mother's birthplace. After the young woman had offered the cobbler the souvenir as a present in an assertion of their shared ethnic difference (he was of Spanish heritage), Mr. Sentat placed his own mark on the mass-produced souvenir by repairing its feet, and thereby made it into a private possession. This public symbol was further moved into private time by his hanging the souvenir next to a statue of Jesus, such that both served as protective icons (Stewart 1984: 138). Always solicitous about my female honor — "You don't know him, Miss" — Mr. Sentat had never pointed the statue out to me before. The ethnic identity asserted by the doctor's daughter in offering the gift was displaced by a solidarity of gender identity in the course of its display, for the men all laughed as Mr. Sentat mentioned its name to me.

After explaining how he had acquired the Belgian souvenir, he left the workbench area and walked towards the left back wall of the workshop, stopping just before the door to the family dining room. From a shelf by the wall he removed two self-referential objects, his war and fireman helmets, to display to the young men and me. Mr. Sentat's discussion of the helmets focused upon their power to symbolize his social integration at the national level, for having performed patriotic duty in military service, and at the local level, for having served as a community fireman for twenty years. The helmets were objects which were cultivated in terms of memories and experiences of a more positive past (Csikszentmihalyi − Rochberg-Halton 1981: 113).

> Young man: What do you have there? A helmet, right?
> Mr. Sentat: Ah, that's my war helmet. So see, I also was a fireman... It's my war helmet, it did seven years of war (taps off dust) it's a little beat up, but it still survives... There's even − there's dust, see, but I'm pleased to show it to you (he turned to his fireman's helmet). And here, see these little lions here, they're lions that I added, here, one on each side, which are, what were on my hussar's hat during the war (his voice took on a noble tone as he uttered these last words), that's it. I used it to do twenty years of service with the firemen, they threw me out of the firemen for political reasons − that got me two and a half years in prison − anyway it doesn't matter − with praise for being a model fireman, that's already not bad ... and we had to leave for war in '39 because... (T-12, April 28, 1982).

At this point he explained how during World War II a local man intervened to keep the Resistance from taking the helmet away from him. This meant that his helmet could remain a sacred symbol of his patriotism from World War I.

> I'll have you know that it's 1985, my regiment number, which fits me just like new (laughter as he tried on his war helmet). So I had, here, the lions were here. Under the chin I had a strap, in, in metal, you know, for the sabre blows, the sabre blows aren't too good, so something in iron, out of metal, it's a kind of steel, understand, to avoid sabre blows to your mug, see. So these are from my hussar's outfit... (T-12, April 28, 1982).

He went on to explain how he had signed up for military duty for love over a girl, whom he lost when his father put an end to the romance while he was off in the service.

The World War I helmet took on a more profound meaning, that of doubly encoding community and nation. It underscored the time when Mr. Sentat's masculine and patriotic identity made for his maximal integration in society. The evocative power of the war helmet continued into the fireman's helmet. Mr. Sentat remade his civilian self by removing two miniature lions from the war helmet and attaching them to his fireman's helmet.[9] The lions could connote the masculine physical strength of warriors and soldiers. By this rearrangement, Mr. Sentat transposed the local back onto the national. His transformation of the mass-produced items of the helmets continued his identity as *bricoleur*.

Mr. Sentat chose an object from a very distant past through which to define himself to the young men in 1982. He referred to his years of military service in World War I, or 70 years earlier, when he had actually used the helmet. By framing himself with respect to World War I in this portion of the videotape, he effaced World War II and its problematic consequences, and so presented his personal rendering of history. As he quoted his regiment number and tried the helmet on, the young men laughed, for the number, 1985, sounded like a very contemporary year. Mr. Sentat's observation that it fit him like new was ironic, for France was not at war, and he was too old to fight. The excitement in his voice and the change in tone were also noticeable as he recalled having been a member of the cavalry group. He evoked his youth and a camaraderie established with other young men in hours of danger, outsiders to the community of Lectoure, yet with whom he deeply identified for the rest of his life, even as he spoke with the three young men who filmed him. They became his peers of many years back as he relived those times. Not having experienced war directly, they could empathize up to a point. But deeply identifying with World War I required membership in Mr. Sentat's age cohort (Hufford 1987: 28; Kirshenblatt-Gimblett 1989: 332), as the cobbler observed at one point during the filming: "So, how can you all understand, there's no way." Formerly objects of action, used and handled, the helmets had become objects of contemplation and material companions which focused memories on past experience (Csikszentmihalyi — Rochberg-Halton 1981: 270). They were gender-marked collective esteem objects for this man, parallel in function to a trophy or medal from a sports competition.

On the right-hand side of the workshop are shelves filled with boxes of scraps of leather and fabric. An old brown bottle filled with locusts in an alcohol solution, frequently shown to schoolchildren who visited the shop on class trips, sits on one of these shelves. Mr. Sentat had preserved the insects as a reminder of an unusual natural occurrence, when a locust invasion devastated the surrounding countryside in the early 1940s. In the center of the workshop stands a machine which Mr. Sentat only learned how to use in the late 1970s, when he himself was in his late 70s. With it he braided ropes of varying widths from the bits of twine that some of his peasant customers brought him. On the right back wall, just before the entrance to the kitchen, hang a row of umbrellas which date from the 1930s. Mr. Sentat collected them and used their wires to repair bicycle wheel spokes. At times they served their original purpose, as on the day when I borrowed one to get me home in a rain storm (N-81, September 30).

The curator of these objects in his living museum (Hufford et al. 1987: 67), Mr. Sentat could entertain visitors too young to have known the nineteenth-century world of the workshop, or even the more recent locust invasion of the early 1940s.

Of shoes and other objects

> To take Aristotle's famous example, a shoe is a shoe, physically, whether it is produced for wear or for sale at a profit with the aim of accumulating capital. But as a commodity the shoe has properties that are in addition to its use-value of providing comfort, ease of walking, pleasure to the eye, or whatever. As a commodity the shoe has the exchange-value function: it can generate profit for its owner and seller over and above the use-value that it holds for the person who eventually buys and wears it (Taussig 1980: 25−26).[10]

In the creation and circulation of objects and poems, Mr. Sentat high-lighted the symbolic dimension of exchange-value, outlined here by Taus-sig through the example of the commodity of the shoe. Mr. Sentat's objects generate social prestige and reputations.[11] In her discussion of the semiotic nature of commodities Stewart (1984: 6) makes a similar point: "... it is necessary ... to note the symbolic nature of the commodity once it is transformed from use value to exchange value and defined within a system of signs and their oppositions." Stewart then quotes Eco:

> It is possible to consider the exchange of commodities as a semiotic phenomenon not because the exchange of goods implies a physical exchange, but because in exchange the *use value* of the goods is transformed into their *exchange value* − and therefore a process of signification or *symbolization* takes place, this later being perfected by the appearance of money, which *stands for something else*... (Stewart 1984: 6).

Although Stewart's quote of Eco refers to commodities, it also holds for a different category of objects, that of gifts. Indeed, Stewart (1984: 144) goes on to note that when offered as gifts, the exchange of commodities is abstracted to the level of social relations and away from the level of materials and processes, as is also the case for souvenirs. This was certainly the case for Mr. Sentat's object-gifts.

Mr. Sentat's material objects reflected knowledge on the part of their maker, but they required other kinds of knowledge on the part of their receivers in order to be "read." As part of a highly situated personal world and a complex symbolic exchange system, Mr. Sentat's objects and poems marked previous encounters and receipt of the gifts of poems or other objects. By offering objects and poems in expressions of solidarity with various groups, Mr. Sentat attempted to create community and circulate a part of himself so as to counter a negative self-image from his political past. His objects were multiply encoded: (1) in terms of solidarities with various social categories such as "the nation," "the community," men, peasants, and Christians; (2) with respect to their overlapping functions as gifts, souvenirs, and at times material companions in his private symbolic economy; and (3) with respect to a personal life-world, and with respect to the social relations of the community. On the one hand, the creation of Mr. Sentat's objects emerged from social relations. On the other hand, they actively reinscribed social relations, centered in a discourse on family and community. The next section will detail how local, national, and gender identities were not only intertwined in the objects' very materiality but also reemerged in the course of their offering and display.

The airplanes

By the spring of 1991 very few of Mr. Sentat's airplane mobiles remained in the store or workshop; most were stored in the shop's basement. Described as made from "plastic bottles, cans, boxes ... like Calder['s]"[12] by one journalist (Gardère 1979: 16), and "fantastic forms made from plastic bottles. Dream missiles or lunar insects, these strange mobiles fly in the wind..." by two others (Carsalade − Durand 1982: 8), the airplane mobiles were first made by Mr. Sentat in the late 1970s in a burst of creative activity which saw intensive writing of poetry and crafting of artistic objects. His most publicly known objects, the mobiles were rarely given away.

The journalists' reference to the mobile artist Alexander Calder and their use of the terms "fantastic," "dream missiles," "lunar insects," and "strange mobiles" are reflected in the town photographer's fascination with the mobiles. François Saint-Pierre took many photographs of them when he first came to Lectoure in the late 1970s. At the time he had a shop near Mr. Sentat and paid frequent visits to his neighbor. Unaware that Mr. Sentat was a creator of other objects, including so much verse,

Saint-Pierre was fascinated by this "poetry," as he called the mobiles in talking about them with me in July 1987. One series of his photographs shows Mr. Sentat adjusting and testing the planes as they fluttered from wires attached to the outside wall above the entrance to the shop. Some focus on the creator's hands, large and care-worn, which lovingly and ever so delicately adjusted the planes. Others show the airplanes at different moments of the day, often in early dusk, with one striking example transforming the slightly blue-gray hue of the mineral water bottle into a fantastic iridescent object. The silvery sheen does make it into a lunar insect, a strange creature from a distant world. Most of Saint-Pierre's photos present the mobiles framed against a blank backdrop. By removing them from the object-filled and dishevelled context in which they were located, this photographer transformed the mobiles into surreal artistic objects ... Calder-like.

The airplane mobiles epitomized Mr. Sentat's multiple identity as artist, *bricoleur*, and engineer.[13] He took an object of consumption, the mineral water bottle, and transformed it into a small-scale airplane, a machine central to the modern world. The discarded mineral water bottles are the refuse of a consumer society and modern cultural practices whereby people drink bottled water from other parts of France rather than their own local water. Once used, it is not apparent how the bottles can be recycled. Mr. Sentat used bottles from his family's personal consumption and those brought to him by friends and neighbors to make the mobiles. The bottles shifted from their original predominantly utilitarian function of holding water to the aesthetic one of refracting light and spinning about, even as they were working models of an actual machine.

The understanding of principles of engineering design needed to transform the bottles into working mobiles reflected Mr. Sentat's interest in mechanics.[14] His overt motivation for building the airplane mobiles was to master engineering principles of locomotion and wind turbulence, for he explained to me that he wanted to learn how to make their wings and tails move and "fly" with the wind. Other instances of his fascination with machines involved his fetishization of shoes, which composed the insides of a clock for a shop display in the late 1920s. On another occasion, shoes appeared to be regurgitated by a conveyor-belt cow for a shop display at a town fair in the late 1930s. In some ways Mr. Sentat's multiple versions of the airplane mobiles — he constructed over fifty of them — underscored the repetitive aspects of work in everyday life, as he labored to master technical principles to make them function.

From a folklorist's perspective, the proliferation of mobiles were variants on a theme in his shop-museum. As Stewart suggests, through their accumulation and arrangement, collections of ephemera made of disposable items might present an aesthetic tableau which no single element could sustain (1984: 166–167). Like Stewart's example of wine bottles placed in a window, the mobiles which hung outside the shop's entrance and from wires in the back garden and which moved constantly with the wind corresponded most to the essence of mobiles as forms of abstract sculpture which aim to depict movement. Mr. Sentat's airplane mobiles contained an element of kitsch as well, defined by Stewart (1984: 167) as split into the contrasting voices of past and present, of mass production and individual subject. Although made from an indistinguishable object, mass-produced mineral water bottles, each airplane mobile was unique in its own way. Replicas of larger airplanes, the mobiles functioned as miniatures. Whereas industrial labor is marked by the prevalence of repetition over skill and part over whole, the miniature object represents an antithetical mode of production, production by hand, a production that is unique and authentic (Stewart 1984: 68).

The airplane as such was also something of a magical object for Mr. Sentat. First developed during his youth, it is a quintessentially twentieth century creation and an example of the human domination of nature, a theme which fascinated Mr. Sentat and regularly appeared in his poems. Mr. Sentat never rode in an airplane himself. He referred to his standard model as the "*Concorde*," inspired by the modern supersonic plane of the same name which the French and British developed in the late 1960s. Mr. Sentat's creation of the airplane mobiles corresponded roughly to the period when the real supersonic machine was being developed. The *Concorde* became a symbol of France's entry in the modern technological world and marked a break with its rural past (Ardagh 1982: 70–72). Its popularity peaked in the late 1970s, after which time political wrangles and severe budgetary problems impeded its further development. Mr. Sentat's choice of the name *Concorde* for his mobile reflected his identification with a national symbol. This model airplane was as well an object of local pride, for the French Aérospatiale factory is located in Toulouse, 87 kilometers east of Lectoure. The *Lectourois* most closely identify with Toulouse as the nearest major city and administrative center. Thus the *Concorde* airplane mobile was both a national and local symbol.

It is quite likely that the airplane mobiles were created as a result of a dialogue between Mr. Sentat and Mr. Thore, another elderly versifier with whom Mr. Sentat began a poetic correspondence towards the end of the 1970s. Their communication began only in old age, since previous political differences had kept them apart. Mr. Thore was fascinated with airplanes and he repeatedly underscored to me and others the role of a *Lectourois* named Louis Damblanc in twentieth-century French aviation. In an interview published in the local newspaper, Mr. Thore commented: "A child of the other century, I saw progress change many things. Aviation was my life dream. And I render homage to all those — aviators, researchers, inventors, who contributed to the conquest of air, space, and the cosmos" (Sarremejean 1986). He went on to note how a man born in Lectoure, Louis Damblanc, had deposited a patent with the United States in 1938 for his invention of a multilayered missile. According to Thore, the Americans then appropriated this patent because France was considered an enemy. After the war an indemnity was finally awarded the inventor so as to avoid any litigation, and in the late 1960s Damblanc accepted another small indemnity as a token for his role in the missile's creation. Mr. Thore and the journalist hailed Damblanc as the "grand-father" of the engendered Ariane missile, to which they both referred as Damblanc's "granddaughter."

Like Mr. Sentat and his *Concorde*, Mr. Thore focused upon the distinctly French contributions to modern aviation via his local hero. The international cooperation between France and Great Britain in creating the *Concorde* was downplayed by Mr. Sentat, while the appropriation of Frenchman Damblanc's airplane patent by the Americans during World War II was played up by Mr. Thore, who wanted the inventor to get his proper national due. Both men underscored the power of airplanes as symbols of unity within the larger context of nationalism. Thus Mr. Sentat's airplane mobiles became objects through which an artisan aligned with the right could communicate with a retired horti-culturalist aligned with the left.

The mobiles, which remained in the shop and rarely circulated beyond its confines, were fixed at the pole of emitter within the communicative chain. The two occasions on which Mr. Sentat gave an airplane mobile as a gift once again encoded his military past and the rift between the rural and modern worlds. In the first instance, he offered an airplane to a young woman who had stopped into his shop as a casual passer-by in mid-September, 1980. In return, her father, who ran a World War I museum in Verdun, sent a set of commemorative World War I postcards to Mr. Sentat as a souvenir and by way of thanks. The second instance took place during my stay (1981–82), when Mr. Sentat offered an airplane mobile to another casual passer-by, a female high school philosophy teacher from Pau to whom he also read his autobiographical poem "Mon Temps Passat." In both cases Mr. Sentat used the model of a contemporary object of technology to communicate messages about the past in a didactic fashion to two young women.[15] In the first case the past was inscribed by memories of the "good" war, World War I,[16] while in the second case the past was inscribed through an earlier rural way of life.

The ropes

In the center of the workshop is a machine that consists of a four-pronged hook at one end and an old bicycle wheel at the other. Mr. Sentat used this machine to braid and wind into ropes of different widths and lengths the twine debris that local peasants and artisans brought him. The finished pieces were looped in circles and stored draped over the top of the machine. Mr. Sentat demonstrated his abilities to make rope on several occasions in the course of my year in Lectoure. Each time he explained that he had only learned how to do this ten years back, or in 1971, when he was 77 years old, and each time he gave his observer the rope as a souvenir. Continuing his identity as *bricoleur* and engineer into old age, he had learned how to use a special machine which required both knowledge and physical strength to make it function.

In late September (N-81, September 23), six weeks into my fieldwork stay, I saw Mr. Sentat give his first demonstration of how to work the machine. He explained that rope made from the machine had a range of practical uses, and focused upon its utility in peasant culture for tying and leading farm animals and harvesting. Turning to a more distant past, he added that peasant women would place a length of coiled rope on top of their heads so as to allow them to properly balance the jugs of water that they had gathered from farm wells. He observed that bits of rope such as these were also used in certain traditional Gascon peasant dances. Each member of a male-female couple were joined together by sharing a piece of rope, integrated into the dance movements. This account of earlier rural courtship practices of the more remote nineteenth century was then collapsed with the present, as he joked that his piece of rope would be an effective lasso for me to catch a husband. During the visit of my friend and fellow graduate student Joan Gross (N-83, April 15), he showed us around the workshop and repeated the demonstration and the joke: "... there you have some souvenirs. If you want to get engaged, you do like that ... a male friend like that (he mimed two young people each taking hold of a rope end) hold on strong, you can also make a tie (he demonstrated how to wind rope), see?" Although he knew that Joan was engaged and did not "need" a rope, Mr. Sentat still offered her one as a souvenir. Several weeks later, when a male American friend visited me, Mr. Sentat again repeated the rope-making demonstration, and presented my friend with the final product. He added with a broad wink that we could each hold onto an end, and therefore form a couple, like in the traditional Gascon folkdance he had described to me back in September. With these words Mr. Sentat once more used the rope to encode male-female relations, a basic social relationship, through an older cultural form, the Gascon folkdance of courtship. He spoke through rope about social relations, past and present.

By collecting twine debris from peasants and artisans in order to make the ropes, Mr. Sentat could mark his solidarity with these social groups in the context of the region's rural culture. By offering rope lengths as gifts, he could circulate part of himself and metaphorically link people together, and in so doing actively attempt to remake community. Like many of his other objects, although their outward appearance was utilitarian, Mr. Sentat's ropes functioned predominantly in the social realm as souvenir-gifts from their maker. He gave the ropes away far more often than he sold them.

The religious crosses

Mr. Sentat kept a crucifix above his work bench at all times. He occasionally made crosses out of bits of wood and metallic cobbler's nails. Like the airplane mobiles, few crosses circulated beyond the workshop. He did give a cross to two women, however: to a nun in 1978, upon learning of the death of her father; and to me, in September 1981, one month after my arrival in Lectoure. In adherence to Christian precepts, the cross is associated with the personal qualities of truth, devotion, and virtue, as well as the communal (Csikszentmihalyi − Rochberg-Halton 1981: 217). By offering this symbol of Christian unity, Mr. Sentat worked to integrate himself into yet another community, this time a spiritual one.

The kinship terms through which the Christian world is often referenced − father, son, mother, sister − take on heightened significance in the exchange between Mr. Sentat and the nun to whom he first offered a cross. Upon hearing of the news of her father's death, Mr. Sentat carved a wooden cross and sent it by messenger to the nun. Her response was a thank-you note penned several months later, on the eve of Pentecost. On the envelope was written "to give to the Gentleman who gave the wooden cross, thank you..." It was accompanied by a prayer card which announced the passing of her father. A portion of the thank-you note read:

> This eve of Pentecost... Very dear Friend of my Papa.
> Excuse my being so late, in thanking you for the wooden cross, made by your hands, and given in memory of my Papa... Thank you again dear Friend for your gesture, so delicate, which touches me so much... I'm going to wear it every day, as a sign of communion in prayer, with you and all your family. It's already twenty-two years ago that one part of our family left the outskirts of Lectoure, but in the plan of God's divine mercy I returned [as a Carmelite] back home on December 17, 1967. This way I was close to Papa these last ten years (Personal correspondence of Pierre Sentat).

The thank-you note spoke through a discourse on family as the nun focused on her role as daughter and how she would wear the cross in prayer for another family, the Sentats. Her sense of genealogical solidarity was reaffirmed at the local level when she explained that, obliged to return to her home town to serve the convent, she also returned to her family. She closed her note by reaffirming the value of "home," which could multiply refer to her biological family; to Lectoure (Mr. Sentat's birthplace), her community of origin; and finally, to the spiritual one of the convent.

Mr. Sentat's cross was a powerful evocative object in personifying the relation between its maker and receiver. That is, the thing given, the cross, was not inert, but alive and bore the imprint of the giver, to use Mauss' (1990: 13) words in speaking about gifts. The cross offered to the nun was a souvenir of individual experience, mapped against her life history, the material sign of an abstract referent, her father's death (Stewart 1984: 139). This simple wooden cross of little material value contained a great "interior significance," to adopt Stewart's (1984: 139) formulation. Stewart (1984: 139) notes that because "of its connection to biography and its place in constituting the notion of the individual life, the memento becomes emblematic of the worth of that life and of the self's capacity to generate worthiness." By creating a self-satisfying art work that evoked a positive response from the nun, Mr. Sentat could unconsciously strengthen his own psychic wholeness and well-being (Greenfield 1984: 140) as he continued to face his problematic past, and as he faced his own death. He was 84 at the time of this exchange.

By offering a hand-made item to mark the ritual moment of death in the life-cycle, Mr. Sentat highlighted familial and religious solidarity through craftsman's knowledge. The nun recognized that its symbolic import derived from its "mode of production" (Riggins 1990: 353), as when she acknowledged that the cross was "made by your own hands." This particular wooden cross had several lives. First, it was a gift, offered by its maker, Mr. Sentat, to the nun. Next, it was a souvenir, an object of contemplation given in someone's memory in the context of a particular life-cycle event. The nun could wear it both in memory of her biological father and in memory of her spiritual father, who had died on the cross. Offered during the period of mourning, Mr. Sentat's cross could be followed by a "psychic rebirth" (Greenfield 1984: 139). By promising to wear it daily, it would be an object of action leading the nun to prayer, and a material companion that connected her with the living and with another family, the Sentats.

Through his offering of the cross, Mr. Sentat appropriated a highly charged collective symbol and individualized it in order to convey certain social messages. These messages involved personal solidarity with the nun and her family during their mourning and a collective solidarity with their shared Christianity. Yet if the cross symbolized community ties between two Christian residents of Lectoure, at the same time it excluded those non-Christians residing in Lectoure who were also part of the "community" of this small town (Riggins 1990: 350). In this exchange Mr. Sentat fetishized the common meaning of the Christian cross as an expression of community, for he represented himself as a non-believer in interviews with me and certain of his poems. He turned to religion only in the last few years of his life, to help him reconcile his political past.

Early in my fieldwork, Mr. Sentat quizzed me closely about my religious practices. I explained that while my father had received some instruction as a Catholic and my mother as a Protestant, I myself had not had a formal religious upbringing. A non-religious person, I hoped that this answer would suffice. In hearing this, Mr. Sentat concluded that I might be confused about the focus of my Christian beliefs. A cross would remedy this potential spiritual confusion, and it would also be a talisman to protect my feminine virtue. Consequently, in mid-September 1981, he presented me with a metal cross made from a pair of old cobblers' nails, which he had strung on heavy cobbler's thread. In so doing, he undertook an aesthetic recycling of a utilitarian item of his daily work world into a meaningful spiritual object (Greenfield 1984: 134). As an elderly Frenchman, he attempted to transcend national boundaries by giving a gift of a collective religious symbol to a young American woman. Many months later, at the end of my field stay, upon meeting an American friend of mine and seeing his beard, Mr. Sentat's first comment to me was "you've got yourself a little Jesus!" He insisted on also giving a cross to this "little Jesus" in an expression of friendship. This cross was parallel in form and content to the one which he had offered me eight months earlier. The cobbler observed that by uniting us spiritually, the crosses could make us into a couple. As with the piece of rope, through presenting an object Mr. Sentat attempted to activate one of society's central relationships, the constitutive unit of the nuclear family. After leaving France, I hung the two crosses among my necklaces in my home. Memory objects, they reminded me of Mr. Sentat each time I glanced at them.

The image of the Christian cross as symbolizing Mr. Sentat's historical and political past was present in the fourth and fifth stanzas of a poem that Mr. Sentat wrote for himself and titled "Thoughts on Saint Martin − 1980." Saint Martin's day, November 11, marked the beginning of the winter season in the traditional rural calendar when a major fair was held in Lectoure and servants were hired out to local farms. It was one of the busiest and most profitable days for the shoe shop. Through the poem's title Mr. Sentat framed the text with respect to the traditional rural calendar which marked saints' days. Mr. Sentat's use of this calendrical date to title a poem which he composed in 1980 meant that his intended audience could only be older people familiar with the earlier system. He wrote an alternate version of this poem, simply titled "To my dear Friends" which he sent to Mr. Thore, his primary poetic correspondent. The variants in the alternate text sent to Thore are indicated in bracketed form in the English translation:[17]

> Comme Vous, moi aussi, Je porte ma croix
> légère ou plus lourde, J'en ais [sic.] pas le choix
> addressons à Dieu nos prierres [sic.]
> un Jour, c'est exact ce sera les dernières.
>
> portons notre croix avec allégresse
> Redressons nous car le temps presse
> sans retard cirons nos chaussures.
> car la fin pour nous, un Jour est sure

[Like *You*, I too, *I* bear my cross
(*I* too *I* bear my cross there)
light or heavier, *I* don't have the choice
(light and more or heavier sometimes I don't have the choice)
let us address to God our prayers
one Day, that's right they will be the last.

let us bear our cross cheerfully
Let's Straighten Up because time presses
(it   )
without delay let us polish our shoes.
(remorse   )
because the end for us, one Day is certain]

In the first stanza Mr. Sentat evoked a common Christian image of Christ's suffering on the cross for humanity's sins. Mr. Thore bore the cross of some family troubles which weighed upon him, while Mr. Sentat bore that of a problematic political past and subsequent social isolation. The second stanza proposes that the two men's suffering be borne cheerfully, as is proper for good Christians. Its second line contains an ambiguous message, for *redressons-nous* can mean "let's straighten up" — from bearing a heavy burden — or "let us right ourselves and make amends with the past." The third line's reference to polishing one's shoes is an appropriate cobbler's metaphor for putting one's spiritual affairs in order before approaching death and preparing to face God.

Like Mr. Sentat's other objects, the cross in the poem and the text itself are framed with respect to a significant date, in this case November 11. In addition to being Saint Martin's day in a traditional calendar, it was also Armistice Day that first marked the end of World War I. After the war Mr. Sentat received a *croix de guerre* or medal for his military service. By referring to November 11 in the title, and by evoking the image of the cross in the fourth stanza of the poem, Mr. Sentat tied the political past of World War II and what had happened in its aftermath into the earlier war which Armistice Day had first commemorated.[18] Multiply encoded through a date which evoked the local agricultural as well as the national political worlds, history was made to move intertextually between object and poem. In this poem, the cross marked "family" for Mr. Thore and "community" and "nation" for Mr. Sentat. Mr. Sentat moved from the national to the personal as he individualized the collective symbol of the cross in terms of his own life-cycle and the inevitable process of aging and facing death.

The handbag

Mr. Sentat's parting gift to me was yet another example of his *bricolage* of the material and the social. In early May 1982, at the end of one of my last visits to the shop, he approached me hesitatingly and said shyly: "It's not much, but I made this for you." He had made me a woman's handbag out of a pair of ladies' boots from the collection of old shoes and boots kept on hand for some future repair. He proudly showed me how he had stitched the bag, added a strap, and made a place for a handkerchief inside. Perhaps he decided to create this gift after remembering how he had restitched my winter boots earlier in the year when they needed repair. Of course he drew upon materials close at hand for inspiration. With some amusement, his daughter observed the object's uniqueness, and added that I would certainly be the only young woman in the United States to have a handbag like this. The bag contains a symmetry of stitches, balanced visually on either side of its center, as were Mr. Sentat's shoe displays.

Yet this object is subliminally engendered, for its shape is reminiscent of a woman's body, with the boots' zippers opening at strategic places. On several occasions throughout the year Mr. Sentat jokingly reminded me how he had been obliged to forcefully remove my damaged boot from my leg in order to repair it. This partial undressing of a young woman could be remedied by giving part of her body back to herself through the gift of the bag. The handbag could also be a tangible metaphor for an unconscious relationship — at times during our conversations Mr. Sentat collapsed time frames and spoke to me as if I were his deceased wife — which would end with my departure.[19] Although his gift of rope to me and my male friend also had cast me in potentially sexual terms, as the member of a romantic couple, but one that excluded Mr. Sentat, the handbag was an even more powerful expression of (possibly his) desire. Like many of the objects which Mr. Sentat made and typically gave away, the bag reveals another quality of Lévi-Strauss'(1966: 21) *bricoleur*, who "speaks" not only *with* things ... but also through the medium of things. It was indeed logical that Mr. Sentat's going-away present to me be a former pair of boots, transformed from their once utilitarian function of keeping feet warm to more aesthetic and symbolic functions, a souvenir in which their maker's and recipient's (sexual) identities were inscribed. Made from a pair of boots, the handbag fetishized the exchange-value of the gift; although potentially functional, this object was much more a souvenir. Like the religious crosses, the bag became a memory object for me. It currently hangs on a door in my study at home and recalls my year of fieldwork (1981 – 82).

Objects of memory

> ... It is important to resist the tendency of collections to be self-sufficient, to suppress their own historical, economic, and political processes of production... At a more intimate level, rather than grasping objects only as cultural signs and artistic icons, we can return to them ... their lost status as fetishes... This tactic, necessarily personal, would accord to things in collections the power to fixate rather than simply the capacity to edify or inform (Clifford 1988: 229).

The preceding discussion has focused upon decoding the meanings of certain objects within the symbolic economy of an individual, framed in terms of the historical and psychological conditions which generated the objects' creation and communication. The example of the ethnographic museum as a world of intimate encounters, with inexplicably fascinating objects, personal fetishes, whose collection is inescapably tied to obsession and to recollection (Clifford 1988: 216), provides a parallel for analysis of Mr. Sentat's workshop-cum-museum and its objects. Although Mr. Sentat was like many folk artists who display and/or give away their hand-crafted objects (Schlereth 1982; Ward 1984), his specificity lay within his socio-political past. His constant re-living of people and places related to his sense of stigma after release from prison. On one level, Mr. Sentat's objects — airplane mobiles, religious crosses, ropes — created a structured environment that substituted its own temporality for the "real time" of historical and productive processes (Clifford, on Baudrillard, 1988: 220), for their period of reference remained obsessively fixed in the 1930s-40s. Yet these objects did in fact emerge from the real time of those historical processes which saw the transformation of the cobbler's profession and the modernization of French society.

Mr. Sentat's passion to create, display and offer objects was articulated in gendered ways as well (Haraway 1985). Thus my own presence has been written into this text, not simply to authenticate the account, but to reveal how Mr. Sentat's gendered subjectivity emerged through encounters with myself and other individuals. Indeed, the ethnographer's presence and that of other outsiders provoked expressions of this man's unconscious, which, lurking just below the surface, readily emerged in his speech and actions, even in chance encounters. Significantly, his objects of memory — airplanes, religious crosses, poems — and of desire — handbag, rope — were most frequently offered to women. These "safe" women included several nuns from the two local convents; a family member; a widowed former client; an elderly fellow lover of the Gascon language; and the single ethnographer. Mr. Sentat spoke with these women through the aforementioned objects and through others such as flowers and poems, via a discourse of family and love, supposedly apolitical domains. In so doing he could compensate for his inability to communicate with men, who would not listen to him, given his problematic past.[20] In the last eight years of his life, his one sustained communication with a man was with Mr. Thore. An elderly peer, Mr. Thore felt equally marginalized, for due to his advanced age he was physically removed from the larger processes of social life.

Mr. Sentat's laboring at self-representation and self-valorization is a dramatic reminder of how objects may provide a measure of the self's social integration, or, in this case, marginality (Riggins 1990: 357). In this respect, the present analysis supports the idealist background of symbolic interactionism that sees the self as "always in the making" (Riggins 1990: 346). By manipulating objects considered to be of negligible and neutral value — in this case, discarded plastic bottles and twine debris — and turning them into personal, expressive structures, both the objects' worth and the individual's self-worth are bolstered, as Verni Greenfield has observed about the catharsis achieved through making objects while in the process of grieving (1984: 140). After his prison years, Mr. Sentat continued to grieve over his lost position in society. His reframing of the utilitarian as aesthetic may be seen as an attempt to redress his psychological confusion. That is, his appropriation of objects meant for one use into *his* chosen use — whether artistic or functional — played out control issues. His fetishization of certain objects, such as shoes and religious crosses, used by him to convey messages about family, community, and nation, suggests a link with the right-wing ideologies of the years of his mature adulthood. Behind the apparent nostalgia of the simplified and rural images of his objects lay a more problematic political situation.

We may return for comparison to the question posed by historian Christian Faure, as mentioned at the beginning of this essay, namely how the political was aestheticized in particular ways during the Vichy years (1989: 175). In Mr. Sentat's case, the reverse operation was at work, namely, his artistic activity was politicized, i. e., put to a "strategic" use. Yet the underlying principle, an operation that separates objects from their use value, is the same (Kaplan on Benjamin 1986: 27). Mr. Sentat's objects were the material products of mental representations. Like much of everyday life, the objects remained invisible to a larger social world, for they formed part of a series of private one-on-one exchanges. Furthermore, their political and gendered encoding was not immediately obvious to the casual observer. This recalls Stephen Riggins' (1990: 359) discussion of a watercolor of a traditional Dutch farmhouse with a thatched roof, located in the entrance to the apartment of a Dutch-Canadian artist émigré residing in Toronto since the mid-1950s. At first glance, the husband's painting evokes the solidarity of village society. But it turns out that the farmhouse's inhabitants were members of the underground resistance to the Nazis, as were the artist couple. This rural image thus encodes a terrifying political reality, a hidden meaning which can only emerge, however, in the artist couple's narrative *about* the painting. Like Mr. Sentat, as twentieth-century Europeans the Dutch-Canadian couple were deeply marked by the historical processes of war, specifically World War II, although at the opposite end of the political spectrum.[21]

To conclude, this essay has linked micro-analysis of the individual with the broader categories of society and the nation. It was shown how objects fashioned through *bricolage* may encode deeper political messages which are not apparent, either through the material surface of the objects themselves, or through their communication. Yet the focus on a stabilizing rural Christian French world encoded within the objects and their exchange does not reveal the origins of Mr. Sentat's life-long confusion about feeling an outsider in French society.[22] Part of his ambivalence about being a Frenchman derived from his own Spanish family background, which was Catalan on his mother's side and Aragonese on his father's side. On the one hand, his childhood memories recalled taunts from other classmates that he was "the son of the Spaniard," even though he and his father were both born in France, and in fact it has been his paternal grandparents who had emigrated to southwestern France after the mid-nineteenth century Carlist wars. In contrast, in his mature adulthood and old age, he reverted to identifying with his Spanish heritage. This strategy offered an ethnic alibi through which he could distance himself from his identification with French right-wing politics during the war years. These ambiguities about ethnicity and citizenship are paralleled in the objects themselves, whose hidden political codings are foregrounded by visual puns. Decoding the objects provides the ethnographer with a method through which to apprehend critical questions about the interrelations between representations of self, history, politics, and culture.

Acknowledgements

The Wenner-Gren Foundation for Anthropological Research, the Fulbright Foundation and the Sigma Xi Society funded my dissertation research in Gascony in 1981 – 82. The Institute for the Arts and Humanistic Studies of the Pennsylvania State University funded follow-up research in the summer of 1987. An earlier version of this essay was delivered at the panel "Signs, Objects, Contexts" of "Crossing the Disciplines: Cultural Studies in the 1990s," held at the University of Oklahoma at Norman in October 1990. All translations from French and Gascon into English are mine. "T" refers to the audiotape number and "N" to fieldnotes from the 1981 – 82 research. I have reproduced the orthography and punctuation of the original French in the poems quoted here. Mary Crain, Pauline Greenhill, Joan Gross, Stephanie Kane, Janet Roesler, and Monique Yaari provided critical readings of an earlier draft of this article.

Notes

1. Mr. Sentat detailed the stresses underlying his identity in these worlds in his lengthy autobiographical poem "Mon temps passat" ["My past life" or "My time spent"], which he composed in Gascon in the late 1970s.
2. In his article on folk art, Henry Glassie makes a brief but tantalizing observation that interest in folk artifacts received official sanction in Nazi Germany and depression America, having earlier achieved a certain status via the antiquarianism of nineteenth-century romantic nationalism (Schlereth 1982: 128). Glassie does not develop this point further.
3. I have analyzed some of Mr. Sentat's poems in terms of a complex and ambivalent discourse about family, represented by him as both a solidarian and an oppressive institution (Mark 1989).
4. In their study of cobblers in nineteenth- and twentieth-century French Canada, Dupont and Mathieu report that these artisans were obliged to engage in other activities to supplement their income. As the profession changed, they increasingly turned to repairs as their primary activity. The cobblers

were often paid in kind, with hay, potatoes, or other products of daily consumption (1981: 195−206).

5. In his interviews with Suzanne Mazé, a hat-maker from the Mayenne who moved to Paris, and who created a garden west of the city, sociologist Maurizio Catani eloquently shows how the garden reflected social relationships:

> It is in her garden that Aunt Suzanne will inscribe, as on a blank page, all the individuals and places close to her heart... Inscription into the earth bears two possibilities: to participate in the garden's building and be inscribed ... in a precise point in space; the space close to the house, veranda, or tunnel being different from those of other parts of the garden where family and friends are inscribed (Catani − Mazé 1982: 428).

Aunt Suzanne remembered: "Lots of people have puttered (*bricolé*) here! Pierre Mazé (her husband's son from a previous marriage), it's he who dug in the beginning." Recalling visits to other family members and friends, she added: "Everywhere we went it was rare that I didn't bring back a little seed. When I planted them I said: 'So, that is for so and so!' I was happy" (Catani − Mazé 1982: 429−430).

6. In his study of the status of present-day artisans and their discourses, conducted in the mid-1970s, Bernard Zarca quotes a cobbler who in talking about how he was a repairer and not a maker of shoes, said: "*J'ai toujours bricolé dans le travail du cordonnier, voilà!*" [I've always puttered around doing cobbler's work, there you go!]. A blacksmith explained how he had learned his trade from his father: "... *je montais souvent à l'atelier avec mon père, et il fallait aider un petit peu à bricoler.*" [... I often went up to the workshop with my father, and I had to help out a little bit puttering around.] (Zarca 1979: 14).

7. Although I do not have precise figures for the mechanization of the French shoe industry, following Dupont and Mathieu, I would suggest the mid-nineteenth century.

8. Although the majority of the videotaping session took place in French, Mr. Sentat read aloud several poems that he had composed in Gascon, the regional language. At times he injected Gascon words or phrases into his French. In this case, what he said in Gascon "*coumo souy dégourdit, bon appétit*" [so since I'm clever, *bon appétit*], was a humorous rhyme. Here he used Gascon rhetorically to valorize himself and his quality of cleverness, which in this case involved using an iron horseshoe as a magnet.

9. Lussier (1987: 153) observes the military cachet of rural firemen in their uniforms and as they performed their maneuvers.

10. I am grateful to Pauline Greenhill for directing me to the Taussig quote.

11. Frequently offered as gifts, they functioned as "social facilitators" which could establish and periodically reactivate social ties and obligations (Riggins 1990: 351).

12. The reference is to Alexander Calder, the American artist, whose early sculptures were made out of wire. Calder eventually added small pieces of colored metal and made objects which, when suspended from the ceiling or supported on a base, turned at the slightest breeze and which he called mobiles. In 1952 he was awarded the grand international sculpture prize in Venice for this work.

13. In their study of material culture associated with World War I, Jones and Howell (1972: 87, 90) note that airplanes and airships were part of the stock-in-trade of the popular artist. Brass-smiths often created model planes during their spare time.

14. Harper notes that one of the first of Willie's creations which revealed his engineering skills was a small wooden airplane, which hung up by the ceiling, nearly hidden between the beams. Willie explained:

    That airplane was made back before many people thought airplanes should look that way. Everyone laughed at me when I was making it. A few years after that was made, airplanes started to look like that. They were all double wingers before that. I made that in 1936... That took first prize in the fair, too. I whittled it out with a knife — every bit of it. I was just a boy. I used shoe nails — cobbler nails they call it — to put it together with. My father used to do all our shoe work... Lost the wheels of it — the landing gear — that got broke off... My idea for that was out of Buck Rogers. I called it a Buck Rogers plane at the time. Your five-passenger planes came out looking like that... I figured that was the safest place to hang it — up there out of sight! You start looking at that and you start reminiscing, though, about school days... (Harper 1987: 171).

    Willie's airplane is an object of knowledge, for it reveals its maker's understanding of technological innovations. Made while still a boy, he took cobbler's nails to attach it; like Mr. Sentat, he easily moved from one work context to another. Buck Rogers, an important comic strip character from mass culture, inspired him to create the plane. In his old age, Willie's wooden airplane is a memory object, taking him back to the past.

15. In her discussion of the aesthetic aspects of fascism, Kaplan (1986: 26—27) details how industrial fetishes such as airplanes and automobiles were used to establish "community," divorced however from their contexts of production and labor, while at the same time a return to an earlier rural society was promoted. Faure (1989) reaches similar conclusions.

16. Mr. Sentat framed technological discoveries associated with space in a language of military conquest, as is evident in the following excerpt from a New Year's greeting card which he sent in January 1974 to one of his buddies from World War I. The first six lines of the letter-poem read:

    Je regarde en ce moment le Joli (Image) représentant
    le 1er cosmonaute, vainqueur du Cosmos
    qui est comme nous entre le ciel et l'enfer —

Nous aussi fumes vainqueurs et le bon ange nous
retira de la *guerre enfer* sur *Terre que cela est.*
guerre à l'etat permanent sur la *planette* [sic.] comme
le ciel et l'enfer. à nous de choisir...
[I'm looking right now at the Beautiful (Image) representing the first
cosmonaut, victor of the Cosmos.
who is like us between heaven and hell —
We also were victors and the good angel
took us out of the *hell* that *war* on *Earth* is.
war is permanent on the *planet* like
heaven and hell. it's up to us to choose...]

In this letter-poem, astronauts are physically caught between sky and earth
just as soldiers are morally caught between heaven and hell. Both attempt to
be conquerors: astronauts of nature, soldiers of humans. With this poem the
author reinscribed his personal history in an event which caught the world's
attention and transcended national boundaries. By offering an airplane mobile to the daughter of a custodian of World War I memories, he could reaffirm the connection between the two types of conquest.

17. I have underscored certain subject pronouns in the English version in order
to translate Mr. Sentat's rhetorical use of capitalization in French and
Gascon. His capitalization functioned to metaphorically aggrandize individuals or significant domains of experience, to use James Fernandez' (1986: 75,
85) formulation in speaking about this strategy in Asturian folk poetry.

18. Derrida (1986: 29) notes that in some circumstances, "to date is equivalent
to signing... To inscribe a date, to record it, is not merely to sign from a
year, a month, a day, an hour ... but also from a place." Mr. Sentat dated
this poem with its title. However, he typically signed his poems with his last
name and birthdate: *Sentat, né le 6 mars 1894.*

19. I am grateful to Janet Roesler for her wording of this image.

20. After Mr. Sentat's return to Lectoure upon release from prison in 1947, many
town residents boycotted the shop, never to return. It was Mr. Sentat's wife
and daughter who remade the family's reputation through their hard work
and devoted service to their customers in the shoe shop. Similarly, in a series
of interviews with the fascist writer Maurice Bardèche, Kaplan learns how
the writings of Bardèche's colleague Paul Morand, banned after World War
II, came back into print some twenty years later: Morand's social and literary
reputation, Bardèche (1986: 178) affirms, was remade "thanks to the cleverness of his wife, a charming woman," a Rumanian aristocrat and friend of
Marcel Proust.

21. Riggins (1990: 364) hints at an ambiguity in the couple's political position
when he notes that in Holland the husband was a political cartoonist for
several years, simultaneously working for newspapers ranging from left to
center to right wing. Copies of these cartoons have been carefully·preserved,
but are not visible in the public space of the living room.

22. In her analysis of the essay "Qu'est-ce qu'un collaborateur," first published
    by Jean-Paul Sartre in August 1945, Kaplan presents Sartre's argument that
    hard-line Paris fascist intellectuals such as Montherlant, Drieu La Rochelle,
    and Brasillach were drawn to this political position because they felt them-
    selves to be outsiders, who had "no real ties with contemporary France, with
    our great political traditions, with a century and a half of our history and
    of our culture" (Kaplan 1986: 14). Although Kaplan disagrees with Sartre's
    position and although her analysis focuses upon intellectuals, the point is
    relevant to understanding Mr. Sentat's motivations, split as he was about his
    Spanish identity and his position in French society. An equally problematic
    element of Mr. Sentat's psychological alienation involved his often stormy
    relationship with his father.

References

Appadurai, Arjun (ed.)
  1986   *The social life of things: Commodities in cultural perspective.* Cam-
          bridge: Cambridge University Press.
Ardagh, John
  1982   *France in the 1980s.* London: Penguin.
Carsalade, Odile — Jacques Durand
  1982   "Lectoure au coeur de la Lomagne," *Connaissance des pays d'oc*
          5 – 9.
Catani, Maurizio — Suzanne Mazé
  1982   *Tante Suzanne: Une histoire de vie sociale.* Paris: Librairie des Méri-
          diens.
Clifford, James
  1988   *The predicament of culture: Twentieth-century ethnography, literature,
          and art.* Cambridge, MA: Harvard University Press.
Csikszentmihalyi, Mihaly — Eugene Rochberg-Halton
  1981   *The meaning of things: Domestic symbols and the self.* Cambridge:
          Cambridge University Press.
Derrida, Jacques
  1986   *Schibboleth: Pour Paul Celan.* Paris: Editions Galilée.
Douglas, Mary — Baron Isherwood
  1979   *The world of goods.* New York: Basic Books.
Dupont, Jean-Claude — Jacques Mathieu
  1981   *Les métiers du cuir.* Quebec: Les Presses de l'Université Laval, Eth-
          nologie de l'Amérique français series.
Faure, Christian
  1989   *Le projet culturel de Vichy: Folklore et révolution nationale 1940 – 44.*
          Lyon: Presses Universitaires de Lyon, Editions du CNRS.

Fernandez, James
1986   *Persuasions and performances: The play of tropes in culture.* Bloomington, IN: Indiana University Press.
Friedländer, Saul
1984   *Reflections of nazism: An essay on kitsch and death.* New York: Harper and Row.
Gardère, Michel
1979   "Lectoure: la paradis des cordonniers!" *Sud 47. Nord 32*, 16.
Glassie, Henry
1982   "Folk art," in: Thomas J. Schlereth (ed.) *Material culture studies in America*, 134–140.
Greenfield, Verni
1984   "Silk purses from sow's ears: An aesthetic approach to recycling," in: Daniel Franklin Ward (ed.), 133–147.
Haraway, Donna
1985   "Teddy bear patriarchy: Taxidermy in the garden of Eden, New York City, 1908–1936," *Social Text*, winter: 20–63.
Harper, Douglas
1987   *Working knowledge.* Chicago: University of Chicago Press.
Hufford, Mary – Marjorie Hunt – Steven Zeitlin
1987   *The grand generation: Memory, mastery, legacy.* Washington, DC: Smithsonian Institution.
Jones, Barbara – Bill Howell
1972   *Popular arts of the first world war.* New York: McGraw-Hill.
Kaplan, Alice Yaeger
1986   *Reproductions of banality: Fascism, literature, and French intellectual life.* Minneapolis: University of Minnesota Press.
Kirshenblatt-Gimblett, Barbara
1989   "Objects of memory: Material culture as life review," in: Elliott Oring (ed.), 329–338.
Laffontan, Michèle
1969   *L'Artisanat rural dans le Gers de 1836 à 1936.* Toulouse: Institut d'Etudes Méridionales, Diplôme d'Etudes Supérieures en Histoire.
Lévi-Strauss, Claude
1966   *The savage mind.* Chicago: University of Chicago Press.
Lussier, Hubert
1987   *Les sapeurs-pompiers au XIXe siècle: Associations volontaires en milieu populaire.* Paris: A. R. F. Editions/Harmattan.
Mark, Vera
1989   "Discours de famille chez un cordonnier-poète gascon," in: Martine Segalen et al. (eds.), 143–151.
Mauss, Marcel
1990   *The gift.* Trans by W. D. Halls. New York: W. W. Norton.

Neary, John
1991   "When rules and drills drive you just plane screwy," *Smithsonian*,
        February, 21(11): 52 – 65.
Oring, Elliott (ed.)
1989   *Folk groups and folklore genres: A reader*. Logan, Utah: Utah State
        University Press.
Rancière, Jacques
1983   "Ronds de fumée: Les poètes ouvriers dans la France de Louis-
        Philippe," *Revue des sciences humaines* 61 (190), avril-juin: 31 – 47.
Riggins, Stephen Harold (ed.)
1990   *Beyond Goffman: Studies on communication, institution, and social
        interaction*. Berlin: Mouton de Gruyter.
Sarremejean, Michel
1986   "L'hommage d'un Lectourois au grand-père d'Ariane" *La Dépêche
        du Midi* (Edition du Gers), September, n.p.
Schlereth, Thomas J. (ed.)
1982   *Material culture studies in America*. Nashville, TN: The American
        Association for State and Local History.
Segalen, Martine – Claude Michelat – Marie-Anne Coadou (eds.)
1989   *Anthropologie sociale et ethnologie de la France: Actes du colloque du
        Centre d'Ethnologie Française et du Muséee National des Arts et
        Traditions Populaires*, 19 – 21 novembre 1987, Louvain-la-neuve: Edi-
        tions Peeters-France.
Stewart, Susan
1984   *On longing: Narratives of the miniature, the gigantic, the souvenir, the
        collection*. Baltimore: Johns Hopkins University Press.
Stocking, George W., Jr. (ed.)
1985   *Objects and others: Essays on museums and material culture*. Madison:
        University of Wisconsin Press.
Taussig, Michael T.
1980   *The devil and commodity fetishism in South America*. Chapel Hill:
        University of North Carolina Press.
Ward, Daniel Franklin (ed.)
1984   *Personal places: Perspectives on informal art environments*. Bowling
        Green: Bowling Green State University Popular Press.
Wright, Patrick
1987   *On living in an old country*. London: Verso.
Zarca, Bernard
1979   "Artisanat et trajectoires sociales," *Actes de la recherche en sciences
        sociales* 29: 3 – 26.

Fieldwork in the living room:
An autoethnographic essay

Stephen Harold Riggins

Introduction

This chapter focuses upon the domestic microcosm and its treasured population of symbolic and functional artifacts. It is about the way the sedentary self articulates its identity socially and materially, both within the household (traditional or otherwise), and with respect to relatives, neighbors, and strangers. In contemporary American culture this dialogic process takes place mostly in an intense interactive space of social contact ambiguously named the "living" room. This architectural feature that is found in practically every house and apartment constitutes a transactional space for the household as well as a stage for selective contacts with the outside world.

Sociology lacks a model which might serve as a guide in gathering the social information conveyed by vernacular interior decoration and assessing its dialogic dimensions. Pioneering studies offer some brilliant insights about interior decoration but in an unsystematic manner (e.g., Goffman 1959; Baudrillard 1981); they concentrate on broad categories of houses, an entire culture or whole social class for example, and ignore the variations within categories (e.g., Bourdieu 1973, 1984; Rainwater et al. 1959); or they note the presence of types of artifacts without being sensitive to their stylistic nuances (Robert 1951; Csikszentmihalyi – Rochberg-Halton 1981). Fieldwork within the living room is at the present an all the more challenging task because the zeitgeist of the decade does not permit the casual positivistic assumptions and ethical insensitivity common earlier in the social sciences.

As a way of introducing the problematic aspects of investigating living rooms, I will critically examine in the first section of this chapter the book *Let Us Now Praise Famous Men* by the novelist and journalist James Agee (1941). Literary scholars agree that this book, which was done in collaboration with the photographer Walker Evans, contains information on the homes of tenant farmers in Alabama in the 1930s that is unrivalled for the author's sensitivity to the symbolism of housing and interior decoration (Stott 1986: 294). For that reason it provides a good point of departure even though it, too, is relatively unsystematic. Agee's work will be used to illustrate the problems of interpreting both artifacts and texts about artifacts. The second section of the chapter discusses the practical and ethical problems involved in invasively scrutinizing inhabited dwellings. Formal categories of analysis will be proposed, derived in part from the work of Erving Goffman on impression management and from some insights into the syntactic and pragmatic dimensions of objects suggested by semiotics.

The concluding section consists of a case study in which the proposed methodology is tentatively applied to the living room of one home. As pointed out above, the living room was chosen as the focus of the research because it is in most American homes the place where the use of artifacts for the purpose of impression management is the most obvious and deliberate.[1] This case study takes the form of an "autoethnography" (Fiske 1990). My decision to attempt to describe and interpret my parents' living room was motivated by two factors. First, my earlier sociological studies of vernacular interior decoration (Riggins 1990) convinced me that such investigations — even though undertaken in a non-judgmental manner — put the self-esteem of informants in jeopardy because of the intimate link that exists between the self and domestic objects. Any questions bearing on the latter are too easily construed as a questioning of the former's social status and personal life. Due to the ethical problems this entails, it has become common in such research to interview friends and relatives. Even Bourdieu (1984) interviewed his own relatives in gathering case studies for his book *Distinction*. Secondly, as a researcher investigating a socially sensitive topic, I felt that I had an obligation to test on my own self the intrusive methodology which I have applied to others. In retrospect, this has been a valuable learning experience. Attempting to describe the house which I felt I knew better than any other made me realize how much I had failed to perceive in the homes of my earlier informants.

Visions of the world / visions of the home

Little in the current education of ethnographers encourages us to pay close attention to the meanings of the material artifacts which we observe in everyday environments even though the topic is relevant to most micro-level inquiries. This defect in our methodological training is probably one of the lingering effects of symbolic interactionism (Blumer 1969), the perspective which has historically exerted so much influence on ethno-graphic studies in sociology. Both symbolic interactionism and drama-turgical analysis (Brissett — Edgley 1990; Riggins 1993) have encouraged researchers to pay far more attention to face-to-face interaction than to physical setting. For example, ethnographic studies in the sociology of the family generally include only a few passing comments about the most obvious features of informants' homes.[2] Such cursory attention seems all the more insufficient when compared with the following description James Agee wrote in *Let Us Now Praise Famous Men* of just one ordinary object, a battered trunk, he saw in a tenant's home:

> It is a small, elderly, once gay, now sober, and very pretty trunk, the lid shallowly domed, somewhat tall and narrow, and thus bearing itself in a kind of severe innocence as certain frame houses and archaic automobiles do. It is surfaced with tin which was once colored bright red and bright blue, and this tin, now almost entirely gone brown, is stamped in a thick complex of daisies and studded with small roundheaded once golden nails; and the body of the trunk is bound with wood and with two recently nailed ribbons of bluish iron. The leather handles are gray-green and half-rotted, the hinges are loose, the lock is wrenched. Opening this light trunk, a fragrance springs from it as if of stale cinnamon and fever powders and its inward casket is unexpectedly bright as if it were a box of tamed sunlight, in its lining of torn white paper streaked with brown, fresh yellow wood grained through the torn places, the bright white lining printed with large and bright mauve centerless daisies (Agee 1960: 160).

Such meticulous descriptions are found throughout Agee's book. Agee discussed the shape, color, location, smell, and aesthetic impressions of artifacts, writing with more subtlety than any ethnographer known to me. Almost any indication of use — dents, scratches, and scuff marks — were considered worthy of mention. His sensitivity to color was remark-able. On one occasion he wrote as much as two pages (Agee 1960: 145 — 146) about the visual effects, "unrepeatable from inch to inch," of unpainted lumber used in the interior construction of a home.[3]

One of Agee's extensive descriptions of a display of objects in which the artifactual rhetoric of self-presentation takes precedence over func-tionality is his account of the objects surrounding a mantelpiece in the tenant housing occupied by the Gudger family (Agee 1960: 162 — 165). The account presents a logical progression of topics, beginning with the props which support the display: the interior wall, the mantelpiece, and the table. In general, Agee shows a preference for structuring descriptive passages by noting appearances from a distance and then moving in more closely. This particular passage includes some information about the means of acquisition of objects and a hint (unfortunately nothing more) of how a member of the family felt about their possessions. Agee acknowledged the symbolic centrality of the mantelpiece upon which the family valuables were concentrated by labelling it an "altar." However, his religious language would appear to falsely frame the Gudgers' values since they seem to give prominence to commercial images from advertisements and calendars.

The pine lumber of the interior wall was noted as being: "narrow and clearly planed wood ... slenderly grained in narrow yellow and rich iron-red golds, very smooth and as if polished, softly glowing and shining, almost mirroring bulks..." Displayed artifacts included: "a small fluted green glass bowl;" a white china swan; "two small twin vases, very simply blown, of pebble-grained iridescent glass;" a fluted saucer (a gift from the mother to one of the daughters who considered it to be one of her favorite possessions), a fringe of tissue paper cut to resemble lace; a faded amateur family photograph; calendar art, popular Catholic pictures of Jesus and the Virgin Mary; pages torn from a children's storybook; and an advertisement "torn from a tin can, a strip of bright scarlet paper with a large white fish on it and the words 'Salomar Extra Quality Mackerel.'" Among all of these items, it was the family photograph which elicited the longest commentary. Agee detected signs of shyness and self-consciousness in the photograph, and a "bearing strong, weary, and noble."

Any object can be conceptualized as existing on a trajectory of time from brand new to discarded and broken. This theme is developed in many of the descriptive passage of *Let Us Now Praise Famous Men* when Agee imaginatively reconstructed the biography of individual artifacts. Although Agee deciphered history using the physical nuances of artifacts, he offered a fictional narrative of artifacts rather than a factual history of either the artifacts or the family.

Understandably, Agee chose to document only one of the three tenant houses in extensive detail. However, one might argue that ideological considerations influenced his choice of the Gudger house because the Gudgers seem to have exerted more control over their possessions than did the other two families:

> ... All really simple and naïve people incline strongly toward exact symmetries, and have some sort of instinctive dislike that any one thing shall

touch any other save what it rests on, so that chairs, beds, bureaus, trunks, vases, trinkets, general odds and ends, are set very plainly and squarely discrete from one another and from walls, at exact centers or as near them as possible, and this kind of spacing gives each object a full strength it would not otherwise have, and gives their several relationships, as they stand on shelves or facing, in a room, the purest power such a relationship can have (Agee 1960: 156).

This passage might be interpreted as implying that the microcosm of the Gudger house is related to the macrocosm of the universe. Just as the laws of nature keep celestial bodies apart to prevent catastrophes, the artifactual order within the Gudger house is not accidental.[4] Order seems to be a joint creation of both the Gudgers and Agee because it is due to the thoughtful spacing of objects and to their temporal depth. The tenant farmers were responsible for the former; Agee was largely responsible for the latter. These characteristics might imply to a reader that although the Gudgers had been victimized by American society, they still had the power to reclaim their dignity through the controlled spacing of the objects with which they populated their private world. In other words, despite the fact that the dwelling represented the most impoverished category of American housing, a reader can still find evidence in Agee's descriptive passages that the Gudgers continued to believe in a core American value − optimism. The idiosyncratic way Agee managed to turn a stigmatized environment into a status symbol could also be read as revealing his strong (although admittedly somewhat ambivalent) commitment to the socialism that was popular in intellectual circles in the 1930s. Such a perception might indicate that he, too, despite being a blasé New York intellectual, shared the Gudgers' faith.[5]

According to the literary critic Kenneth Burke (1989), part of the commonsense knowledge readers bring to their understanding of fiction is that character and environment are related. Readers expect to discover moral characters living in a humane environment or evil characters in a brutal environment. People who escape being affected by the brutal environment which surrounds them seem to defy commonsense. Agee was very sympathetic to the Gudgers. If he had observed only the negative aspects of tenant housing, readers would have been puzzled about the negation of their commonsense expectations. If Agee had observed only the positive, he would have undermined his readers' moral outrage and thus their tendencies to social activism. Agee's solution to this dilemma was to state unequivocally that the housing was unfit for human habitation, but at the same time to devote most of his text to their unintentional beauty. References to the learned genres of the fine arts and to prestigious cultural artifacts were continually used to inflate the status of the houses. Objects in the Gudger house reminded Agee of "fugues" (Agee 1960: 144–145, 184), "tragic poetry" (Agee 1960: 204), "holy effigies" (Agee 1960: 141), "Doric architecture" (Agee 1960: 144), "jazz recordings" (Agee 1960: 161), "shrines" (Agee 1960: 162), "ivory" (Agee: 1960 180), and "silk" (Agee 1960: 131, 146). Furthermore, the exhaustiveness of Agee's descriptions was in itself a political act. Humble and anonymous architecture received the concentrated attention normally reserved for the fine arts.

Objects in dialogue: Methodological issues

Perhaps the major lesson Agee can teach ethnographers is to sensitize us to the richness of the information that can be read into or inferred from artifacts. But, unfortunately, when one moves beyond this basic lesson, Agee's example becomes quite problematic. Since Agee's methodological procedures were impressionistic and intuitive, his work cannot serve as an ideal model for academic specialties that are more theoretically grounded than are literature and journalism. Moreover, *Let Us Now Praise Famous Men* betrays an unresolved tension between the positivistic ideals of a neutral, value-free language and the radical subjectivity of idealism. While this tension may be an inescapable characteristic of all ethnography (Van Maanen 1988), it is exceptionally strong in Agee's case because of his highly idiosyncratic language and the continual intrusion into the descriptive passages of his own insecurities, moral dilemmas, and aesthetic preferences.

A positivistic outlook is evident in Agee's (1960: 13) desire to let domestic artifacts speak for themselves. He wanted to give the public a selection of photographs and bits of objects from tenants' houses, a kind of museum display, so that the sampled artifacts could be directly experienced without the distortions produced by verbal descriptions. Additional evidence of the same attitude is his tendency to sometimes give unembellished lists of objects and their characteristics. But, on the other hand, Agee knew that any museum display was in itself a form of distortion because objects ripped from their context acquired new meanings. Agee did not hesitate to utilize poetic language or to make farfetched analogies, such as the reference in the preceding quotation to the "innocence" of frame houses and archaic automobiles. Nor did he make an effort to distance himself from the houses he observed. Readers become so aware of Agee's ego as the center from which the houses were experienced that the book could be cited — unfavorably — as an example of the "confessional" (Van Maanen 1988: 73 – 100) or "I-witnessing" (Geertz 1988: 84) types of ethnography.

It is Agee's failure to make formal interviews that is probably the most glaring flaw in his approach to understanding the social significance of interior decoration. All that readers learn about the tenants' perception of their homes is a few prosaic comments: "Oh, I do *hate* this house *so bad*! Seems like they ain't nothing in the whole world I can do to make it pretty" (Agee 1960: 210). A trained ethnographer would more likely have realized from the very outset of the research that one cannot begin to grasp the full significance of domestic objects when information is not elicited directly from members of a household through conversations and interviews. Much of the bricabrac in homes, travel souvenirs, gifts, knick-knacks, etc. symbolize relationships with people. Which objects are chosen for display and the styles of display provide interesting clues about interpersonal dynamics within households and beyond. Much of this knowledge cannot be acquired simply from observing objects. Thus, it is not just Agee's style of writing that makes *Let Us Now Praise Famous Men* radically subjective, it is also due to his failure to interview the tenants. If he had not written so much about himself, he would have had practically nothing to say!

At least at a superficial level, interviewing people about their home is not difficult. It is obvious that many people, male and female, enjoy talking about their home. Open-ended, unstructured questions about the means of acquisition and symbolism of domestic objects are usually sufficient to prompt informants to tell lengthy stories. For instance, Csikszentmihalyi and Rochberg-Halton (1981: 56) elicited detailed comments by asking informants to describe the mood of their home and its basic physical characteristics, and posing the question: "What are the things in your home that are special to you?" Ellen Pader (1993), in a study comparing the domestic use of space in Mexico and the United States, drew detailed interior plans that included some reference to furniture and domestic artifacts and then asked the informants who lived in the house to comment on the plans.

However, some reflection on the types of information that can be elicited from conversations or formal interviews is in order because an interview is not an unproblematic, straightforward dialogue. Interviews document intersubjective relationships between interviewer and informant rather than yield direct information about artifacts and their relations to their owner. Why should informants be thorough and truthful in their answers when they can avoid questions by providing standard or alternative stories instead of disclosing intimate or secret aspects of their self? Is direct questioning from a stranger congruent with the high emotive charge of displayed objects that are linked with deceased or absent family members or close friends?

During interviews material artifacts become discursive objects or arguments in the strategies used by both sides to establish their "expertise." The interviewer is always in a position of self-assumed authority. Informants – more often than not women since interior decoration is seen as an aspect of traditional femininity – must negotiate a process of interaction through which their own worldview is intrusively challenged in the form of questions about their relationship to objects. While informants may provide comments that are a little more formal and explicit than during everyday conversations, they cannot be expected to step outside their commonsense world and sever all relationships between self and personal artifacts for the purpose of an "objective" investigation. Nonetheless, if close reflexive attention is paid to the hidden agendas of the interview process, valuable insight can be gained concerning the role of domestic objects in the social construction of the self.

It should be recognized by the ethnographer that "truth" exists in many forms. Consequently, the analysis made by the ethnographer should not be understood as a more accurate account of the home than that provided by the informants. Perhaps it is best to view both the ethnographer and the informants as "authorities" even though their sources of authority differ because they come from a knowledge of different types of discourse. The authority of the informants might be summarized by the statement "I know best because I live with these objects," the ethnographer's authority by the statement "I know best because I have read so many books on sociology and interior decoration." Informants are in fact the expert with respect to the narratives about their home because the researcher cannot possibly know the contents and stories which they elicit as well as the informants do, unless, of course, the researcher writes about his or her own home. Otherwise, there will always be more stories about the home which informants could tell the ethnographer or more complicating factors in the stories which have already been told. This "multivocal" understanding of the truth can be reflected in published

research if as much speaking space as possible is allocated to the informants through direct quotations.

Comments elicited from informants might be divided into two broad
categories of information: referencing, and mapping (Riggins 1990). The
term *referencing* would apply to all of the content which is about the
history, aesthetics or customary uses of an object. However, in general
this type of information tends to be relatively brief and superficial; even
college-educated informants generally have little knowledge of this sort
about the artifacts in their own homes. Instead, domestic artifacts are
more likely to serve as entry points for the telling of stories about the
self and its personal relationships. All such content will be referred to as
mapping, meaning by this that the self uses the displayed objects (gifts,
heirlooms, photographs, etc.) as a way of plotting its social network,
representing its cosmology and ideology, and projecting its history onto
the world's map, its spatial spread so to speak. This is indeed what objects
are — dots on a map and connecting links which can be retraced in any
direction.

The realization that whenever people talk about domestic objects they
are articulating and explicating their own selves may encourage an attitude of tolerance with respect to what might at first seem to be long-
winded digressions into family and personal history on the part of the
informants. Nonetheless, while a study which documents an informant's
mapping of the social relationships embodied in domestic objects may
indeed be a significant piece of research, it may make a greater contribution to the sociology of the family, gender, or intimate relations than
to material culture studies. To avoid this, it is essential for the ethnographer to exceed the informant's often rather minimal level of referencing.

Occupants of the same home are unlikely to tell identical stories about
their shared possessions even though the decoration of homes typically
involves a process of negotiation by at least two people in interaction.
This phenomenon is similar to the concept of "his and her marriages"
proposed by sociologists of the family. Bernard (1971) suggested that
within each nuclear family there are actually two families, his and hers,
because couples have such divergent memories of many facets of their
life together. With respect to domestic artifacts, some of the nuances of
this selective memory may be lost if family members are interviewed
together. In separate interviews discrepancies can be expected not only
with respect to the mapping function of objects but also with respect to
referencing because gender differences entail a number of gender-specific
objects and forms of expertise.

If Agee is to be considered a model for investigating human-object interaction, then it is obviously expected that the ethnographer will demonstrate a sharp eye for the physical details of artifacts. Photography is an essential tool in this process. Many of the subtleties of domestic artifacts will elude the researcher unless it is possible to closely examine photographs. Consequently, each room must be thoroughly photographed. Unlike the practice followed by the professional photographers employed by decorating and architectural magazines of removing all ephemeral traces left by users and inhabitants in order to avoid dating the photographs, ethnographers should make an effort to include the permanent as well as the ephemeral. Both are relevant to the research. To be realistic, the researcher may have to recognize that efforts to discourage informants from cleaning and tidying up homes before interviews may not succeed. When that happens, the researcher should try to form an impression of the normal appearance of the home.

One might want to begin the written account of a room with the first object visitors are likely to notice upon entering (something directly opposite the door or some other highlighted space) and from that point proceed systematically around the room. The same procedure should be applied to the contents of cabinets or shelves. Begin with the object farthest to the right or the left and proceed down the shelf. Skipping from area to area throughout a room or from shelf to shelf within a cabinet may confuse readers and make it more difficult to form an accurate mental representation of the space. Keeping in mind the categories of display syntax (discussed below), especially the notion of co-location, can assist writers in conveying an impression of the artifactual ecology of objects.

Given the way gender influences the perception of domestic objects, a researcher with traditional male values should be warned that he may underestimate the amount of social information encoded in tableware and knickknacks. Confronted with a large cabinet packed with heirloom dishes, he may be tempted to lighten the burden of description by reducing everything to broad categories. But the stylistic nuances of glass, china, and knickknacks reveal almost as much about social values as does the art displayed on walls. The possession of heirloom china is frequently a source of conflict within families and provides clues about how power is exercised across generations. The time that may be required to write a description of each piece, handling it in order to note measurements and inscriptions, offers opportunities to solicit stories from the interviewee. When knickknacks are too numerous to treat in the text, their characteristics may be summarized in the form of detailed appendices. Micro-sociology cannot avoid such microscopic examinations, if one is to understand the degree to which the self is constructed through the medium of things whose social meanings overshadow their physical features and economic value.

Finally, in view of the academic over-specialization that is presently encouraged, it should be noted that it is counterproductive for researchers in the sociology of vernacular interior decoration to restrict their reading to the social sciences, overlooking the vast number of publications produced by professional decorators, and designers and manufacturers of household objects. All of these sources of information provide technical vocabularies which should be incorporated into a sociological analysis.

Analytical categories

In the first of the following sets of categories the focus is upon the features of individual objects. In the second set it is upon the features of objects perceived in relation to each other. In neither case are the categories mutually exclusive. Depending upon the way an object appears to function within a household, it could be defined by the intersection of numerous categories. (For a more detailed analysis of these categories see Riggins 1990.)

Agency and *mode*. The concept of "agency" distinguishes between the active and passive use of objects, that is, between objects to be handled and objects to be contemplated. The term *intrinsically active* refers to objects which designers and manufacturers assume will be physically manipulated. For example, a corkscrew and a deck of cards are meant to be handled. *Intrinsically passive* refers to objects which designers and manufacturers assume will be contemplated (for example, a poster or painting). However, the semiotic treatment of objects within a household may not correspond with these intentions. Thus, the concept of "mode" provides a more subtle differentiation. *Active mode* refers to objects that are being touched, caressed, or moved within a household regardless of the intended use. *Passive mode* refers to objects that are being contemplated irrespective of original intentions. For instance, an old manual coffee grinder is an intrinsically active object, but if it is displayed as an antique in a living room, its mode is probably passive. Conversely, an intrinsically passive object like a small sculpture can be treated in the active mode as a paperweight.

Normal use and *alien use*. These concepts also refer to the shifting of categories in the use of artifacts, but they are more narrow concepts than the preceding. The term normal use covers an artifact's intended use at the time it was made. Alien use refers to some non-standard or unanticipated use that may vary from objects recycled because of poverty to objects refashioned in response to purely creative concerns. An ashtray which serves as a receptacle for loose change is an example of alien use. "Found art," artifacts whose aesthetic qualities are due to accidents such as weathering rather than human intention, is an extreme example of alien use.

Status objects. Objects can also be semiotically interpreted and manipulated as indices of social status. Since all domestic artifacts express a style of life and cultural values, they contribute information relevant to the ranking of people. All domestic objects could thus be conceptualized as serving political functions. Although the cost of objects is an important component of status ranking, actual cost is rarely known or ascertainable. *Apparent cost* may be a more accurate term.

Esteem objects. This category refers first to the personal self-esteem an individual has achieved in the intimate spheres of life such as parenthood or marriage, secondly to prizes and awards indicative of public recognition or communal gratitude. Displays of greeting cards, trophies, or children's art are some of the most common examples.

Collective objects. Some artifacts may represent ties with groups outside the family. This would include national symbols, memorabilia from social movements, and signs of membership in volunteer associations. Family heirlooms might also be classified in this category if they are considered by the informant to represent ethnicity, religion, or tradition, and not just personal or family identity.

Stigma objects. Households contain material artifacts associated with "spoiled" identities. Probably the most common examples in living rooms are objects associated with aging, but other examples might include medical supplies, items used in "disreputable pleasures," and signs of poverty. Most living rooms contain relatively few stigma objects; more can be found in the private areas of the home, notably bathrooms and bedrooms. Tidying up a living room often means removing stigma objects.

Disidentifying objects. From the pragmatic point of view, objects can be assigned a variety of specific functions including deliberate self-misrepresentation. The concept of disidentification refers to objects representing such false claims, for instance, those which inflate status. Fake antiques and books no one reads may be the most common. In some instances, it might be argued that the overall flavor of a home contributes in a substantial way to such misrepresentation. Baudrillard (1981: 37) distinguishes between "unrealistic objects," those which are not an accurate indicator of an informant's status, and "witnessing objects," those which do provide an accurate reflection. The distinction is, naturally, very subjective. The notion of disidentifying objects differs from those of Baudrillard in that it is not linked solely to status. Informants may distance themselves from a variety of social categories, one of which could be status.

Social facilitators. Objects can be used by groups of people to turn each other into temporary partners and opponents (e.g., card games, chess), or to facilitate public demonstrations of skill and knowledge (e.g., puzzles, Rubic's cube). Such social facilitators structure face-to-face interaction in the immediate present.

Occupational objects. The display of tools or some material reference to occupations is not uncommon in living room decoration. These tools may be somehow atypical, antique, handmade, or constructed in unusual dimensions. They may orient conversations toward a topic that members of the household know best.

Indigenous objects and *exotic objects.* Households contain both locally made objects and those made in geographically distant areas. The proportion of exotic to indigenous objects may provide information about several topics: an informant's reference groups, attitudes toward the local society, as well as status.

Time indicators. This category refers to any sign of time in the decoration, for instance, stylistic features of objects which place them in an historical era, or an artist's dating of a work of art. *Temporal homogeneity* refers to a room in which most of the artifacts appear to have been made at the same time. *Temporal heterogeneity* refers to the mixing of objects of obviously different historical eras. The category tells one about the self's position in time; attitudes toward history, tradition, change and continuity; and the active presence of several generations in the house.

Size and *proportions.* The potential interpretation of objects is influenced by their size. Objects of non-standard size or proportion carry a different meaning than do those of customary size. Miniaturization and monumentality represent the extremes of the category.

Way of production. This category distinguishes between handmade and machine-made objects. Although the vast majority of domestic artifacts are now manufactured in factories, the home remains a refuge for hand-made artifacts because they embody so well signs of individuality, esteem, and personal relationships. Many people are quite sentimental about handmade objects and for this reasons they tend to be a fertile source of narratives.[6]

The next set of categories refers to *display syntax*, that is the way objects are displayed in relation to each other:

Co-location. The meaning of an artifact is influenced by the qualities of the surrounding or co-located artifacts. Consequently, the same artifact may elicit radically different readings depending upon the setting in which it is displayed.

Highlighting and *understating*. The artifacts within homes cannot be displayed in such a way that each attracts an equal amount of attention. Some things must be more prominent than others. Highlighting refers to techniques of display which attract attention to objects. Highlighting technics include: hanging objects at eyelevel, framing pictures or artifacts, putting plants on plant stands, setting something at the center of a mantelpiece, putting one antique in a contemporary setting, etc. Under-stating refers to any technic of display which deflects attention away from artifacts: placing something above or below eyelevel or in an obscure corner. Consciously displaying an expensive artifact in an apparently casual manner may reinforce claims to prestige. Such understating may paradoxically result in the self's status being highlighted.

Clustering and *dispersing*. This category refers to the manipulation of space which separates objects. Artifacts are clustered when they are grouped together. Scattering objects in a large volume of space, one artifact on a bare table for example, is referred to as dispersing. Clustering may highlight a group of objects. Dispersing may highlight individual objects.

Status consistency and *status inconsistency*. When most objects in a room convey the same level of status, because they are all apparently costly or apparently inexpensive, it could be said that the room is characterized by status consistency. However, many homes seem to be a mixture of apparently costly things and those which are inexpensive but sentimentally precious. Such homes display status inconsistency. Either characteristic is an indicator of political attitudes and may be related to notions of egalitarianism or elitism (Laumann — House 1970).

Degree of conformity. As one would assume from this term, the concept refers to the extent to which a household conforms to the current tacit rules of interior decoration. Even though there is at present evidence of a wide diversity of styles of interior decoration, shared notions of appropriateness remain, such as those relating to functional specialization, orderliness, color, comfort, and decorative complexity. Some styles of design and decoration which might have undermined these notions most dramatically, for example the playfulness of postmodernism (Buchanan 1989: 102) or the primitivist style of the hippies (Weisner — Weibel 1981: 418 – 419) have not succeeded in attracting a wide public.

Flavor. All of the preceding categories should be seen as subcategories of flavor, a term that summarizes the general impression conveyed by a room. Flavor is similar to the popular terms "atmosphere" and "character." Flavor refers to taste, a sense which for most people is less well developed than sight. Flavor refers to a range of identifiable but elusive qualities whose reality is undeniable. Examples of flavor include: cosy, conservative, impersonal, chaotic, formal, casual, deprived, bohemian, nostalgic, extravagant, and so on.

To give an impression of the way these categories could be related, it might be hypothesized that the more information a domestic environment conveys, the higher the status (but not necessarily in purely economic terms) of the occupants. A high-status living room may have more surprising and unexpected co-locations, more objects may demand an explanation because of their unusual placement, exoticism, or prominence.

A living room: An autoethnographic essay

In 1937 my parents purchased a house in the small town of Loogootee, Indiana, which is located in one of the less prosperous counties of rural southern Indiana.[7] A wooden frame structure built about 1905, the house is a one-story residence characteristic of working-class housing of its time and place. This has been their home for practically all of their married life. In the 1950s two rooms were added to what was originally a five-room house by enclosing the front and back porches; however, the enclosed areas continue to retain much of the flavor of a porch and are not fully integrated into the house. Since the death of my father in 1986, mother has lived here alone but has made only minor changes in the interior decoration. The artifacts in both the living room and dining room will be described in this chapter because the functional distinction between these two spaces is largely fictitious. No real physical boundary separates them other than a partition wall with an opening the size of double doors. The "living-dining room" is the principal room in the house. There is no additional den, family room or parlor.

In terms of social class, the house might be placed at some point near the boundary between working class and lower-middle class. The original absence of a buffer area between the public space outside and the private space indoors, the relative lack of privacy throughout the house, and the way the two bedrooms directly connect with the living room are typical of the working-class character of the structure. The status connotations of the interior decoration, however, are higher than those of the structure and might be consistent with the generalization that working-class families tend to place more emphasis upon the interior appearance of their home than upon the exterior (Cohen 1982: 305; Rainwater et al. 1959: 171). As will be shown later, the living room conveys a high level of concern for impression management, but there is also evidence of a preoccupation with preserving furniture and carpets more characteristic of the less affluent and the past. (My parents were married a month before the economic crash of October 1929.)

Since interior decoration is influenced in part by the type of visitors one expects (Duncan − Duncan 1976b), it should be noted that visitors were, and still are, most likely to be family members. As the youngest and only surviving sibling of a family of nine children, mother had become by the time of this inquiry in July, 1992, a kind of matriarch for a large extended family of cousins, nieces, nephews, and their descendants. In 1992 my mother perceived the "living-dining room" as possessing the qualities she appreciated most in homes, "comfort" and "modesty."[8]

The last time the house was decorated was in 1967 when my parents were preparing for retirement. The decoration was influenced by the choices in furnishings available at stores in some small southern Indiana towns between the early 1930s and 1967. All of the furniture was purchased in Loogootee, a town that has declined so much economically that at the present most residents have to buy their furniture in nearby, more important towns. The only advice mother received from decorators was a suggestion from an individual one might classify as a "semi-professional" about where to hang the Beckmann and Bartlett pictures mentioned below. Although she subscribed for several years to one mass-circulation magazine about interior decoration, *Better Homes and Gardens*, she claims that she intuitively understands how to match styles and colors: "I just have a hunch about things that go together." The nearest department store that might have considered educating consumers in the art of interior decoration to be part of its "cultural mission" (Saisselin 1985: 33 – 49) was in Indianapolis, one hundred miles away.

Except for 10-foot ceilings, the dimensions of the house are small. The living room and dining room are each 13 feet wide and 15 feet long. These dimensions and the number of windows and doorways in the living room limit decorating options, particularly the placement of a sofa. There are three doors in the living room (two opening to bedrooms and the third to the enclosed front porch), two windows, and the partition wall which marks the symbolic boundary with the dining room.

Furniture crowds the living room, although not uncomfortably so, solid, sturdy pieces of furniture in unbroken colors and with relatively little ornamentation. The major colors in the room are subdued. The wall-to-wall, sculptured, pile carpet is a medium tone of gold. The colors of the largest pieces of furniture are gold, brown, and green. In the language of interior decorators (Pile 1988), the room has been decorated with "cool," restful colors. Green is considered a cool color, and gold is one of the coolest of the warm colors. "Browns ... have a traditional association with a snug, clubby atmosphere," according to Pile. "They appear homelike in their mildest tones, masculine in their heavier values" (Pile 1988: 250). The brown in this case is heavy toned. Some of the areas most likely to become soiled are protected with small throw rugs, one in stripes of four colors: dark and medium blue, sandstone and limestone gray; the other in brown, tan, and beige stripes. The walls are decorated with a near white, gray-toned wallpaper, flecked with white and gold. The ceiling is covered with plain white wallpaper. The door frames and wooden trim, with few ornamental details other than simple egg and dart cornices, have been painted white.

The separation between the living room and the outside environment is greater in this house than is characteristic of more modern housing (Spigel 1992: 187). The sheer curtains in the east window are permanently drawn and those in the south window are frequently left closed during the day. Although Alexander et al. (1977: 891) write that the amount of preferred window space varies culturally and geographically, they suggest a floor/window ratio of 25% to 50%. For every 100 feet of floor space, there should be 25 to 50 feet of windows. When only the sheer curtains in the south window are open, the floor/window ratio would be a mere 6%. The floor and table lamps in the living room were made by the Rembrandt Corporation, according to mother. There are two floor lamps, one an upright (with an off-white, cloth shade) that provides diffuse and indirect light, the other (with a brown shade of burlap-like material) has

Plate 1. Living room of Harold and Eithel Riggins, 403 Walker Street, Loogootee, Indiana. Photograph by Bill Whorrall.

a flexible neck that directs light downward. Two identical, upright, table lamps (both with off-white, cloth shades) also provide indirect light. Hanging from the middle of the ceiling is a five-light ceiling fixture, a dark metal body and tan-colored glass shades, purchased in the late 1930s. The fixture hangs from a chain at the end of which is a small, plain, metal sphere, with a horizontal circular band of ribbing, and below the sphere a vertically ribbed, metal tube. A circular metal frame holds five, vertically ribbed, glass shades which reflect light upward. Metal bands between the shades are also ribbed vertically. On the underside of the frame are three, stepped, concentric circles in metal that terminate in a point of two ribbed circles and an unembellished center.

A visitor to the house cannot fail to notice a dark-stained, l-shaped, oak bookcase in the far left corner opposite the outside door. Because this corner is one of the most prominent display areas in the living room, my description will span the room counterclockwise beginning at this focal point. The bookcase was handmade for me when I was in high school in the early 1960s by my father's brother, Ival Riggins, a professional carpenter and cabinetmaker. Like the other furniture which my uncle made for this house it has a straightforward functionality rather than the flourishes, bowed cabriole legs for example, of the manufactured furniture. In Baudrillard's (1981: 37) terms, the bookcase might be called a "witnessing object," an artifact testifying to the family's actual social class. The manufactured furniture, on the other hand, might be considered an "unrealistic object" because it carries signs of higher social aspirations.

On top of the bookcase is a framed, professional photograph of me in my early 20s. This is the classic studio portrait in which I am carefully posed, formally dressed, and serious. Beside the portrait is an ostentatious edition of the Bible which I purchased in high school. It is so heavy that it is cumbersome to handle and might be displayed more appropriately on a church lectern. The Bible has gilded pages; a thick, tooled, leather cover; and is illustrated with reproductions of engravings and paintings by Rembrandt. The pages show no sign of use. The genealogical tables at the beginning are blank. Next is a brass handbell, one of the gifts my parents received for their fiftieth wedding anniversary. Beside the handbell is a handmade clock in a plain rectangular wooden case. Gold-colored thumbtacks mark the hours; the hands are disciplined curlicues. The wooden case is the work of my father, who was a carpenter for part of his life. The clock mechanism and hands were sold as a kit to people who engaged in carpentry as a pastime. It is consistent with my understanding of his character that his creative work in this clock calls so little attention to itself. The clock might be considered an occupational object in that it so naturally provides a topic of conversation that would lead to discussing carpentry. A book which I edited, another occupational object, is highlighted by its placement at the very center of the bookcase. Behind it is a polished brass lamp. The body of the lamp is a tapered, fluted shaft, the grooves of the shaft white, the fillets unpainted brass. The shaft terminates in a large, white sphere, encircled by a polished brass band, and below that a smaller, polished brass tube. At the very bottom is a flat, octagonal, white base. Beside this lamp is a thin, clear blue, blown-glass vase that adds a touch of color. Twenty-six inches high, its narrow neck is stretched to such a length that it can serve only decorative purposes. The vase has a somewhat anthropomorphic appearance, a sort of protruding belly on top of shapes not unlike human shoes. Strictly speaking, the vase would probably not be considered an example of either "joke glass" or "grotesque glassware" (Newman 1977: 141, 168), but it is not distant from such classifications.

The final object on top of the bookcase is a snapshot of my father and me sitting beside the backyard well when he was in his mid-40s and I was about four years old. The snapshot is less conspicuous than the professional portrait because of its smaller size. Unframed, it is displayed in a temporary cardboard and plastic holder. My father and I are carefully posing as if this, too, were a studio portrait. He has turned his head slightly away from the camera; I look directly at it. The thinness of his body and his wire-frame glasses convey an ascetic impression. His facial expression may indicate that he has been made somewhat uneasy by the attention (or perhaps the sun). His jet black hair is meticulously parted, his ears prominent. He wears a casual shirt. Dressed in shorts and t-shirt, I smile and offer to the person holding the camera a prosaic Midwestern flower, a zinnia. For a few years officials in Loogootee attempted to promote the town by giving it the nickname "Zinnia City, U. S. A."

On the two walls directly above the bookcase are a framed picture and a cloth wall hanging. In a wood and gold-leaf frame, a bit old fashioned as a frame for modern art, is a reproduction of a painting by the German expressionist painter Max Beckmann (1884−1950). The painting is titled "Summer Day (View of Lake Chiemsee)." This is a picture of a lush summer landscape in which farmers gather hay in pastures beside a lake. It avoids the social commentary characteristic of most of Beckmann's art. The cloth wall hanging is a recent Christmas gift I gave my mother. It shows a cat sitting on a window sill beside a pot of red flowers and looking out at some of the icons of popular

Plate 2. Corner bookcase in the living room of Harold and Eithel Riggins. Photograph by Bill Whorrall.

Newfoundland art, a distant lighthouse and a small boat. The wall hanging has been crafted in a slightly clumsy manner to signify its handmade origins. On the floor beside the bookcase is a foot-high Japanese vase decorated with pictures of irises and colorful exotic birds.

All of the books in the house are mine. They are clustered in two restricted areas in the living room and dining room (the corner bookcase and the top of the piano) as though they are contained there in my absence. They constitute a kind of interactional backdrop. Like most Americans of their class, my parents have lived in a largely oral culture supplemented by the reading of daily newspapers and occasional magazines. The books which I have left in the house are those which are of only superficial interest to me. Mostly published in the early 1960s, many reflect current interest in social issues. There are also popular "middle-brow" novels, such as those by Irving Stone, short stories by Hemingway and Twain, and a series of books on world religions. Inside the bookcase are two of my treasured childhood collections, one of rocks and another of sea shells.

To me, the encyclopedia in the bookcase is one of the objects in the house which is most symbolic of the cultural gap between myself and my parents that is due to intergenerational social mobility. For that reason I would classify it as a stigma object. It is a 16-volume edition of the *American International Encyclopedia* published in 1954 by the J. J. Little and Ives Company of New York. This crudely printed encyclopedia was offered as an incentive to shop in a local grocery store. The entries are brief and lack the erudition of more professional encyclopedias. But for my mother this edition has "just the right amount of information." Its presence authenticates her claims to sound and comprehensive knowledge upon which to base her commonsense attitudes and judgments.

The stories mother tells about the house do not have social mobility as a theme. Her stories often tend to be about absent objects and persons, broaching on the theme of lost opportunities: old things she failed to save because she never anticipated their present value, the type of fur-nishings she wishes she could have purchased. A wine decanter, a gift from her deceased employer who was a dentist, elicits a story about inappropriate gifts. But at other times, and generally more implicitly than explicitly, the contents of the living-dining room are used to validate social status. Domestic artifacts are authenticating evidence supporting claims made in conversations. For older people deprived to some extent of the self-validating effects of work and social connections, objects are a vital source of status.

The knickknacks on the shelves of the bookcase are an assortment of historic mementos, travel souvenirs, curios, collective and esteem objects. On the far left of the first shelf is a medallion commemorating the inauguration of President John F. Kennedy, an artifact that might be considered a collective symbol of American patriotism. Attached to a flat stone is a cast metal sculpture of a raccoon washing its food. To me an esteem object, this work of art was a gift I gave my father to remind him of the time when he had pet raccoons in the backyard. Crafted by Siggy Puchta, this signed, limited edition sculpture might be contrasted with another representation of an animal on the bookcase shelves, a handmade ceramic Grizzly Bear. A fish is strapped around its neck with a rubber band. The bear was a gift from some of my mother's relatives. There is also a postcard view of the town of Riggins, Idaho; a limb of petrified wood from the American West, gathered by some of mother's relatives; a pink wooden pig with an oversized red heart like a valentine (a handmade esteem object a nephew gave my mother); and a miniature metallic model of a Spanish canon from the 16th century, one of my high school travel souvenirs.

In front of the bookcase is a padded armchair, purchased in the mid-1930s, and periodically reupholstered, now in a green tapestry fabric of flowers and curving lines in raised relief. Prior to the purchase of the brown reclining chairs (manufactured by Style-craft Inc., Milford Iowa), which changed the sense of territoriality in the room, this was my father's favorite chair. The windows are framed with antique satin, cream-colored draperies and white sheer curtains. The draperies are tied back with a braided gold cord from which hangs a tassel. Through the window one can see a few feet of the yard, an adolescent oak tree, and the side of the neighbor's house. To some extent the view is obscured by the brown reclining armchair having been moved as close to the television set as possible. The back of the chair is protected by a brown hand towel.

On the floor within easy reach of the armchair are a number of objects for entertainment which have stigmatized connotations since their presence is a sign of the failing eyesight of old age. Alternatively, one might argue that these things convey status rather than stigma because they indicate the strength of character which an old person requires to live independently: a special cassette player for "talking books" distributed by the state to the visually impaired, a pile of cassettes in the green plastic boxes the state uses in distributing cassettes, and an illuminated magnifier. There is also a plastic letter opener and a fingernail file. The floor lamp is plugged into a gold-colored, plastic wallplate, decorated with a moulded foliage border. All the other wallplates and switchplates are similar.

The television set in my parents' home is in a corner of the living room, but clearly visible from the sofa and two armchairs. Baudrillard (1981: 56−57) and Fiske (1990: 87−88) comment on the treatment accorded the television set in modern homes. Baudrillard writes about the way the introduction of the television destroyed the "traditional centrality" of the living room.[9] Placing the set in a highly visible location tends to be correlated with heavy use and thus with low social status. Placing it in a far corner or hiding it inside a cabinet are assumed to be correlated with less frequent viewing and thus with higher social status. Fiske writes about the artifactual context in which he placed his own television set. He placed academic books, frivolous children's toys, and left-wing cartoon figures around the set, thus merging academic and popular cultures. He thought that this unintentionally paralleled his interpretation of television programs such as the Newlywed Game, a "pleasurable mix of progressive politics, fun, offensiveness, and a populist vulgarity" (Fiske 1990: 88 – 89).

My parents purchased, to quote the term used by the manufacturing company in its advertising, a "traditional style" television set. This is an RCA, 24-inch, console, color television (Model XL-100 Solid State). Since the set is now about 25 years old, it would have to be considered "low tech," at least in comparison with products presently available. Stylistic elements recall premodern styles of furniture. Adorning each side of the screen are pilaster-like wooden shapes which resemble furniture legs that have ribbing and spooling. Below the screen are two false wooden drawers with curved Italianate brass handles behind which are straight backplates that end in a fleur de lys. The veneer on the television cabinet is slightly cracked due to water damage. Displayed on top of the television set is: a glass basket with orange-colored silk flowers; an alarm clock; a solid plastic cube containing labelled fragments of 24 minerals from Canada, a gift I brought to my father when I was studying in Toronto; and an antenna rotator, a folded brown towel underneath protecting the veneer.

At first glance there appears to be a conventional open book on top of the television set highlighted by the easel which supports it. However, the volume has been glued shut except for the two opened pages, and pasted on top of them is an extraneous picture and text. The picture is one of the most common religious images in Protestant homes, "The Good Shepherd," by an artist named Plockhorst. It refers to one of the best known parables about God's mercy. On the opposite page is the complete 23rd Psalm in the King James translation: "The Lord is my shepherd; I shall not want. He maketh me to lie down in green pastures; he leadeth me beside the still waters..." The volume has a false patina of age. The cover and the edges of the pages have been gilded, some of the paint scratched away to create an antique appearance. Paper doilies have been glued to the cover. The Biblical references — which some might interpret as the ultimate truth — are pasted over a secular book. For my mother this is a strong collective object, a visual affirmation of her membership in a local church community. However, from the point of view of "medium theory" (Meyrowitz 1985), a specialty in mass communications research which explores the relation between a society's most popular medium of communication and its prevailing values, this partic-

Plate 3. Television set in the home of Harold and Eithel Riggins, Loogootee, Indiana. Photograph by Bill Whorrall.

ular co-location is revealing of a transitional anxiety: America's past source of authority, the (religious) book, has been placed atop the contemporary source of authority that has replaced print media, the (secular) television.

Beside the television is a veneer end table with cabriole legs and brass handles (manufactured by Mersman Tables, Somers Corporation), one more rejection of pure functionality like the decorative television set. But although the end table has traditional stylistic references, they are not identical to those on the television cabinet. The handles have colonial American backplates suggestive of an Eagle with open wings. The exterior also incorporates false decorative features because the doubling of the handles gives the impression that the end table consists of two shallow drawers when in fact there is only one. The end table is cluttered with cassettes in plastic boxes and cardboard boxes, envelopes, and a commercial cassette player. The armchair and matching footstool, a wedding present received in 1929, are among the oldest pieces of furniture in the two rooms. They are presently covered in a gold-colored, nylon frisé fabric. There is a green silk throw cushion on the chair. Newspapers (now only local ones but in earlier years the *Indianapolis Star* would have been among them); magazines such as *National Geographic*, and *Modern Maturity*; and letters are usually piled on the footstool.

The exterior door to the living room is panelled, the top half glass covered by sheer curtains. It appears that the door's original lock — certainly ineffective by today's urban standards — is still in use, as is the original black china doorknob. Hanging from the lock is an old fashioned key, three inches long, with standard bow and bit. Attached to it is a buckeye on a short chain.

Between the two doors to the bedrooms is a three-seater sofa with a fixed back and movable seat cushions covered in a green tapestry fabric identical to the previously mentioned armchair. A handwoven, striped afghan rests on top of the sofa. The stripes are green, brown, red, and beige. A brown hand towel is sometimes used to protect the pillows, other times to protect an arm of the sofa. There are four yellow silk throw cushions with black tassels at each corner. A second magnifier is stored for quick retrieval in a corner of the sofa.

Above the sofa is a round, recessed, antique picture frame containing a reproduction of the bust from Ingres' portrait of Charles-Joseph-Laurent Cordier. In such a small fragment of the original painting, Cordier's aristocratic ancestry can still be inferred from his penetrating eyes and his lace tie which is called a jabot. Underneath the frame is a small, dark-gold wall bracket with ornamental moulded plaster. This is a display device for a treasured ornament. Since the bracket is below eye level when viewed from a standing position, its ornamental details appear from a few feet away to consist of only foliage and curlicues, but hidden among the foliage is a snarling dragon. Sitting on the bracket is a handmade vase, wool woven around a plastic frame, that holds artificial flowers. Covered in glitter and frosting, these flowers are the most unrealistic ones in a house in which most plants are artificial. The round frame and the bracket share one similarity. Ironically, both attract more attention to themselves than the objects they are supposed to highlight, a shift of focus indicative of working-class aesthetics. In aristocratic contexts frames are supposed to be appropriate for the value of the framed object and not displayed for themselves.

There are four delicately detailed, mid-nineteenth-century engravings of Swiss scenery by William H. Bartlett (1809–1854), a British illustrator who specialized in travel art and whose engravings epitomize Victorian notions of the picturesque and sublime: "Mt. Sion from the West;" the

"Hofbrücke in Lucern;" "Kandersteg, Canton Bern;" and the "Castle of Granson." These engravings present wide, panoramic views of grandiose scenery in which humans and nature coexist in harmony. The precision and exactness of the engravings and the fact that Bartlett has depicted human figures leisurely working in traditional costumes reassuringly domesticate the dangers hidden in wild mountainous landscapes.

I gave my parents the pictures by Bartlett and the antique picture frame in order to replace an inexpensive reproduction of a painting, "May Morning," by an obscure commercial artist named Carl Woermer. (The overly decorative bracket was suggested by the interior decorator when mother consulted him about the placement of the Bartlett engravings.) The Woermer painting, two ancient apple trees in bloom on a perfect sunny spring day, had been purchased by my mother because it reminded her of the small apple orchard on her parents' farm. The Beckmann reproduction, which I bought as a souvenir of studying at the University of Munich, is also a landscape showing an agricultural setting in ideal conditions. Both artists found poetry in the commonplace. In both pictures nostalgia is a prominent element. The difference between the paintings does not lie in the subject matter but in the treatment accorded it. Woermer imitated nature more closely than did Beckmann whose style is more expressionistic and schematic.

In front of the sofa is a drop-leaf coffee table, with cabriole legs, which matches the end table. The coffee table functions as a sort of "landing pad" for small new objects arriving in the house. Visitors cannot miss seeing what is displayed here, generally the most recent esteem objects, such as greeting cards, letters, and gifts. At present the gifts are exotic objects geographically most remote from the Midwest: an alabaster box from India inlaid with colored stones that form a flower motif; and a ceramic "welcoming cat" from Japan (a "maneki neko"), a symbol of good luck. In addition, the coffee table displays a pebble milk-glass ashtray used in an alien manner to contain keys, antacid tablets, cough drops, and a "twiddler" (a handmade wooden toy to hold while twiddling thumbs) that functions as a social facilitator. A brass bowl contains pink silk roses. Between the sofa and the second brown reclining armchair is the previously-mentioned brass floor lamp with the flexible neck. This armchair, too, is protected by a brown hand towel. The chair somewhat obstructs the door to one of the bedrooms.

Although the dining room is now rarely used for meals, most areas are in full view of visitors and it displays regular dining-room furniture. The table remains in the center of the room. Leisure activities take place along the room's periphery, the location of the desk and piano: talking to relatives and friends on the telephone, writing letters and paying bills, and playing the piano. A lower level of impression management is evident in the dining room except for the fact that it is "displayed" as a special room distinct from both kitchen and living room. While functional specialization can be an indicator of high status in American homes (Pader 1993), this dining room is actually a multi-purpose area, a buffer space between the kitchen, the living room, and the bathroom. The corners of the room are used for storage. Popular styles of art are displayed on the walls. Scratches and scuff marks are noticeable on a few pieces of furniture.

The color scheme is the same as in the living room: gold, green, and brown. The sheer curtains in the west window are permanently shut since the window now faces the enclosed back porch. The curtains in the south window are always open. Strong sunlight streams through the south window which is not shaded by trees. No furniture is oriented to the window despite the pleasant view, a long expanse of neighbors' backyards. There is a brass light on the piano and on the desk. An overhead light fixture identical to the one in the living room hangs in the middle of the ceiling.

A red mahogany drop-leaf table (manufactured by the Craddock Company, Evansville, In.), kept to its minimal dimensions, is in the center of the room. Two of five matching dining chairs are placed at the table. The cloth-covered chair seats are printed with an imitation of embroidery, flowers on a black background, and have faded to some extent because of the harsh sunlight. Carved on the back rail of the chairs is a camellia-like flower. The table legs are slightly scratched, apparently when the chairs are returned to their resting places. On the table is a crocheted doily with prominent pineapple stitching along the border; a straw basket containing a variety of cloth flowers in pastel colors (roses, daisies, lilies); a silver and glass coffee warmer; and two matching, short-stemmed, silver candlesticks with circular bases.

A reclining "La-Z Boy" armchair, upholstered in green imitation leather with a simple button back, might attract attention because it is in front of the wall opposite the living room. This chair became part of the household property by accident. Mother purchased it for one of her brothers who used it for a few months, and when it was no longer of use to him, she chose to keep the chair rather than sell it at a fraction of its original cost. On the wall is a framed, colored-pencil sketch by Khoa Pham of my father asleep in this armchair in the last year of his life.

Plate 4. The dining room of Harold and Eithel Riggins, Loogootee, Indiana. Photograph by Bill Whorrall.

Pham is a professional architect and personal friend who prefers to make abstract art, but does realistic portraits as a favor for friends. His portraits "tend to accentuate the expressions that are questioning or defiant, taciturn or defensive; aspects which generally are not seen as 'flattering' to the person" (correspondence, Aug. 13, 1984). However, the sketch of my father seems to me to represent a resigned acceptance of stillness and vulnerability.

Noting the rest of the room's contents beginning counterclockwise from the armchair, one sees a wooden desk whose rounded contours counteract its connotations as office furniture. Some scuff marks can be seen on the finish and the surface of the desk is protected by a pane of cracked glass held together with tape. Under the glass are addresses to contact in case of an emergency. On the desk are utilitarian office supplies: a cheap stapler; a pebbled, clear-glass ashtray filled with rubber bands, paper clips, and light bulbs used in illuminated magnifiers. There is a wooden box, the size of filing cards, made by my father; and a white and green Varron brand plastic tumbler ("vacuum tumbler, Bopp-decker, Plastics Inc.") that holds pencils and ink pens. A round, polished-brass container holds a roll of stamps. In addition, there are neat piles of old papers, letters, receipts, and out-of-date telephone books saved because they contain addresses of family members. A brass letter holder formed by the words "do it NOW" is tightly stuffed with old mail above which prominently sticks the one item which does get prompt and frequent attention, a small black bankbook. Two telephones have been placed on the desk, a cordless Cobra INTENNA and an AT&T Big Button Telephone for the visually impaired. Above the desk is a Black Forest, wooden, cuckoo clock of standard design. The case is perfectly preserved but the internal mechanism is broken. To the side of the desk is this year's calendar which depicts Scottish scenery, a reference to the Scottish origins of mother's family who, according to our genealogical research, immigrated to the United States in the mid-1700s. This is the only explicit reference in the two rooms to her pre-American ancestry. With one other exception (the stoneware jar mentioned below), the historical depth of artifactual references to ancestors, whether maternal or paternal, is very shallow and stops with my grandparents. One wooden chair is in front of the desk, underneath is a dark red throw rug, and to the side one of the matching dining chairs. Underneath this chair is a gold-colored wastepaper basket. Hidden under the desk are three shoe boxes containing cancelled checks and an empty clear plastic bowl that originally held a fruit basket given as a Christmas gift.

Plate 5. Desk in the dining room of Harold and Eithel Riggins, Loogootee, Indiana. Photograph by Bill Whorrall.

The dining room contains four mass-produced pictures by the artist Paul Detlefsen that present nostalgic visions of turn-of-the-century farming and small-town life. I would interpret these pictures as showing manual labor without drudgery, the reassurance of technological simplicity; the satisfactions of the harvest, and the excitement of firemen racing to put out an unseen fire in the distance (also reassuring because there is no hint of tragedy). These pictures are printed on an unusual material, foil paper. The two pictures beside the desk are titled: "Old River Days," a view of steamboats on the Mississippi; and "Iron Horse," a picture of a steam-powered train. Although mother grew up on a farm and my father spend some of the formative years of his childhood on a

farm which his father rented, the two rooms contain few "country antiques" (Fiske 1990: 87), artifacts whose rustic and hand-crafted forms
might appeal to an intellectual's left-wing sentiments.

The only live plant in the two rooms, an overgrown poinsettia no
longer blooming, has been placed in front of the window. Hidden somewhat by the poinsettia is a late-nineteenth-century stoneware jar used in
an alien manner as a vase to hold dried Fox Tails, Dollar Plants, and
lilies made of a printed cloth that might be appropriate for aprons. This
ten-inch high jar is covered in an oatmeal-gray glaze and is a functional
object with no decoration other than a hastily-drawn blue circle that
serves as a trademark. The jar is displayed in an understated manner,
but is of some significance because it is one of the most ancient objects
in the house. Having originally been the property of my mother's paternal
grandmother, the jar is the only object in the two rooms linked with any
generation of the Ledgerwood family older than mother's parents.

The six-foot display cabinet consists of three glass-enclosed shelves, a
drawer, and two shelves hidden by panelled doors. The cabinet functions
as both a shrine (to the past and to good dining) as well as a catchall. I
use the term "shrine" to refer to the glass-enclosed shelves whose contents
are visible, and the term "catchall" to refer to the hidden space, the
drawer and the shelves behind panelled doors. Mother has collected and
placed on display traditional objects of femininity: antique china (from
my father's family for the most part) and cut-glass (from her family). On
display is the densest cluster of associations with ancestors and with
people of my parents' generation anywhere in the two rooms. Nonetheless, prior to my undertaking this research, the contents of the shrine
were to me simply an interactional backdrop, functioning in a way similar
to that of my books in my parents' eyes. While I knew the china and
glass symbolized cherished relationships with other people, my knowledge
of the manner of acquisition of most of these objects was vague. The
catchall portion of the display cabinet has become the repository for the
less attractive or bulkier dishes, napkins, coasters, candles, bridge cards,
sewing supplies, a manicure set, old eyeglasses, and Christmas decora-
tions.

Most of the items on display were given to my mother or were
inherited. The few exceptions, which have been purchased, tend to be
more recent travel souvenirs. Here is the kind of late-nineteenth and
early-twentieth-century fancy china and glassware which was preserved
for special social occasions. They carry the standard decorative features
of the era: clear glass with stars and thumbprints; hand-painted china

with pastel roses, lilies, pansies, and fleurs de lys; pictures of deer and gnomes; gilded and painted rims. Although the trademarks show that several of the older pieces were manufactured in Germany, this is probably a reflection of conditions in international china and glass industries rather than conscious family identification with German culture. Perhaps the two most artistic pieces are a plate of Haviland china decorated with pictures of red and black raspberries and leaves; and a Ginori cake plate decorated with pink and white lilacs. The most frequent type of tableware are plates of various sorts, twelve of the sixty-six items. Some of these things are from categories of dishes which are so old that they are no longer used in dining: three clear-glass salt cellars, and two cut-glass spoon holders.

Although antiques predominate, the shelves do contain on closer inspection an eclectic mix of styles and types of objects: reproductions as well as genuine antiques; memorial china (from the golden wedding anniversary); a cheap blue pitcher decorated with a picture of the child actress Shirley Temple; a real pine cone from Bavaria; a marble pebble, a travel souvenir of unknown origin; a snail shell; an Inuit soapstone carving from Canada; a reproduction of a colonial bottle from James-town, Virginia; and a plastic needle threader whose location in the china cabinet makes it easy to find. There is also a clear-glass beer stein illustrated with figures in relief, people in costumes typical of heros and heroines in historic operas. Originally sold as a container for food, the beer stein was used by my grandmother as a flower vase. Since it is displayed as a decorative item in a household of teetotallers, its message is ironic: "Massig trinken lieder singen half vonje zu guten dingen." In proper German the message should read: "Mässig trinken, Lieder singen, halb von jedem zu guten Dingen." [Drink moderately and sing songs in order to achieve good things.] The few pieces of modern tableware were gifts from me: a Delft china flask and vase, and Arabia Ware egg cups. Items for use in social contexts more prestigious than family dinners on Sunday afternoons are also sometimes from me. An example is an antique clear-glass perfume bottle encased in a silver holder of lilies of the valley.

Once again an insignificant-looking item is sentimentally valued, an obviously cheap mug decorated with a wreath of pansies and a gnome. It was used as a shaving mug by my paternal grandfather, Harve Riggins (1881 − 1917). For me, this appreciated emblem of masculinity is a sign of a broken bond with the past. It might also steer a conversation toward the topic of gender, documenting my belief that traditional female values are superior to the traditional values of men. My reference would be the literature summarized by Rubin (1983) about the difficulty adult men experience in maintaining intimate relationships. Rubin traces the relative social incompetence of men in intimate relationships to the structure of the family during childhood, the fact that "mothering" or caregiving is the work primarily of women, the same sex for girls, the opposite sex for boys. Psychoanalytically-inspired feminists, such as Rubin, believe that this pattern of caregiving fosters excessively strong ego boundaries for boys as well as a discontinuous gender development. When mothers psychologically push young sons away in order to encourage a male identity, sons misperceive this as "abandonment." Apparently, such misperceptions remain lodged in the unconscious and are among the reasons why adult men insist on asserting their separateness and detachment from others.

The shaving mug with the pansies and the gnome belonged to my paternal grandfather, whose political views might be an inspiration to me if I knew more about them. I have spent a considerable amount of time writing about the personal lives and farming technics of my mother's family (Riggins 1983a, 1991). This was not because I necessarily identified with the politics of the Ledgerwoods, but because mother, being more connected psychologically to others, remembered so many of the stories about her extended family that she had heard as a child. Even if one is tracing the line of male ancestors, family history is largely women's history because it is women who tend to remember the information they hear. In the case of Harve Riggins selective memory due to gender has reduced the story of his life to a few sentences. Despite being a farmer, he is supposed to have been sympathetic to the labor organizer and socialist Eugene V. Debs and he threatened to become a pacifist if the United States entered World War I. Harve drowned, however, in a fishing accident before he had the opportunity to take a public stance as a pacifist.

The top of the china cabinet is a visible but out-of-the-way place for "parking things," as mother says. An electric insulator in green glass, an object considered to be a collector's item (Rinker 1984: 277–279), was saved by my father to be used in the making of a night light. There is also a coal oil lamp ("Queen Anne no. 1. Scovill Mfg. Co.") originally belonging to mother's parents. The other objects are recent gifts – rather impractical now due to the rarity of formal entertaining in old age – but they need to be on display because of the relationships they represent: a modern, Finnish, clear-glass water pitcher; an antique, clear-glass cake stand; a modern, clear-glass bowl; and a silver water pitcher wrapped in a plastic bag.

Beside the china cabinet is a music cabinet in veneer, a rigid rectangular box on straight legs, built to hold music and phonograph records. As the work of my father's brother, it has the same functional qualities as the bookcase, referred to earlier as a witnessing object. The small objects on the music cabinet are an empty wine decanter, a brown ceramic object that resembles an egg cup (mother has forgotten its purpose but not who gave it to her), a magnifier used in an alien manner as a paper weight to hold down some family snapshots, a small box containing an unused salt and pepper shaker, and a broken thermometer. On the wall above the music cabinet are the other two Detlefsen pictures on foil paper: "Fire Wagon," an image of horses galloping down the street pulling a fire engine; and nearly invisible behind the clock, "Harvest Time," a picture of children watching a steam-driven threshing machine. Underneath the music cabinet is a pile of catalogues for ordering recorded books. In the corner formed by the two cabinets is one of the matching dining-room chairs. Sometimes referred to as a "carver," this is the only chair in the set which has arms. Presumably, the man who sat in it would carve the meat. A more politically conscious family might prefer two carvers or none at all.

On the music stand is a shelf clock made by one of the leading manufacturers of clocks in nineteenth-century America, the Seth Thomas Company of Connecticut. It is a spring-driven, eight-day, pendulum clock, which strikes each half-hour. On the back is a label which reads "number 298." This clock was received as a wedding present by my father's parents who married in about 1901. The case is manufactured of pressed oak wood decorated with the face of an old man, Father Time presumably, and a roaring feline, perhaps a reference to the swiftness with which time passes. Father Time's beard and the mane of the feline are so stylized that they have evolved into vine-like shapes. The glass door protecting the clock is covered with stencilled gold-leaf grillwork. Although originally inexpensive, the high sentimental value of such shelf clocks today is due in part to the fact that at the turn of the century they would have been one of the few ornaments in the parlors or kitchens of farmers and manual laborers. Unlike modern clocks, its slow deliberate ticking makes one very aware of the passage of time. Hanging on one corner of the clock is the tassel from the cap I wore at my high school graduation ceremony. This clock is practically the only furniture which my father preserved from his parents' household property. He may have liked it because it could be placed, as a mechanical gadget, in the realm of traditional male objects. The clock has been restored and is in good working condition, but my father was the only person who knew how to coordinate the chiming mechanism with the time. It has struck the wrong hour ever since his death.

Attached to the partition wall that separates the living and dining rooms is a horn-shaped, yellow vase with a gilded rim. Now empty, it once held a hanging vine. There is a black, metal TV-tray from the 1950s. It is decorated with white and turquoise leaves which are intentionally misregistered. In other words, it appears that a mistake has been made in the printing process because the outlines of the leaves and the veins are not perfectly aligned with the body of the leaves. It has been suggested that in the 1950s the popular awareness of the atomic components of matter made people highly sensitive to the fact that things are not as solid as they appear to be. This awareness had an effect on decoration and art and may be reflected in the intentional misregistration on the TV-tray. Another TV-tray, this one wood and made by hand by one of mother's nephews, leans against the partition wall. Above the partition wall are the chimes of the doorbell. In the corner by the piano is a Sears brand humidifier. When not in use, the humidifier serves as a place for collecting cassette tapes and papers. On the wall behind it is a mahogany wheel barometer and thermometer in a banjo-shaped case with a broken arch pediment and a brass finial suggestive of colonial furniture. In recent years the barometer is sometimes accidentally hung upside down.

The piano in the dining room was manufactured by the Hobart M. Cable company. Among mass-produced upright pianos, it might be considered to be of medium quality. At the moment the classical music on the piano includes Debussy's "Suite Pour le Piano," Kabalevsky's "Sonatina," "Piano Masterpieces of Maurice Ravel," Bach's "The Well-Tempered Clavier," and a book of Mozart Sonatas. In addition, there is a considerable amount of popular music which reflects my parents' taste but not my own. The religious music includes two Methodist hymnals, "He Touched Me" by William J. Gaither, "Thank You" by Roy Boltz, "Faith Unlocks the Door" by Samuel T. Scott and Robert L. Sand, "The Holy City" by Stephen Adams, and "He" by M. Jack Richards. The secular music consists of "Everything is Beautiful" by Ray Stevens, "Doll Dance" by N. B. Brown, "Somewhere my Love" by Maurice Jarre, "White Christmas" by Irving Berlin, and "My Funny Valentine" by Richard Rodgers.

Plate 6. Piano in the dining room of Harold and Eithel Riggins, Loogootee, Indiana. Photograph by Bill Whorrall.

When I was a child, this kind of popular music (whether sacred or secular) was highly discredited in the eyes of the young and was certainly not publicly validated — like rock music — by associations with youth, fashion, or teenage fun. Locally, classical music was appreciated even less but was highly valued in my eyes. The piano was thus the site of some rather intense family conflicts in which compromises in musical taste represented, on one hand, the negation of a child's fragilely maintained self-identity, and on the other hand, an indication of the ungratefulness for the advantages the child had received from self-sacrificing parents. The sacrifices included a 100-mile round trip for weekly piano lessons throughout high school with an Indiana University faculty member (Frederick Baldwin) and the wife of a faculty member (Mrs. Walter Robert).

A number of objects unrelated to music are on top of the piano: a mottled-brown, earthenware pitcher that belonged to my maternal grandmother; a blue ceramic beer stein decorated with a picture of a stag (a travel souvenir from Bavaria); a series of unread classic hardbound books in cardboard slipcases (the authors include Balzac, Cervantes, Tolstoy, and Twain); a bound copy of my Ph.D. dissertation; two bright-yellow, wooden salt and pepper shakers (more gifts that need to be displayed because of the person who gave them); and a magnifier. The brass light on the piano rests on a hot pad depicting a Dutch windmill on a cloudy moonlit night. The wooden piano bench is covered in a green and blue woven material that suggests burlap. The bottom of the bench is beginning to sag from the weight of its contents, most of my letters from distant places.

Above the piano is a Wormy Chestnut picture frame (made by my father's brother) that holds a travel souvenir I bought during a trip to a Boy Scout Jamboree in Colorado. This is a reproduction of a painting by the well-known Western artist C. M. Russell (1864 – 1926). An experienced cowboy, Russell specialized in making genre and anecdotal paintings of cowboys and Indians and other Western scenes in Montana and the surrounding territory. This picture shows two mountaineers returning to their campsite at the end of a day hunting deer. One mountaineer makes a gesture to silence his partner because he sees skunks foraging for food among the utensils around their campfire.

Beside the piano is the fifth of the matching chairs. Hanging across the top rail is a cloth calendar for the year 1971 which depicts a jolly mustached man cooking on an antique wood stove. The purse mother is presently using is on the chair. An Everyready, yellow and black, plastic flashlight; a pint-sized Donvier ice cream maker; and one of mother's old used purses are on the floor underneath the chair. Recently ironed shirts hang from the black china doorknob of the kitchen door. Hidden behind this open door is an antique record player, a Columbia Grafonola, purchased in the mid-1930s. The Grafonola may be technologically interesting, but it is a crude rectangular box on spindly legs that is not especially attractive and has thus been shunned to the side. The record shelves inside contain every piece of art I drew or colored in the first three grades of primary school. On top are a jumble of old calendars, some as old as the late 1970s, which have been preserved for their illustrations, and an electric hair dryer still in its original styrofoam package. Resting on a sheet of aluminum foil underneath the Grafonola are two dust-covered boxes full of esteem objects that are much too old to display: Christmas cards, some dating back to the early 1970s; a box of golden-wedding anniversary cards from 1979; and a night light which my father made out of a block of wood and a green-glass insulator.

Conclusion

It must have been obvious to the reader that my account of my parents' living room betrays a tension between two points of view, mostly my mother's and mine. Her own perception and self-validation appear in the text as direct or indirect quotations. In spite of all my effort to be "objective" and systematic in the description, I found it impossible to avoid value judgments which operate in the text as distancing devices, and which could be considered sociologically as a measure of social mobility. It is in particular noticeable that my own input in the account tends to take the form of referencing while my mother's input concerns almost exclusively the mapping of personal or family events and relations onto the displayed objects. Such discrepancies provide an example of what is probably one of the most constant features of living-room decoration: a conflictual space of marks and interpretations, a negotiated symbolic space in which value discrepancies and generational tensions are mediated and stabilized. After all it has been — and still is to a certain extent — my living room, a space where I am present both as a symbolic object of status (photographs, objects, publications) and as an agency, who over the years strove to modify the symbolic economy of the objects displayed and shifted their relevances toward high culture and cosmopolitanism.

In my account, the clash in aesthetic tastes in the two rooms is understated to some extent and at several points in the chapter I tried to emphasize the underlying similarities between myself and my parents. Few individuals are able to choose and control all the objects in their home; compromises are made for both economic and personal reasons. Thus, an element of eclecticism and inconsistency is introduced by gifts which do not correspond exactly with my parents' taste but which must be displayed in recognition of the relationships they symbolize. Because my parents have a more sentimental than aesthetic or economic appreciation of objects, this establishes relatively flexible boundaries with respect to taste but relatively inflexible ones with respect to people. Except for a few dishes in the cabinet that were gifts from friends, all the symbolic references are to family members.

The living room betrays an indulgent attitude towards children, but this is not obvious until objects are mapped, disclosing how many are related to me as iconic representations, gifts, or childhood possessions. The exotic objects which I have introduced evoke the American West,

Germany, Switzerland, Holland, Canada, India, and Japan. However, most of these are related in some way to me; they map my having been there. Most of the exotic objects — and all of those which are the most foreign — are in the living room. The status inconsistency in the home that is due to the number of exotic objects is kept in check by their systematic co-location with childhood memorabilia, thus framing the unknown within the securely controlled.

By centering artifactual displays on objects related to the offspring, status artifacts are highlighted. One might argue that these things represent my parents' aspirations for social mobility. Some blue-collar workers are thought to compensate for blocked social mobility by excessive expenditures on material goods. Caplovitz (1964: 119) refers to this as "compensatory consumption." While excessive expenditures have been avoided by my parents, the way the living room highlights the child's achievements may in part be a compensatory mechanism. In upper-class families in Western as well as in some non-western societies such as India, where status comes from birth and family origins, portraits of ancestors rather than descendants are displayed in living rooms (Duncan — Duncan 1976a: 208). In contrast, American middle-class living rooms are often decorated with pictures, memorabilia, and esteem objects from children and grandchildren. In a society which emphasizes occupational mobility, children's accomplishments — to some extent achievements of the parents after all — convey more status than do those of the ancestors. In this respect the noticeable indulgence of my parents' living room is a general societal feature which is simply aggrandized by the fact that they had their first and only child after seventeen years of marriage.

Despite mother being the amateur historian of her family, the rooms appear, at least in my eyes, to be characterized by temporal homogeneity rather than temporal heterogeneity. Objects older than 1930 are few in number, relatively small, and confined to limited areas, notably the china cabinet. Objects purchased by my parents tend to have a conventional lower-middle class or working-class flavor (Rainwater et al. 1959: 184 – 202). This can be seen in the "rugged sturdiness" of the furniture, the avoidance of ostentation, the home's cosiness, and the preference for the modern and the easy to clean. The two rooms are characterized by a high level of conformity to the current tacit rules of interior decoration: they contain no unexpected artifacts or oddly co-located objects; all of the examples of the alien use of objects are indications of practical concerns rather than creativity or nonconformity. Nothing explicitly evokes the state of Indiana or the picturesque county where the home is located despite my parents' rootedness in the area. Both were born about a dozen miles from the home's location. The most prominent objects conveying indigenous references are the two pictures on foil paper which might be interpreted as Midwestern scenes, but they are visually lost in the dining-room backdrop. In addition, the religious artifacts, which I classified as collective objects, might be considered indigenous references in that they are related to small-town Midwestern values from the era of my parents' youth.

Since sociologists delight in debunking the impression management of others, there is a theoretical justification in admitting that this account is not devoid of misrepresentations. I was unwilling to be disloyal to my parents in print. Thus, any criticism of their values is quite minor in nature. Nor did I scrupulously follow all of the recommended methodological procedures. I tidied up the rooms before photographing them. I removed William Shirer's academic study of the Third Reich from the bookcase because the swastika on the spine was very prominent and I worried that it might mislead some inattentive reader about my parents' conventional middle-of-the-road political views. I also removed one small picture which I considered too personal to analyze in print.

Postmodern social theory conveys an image of society as being in constant flux. Featherstone (1992: 270) refers to "... the rapid flow of signs and images which saturate the fabric of everyday life in contemporary society." This perspective has been constructed by concentrating primarily on studies of public life: the street life of metropolitan cities, tourism, consumer culture, popular entertainment such as fairs and carnivals, and the informational overload of the mass media. But American homes are not department stores with continually changing exhibits. Domestic artifacts appear to give personal identity a stability it would otherwise lack, and a refuge from the unstable, fragile flux of public life. The case study presented in this chapter may be an extreme example because of the exceptional stability it documents, but even among people who frequently redecorate their homes artifacts still seem to function in this manner, like a score that the self can follow to endlessly retell the stories through which its social identity is selectively constructed.

Notes

1. The link between the self and interior decoration is recognized to varying degrees by manuals of popular advice. Kraft (1971:15–16) writes:
    "No woman ever thinks of her home as a stage set. And yet it's true that you are complemented by your surroundings, just as actresses are. It is

worthwhile, therefore, particularly where color is concerned, to give a
thought to what kind of decorating scheme is becoming to you personally.
That is not as vain as it sounds. To your guests, and even to your own
family, the mistress of the house is an element in its decorative effect. Your
own living room should not upstage you, clash with you, or put you —
literally — in an unfavorable light. You and your home should show each
other off. Keep that thought in the back of your mind while you're
decorating, but don't let it run away with you."

2. It is customary to provide a brief account of a standard domestic interior
   (Caplow et al. 1982: 106), to mention the general condition of a house (Stack
   1974: 5), and to make some inferences about an informant's character from
   the treatment accorded furniture or decoration (Hochschild 1989: 59). The
   implications of the perception that objects are inherently social remains largely
   unexplored in the ethnographic literature on family life. With few exceptions
   (e.g., Weisner — Weibel 1981), practically no one in the field is presently
   writing about the way domestic artifacts reflect household cosmologies; generational, gender, and individual inequalities; or attitudes towards history and
   tradition.

3. One can only speculate about what might have been responsible for Agee's
   hypersensitivity to objects. The literary scholar J. A. Ward (1985) in his book
   on silence in realist art and literature noted that Agee was a visually oriented
   person who showed great appreciation for the aesthetic power of silent film
   and photographs. For Agee, silence was indeed more profound than the
   circumscribed topics of normal conversation. Silence also provides a contem-
   plative space in which it is perhaps easier to sense the physical nature of
   things, something easily lost in the distractions of interaction.

4. The idea that there is a similarity between a culture's understanding of the
   universe and the symbolic features of its homes was discussed by Eliade (1959)
   in his history of religious thought, *The Sacred and the Profane*: "The house is
   not an object, a 'machine to live in'; it is a universe that man constructs for
   himself by imitating the paradigmatic creation of the gods, the cosmogony"
   (as quoted in Cooper 1974: 143).

5. Agee's political views are generally considered to be complex and contradictory
   (see Bergreen 1984).

6. Attitudes toward handicrafts are related to a society's mode of production.
   In a modern industrialized society handicrafts have become luxury items. The
   folklorist Michael Owen Jones (1989: 31−32, 102) comments that the wife of
   a traditional chair maker in Kentucky insisted on replacing his handmade
   chairs with modern factory-made reproductions of antiques: "For many people
   whom I met ... handicrafts were too much a reminder of an older way of life
   characterized by poverty and deprivation, which they sought to escape" (Jones
   1989: 94).

7. The county has been the focus of a series of studies about folklore and social
   history (Riggins 1983a, 1983b, 1988, 1991; Whorrall 1991, 1992, 1993).

8. According to Rainwater et al. (1959: 185), working-class women: "tend to like something or dislike it without relating these preferences to general principles of what they like or dislike. About the only principle they themselves recognize is that some of their aesthetic tastes are aimed to conform with their general estimate of what they can afford, or their conception of themselves as plain and simple people."

9. When television became part of the expected furniture of American homes in the 1950s, this alteration of the space within living rooms was also noted in contemporary decorating magazines (Spigel 1988).

References

Agee, James — Walker Evans
  1941 [1960] *Let us now praise famous men*. Boston: Houghton Mifflin.
Alexander, Christopher — Sara Ishikawa — Murray Silverstein — with Max Jacobson — Ingrid Fiksdahl-King — Shlomo Angel
  1977   *A pattern language: Towns, buildings, construction*. New York: Oxford University Press.
Baudrillard, Jean
  1981   *For a critique of the political economy of the sign*. St. Louis, MO: Telos Press.
Bergreen, Laurence
  1984   *James Agee: A life*. New York: E. P. Dutton.
Bernard, Jessie
  1971   "The paradox of the happy marriage," in: Vivian Gornick — Barbara K. Morran (eds.), 85—98.
Blumer, Herbert
  1969   *Symbolic interactionism: Perspective and method*. Englewood Cliffs, NJ: Prentice-Hall.
Bourdieu, Pierre
  1973   "The Berber house," in: Mary Douglas (ed.), 98—110.
  1984   *Distinction: A social critique of the judgement of taste*. Cambridge, MA: Harvard University Press.
Brissett, Dennis — Charles Edgley (eds.)
  1990   *Life as theater: A dramaturgical sourcebook*. New York: Aldine de Gruyter.
Buchanan, Richard
  1989   "Declaration by design: Rhetoric, argument, and demonstration in design practice," in: Victor Margolin (ed.), 91—109.
Burke, Kenneth
  1989   *On symbols and society*. Joseph R. Gusfield (ed.). Chicago: University of Chicago Press.

Caplovitz, David
   1964   "The problems of blue-collar consumers," in: Arthur B. Shostak —
           William Gomberg (eds.), 110—120.
Caplow, Theodore
   1982   *Middletown families: Fifty years of change and continuity.* Minneap-
           olis: University of Minnesota Press.
Cohen, Lizabeth A.
   1982   "Embellishing a life of labor: An interpretation of the material culture
           of American working-class homes, 1885—1915," in: Thomas
           J. Schlereth (ed.), 289—305.
Colomina, Beatriz (ed.)
   1992   *Sexuality and space.* New York: Princeton University Press.
Cooper, Clare
   1974   "The house as symbol of the self," in: Jon Lang et al. (eds.), 130—146.
Csikszentmihalyi, Mihaly — Eugene Rochberg-Halton
   1981   *The meaning of things: Domestic symbols and the self.* Cambridge:
           University of Cambridge Press.
Curtis, Tony (ed.)
   1992   *The Lyle official antiques review.* Lyle Publications: Glenmayne, Scot-
           land.
Douglas, Mary (ed.)
   1973   *Rules and meanings.* Harmondsworth: Penguin.
Duncan, James S. — Nancy G. Duncan
   1976a   "Social worlds, status passage, and environmental perspectives," in:
           Gary T. Moore — Reginald G. Golledge (eds.), 206—213.
   1976b   "Housing as presentation of self and the structure of social net-
           works," in: Gary T. Moore — Reginald G. Golledge (eds.), 247—253.
Eliade, Mircea
   1959   *The sacred and the profane: The nature of religion.* New York: Har-
           court.
Featherstone, Mike
   1992   "Postmodernism and the aestheticization of everyday life," in: Scott
           Lash — Jonathan Friedman (eds.), 265—290.
Fiske, John
   1990   "Ethnosemiotics: Some personal and theoretical reflections," *Cultural
           Studies* 4(1), 85—99.
Geertz, Clifford
   1988   *Works and lives: The anthropologist as author.* Stanford, CA: Stanford
           University Press.
Goffman, Erving
   1959   *The presentation of self in everyday life.* Garden City, NY: Doubleday
           Anchor.
Gornick, Vivian — Barbara K. Moran (eds.)
   1971   *Woman in sexist society: Studies in power and powerlessness.* New
           York: Basic.

Hochschild, Arlie
  1989   *The second shift: Working parents and the revolution at home.* New York: Viking.
Jones, Michael Owen
  1989   *Craftsman of the Cumberlands: Tradition and creativity.* Lexington: University Press of Kentucky.
Kraft, Mary
  1971   *Good housekeeping complete book of decoration.* New York: Good Housekeeping Books.
Kron, Joan
  1983   *Home-psych: The social psychology of home and decoration.* New York: Clarkson N. Potter.
Lang, Jon — Charles Burnette — Walter Moleski — David Vachon (eds.)
  1974   *Designing for human behavior: Architecture and the behavioral sciences.* Stoudsbury, PA: Dowden, Hutchinson and Ross.
Lash, Scott — Jonathan Friedman
  1992   *Modernity and identity.* Oxford: Blackwell.
Laumann, Edward — James House
  1970   "Living room styles and social attributes: The patterning of material artifacts in a modern urban community," *Sociology and Social Research* 54: 321 – 342.
Maril, Nadja
  1989   *American lighting: 1840 – 1940.* West Chester, PA: Schiffer Publishing Ltd.
Margolin, Victor
  1989   *Design discourse: History/theory/criticism.* Chicago: University of Chicago Press.
McKearin, George S. — Helen McKearin
  1968   *American glass.* New York: Crown.
Meyrowitz, Joshua
  1985   *No sense of place: The impact of electronic media on social behavior.* New York: Oxford University Press.
Moore, Gary T. — Reginald G. Golledge (eds.)
  1976   *Environmental knowing: Theories, research, and methods.* Stroudsburg, PA: Dowden, Hutchinson and Ross.
Newman, Harold
  1977   *An illustrated dictionary of glass.* London: Thames and Hudson.
Ohlin, Peter H.
  1966   *Agee.* New York: Ivan Obolensky.
Pader, Ellen
  1993   "Spatial and social change: Domestic space use in Mexico and the United States," *American Ethnologist* 20(1): 114 – 137.
Pile, John F.
  1988   *Interior design.* New York: Harry N. Abrams.

Rainwater, Lee — Richard P. Coleman — Gerald Handel
  1959   *Workingman's wife: Her personality, world and life style.* New York: Oceana Publications.
Riggins, Stephen Harold
  1983a   *Country lilacs: Eithel Riggins' account of the Nathaniel Ledgerwood family in southern Indiana, 1830 — 1930.* Toronto: privately published.
  1983b   "Notes toward a portrait of Reba (Brown) Chandler," in: Bill Whorrall (ed.), n.p.
  1985   "The semiotics of things: Towards a sociology of human-object interaction," *Recherches Sémiotiques / Semiotic Inquiry* (RS/SI) V: 69 — 77.
  1988   "The spirit of commerce in the journalism of Carlos McCarty," *Indiana Magazine of History* LXXXIV: 262-281.
  1990   "The power of things: The role of domestic objects in the presentation of self," in: Stephen Harold Riggins (ed.), 341 — 367.
  1991   "If work made people rich: An oral history of general farming, 1905 — 1925," *Midwestern Folklore* 17: 73 — 109.
  1993   "Life as a metaphor: Current issues in dramaturgical analysis," *Semiotica* 95 (1 — 2), 153 — 165.
Riggins, Stephen Harold (ed.)
  1990   *Beyond Goffman: Studies on communication, institution and social interaction.* Berlin: Mouton de Gruyter.
Rinker, Harry L. (ed.)
  1984   *Warman's Americana and collectibles.* Elkins Park, PA: Warman Publishing Co.
Robert, John M.
  1951   *Three Navaho households: A comparative study in small group culture.* Cambridge, MA: Peabody Museum of American Archaeology and Ethnography, Harvard University.
Rubin, Lillian B.
  1983   *Intimate strangers: Men and women together.* New York: Harper Colophon Books.
Saisselin, Remy G.
  1985   *Bricabracomania: The bourgeois and the bibelot.* London: Thames and Hudson.
Shostak, Arthur B. — William Gomberg (eds.)
  1964   *Blue-collar world: Studies of the American worker.* Englewood Cliffs, NJ: Prentice Hall.
Spigel, Lynn
  1988   "Installing the television set: Popular discourses on television and domestic space, 1948 — 55," *Camera obscura* 16, March, 11 — 47.
  1992   "The suburban home companion: Television and the neighborhood ideal in postwar America," in: Beatriz Colomina (ed.), 185 — 217.

Stack, Carol B.
  1974   *All our kin: Strategies for survival in a Black community*. New York: Harper and Row.
Stott, William
  1986   *Documentary expression and thirties America*. Chicago: University of Chicago Press.
Van Maanen, John
  1988   *Tales of the field: On writing ethnography*. Chicago: University of Chicago Press.
Ward, J. A.
  1985   *American silences: The realism of James Agee, Walker Evans, and Edward Hopper*. Baton Rouge: Louisiana State University Press.
Weisner, Thomas S. — Joan C. Weibel
  1981   "Home environments and family lifestyles in California," *Environment and Behavior* 13(4): 417 – 460.
Whorrall, Bill
  1991   *Woven hills and quilted rocks: Folk artists in Martin County, Indiana*. Shoals, IN: privately published.
  1992   *Martin County Indiana USA: A photo documentation*. Shoals, IN: privately published.
Whorrall Bill, with contributions by Stephen Harold Riggins and Thomas Rogers
  1993   *A photographic history of Martin County: Indiana Album*. Shoals, IN: privately published.
Whorrall, Bill (ed.)
  1983   *The republic of Indiana*, II. Shoals, IN: privately published.

Bridewealth revisited

George Park

The Kinga of Tanzania

In this essay I inspect the way native Kinga artifacts in southwestern Tanzania during the final decade of British rule were supplanted in the local imagination by products of the industrial world. The main point of interest is not the economic impact of new goods but how old meanings which Kinga men and women attached to these goods affected the course of local cultural change. Kinga were a mountain slope and valley people, relatively remote from colonial administrative centers after World War I, but given to migratory labor. In the main, migration was an option exercised by young men singly. At the plantations or towns they generally lived in company housing, differed from many other migrants in needing no heterosexual contacts, and saved money. In effect, some new things young men brought back from the towns were used to reconstruct old institutions.

Central to this piece is the meaning of bridewealths in a marriage system like the Kinga. Small amounts of cash were moved into Kingaland by men subject to the British head tax — only females, children, and the very old were exempt, and the source of cash was only in the outside world. But bridewealths in the generation or two before independence in 1961 rose to dazzling intensities, leaving the colonial taxes in shadow. Explaining this calls for enlarged understanding of the relation of kinship and friendship in a society which, in precolonial times, had departed from the usual paradigm of a "kinship society" in favor of social groupings based on principles of amity. In a kinship society, the "axiom of amity" shelters under the cover of consanguinity, extending only by contract to non-kin (cf. Fortes 1969); in Kinga society the sheltering function was reversed. I find that Kinga made a successful initial adjustment to a money economy by selectively re-emphasizing kinship ties in connection with their spectacular inflation of bridewealths. Money was "banked" as bridewealth and so diverted from short-lived luxury goods to consumer capital. Generational and gender relations underwent subtle transformation in the process, which can be conceived either as a semiotic or a political one — the differential allocation of values and qualities to an array of things, or the differential allocation of things of value to persons arrayed by quality.

Kinga after World War II were witness, albeit from great distance, to the economic recovery of Ulaya, the Great Society I and my kind came from, and many young men had fixed ideas about the way Ulaya was to affect the Kinga future. When Tiyani asked me, in a quiet moment, whether as an American I did not admire "John Wayne" I was ignorant enough of my own mythlore to have to turn the question around. As I gradually managed to form a picture of "John Wayne" I learned how on a visit to Dar es Salaam Tiyani and friends had come to admire a cinematic cowboy and identify him as an American social type. They had not seen him as Lawman but Leader. They found their hero in a world beset by troublemakers lacking his scope and vision. The films showed how he could rally men about him and clean the world of troublemakers. He had the advantage of superior organization. Things — weapons, saddle-horses, uniforms, telegrams — were part of this. Two aspects of Tiyani's perception of the John Wayne Western strike me as telling: (a) All the amenities which elevated the American world to heroic status were within the range Tiyani had seen laid on for the rural Boma crowd, the club from Ulaya who had formed the governing elite during colonial times. By contrast to the world of whores, shopkeepers, and office workers of Dar es Salaam, American reality was as close to nature as the Kinga. Men worked with their hands. (b) In the films the same amenities seemed to be laid on for everyone. Tiyani needed no theory of class or colonialism, no dream of classlessness, to see the difference and choose a rural model of development.

When, much later on, Tiyani pressed me to say how long it would be before Kinga had things ordinary folk in Ulaya had, his urgency sprang less from private than public ambition. I had come to know him as a self-selected *évolué* who had gone beyond an initial interest in owning things like mine. Young men like him in every community were now in the habit of playing spokesman for their people. First the Independence Movement and later the Government Party TANU had been encouraging this. It was, in the poignant phrase of William McCord (1965), their springtime of freedom. Tiyani felt the Kinga wanted again a world like the one his father had lost, with leaders who could set things right. It was only some years after I had left the field that I began to see it was not sophisticated young men like Tiyani who had been taking the r effective steps to set things right but their stay-at-home fathers. Bride-wealth was the instrument.

My first formal paper on the Kinga (1962) was written in the field for a regional conference and dealt with the bridewealth inflation. I argued that a fair variety of plausible hypotheses might be invoked to help "explain" the soaring curve of the settlements demanded by a bride's family. These had in some communities been magnified in a single generation by a factor of forty or fifty. I argued that, although using a bagful of conceptually distinct analytical frames might not yield a cogent and singular "explanation," such an eclectic approach would illuminate aspects of the problem which any single frame could not take into account. So I came down *for* multiplying hypotheses. But one aspect of the problem was particularly intriguing and has kept recurring to me. Why were the highest bridewealths to be found in remote, quietly conservative valleys?

The answer I have found most satisfactory is the paradoxical one that the traditional order was strongest there. You have to appreciate the importance of the power of definition traditionally conceded to older men. The main and obvious source was their court of law. This remained as in earlier times the central institution in the men's public life and, in the near absence of a family system, the one arena where men could regularly exercise that mandatory intellectual tyranny over women and youths which mature men of their civilization expected. But in the more accessible Kinga communities by 1960 young men were coming and going with great frequency and mixing with sophisticated chums from other localities. The power of the senior mind and the grounding reality of the local scene were harder to assert. When bachelor men are sojourners soon to migrate again, when they have paid their taxes elsewhere and covet access neither to land or to other men's wives, the court will be less of a feature in their lives and the authority of elders be less apparent. In like manner, where elders in a less remote community are themselves affected by direct experience of the outside world and its markets, their subtly won solidarity as an elite will be diminished.

It is a minor irony that legal limits put on bridewealths by the colonial government, intended to stem the inflation, were expected to be enforced by the local courts — in effect, the men who stood to profit from ignoring them. In the more trafficked communities young men did complain, and the court had to order (nominal) compliance with the law. This could result in an eventual off-the-record compromise, dragging the amount of the transaction down a little, or simply in cancelling plans. In Kinga culture there was no spinsterhood to be feared and little probability that a marriage would be precipitated by a pregnancy. This put the bachelor girl's father in a strong position. But another feature of the traditional culture was all-important when an actual contract ran at three times the value officially guaranteed by court documents. Most Kinga marriages are monogamous and stable.

In the traditional culture a bridewealth was a set prestation scaled to the giver's wealth. In the normative model the giver would be the father of the groom, his wealth visible. In effect that would be the herd of goats the same youth had cared for as a boy. A bridewealth would consist of a couple of goats from this herd, and a couple of iron hoes worked at the smithy by the son, more or less of each depending on the arrangements negotiated. The parties were, in the model, the two future fathers-in-law. Nominally, a bridewealth passed from the older generation on the groom's side to the same generation on the bride's. To have done the thing otherwise would have been to downgrade the transaction from social institution to private arrangement. But the young man was free to feel (and did) that the bridewealth was his own, only under the care of a guardian and, more remotely, the court.

Among the seminal changes a cash economy brings with it is the possibility of hiding wealth. In a society where kinsmen have a claim on your goods, hoarding is the basis of capital accumulation. But there are two ways to hoard capital, under ground and under bond. Pastoralists can sometimes "hide" wealth by distributing cattle among the herds of close kinsmen on a reciprocal basis, but they are hiding their wealth from the depredations of enemies, natural or human, not from neighbors. Kinga were hardly pastoralists, in any event, and their personal things were so few and recognizable as to render theft all but unthinkable within a face-to-face community. Apart from certain avoidances, the rule of hospitality was such that prepared food might hardly be denied anyone − kinsman, friend, or traveller. While stored food might always be the object of theft, it was rare. The culprit lost all civil rights and faced death by stoning if caught in the act. In short, a man's or a woman's wealth or poverty was public knowledge. An old man with no young boys and no herds might be supposed to have medicines hidden away, to give him parity with wealthier peers. Money hoards hardly existed before British times, after the 1914−18 war, and would have had no importance for ordinary folk until a decade later. But by 1930 the special value put on small pieces of silver was known to the smallest child, and suspicion in the case of an ego-bound old man would as likely turn to buried coin as to the stuff of sorcery. In the prevailing myth of paths to recognition, money seemed to be taking over from medicines. There is a point of diminishing returns when an old man's sense of risk in putting another ten shillings under ground overmatches any added sense of security; then putting money carefully out at loan is sensible.

One way to conceptualize this secularization of semantic space is represented in Figure 1.

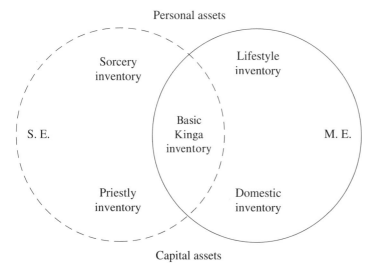

Figure 1. Prime categories of the old (broken line) and new economies. S. E. = Subsistence economy. M. E. = Money economy. Basic Kinga inventory includes locally wrought iron tools, livestock, and housing. The timeline represented is the sixty years of the German, then British colonial *pax*.

Kinship cannot be strong where filial bonds are not. Kinga stress fraternal solidarity but only as an intensified form of peer harmony, leaving kinship almost to spontaneous initiative. They construct community on a foundation of amity, male to male, female to female, reinforced by non-possessive love. Supporting this strategy is a pattern of late marriage — both genders traditionally married a decade or more later than most neighbor peoples. Late marriage leaves little room, demographically, for plural marriage, and polygyny was mainly for rulers. Especially for men, the bachelor period was one of openness to new friendships and easy movement among the barracks houses of the several small courts comprising one of the four Kinga realms. Marriage came with the readiness to settle down, and plans were often made to settle with friends. If a new hamlet was formed by a small group of peers sharing a surname, as was not unlikely, it would pass for a local agnatic descent group, as such matters are conventionally seen by anthropologists. But at bottom it would be a group of friends, as stable as their mutual good will. A political implication of this is that local groups were not especially truculent. The nature of the kinship bond is that it cannot be questioned, meaning that when hostility deepens within a local descent group Ego is in no position to deny the moral claims of others. Kinga had a form of social organization I (Park 1988: 161) have dubbed "antipolitan" — the kind where loyalties are intense enough but volatile, and men would usually rather move than fight. I think it likely, though requisite observations can no longer be made, that all but the most tightly organized peoples of folk tradition, African or other, knew the antipolitan ethos.

Two features of the colonial *pax* were particularly important for the Kinga. Loss of the war pattern, which had been well institutionalized, brought disuse of barracking at the royal courts and loss of the discipline sanctioned there. Young men were later quick enough, as a plantation economy took hold, in turning to migrant labor. What needs to be said is that they made themselves at home in the barracks life of the tea or wattle estates, gaining a reputation for steadiness. Few took the (economically rational) view that your work was done when you had earned your taxes and the bus fare back to Kingaland. Staying on, they were in a position either to squander money or accumulate savings, and their rationale for doing the latter came to be the rising cost of a bridewealth. This in turn was a reflection of the strength of their common commitment to an eventual return and marriage. Ethnicity played only a limited role, as Kinga in their travels never minded passing as members of one of the better-known groups in the region. The main thing to see is that Kinga workers were enjoying the bachelor stage of what they regarded as a man's normal career, as their forebears had for generations before the *pax*, and were glad to extend "youth" into the fourth decade of life. It is easy enough to see that the *pax* had set the stage for this kind of change by offering a barracks life away from home; but men were living away from the old social system and exposed to new attractions well designed for separating rural men from their savings. Why did the money continue to flow back home?

After a closer look at the way community was constructed by Kinga, I will argue that the steadily inflating bridewealths of the plantation period were part of a successful decentralization of power through the creation of new networks of debt.

Filiation reborn

The old pattern of late marriage meant that a father was often dead before his eldest son married; as adults in a homophilic society the two avoided any show of intimacy; from his weaning, a son might never share a roof with his father. You do not have to assume that structure has psychological roots to see that filiation in such a set-up wants social reinforcement and exists more in name than actuality. The respect young men showed their elders in the old culture was political not filial. But with the *pax* that whole structural dimension was bound to collapse. In some neighboring societies there remained a robust agnatic kinship system, at least at a minimal lineage level, to fall back upon. But for Kinga elders it would take a new departure, a reconstruction of filiation and the nexus of kinship.

In the old culture the bridewealth transaction was essentially dyadic. Typically a couple of hoe blades and a couple of goats were put up by the guardian of the groom (father, older brother, or father's brother). One of the goats would be taken by the court — this was the principal tax. The other goat was earmarked for a more private feast at which the recipient was host, the bestower and wife were guests, and seniors among the close bilateral kinsmen of the bride were privileged participants. The point was to put the stamp of amity on a network centered in the bride's natal household. Where the social function of a bridewealth system is often thought to lie in establishing mutual debt/obligation bonds guaranteeing the marriage and legally establishing the mutual interest of these elders in the offspring, in the Kinga case parental authority was nominal at best. The main guarantee of their marriages was the maturity of the principals, helped by the modest level of emotional intensity expected in the new relationship. So the bridewealth custom reflected the signal importance of private amity and public loyalty to a royal court.

A psychological parameter in the father-son relationship was the element of distrust inherent in the possibility of father-son incest, expressed in the taboos of physical (especially suggestions of anal) contact. A father would not frequent his wife's domicile until a child of either sex was old enough to fetch and carry — authority at that level was part of the general conceptual scheme. But after a year or two of this the child would be weaned, the wife made pregnant again, and the man was free to resume living at the barracks. Efforts I could observe (in the early 1960s) by fathers to exert authority over weaned children even in Christian communities were often frustrated and sometimes bizarre — the kind of authority which prevails over counter-argument seemed not to be part of the cultural program. Boys were attuned to heeding their senior peers and treating the ascending generation at best with diffidence. Among themselves they loved to parody the ineffectual deportment of their elders. An index of the moral segregation of the generations is to be seen in the rules which governed a boy's relationship to an uncle who was his age peer: right up to the uncle's marriage, he would be treated like any friend eligible for intimate relations; but with the marriage strict taboos descended.

What happened under conditions of the *pax* was a pulling together of men in any community who were home "running things" while (mainly) younger men were away at the plantations and towns taking wage work. Language played a part, as Swahili was the language of such work. Even after Independence most elders in conservative Kinga communities were unable to communicate in Swahili, while virtually all young men could — the exception would be a smith's apprentice with no need to travel. Though Swahili was the written language of the courts, a local dialect of Kikinga was always the spoken tongue. Until elders were uniformly masters of the national *lingua franca* they could hardly have allowed Swahili a toehold in their forum. The British, having no interest in "nation building" and no taste for the development of responsive government at the grass roots, were in no hurry to promulgate a national language or the universal literacy which that would make possible. To that extent their program favored the court elders; but on the specific matter of bridewealth inflation Boma policy was inspired by a simple stereotype — crafty old men, selling their daughters in a distorted market, were mulcting the credulous young.

A more sympathetic, more informed, and probably better balanced view would be that Kinga ethnicity as such was not enough of a centripetal force to prevent the young men from disappearing into their diaspora, but marriage could be if the right value were put on it. Of course, a man with a clutch of daughters and no sons stood to gain a fortune. One man who had quite disappeared in early British times reappeared in 1960 with two culturally Swahili daughters; it was no secret that when he had married them off he would be away again — in short, his motives were un-Kinga. I never heard how these city girls made out — they distinctly had the requisite charms, but could they hoe? One reason the high bridewealth system was working was that Kinga women were diligent to a fault and modest in their demands upon a husband's income.

Usually, the bridewealth was to be paid in full at the marriage, leaving a lad deeply in debt to a consortium of kinsmen, mostly agnates of an ascending generation. Once his wife was pregnant he would go back to plantation work to pay off these creditors. Once he had framed up and roofed a house for her, a young wife was all but self-sufficient. Providing she soon found friends in her new community, he could expect to be free of trouble at home. He could stay away at work for a year or two at a stretch, keeping in touch through the many friends travelling back and forth. Kinga had the advantage here of a culture which puts both genders most at ease with own-sex peers, even while conceiving marriage as the natural outcome of a (slow) maturation process for both men and women.

For his part in all of this a young man might put in a few years of work to acquire a few things for himself, his mother, his sister — then some years more saving for a promised marriage, after which there would be a good many more years making the bridewealth good, always with some breaks spent at home. The variations were many. Some men sent for their wives instead of taking off work when it was time to establish a new pregnancy; but women could not leave their fields for long and generally failed to thrive on such visits. A man might fail to settle his wife well and, taking her for granted, lose her early to a runaway affair; then the matter of bridewealth repayment would have to be adjudicated, and her new man would have to make the proper arrangements — but Kinga were not characteristically aggressive in pursuing women. Sometimes they were prepared even to admit neglect in the loss of a wife, once the surprise was past. Kinga men could drop the I-Thou mode of speech (the court could say "she's your meat" meaning you have full sexual rights) in reference to a wife, but were less sure about turning macho talk into action.

What the elders had been doing all through the 1940s and 1950s was to mend the generation gap by putting the right social value on marriage. Marriage *choice* had always been exercised freely, being a matter of proposal and consent, by most Kinga. Betrothals were always unofficial but traditionally long lived. Men subscribed to the theory that a maiden who had a man's keepsake was not free to take another until she had waited seven years — a detail I would think should interest our folklorists. But as money earnings became important the slender thread of romantic trust, what in Western bourgeois culture is so fully institutionalized as "engagement," came to be the basis for rebuilding filiation. A youth would entrust his earnings to his elders. Though his savings bore no interest, the money was out of harm's way and invested in a bond of

trust which could claim to be more substantial than informal peer relations and more realistic than that thread of promissory love the youth
had contracted with a girl. In fact, a young man's romantic arrangements
might fall through without really overthrowing his plans for marriage —
he only had to find himself another maiden, a pleasing project for the
next visit home. I do not mean to make light of romance, only to point
out that kinship can claim as strong a base in nature, and a less capricious
one. I suppose this was the nub of the counsel which tended to pass from
elder to younger man in the unrecorded conversations which must have
gone into those marriage arrangements, so preoccupying to migrant
workers from Kingaland during the *pax*. That a money economy should
have so come to the aid of a floundering kinship system may seem to
offer ground for wonder — the two systems of debt more often seem to
work on conflicting principles.

It was not strictly the filial bond which was strengthened by this
romantic banking arrangement. Whoever was guardian to a bachelor
youth was only a node in the credit network preparing to put up his
bridewealth or, after the fact, judiciously allocate or solicit payments on
the debt. Apart from the father-son relationship which in the model case
is central for dealings within the groom's camp, there is reinforcement of
the father-daughter relationship at the receiving end, as well as the ties
of the maid to her maternal kinsmen. If they can claim to have been
care-givers they can claim each a small share in the bridewealth. As with
a funeral, a wedding is a time for reminding others of past obligations,
met or shirked, and strengthening weak ties or cutting them. But a
mother's brother who would not put up a sum to help with a young
man's plans last year is in a poor position to claim some part of the
sister's bridewealth at the next turnaround — the concern with money
becomes a general concern. Increasingly it preoccupies those masculine
fiduciary networks which comprise the social structure at the proto-
political level, where moral strategies are ruled by kinship and amity,
estrangement and animosity.

Peers were also expected to help bankroll a bridewealth, so a youth
might from time to time find himself allocating money to a friend's cause
which otherwise might have gone to his own. The network of mediators
who would put the touch on a youth is not difficult to visualize — the
management of a young man's affairs had become a community concern
as much as a private one. About money hoards there was speculation on
every hand and little hard evidence, but when a landslide took away one
key elder and all trace of his treasure the loss of both was felt by more

than near kin. One of my special tasks in the field was giving hard cash for paper money. The flow to a hoard, as I so glimpsed it, was in small and irregular amounts which over the months and years would be carefully added up. But the flow *from* any hoard, in payments or investments, must have been nearly as considerable. When a man died his debts and credits would not have died with him, but sorting it all out in a case as sudden as the landslide must have required a long collaboration over many pots of beer.

As money moved within the "Bank of Kingaland" name after name was engraved on it. When the money was finally used to *purchase* a thing from strangers the money was gone but the trail of names remained, only to be cancelled one by one with the passage of new money back along the trail. Conservative Kinga did not use money to purchase goods from Kinga where barter or an exchange of services would do. But for younger men the tastes acquired in travel were brought home. So there were lads who bought peppermint knobs or bottles of soda at the store Amin had set up on the main road, and salaried or otherwise sophisticated men (and two or three unusual women) who bought native beer at the concession just off the grounds of the high court. At two or three places regular country market days were approved. The sellers were women with their foodstuffs, maidens with fruit head-carried up from the lowlands, and occasionally a man with specialty goods brought in. But the buyers were wage-earning folk, and these markets only functioned in *kiangazi* the season for sojourners. Such were the forces — market forces in the most elementary sense — which the bridewealth movement was meant to hold in check. Away from the markets money was not treated as tender but wealth on a par with such other transferable capital goods as hoes, goats, and cattle, the traditional components of bridewealth. It is important to see that in making up a bridewealth capital is not spent but invested. Women produce all the garden food as well as all the children.

Goods and meanings

Kinga goods, new or old, do not nicely sort into the frivolous and the utilitarian, objects of purely personal and genuinely social value. How should I class a pair of plastic sandals? With very careful use they might last two months or more; but they are not repairable. Canvas shoes cost a bit more and give more value; they help keep jiggers off; but they are best used with socks, which are troublesome and expensive; and they will eventually soften the horny sole of the foot, so that footgear becomes indispensable. The nearest thing to universal footgear for Kinga conditions in 1960 was the desert boot, the choice of most visitors from Ulaya or Dar es Salaam but, for good reasons, few Kinga. At some date after 1960 there would begin to emerge a consensus on the need for footgear, and a rough set of priorities based on experience and adjusted to personal means. When the world has been made over in favor of the shod, bare feet will put a person at a social disadvantage — footgear will become a "necessity." The same considerations apply to tailored trousers, dresses, shirts; or to alternative styles in clothing the body. In 1960 quite a majority of men might have said they "needed" tailored shorts for the pockets, while only a few "needed" footgear and hardly any would claim to "need" a wristwatch. The kind of watch available was unlikely to keep working for more than a few weeks under prevailing conditions of use in rural areas. Yet watch repairmen with little collections of used parts were beginning to appear at the market towns Kinga migrants visited. Battery-powered radios were clumsily big at the time and plainly frivolous as they only brought in foreign gabble and pop music from Katanga; but as the technology changed and national political broadcasting became more important, radios would begin to have redeeming social value.

The semantic space these considerations suggest can be pictured as a normal curve of distribution with the range from private to public value running across the base. Most market goods would be found clustering near the center of the range, but the shape of the curve would be rather flat; and in the kind of open market which then prevailed the curve would be skewed, if meant to represent the youngest wage-workers' view, toward the frivolous end. The things young men were proudest to bring home were useful gifts for a sister, a mother, aunt, or fiancée — print cloths, aluminum cooking pots, sugar. There were a number of things they might have brought but usually did not. A commercial-style knife was still a specialty tool — if it was not as foreign as a fork or spoon it was a thing no kitchen needed. A youth would hardly bring a watch for his beloved though he would have one (working or not) on his own wrist. As for changes of clothing, a youth would carry none at all or a few small things knotted in a kerchief. Two items a young man would probably *not* think of on his own were blankets (wagework areas were tropical) and mechanical corn mills (men never ground it). The bridewealth inventories would feature these rare goods as frosting.

Picture now a normal curve representing market items available to a migrant in the towns he passes through or visits from his place of employment, but picture a little rainbow arched over the baseline, inside the curve of goods. The rainbow illuminates things particularly valued (and increasingly found) in Kingaland. On the left we have things a young man's peers would admire. Across the center are a range of things which, because they would enhance a woman's self esteem, he would proudly bring as gifts. On the right are things coveted by neither his peers nor his women, as he conceives them. The blankets and the corn mills, though we seem to know women would prize them, belong to this group.

A young man would no more bring a *gift* to his father than you would to your banker. The kinds of things we have found on the rainbow are three: things with egoistic value, things with alter-egoistic value, and things with a value ego cannot properly feel. These last are things which, if they are not somehow invested with "social value," will stay on the merchant's shelf. It was by including some of them in the bridewealth inventories that Kinga elders managed so to invest them. They are important not for the proportion of the bridewealth they represent but for the sign they put upon it.

Structures of debt

Once my wife managed to stimulate a little crowd of wee girls, stopping by our courtyard to look at the children from Ulaya, to boast about their bridewealths. They were only eight or nine years old, not half the way to marriageability, but each one possessed exact knowledge of what her bridewealth was meant to be. Nothing on any of the lists would ever belong to the girl herself; the point was she felt she would be socially weighed against these things and not found wanting. So the co-operation of the maiden in the bridewealth project was early secured. There could be small rebellions later, when her intended expressed his frustration with long delays, but how would he truly convince the child in her that the vast outlay expected of him was not to be taken as his measure of her worth?

It is particularly instructive to compare this situation to one just across the Rumakali river, a corner of Kingaland ethnically distinct from the rest. The people of Magoma never experienced a bridewealth inflation.

Instead, comparably huge sums of money passed from the hands of young men into the coffers of their elders in the form of penalties for adultery. Kinga magistrates were convinced, not without ample testimony and some clear evidence in court, that most of the cases they tried for adultery in Magoma country were setups. While the young men were away at wage work their old girl friends were being married by the polygynists left at home — such was the scenario — and put to luring lads with cash in pocket into compromising intimacy. However much adultery was actually set up in such a way, the difference in court statistics on damage payments between a Magoma and a typical Kinga community was quite enough to compensate for the difference in bridewealths, supposing the two groups of elders were choosing alternative routes to the same economic end.

The Kinga route was undoubtedly the more subtle one, although it did not always follow the strait path of negotiated settlement. In 1960 Unsala had promised through his father Shs. 1400 in coin, 3 cows, and 6 goats, making his bridewealth worth Shs. 2180. But shortly before the wedding his prospective in-laws arrived in force at Unsala's little house and confiscated his personal stores of cloths, lamps, cups, and tumblers. These things represented two or three months earnings. But it was only when the men tried confiscating his bicycle that he put up such a stink they let him be. Government unskilled labor rates at the time started at a shilling a day, with as much again in rations and housing. The "raiders" could have figured that as a clerk (of sorts) Unsala would have been clearing Shs. 200 a month, and spurred on by grapevine news of spiralling bridewealths elsewhere decided to take what they could while they could. As "bankers" for their own young men they may have felt they had a moral right to reconsider the deal they would make with Unsala's father, but there was no legal or traditional basis for what they did. They just knew Unsala would cool down before taking them to court. When he told me the tale he was not angry about the stores he had meant for his (wife's) own household; his relationship to those things was of the alter-egoistic kind. But the bicycle, a true investment in self, was not in the same category. I suppose the little razzia group understood this and made peace accordingly.

It is only when bridewealth can be seen to operate in a system of generalized exchange, brides circulating one way, cattle the other in a comprehensive circle of local descent groups, that bridewealth is an efficient sanction of *kinship* at the level of macrostructure. One and only one monograph (Krige — Krige 1943) from all of Africa substantiates

that theoretical possibility. For Kinga the affinal bond in the old culture
was no more than an interdomestic one, a small pledge of the ritual kind
by interested elders to keep the peace, to take no sides in a lovers' quarrel
but help cool it. Even the name on the bridewealth before it passed over
was ambiguous: we might think the young man not the father had earned
it all. Yet as money and market goods made themselves felt, they conferred
a radical sort of independence on youth. In Magoma this produced open
war between the generations; in other Kinga communities, especially the
more trafficked ones, the din of war could surface from time to time; but
in those conservative communities which had been stable court centers
the bridewealth movement was astonishingly successful. An ordinary
laborer would have to work steadily for more than a decade, spending
nothing on himself, to pay off a marriage. Of course, what made this
possible was the fact that the money and goods he brought home continued to circulate there, and his own prospects there were, if not always in
the short run, enhanced as he himself moved into the circle of the elders.
But an absolute condition of all this was that Kinga elders themselves
would not move, as the perfectly heterosexual Magoma did, to take the
maidens themselves.

Unsala's father married in the 1930s for a bridewealth of Shs. 60 and
a cow, for a total value of Shs. 80. His father before him would have
married under the old regime for two Kinga hoe blades and a couple of
goats. These marriages never entailed the heavy debt structure, with its
lateral spread, which evolved in the postwar period. It was possible to
view this interlacing pattern of debt, this wide web of financial involvement, as *the* indigenous structure of Kinga society at the time of my
fieldwork.

Among Kachin peoples in highland Burma *hka* "debt" is greatly
inflated in the hierarchical communities but deflates rapidly where hierarchy has been set aside (Leach 1954). The reason is that in a polyglot
community kinship obligations cannot effectively extend into the public
sphere, and another kind of obligation is required to produce stable
structures. In the Burmese case this is achieved through a variety of
contractual arrangements built around marriage. Oddly enough, in the
anthropology of the 1960s "alliance theory" based in models of generalized wife exchange, which requires a "pure" system of local descent
groups, was largely inspired by the Kachins' own model of such an ideal
system — anthropologists were concentrating on one kind of structure,
kinship, to the exclusion of others. But in a plainly multicultural region
this concentration was bound to make a greater contribution to "pure"

theory than to our understanding of Kachin social structures as they were lived on the ground. Kinga were much less multicultural — at the coming of the *pax* they were close to the establishment of a comprehensive system of government (a segmentary state), and dialect differences among the several realms were no barrier to communication. But Kinga social structure was just as firmly politicized as the Kachin. There was no prospect of resurrecting a "pure" kinship order. With the deflation of their militarism, royal rulers became inglorious tax collectors, and the authority of the courts no longer extended to life-and-death issues. Magoma society simply fell apart, reduced to dependence on a magistracy and a policing authority which everyone regarded as instruments of the colonial powers. Kinga retained their sense of policing themselves, gradually building up a looser kind of social structure based on the affinal contract.

Alliance and amity

Marriage is a contract to share the reproductive life of an unrelated person on the moral basis of amity. This does not usually entail equality, and the contractual nature of the marital relationship is never quite erased by time and familiarity. Kinship bonds are "of Nature" but affinal bonds are at most "of God." Put simply, the principle of amity is the obligation to maintain good faith with another person, and this requires jural sanctioning — a set of *mutual* rights and obligations — already in place. Affinal relations *must* be regulated in kinship societies because exogamous rules mean adults will normally form such contracts, and find them in competition with existing good-faith kin relations. In the old regime a Kinga prince often had to *give* a royal daughter to a warrior in order to retire him when he seemed to deserve it or simply was aging — the bachelor life was not naturally aimed at marriage. How sure can we be that it ever has been?

Any effort to discover the structural meaning of bridewealth from its distribution, even just among Eastern Bantu peoples, seems doomed to frustration. Bridewealth is found as often in matrilineal as patrilineal societies, shows no respect for the political weight of descent groups, and appears even among the band-organized Hadza. The insistence of Lévi-Strauss (1958: 56) that the basic building block of kinship (*l'atome de parenté*) includes an affinal link (*relation d'alliance*) is well known and accepted. It amounts to defining "kinship system" so as to include an element of marital politics. All that is banished by this is the mythical case of a bunch of exogamous tribes living on an island and marrying by unregulated capture. Unfortunately, the models of kinship societies which Lévi-Strauss built from his basic blocks were premised on an exceedingly narrow insight. For a very few societies you can plausibly argue that women are "goods in scarce supply" and men are in position to use these goods to cement alliances between structurally impressive segments of the cultural community. This is politics flowing from the brain of Economic Man and requires a full-blown system of prescriptive marriage. From the very few cases which match a blue-sky model meeting these specifications it is difficult to see how you would derive any cultural universals. The facts on-the-ground have stubbornly refused to fit the models, and the structuralist program on socio-political systems has not been much advanced from the time of its original presentation. But setting aside the ideal of universal relevance inherent in the structuralist enterprise allows us to focus on a feature of the marital "exchange" which has a restricted distribution; and setting aside the concern with prescriptive marriage systems allows us to see ordinary cases as examples of situated action. This more modest theoretical stance permits us to inquire into the changing meanings of a Kinga bridewealth and relate the change to the semiotic roots of a social structure. We are also free to see that marriages are normally rather private arrangements – "alliances" are not usually frozen into the macrostructure.

The public or manifestly political side of a Kinga marriage under the old culture was the bridewealth tax, a goat, and the feast on its meat at court. The tax was collected by a party from the court and levied on the father of the bride at the court's convenience some time after the marriage. Matching arrangements were certainly private otherwise, unless in the case of a royal princess, who by reason of her segregation was unlikely to be promised. It was the British who put an end to the old bridewealth tax (*imongo*), wanting no competition with their own imposts. The public or structural importance of a grossly inflated bridewealth lay in the wider, overlapping networks of debt which were created, and the implications of the system for age stratification. In effect, young men were working for their elders as truly as for themselves. A new emphasis on father-son filiation was one mechanism, and on the other side of the contract, father-daughter filiation. But these ties had little to say on the score of *descent*. It is the oblique dimension of the affinal bond which wants our attention.

The aspect of filiation to be stressed is the fiduciary one. Kinga fathers claimed a right to boss small sons about and scold them if they let a goat invade a neighbor's field; but the rule of avoiding intimacy was not narrowly construed, and filiation was free of moral intensity once the boyhood stage of herding and running errands was past. A daily concern for a lad was keeping out of his father's sight — in the Kinga Republic of Youth there were no elders. But the "banking system" turned that around. A father was actually in position to capitalize on the cool nature of his tie to a son, combined with its constitutional permanence.

The father-daughter tie was a different matter, as in the old culture bachelor women were thought competent to take care of each other in everyday matters without recourse to parental protection. The young women lived in self-governing house-groups, worked their fields in peer gangs, and regulated visits by courting youths to their own satisfaction. Making a "structural" thing of the bridewealth meant that guardian status took on importance and was even something to covet — as between an older brother, for instance, and a father's brother. A half-orphaned girl who had never met her "guardians" when she was only a small mouth to feed could be confronted on the path, when she had entered the courtship stage, by a party of magnanimous men bearing cloths. There are tales of maidens, forewarned, who let the gifts lie on the ground. In Christian communities first, and most others subsequently, fathers took to building special houses for nubile daughters, near the mother's. Increasingly, the whole domestic pattern changed. Men's houses declined, married men took to living with their wives, young men took to living in twos and threes in what my children saw as "gingerbread houses," and young women did the same but usually in proximity to some kind of sponsoring protection. It would be too much to say they were becoming the very "objects of exchange" of Lévi-Straussian theory. But the diagonal or "avuncular" dimension of the expected marriage was being set up, and in their own circles the maidens were well aware of it, even if the political economy of marriage was seldom really forward in their minds.

A radical departure in architecture had even occurred in two communities I visited, where Christian fathers had built two-room houses, letting their children sleep in the kitchen. But a Kinga boy or girl would only put up with that arrangement to a certain age. Well before puberty they would have insisted on moving out with peers. Still it could only be a matter of time before overlapping networks of agnatic-and-affinal kinship came to be as characteristic for Kinga social structure as for neighbor peoples. In the old culture there had been a vertical dimension which was simply political and a horizontal emphasis on living with peers which, as a program for local settlement, passed for kinship. In the new culture women were being weighed against bridewealths; young men debated whether a wife could be worth as much as a used Land Rover. Were the elders making a new, chauvinistic world?

It was a world which would be tempered by a continued disjunction of men's and women's social spheres. Even the traditional exclusion of women from serious debate in open court served as much to maintain women's independence as a group, as to subject individual women to men's judgements. Because women were not expected to give more than factual evidence in court they were not expected to air their deeper moral perspectives to men or expose their personal strategies to cross examination. In his famous studies of Barotse court practice, Gluckman (1967, 1972) makes much of the forensic role of the Reasonable Man argument − would the Reasonable Man have behaved as Saywa did? Then Saywa could not be found gravely at fault. In practice, this entails the kind of examination of motives a mother in our culture may be inspired to conduct on a wayward child. Kinga court procedures rely on the same kind of sharp inquiry into character, but even in adultery hearings in Magoma no Reasonable Woman argument was mounted. Women had no hoards and attracted no litigation. Perhaps our phrase should be they knew how to mind their own business.

The new bridewealths were not noticeably turning women into chattels. The same young men who thought (against, I may say, my own expert testimony) that a Land Rover could be a better investment than a wife could be caught the next afternoon in a state of pitiful erotic suspense as they tried to cope with the teasing wit of a band of maidens with whom they had lightly agreed to share a harvesting task. In the bachelor world women exercised a far more successful solidarity than men, and tended to dominate.

What the bridewealth did do was turn the bride's father into a banker. What he received and how much of it he kept was public knowledge. What good it might eventually be to others was a matter of speculative discussion. Young animals were required and, with luck, would reproduce and allow culling the herd of older individuals. Some money would go into a long-term hoard and some might be spent on small acquisitions (utensils, grinders, sugar, tea, tobacco) mainly meant to improve the lot of the bride's mother, but most of the cash half of the bridewealth would probably continue to circulate on the same sort of errand which had brought it in. This would happen because the circulation of wealth had become an essential instrument of amity in the lateral structure of network relations among elders of each local court or moot. To own a hoard and deny it meant denying the claims of amity. A man truly isolated from close kin might be found, but Kinga use their terms for kin in a broadly classificatory manner and know how to fill in the blanks on a family tree by succession, so that a man wanting friends will soon find kin.

The gradual but constant inflationary trend in bridewealths negotiated in any particular court community meant that each cohort of bachelors going out to wage work was bound to bring new wealth in. Trade items actually listed in the marriage contract brought in a new form of wealth; fresh animals would be joined to those recirculated by debt-purchase within the court. The principle of usury had not made an appearance; but the acquisition of a young breed cow would allow a man to slaughter an older animal and, in progressive communities, sell the meat at a shilling a pound (everything from viscera to tenderloin at one price) and strike a profit. In the case of a goat I think the meat never would have been sold. In that case a man's profit is the moral debt of his neighbors, with whom he is obliged to share. But sheep (unless black) had no such ritual standing.

Bridewealth systems everywhere may have more in common with the Kinga than supposed in the conventional wisdom of social anthropologists. What happens with the Kinga marriages of my sample is that a young woman is lost to her peers in one small community and removed to another where her status will be different and the product of her labor shared with a new family set. To say she is lost to her natal family, since she freely visits her mother, is not an accurate description. Paradoxically, high bridewealths actually connect the girl more firmly than she had been as a bachelor to her agnatic kin. On the groom's side a huge debt is acquired, which will keep him busy for the foreseeable future and, since his agnatic guardians are brokers and bankers for his debt, keep him tied by a renewed filial bond to the specific community of his birth.

It is another and parallel transaction which occurs as between elders of the same communities. On receipt of a bridewealth the father, uncle, or brother of the maid is at last in position to settle debts that may remain from his own marriage and doubtless others, restore his herds, and gain the special respect due a man of means from sons and nephews. In the other community the father of the groom has seen no real change in his own economic condition. He is not personally responsible for the debts he mediated; for his own good name as broker he need only be concerned for the continued health and earning power of his son — a concern quite befitting his renewed status as father. Kinga father and son are not the living members of a corporate group exchanging wealth for a woman from another such group down the valley. The woman moves to the son; her economic responsibilities remain to her own and a descending generation. Her productive powers thus move diagonally downward on an interdomestic grid. In response the wealth moves diagonally upward from the young man to the ascending generation. Of a dozen cows, a young man will probably purchase or owe for all of them; of a dozen goats he may be granted the half as patrimony; of twelve hundred shillings he will eventually bring the whole sum in from wages or business earnings.

Seen in the light of networks of debt and demand right, a bridewealth marriage system is probably never close to being one of alliance between corporate descent groups owning and exchanging women. For Lévi-Strauss there was "a fact virtually universal in human societies: for a man to take a wife, she must be surrendered, directly or indirectly, by another man who, in the simplest cases, is in the status of (*en position de*) father or brother to her" (1973: 104, my translation). This is not a conclusion but a premise of the most recent example of Grand Theory in social analysis. In the (distinctly Freudian) myth of origin of kinship which Lévi-Strauss (1969: 12 ff.) tenders by way of explanation, the internal structure of *family* can be seen to belong to Nature; for only with the adoption of incest taboos does the first "*atome de parenté*" (and so the possibility of Culture) spring into being. Yet incest taboos are rules presupposing a well-defined family *structure*, and necessarily attuned to the specifics of that structure in a given *culture*. Evidently Nature in this Grand Theory prevails even today within the family, as no other explanation is forthcoming for the universality of the supposed male ownership of females on which Structuralism has the world construct kinship. In Nature as most of us understand it there are no fathers or brothers — one is reminded of the dog in the comic strip all unwittingly ordered to "go find its father." *Status* is not prior to Culture but follows from it; the French *position* achieves an illusory ambiguity.

But if we set aside some of these Grand Atavistic Thoughts and start with other premises, the formalities connected with marriage may look less like a natural family's "surrender" of a maiden's fertility to strangers and more like a responsible interdomestic system for keeping your own among friends. Bridewealths are normally returnable when a woman leaves a man for cause. At least where cattle are concerned the mark of ownership does not wash off. On the other side of the same coin a bridewealth holds in place the transfer of rights over and duties toward the woman, putting a measured distance between her and her consanguineous kin. As for Grand Theory, a working prescriptive marriage system if it could be found would mean wife-givers could shut off the supply of women if any were mistreated. The "savage mind" is not more given than others to geometry in politics. Marriage contracts of any kind establish identity and underscore responsibility. Dowries move obliquely down the generations, bridewealths and bride service obliquely up, always juxtaposed with the filtering down of wealth according to rules of descent. Both bridewealth and dowry bear the message that filiation — structurally framed parenthood — is by contract not by nature *or* prescription. Unsala has contracted dearly for the privilege of being father to a son or daughter; even as the children grow to maturity he will be working off their debt, so the meaning of the bridewealth is written on the relationship of filiation. The structural change this reborn parental tie will work in the Kinga social fabric can only be profound. As the inflationary stage comes to an end and the Kinga bridewealth takes on a "normal" configuration, the movement of goods will more truly be horizontal, from the groom's guardian(s) to the maid's; and the maid, switched for the wealth, will more plainly be seen as the pre-mortem patrimony of the son. In Nyasaland a man can say he does not inherit from his father "*because* there is no bridewealth" (Goody 1973: 1–4). In the old Kinga culture descent was embodied in a surname, scarcely at all in objects — it was nominal.

In Polygynous Eastern Bantu societies there is chronic generational conflict over the stuff of bridewealths, as each generation seeks to prolong its hold on wealth and standing, withholding these goods from the next. But it is just because the males of that next generation are fixated by the wealth of their fathers, knowing they have a demand right on it and no other wealth, that a polygynous compound *looks* like a corporate group, a temporal section of a timeless lineage embodying the ethos of an ancestor-fixated culture. But I have questioned whether we can be right in reading the surface signs that way. It is ironic that for Kinga during their inflationary phase, the reconstruction of their "agnatic kinship system" was achieved by making the wealth flow temporarily *up* the generational ladder not down. For each marriage two old men and their separate sets of cronies impose a demand right upon the past and future earnings of a young groom. But as the wealth continues to trickle in to accumulate in the hands of his lineal elders, and with growing certainty that the same wealth will soon begin to flow downward again, the ties of filiation will grow stronger. Shortly after my fieldwork was done

Tanzanian policy began to focus on moving migrants back home. The idea was to have them bring their sophistication with them and begin to make use of it in the social and economic development of their special place in a marginal region. Kinga were ready for this, not least because half of a substantial bridewealth was being taken in cash and imported goods.

The decay of the royal courts and their military agenda with the *pax* had to provoke a crisis in Kinga society because grass-roots social organization had previously been allowed to decay under the feudal warrants of the courts. The nuclear family hardly existed, and peer solidarity had more weight than consanguinity. The introduction of money and market goods from abroad was seized upon in a re-emphasis of affinal and consanguineal networks of obligation, with bridewealth as the vehicle. Money earned by young men was "banked" by their elders as bridewealth and so diverted from frivolous consumption or short-lived luxury goods like soap and lamp oil, cigarettes and tea to building domestic capital. The typical moral strategy of the migrant worker was in this way redirected from making a career abroad to making one at home, even while — irony vying with paradox — the young men were kept away earning year after year. Generational and gender relations underwent their subtle transformations so quietly that no one talked of change or deplored the passing of custom. As indexed by inflation of bridewealths the process of change once begun was progressive over a period of more than three decades.

The basic movement can be conceived as the adoption of a fresh management strategy by the informal oligarchy of elders which always had presided over the semantic field of politics, through the mechanisms of court and ritual theater. In the scenario I have provided, the moving force is doubtless anxiety: how will the elders maintain a privileged position in face of the new independence of youth? But where elders in Magoma could be seen baldly to covet and grab a share of the new wealth, relying on their *de facto* domination of the legal arena, most Kinga elders did more, taking charge of the way wealth must be construed in their culture by young and old alike.

References

Fortes, Meyer
    1969   *Kinship and the social order*. Chicago: Aldine.

Gluckman, Max
   1967   *The judicial process among the Barotse of Northern Rhodesia (Zambia)*. 2nd edition. Manchester: Manchester University Press.
   1972   *The ideas in Barotse jurisprudence*. Manchester: Manchester University Press.
Goody, Jack — S. J. Tambiah
   1973   *Bridewealth and dowry*. Cambridge: Cambridge University Press.
Krige, Eileen Jensen — J. D. Krige
   1943   *The realm of a rain-queen*. Oxford: Oxford University Press.
Leach, Edmund R.
   1954   *Political systems of highland Burma*. London: Bell.
Lévi-Strauss, Claude
   1958   *Anthropologie structurale*. Paris: Librairie Plon.
   1969   *The elementary structures of kinship*. Rev. edition. Boston: Beacon Press.
   1973   *Anthropologie structurale deux*. Paris: Librairie Plon.
McCord, William
   1965   *The springtime of freedom*. Oxford: Oxford University Press.
Park, George
   1962   Kinga bridewealth. Kampala: EAISR Conference Papers II.
   1988   "Evolution of a regional culture in East Africa," *Sprache und Geschichte in Afrika* 9: 117–204.

Melanesian artifacts as cultural markers:
A micro-anthropological study

Nick Stanley

Introduction

In contemporary anthropology, strongly influenced by modern critical thought, the authority of the ethnographer is gradually giving way to a text which represents a "dialogue between the ethnographer and informants, where textual space is arranged for the informants to have their own voices" (Marcus — Fisher 1986: 67). Unfortunately, specialists in the study of material culture are still a long way from conducting a satisfactory "dialogue" with artifacts. One possible exception might be McLung Fleming's (1982) methodology for deciphering the rich symbolic meanings attached to artifacts. Although originally published in 1974, Fleming's procedures remain a model that is worth emulating because they offer a broad, humanistic approach to unpacking symbolic meanings. Furthermore, this is a perspective that remains centered on the object itself but not divorced from other related cultural material whether literary or artifactual.

The first step discussed by Fleming, *identification*, involves many of the topics associated with classical description: the construction of the object, its function, its history, etc. The second stage, *evaluation*, consists of a range of comparisons: comparisons with other objects of the same kind, with objects made by the same or different craftpersons, things made in the same region, and so on. Evaluation is followed by *cultural analysis*. At this stage more general theoretical inferences are made about the social functions of the artifact and what can be learned from it about the nature of the society in which it was produced. In the final stage, *interpretation*, an account is offered of the contemporary significance of the object. At this point the object is related to ourselves and to present concerns.

Perhaps the most interesting of Fleming's terms are the ones that he adopted from George Kubler, "real intersection" and "virtual intersection." The former refers to close and clearly demonstrable connections such as the link between economic history and silversmithing that would be evident in silver coins. In contrast, virtual intersection refers to "noncausal, unprovable, but possible correspondences and conformities between artifacts and cultural constructs" (Fleming 1982: 171). An example might be relating the form of silver tea pots to popular concepts of charity, gender, and nurturing (Prown 1991).

Fleming's schema has been further refined by Igor Kopytoff's (1986) development of what he called the "cultural biography of a thing," the recording of the continually shifting social definition of an artifact from the status of a commodity to its treatment as a singular and unique entity. In this approach objects are treated as if they were people; similar questions are posed about an object as would be asked in gathering information for a person's biography: origins, ideal and actual careers, socially recognized age grades, changes in function due to age, decline and eventual death, etc. Such an approach, Kopytoff argued, can be particularly useful at a time of cultural contact. The biography of an object can show that "what is significant about the adoption of alien objects – as of alien ideas – is not the fact that they are adopted, but the way they are culturally redefined and put to use" (Kopytoff 1986: 67). Objects can have, in Kopytoff's schema, new careers if not new lives.

This biographical approach has been applied with considerable success to such simple and everyday objects as the styrofoam cup, the tin mug, and the Coca-cola bottle. It is possible, as John Shuh (1982) demonstrated, to conduct a moral, economic, and political debate about the nature of contemporary urban life by contrasting the disposable styrofoam cup with the continuity of the tin mug in our grandparents' world. A more formal cultural analysis was given by Craig Gilborn (1982) in his monograph on the Coca-Cola bottle. Such bottles, he maintained, offer admirable examples to handle and study as "they are inexpensive, expendable, durable, and possess sculptural and optical qualities of great complexity" (Gilborn 1982: 185). Using objects as initial clues for the study of another culture has a prominent role in development education (Thomas 1983: 4). In all of these cases the procedure is similar. The object provides – like a detective story – a continually wider and more inclusive tale that takes the viewer or reader to an increasingly convincing explanation of its existence and function. The more sophisticated versions of the biographical approach claim that the artifact has two separate existences – one in its original context, and a new one in collections, exhibitions, and catalogs (Pearce 1986: 199).

As our confidence in the single historical account wanes, it might be logical to assume that we are moving in material culture studies into a postmodernist phase. Certainly, Kopytoff's (1986: 64) warning that what is considered to be a commodity by one person may have an entirely different meaning for another introduces the possibility of multiple meanings and incompatible views. We may be entering a new age where all the old ethnographic certainties and taxonomic orthodoxy remain but a dim memory. But I want to suggest that, rather than proceeding in such a logically tidy direction, there may be strong reasons for concluding that we may even be in danger of regress. In the concluding pages of this chapter I will attempt to develop this argument by noting the similarities between, on the one hand, missionary exhibitions from the early decades of the twentieth century and, on the other hand, contemporary museum displays, modern tourist art, and the state promotion of indigenous minority cultures.

What is a collection?

One small case study will illustrate my point. I claim no special virtue for the collection which my chapter examines. It is a very ordinary collection. This is not to disparage it, but to argue that it may, in its very mundaneness, provide a useful exemplar and one which is typical of countless other collections found in our museums. The collection was presented to the Birmingham Museums and Art Gallery by Ida Wench in 1930. She was a teacher working from 1909 to 1936 for the Melanesian Mission in what was then the New Hebrides Islands (since 1980 the Republic of Vanuatu) and the Solomon Islands. The collection is small. Wench's own inventory lists a mere one hundred and sixty-one items. Her short notes on provenance are the only documentation that the collection possesses. These notes usually provide a single term description — ornament, bowl, mat, earstick, etc. For one-half of the items there is also an indication of original location. Occasionally Wench attached a handwritten label to the object, but again these offer the most laconic comments.

The question I wish to ask of the collection is, frankly, what is it? What does it represent? Does it lend itself to a positivist or a postmodern reading? Perhaps this is merely an incoherent jumble of objects swept together by accident and united only by geographical provenance? Or is there, to renew the parallel with the detective story, a plot to unravel? I wish to argue that the answers we seek are complex. It may be that we will have to revise the clean and simple division of the "two lives" of artifacts, previously mentioned, at least for the collection under scrutiny.

It would be pleasant to record that Wench's collection represents a well ordered and personal response to academic anthropology and the agenda set by the Royal Anthropological Institute's (1929) *Notes and Queries on Anthropology*. The surprise is that in some ways it does. The major anthropological writer on Melanesia at the end of the nineteenth century was R. H. Codrington, who was also a cleric of major importance working for the Melanesian Mission. His analysis of Melanesian culture, *The Melanesians* (1969 [1891]), follows a recognizably standard format. Codrington's own collection has been dispersed to a number of locations. The major holdings are those at the British Museum (EOC 4663) and the Pitt Rivers Museum, Oxford (1920.100). The former contains 93 entries, the latter approximately 400. Some of the items in both museums have arrived through another donor or as part of another collection. The broad span of time during which the objects were acquired and the particularly protracted period over which items were accessioned (1875 – 1944) throws into question the assumption that Codrington's collection was a complete entity at any one time. The collection did offer material, however, for his anthropological study. For example, one of the items at the British Museum, a black and white dress with fiber fringe and feathers from the Banks Islands (Republic of Vanuatu) is specifically illustrated in his work (Codrington 1891: 108). The ordering of the older items in the Pitt Rivers inventory follows closely the chapter headings in the *Notes and Queries on Anthropology*. One group consists of weapons (including bows, arrows, clubs, and sticks). Another is entitled tools (adzes, pounders, drills, beaters, and knives). The group associated with fishing (including the celebrated Solomon Islands fishing kite) is extensive (24 items). There is a heading for domestic items (pudding knives, coconut scrapers, head-rests, and water gourds); another for mats (including bark cloth, and fringed mats); and a large number of items gathered under the heading "dress and personal adornment" which are further subdivided into clothing, combs, armlets, necklets, ear and nose ornaments. Codrington's collection concludes with decorative arts, musical instruments, toys, and charms.

Many of Wench's items replicate the material discussed in Codrington's book. In fact her collection is — although smaller and with poorer specimens — remarkably similar to the items Codrington gathered. There is a fine collection of thirty arrows from Santa Cruz, an aesthetically satisfying exhibit in its own right. Domestic items are well represented by bowls, cups, pudding knives, spoons, and water gourds. Items of personal adornment are similarly to be found (combs, wristlets, armlets, ear plugs, earsticks, nose pins). There are also several items of woven fiber (bags, mats, and baskets) in addition to items of customary exchange (shell and feather money, beaded belts, and ornaments for ritual occasions). There are the obligatory items enigmatically labeled "charms." As in Codrington's collection, cultural practices are also represented, such as the chewing of betel nut (lime, gourds, and boxes), and several items connected with fishing. Wench's collection is the more recent of the two. It is difficult to escape the suspicion that her collection represents an accretion of elements first assembled elsewhere. The arrows are so similar stylistically that they encourage one to think of them as a sub-collection. The same may hold for the impressive range of designs in her collection of pudding knives. Many of Wrench's other items, however, do not suggest a similar logic or tutored eye.

The Santa Cruz arrows raise an interesting point. In general, Santa Cruz artifacts appear to be over-represented in many Melanesian collections. Perhaps Walter Ivens provided part of the explanation in his account of the rare visits of ships to the island in the early days of the Mission when Cruzians would bring goods for barter. Ivens' list is instructive:

> ... bows and bundles of arrows, paddles, dancing clubs, mats, kits, looms, fishing nets and lines, lassoes for shark catching, flying fish floats, shell armlets, shells and shell spoons for scraping coconut, bundles of smoked canarium nuts, coconuts, dried and green breadfruit, a few yams and pana, areca nuts and pepper leaves, wild wood pigeons, parrots, and native fowls (Ivens 1918: 241).

This list in turn raises further vital but unanswered questions: to what extent were the Cruzians responding to already well known visitors' preferences or were they trying to anticipate their preferences? Were they providing a "normal" set of merchandise used in regular inter-island trading?

The Melanesian Mission gave several collections to the British Museum. Others came from private collectors. There are now at least sixteen Melanesian collections in the British Museum, nearly all of them from clerics. Eleven of these contain less than ten items. These tend to consist of items of adornment (such as nose ornaments and necklaces) or other shell implements (bailers, spoons, knives). Four of the collections are larger: Ivens (21 objects); Nind (20); Robin (23); and another that invites comparison with Wench, Comins (68). Ivens' artifacts are largely fish hooks, ornaments, and bowls. Nind provides fishing items, ornaments, and shell currency, while Robin offers a wider variety of reference including (beside fishing materials) ornaments, domestic utensils, a range of charms, and human hair and bone. Ivens and Robin had, like Wench, good reason to form collections. Both were Organizing Secretaries (a duty involving the promotion of the Mission): Ivens in New Zealand 1909 — 10, Robin in England 1899 — 1905. However, none of these collections achieves the range and variety of Wench's collection.

Some information concerning Wench's motives and means of collecting come to light in her autobiography, *Mission to Melanesia* (Wench 1961). The first form of acquisition appears to have been gift. Concerning an early visit to Maravovo on Guadalcanal she wrote:

> On emerging from the church, we were confronted by a crowd of smiling villagers, most of whom had come along with gifts for the white visitors. We were reluctant to accept their presents, but the people would have been so bitterly disappointed that we allowed ourselves to be laden with everything they had brought. Amongst other things we received baskets, native skirts and umbrellas, yams and two monstrous stalks of bananas (Wench 1961: 133).

A second, and for the purposes of this paper, a more interesting means of acquisition was what Wench termed "make and earn." The very title suggests capitalist or mercantile values. The system derived from the "unsatisfactory state of affairs" in Melanesia where the great majority of the population — including her own pupils — were outside the cash economy. This created a particular problem with respect to offerings collected at Christian religious services. Wench remarked:

> I suppose we could have provided the girls with money for the offertory, but we felt that to have done so would not have taught them the spirit and nature of giving. Then, we hit on a system that had much to commend it. We invited them to manufacture useful articles, such as brooms, coco-nut leaf mats and loosely woven bags, which we promised to buy from them ... Our pupils responded magnificently. The Mala girls made flat bags, those from Gela fashioned folding umbrellas, some wove mats, and a couple of Reef islanders put together a pretty little sewing kit... The San Cristovalites became particularly adept at manufacturing cups from coconut shells and others soon picked up the technique (Wench 1961: 185).

This vignette provides an interesting insight into stylistic diffusion associated with the advent of exogenous change. It also provides a link between the two contexts in which the meaning of artifacts is established.

Articles made by this method were sent home by Wench to her family and to others associated with the Mission. The parallel systems of monetary and non-monetary exchange continued to operate well into the 1960s. As a teacher at Patteson College, Guadalcanal, remembers, when students were unable to offer their tuition fees in cash, they paid with traditional shell currency (Rev. J. Pinder, personal communication). Such an arrangement would certainly have been more regularly employed earlier in conjunction with gift exchange.

One of the objects in the collection, a tapa cloth, furnishes evidence of another means of acquisition. It carries a tag on which is written "Birmingham Missionary Exhibition." No other object in the collection is similarly tagged but it seems a fairly safe assumption – in light of the damage that many of the objects have suffered at some time in their existence – that they too have travelled extensively. Similar clues are to be found in the British Museum collections. Two pieces of tapa cloth bear labels for the "Missionary Loan Exhibition, Shrewsbury" (Q80.Oc.470), and "Missionary Exhibition, Taunton" (Q81.Oc.1572). These labels offer little information and are a particularly insecure means of identification. Missionary exhibitions provided a second life for these objects prior to entering the world of the museum. Missionary exhibitions were very popular forms of instruction, evangelism, and entertainment in Britain, in parts of continental Europe, and in North America from the 1890s until the Second World War. According to the Church Missionary Society (CMS):

> A missionary exhibition is a huge "living picture" of the peoples of Africa and the East – their daily life, their surroundings, their customs, their religion. To those who cannot go personally to Africa, India, China, the missionary exhibition offers the best means of getting into close touch with the life and thought, the opportunities and needs of these and other lands (CMS Archive 1928 H H30E 1D/E).

The missionary exhibition did not appear fully formed out of the blue. From its early days the Melanesian Mission contributed to exhibitions of curios in national and international expositions, particularly in New Zealand. The Rev. J. Palmer, acting head of the Melanesian Mission, for example, exhibited "curios, baskets, etc." from the Banks Island and "exhibits from Santa Cruz" at the New Zealand and South Seas Exhibition of 1889/90 (Official Catalogue: 187). At the South Seas Exhibition in Wellington in 1891 the Bishop of Melanesia, J. R. Selwyn, provided a cornucopia of items from Santa Cruz and the New Hebrides group of islands, including among other artifacts:

Belts used for money, many yards in length, beautifully decorated with red feathers and small strings of white opercula; sandals made of coarse cord, Reef Islands; dancing rattle of hollow nut-shells strung together; small loom for making bags; two large looms, for native cloth; bow and poisoned arrows, painted, carved and tipped with human bone; model of canoe with outrigger; man's bag, slung round the neck and used for holding betel-nut, lime, fishing lines, etc., and beautifully woven, dyed and ornamented with shells and palm leaves (Hastings 1891: 244).

The collection also contained drinking bottles, spoons, a "belt made from finely plaited human hair," breast ornaments, armlets, a wooden pillow, fishing gear, dresses, and tapa cloth. The echo of authorial voice is just audible: a sense of pride in the aesthetic quality of the work ("beautifully decorated" and "beautifully woven") is tempered with a hint of the exotic ("finely plaited strands of human hair") and the somber entry of poisoned arrows "tipped with human bone." The bishop also contributed articles from the Solomon Islands:

Two large canoe prows, stained black and inlaid with mother-of-pearl; very large food bowl, inlaid with white shell; musical instrument, Paris pipes; wooden finials for gable of house, with carvings of men in a crouching attitude, and of monkeys; turtle-shell nose ornament, San Cristoval; two hair-combs, Ulawa; sleeping coverlet, made from Pandanus leaves sewed together, Florida (Hastings 1891: 244).

What makes this description unusual is the geographic attributions. Few other contributors to the exhibition had such detailed catalog entries. Attached to Rev. Palmer's contribution are the indigenous names of articles from Banks Island. In addition, hints about the minister's aesthetic taste can be found in the entry:

Gete, a large basket used for carrying yams, etc.; tapera, wooden dish chiefly used for mashing taro; tapera gae, flat basket with rim, used as a dish; targelut, stick used for mashing taro and breadfruit; four beautifully plaited baskets (Hastings 1891: 244).

A more systematic missionary presence is recorded by the second decade of the twentieth century. The Church Missionary Society exhibition in Auckland in December, 1917, provided a shop window display of some complexity. This display offers two contrasting readings which correspond closely to the distinction made by Kirshenblatt-Gimblett (1991: 388) between "in situ" and "in context" presentations. She writes of exhibition classifications:

Whether they guide the physical arrangement of objects or structure the way viewers look at otherwise amorphous accumulations, exhibition classifications create serious interest where it might be lacking. For instruction to redeem amusement, viewers need principles for looking. They require a context, or framework, for transforming otherwise grotesque, rude, strange, and vulgar artifacts into object lessons (Kirshenblatt-Gimblett 1991: 390).

Plate 1. Melanesian Court 1917, Auckland Missionary Exhibition. A. J. Palmer Collection. Auckland Institute and Museum c24,962.

The Auckland display of 1917 can be seen as an example of an "in situ" construction in so far as it suggests metonymy and mimesis. The natural surroundings in which objects were typically found were reproduced; configurations of objects represented the experience, the "reality" of Melanesia. There were the items, or their near equivalents, appearing in the earlier displays: the model canoe, belts, tapa cloth, poisoned arrows, breast ornaments, bags, "Paris pipes," cups and combs, and at the top left, the ubiquitous loom. To anchor the viewer in the missionary experience a portrait of the martyr of Melanesia, Bishop Patteson, was prominently displayed as well as two boards of photographs, one of which contained an immediately recognizable image used for a postcard sold by the Melanesian Mission. To complete the viewer's identification with the scene, a large map at the center of the display situated the mission field geographically. The cross beneath, one of a range of "intermediary objects" (created for Christian religious use but utilizing local craft traditions), focused attention on the merging of the old and the new, the Christian and the Melanesian, to create a new but "appropriate" tradition.

Yet the display also had strong "in context" connotations because of the arrangement of the artifacts in taxonomic categories. Objects were grouped and balanced − fish hooks to the right of the back panel, rings to the left; combs (labelled) to the right and combs again to the left; spears and arrows symmetrically displayed on both sides of the map, each grouping accompanied by a set of eight or nine photographs. The mounted display insisted on the importance of comparative presentations − the combs, the rings, the hooks. The Auckland exhibition provided both the taxonomic respectability required of serious display together with the romantic invitation to partake, if at a symbolic level, in the work of the mission.

In the interwar years the Melanesian Mission participated in similar large-scale exhibitions. The 1926 East and West Great Missionary Exhibition was particularly significant. The exhibition was held in Auckland Town Hall for one week in August. It was a joint exhibition which had courts devoted to Egypt, Zanzibar, Japan, China, and Melanesia. The general tone of the exhibition might be termed "domestic exoticism." The promotion announced:

> At the opening of each evening session there will be a Pageant Procession, in which all workers are asked to take part in the national costume of some country represented in the exhibition ... such costumes need by no means be gorgeously elaborate but such as would naturally be worn in the streets, e.g., Cairo, Zanzibar, Tokyo, Peking, etc. What is wanted is colour, and plenty of it (Anglican Church, *Church Gazette*, 2 Aug. 1926).

The exhibition offered, then, a form of romantic naturalism developed through the participation of members of the local parish. A review of the exhibition noted:

> The Melanesian Court may be said to be the outstanding feature of the exhibition. Before a verdure-clad island washed by the blue tropical sea is set out an array of the arts and crafts of the natives ranging from weapons of war to the gourds and other articles of domestic utility. There are wood carvings and shell ornaments, some the product of the pre-missionary era and some the product of the native schools conducted by the European and native teachers (Ross 1983: 66).

By the 1920s the organization of the missionary exhibition had been standardized. Two features are particularly worth noting − the "courts" and "court sketches." The Church Missionary Society explained that the exhibition hall would "be arranged in a series of courts with houses and lean-to's showing life and customs... The exhibits will include specimens of the native dress, ornaments, household utensils, weapons, idols and other interesting objects, illustrative of everyday life" (CMS archive 1928 1D/E). These court scenes were to be interpreted through talks by missionaries and others. Interpretation became the key to such exhibitions and much work went into preparing speakers. "Court sketches" in particular were employed to give visual reference for verbal interpretation.

The structure of "courts" is clearly visible from the photographic records of the Missionary Exhibition at Hamilton in June, 1932. As might be expected, there was a Maori Court with patu clubs, a kotiate club, spears, a lizard moko, and flax skirts on a trestle table with a back screen. The African Court appeared more like a hunter's trophy room with mounted heads of assorted wild game and a frontispiece painted to show "African" huts with emaciated figures prominently displayed. The third court was obviously something of a geographic compromise offering a range of textiles from "India, Polynesia and Palestine." The fourth was devoted to Melanesia.

The Hamilton Exhibition display of 1932 contrasts markedly with the Auckland exhibition of 1917. The "in context" classificatory scheme has been almost entirely abandoned in favor of a large diorama depicting coconut-clad islands roughly painted on a backdrop. What could be a couple of historically important objects, Santa Cruz duka (or ancestor figures), appear on the trestle. Pride of place is given to inlaid crosses. Publications on the left of the display are balanced by "baskets" or bags for sale on the right. These are the sort of products that missionary schools would be involved in manufacturing. The overall tone of the display is that of a spare, wistful, and somber spectacle more reminiscent of a film set than a museum case.

Yet these displays undoubtedly did contribute to museums. Extant labels still attached to objects can be found not only in Wench's collection but also in the Melanesian Mission Museum now held in the Auckland Institute and Museum. After the East and West exhibition it was decided to create a permanent exhibition of the Mission and Melanesian culture at Mission Bay, Auckland, bringing together material from the exhibition, from Bishop Patteson's memorabilia, and other items collected or donated to the Mission. From 1929 until 1974 the Melanesian Mission Museum provided an annotated display of these religious memorabilia and traditional cultural items from the region of the Mission's operation.

Plate 2. Melanesian Court, Hamilton Exhibition, June 1932. Provincial Archives Committee, St. John's College, Auckland.

Interestingly, the problems of attribution associated with Wench's collection are nothing compared with those confronting the Missionary Museum. Although at its inception labels were in all probability placed beside exhibit items, by the time the museum was professionally inspected in 1977 "a few identification labels from the Missionary Exhibition, Auckland, 1926, were found in a cupboard along with a copy of the official exhibition handbook" (Ross 1983: 67). The inspector then confronted the worst nightmare facing a curator. In the 30 some years since the opening of the museum:

> there may well have been some chopping and changing in the arrangement and the labelling of exhibits, and therefore, inadvertently or otherwise, some confusion about what display card(s) refer to which exhibit(s). Thus, even when some display cards appear to refer to particular exhibits (and this is not so in many instances), there is no guarantee that, even in these instances, the exhibits are correctly labelled. On the other hand, who is there who could (a) detect errors in labelling and (b) correct those errors? (Auckland Institute Library, Ross papers, MS 1442 52(6)).

Such candor is seldom encountered in discussions about accessions. It represents both a salutary warning to taxonomists as well as an implicit rebuttal of the school of display that privileges texts and labels over objects (Kirshenblatt-Gimblett 1991: 394). Inadvertently, the missionary exhibition, in its earnestness, its desire to make an impressive show, and its limited recognition of either the traditional symbolic significance of an object or the reasons for its collection, risked not only obscuring prior scholarship or knowledge but provided a ready opportunity for thoroughgoing transpositions.

The rhetoric of displayed artifacts

It is in the context of missionary exhibitions that much of Wench's collection has to be considered. It is perhaps worth returning to the issue of meaning afresh. Ida Wench was immersed in the culture of the Melanesian Mission which itself employed for its own uses a range of pre-existent stereotypes and built them into a systematic edifice. The principal pillar in such a construction was the marking and symbolization of difference. The whole tone of Melanesian Missionary literature was set in the very name of Melanesia − the "dark isles" − islands of deadly illness and a cataclysmic population decline. The contrast between primitiveness/heathenness and civilization/Christianity provides a tension between the misery of superstition, visually manifested in the emblematic significance of "curios" (and particularly of "charms," a designation applied to ambiguous objects of symbolic significance), and the heroism of the missionary:

> How the very name [Melanesia] rings of Christian heroism! Whether we think of its roll of apostolic bishops with their slender yet devoted band of missionary clergy, or of the brave Englishwomen, who taking their lives in their hands, go to the islands for the sake of their dark sisters... We can hardly hear the name of Melanesia without a thrill, a glow of enthusiasm (Suter 1935: n.p.).

Wench imbibed not only these romantic aspects of cultural contrast, she also picked up the more sinister and shocking undertone in missionary propaganda as her reminiscence shows, an amplification of fears channelled into a stereotyped fantasy: "How then would they [my parents] react when I announced that I intended to go and live half a hemisphere away? Worse than that, they would immediately picture me − their little girl, small, slightly built and helpless − surrounded by black, frizzy-haired heathens, whose ancestors had assuredly gorged on human flesh"

(Wench 1961: 7). This tone was also conveyed in the missionary exhibitions in which posters depicted "cannibal forks" and other talismans of idolatry well into the 1950s.

Plate 3. Melanesian mission poster, 1950s. Courtesy of Melanesian Mission, English Committee Records.

To be effective, stereotyping needs symbolic visual references that can be recalled swiftly and in detail because they evoke an immediate emotional response. In 1905 the Melanesian Mission obtained just such a combination, albeit unwittingly. Bishop Cecil Wilson invited John Watt Beattie, a well known topographical photographer from Hobart, Tasmania, to accompany the mission ship on a tour of the diocese. Beattie spent four months travelling with the bishop from station to station photographing extensively. He also kept a journal of his trip. A large archive of pictures was deposited with the Melanesian Mission. This became a bank of images that was regularly employed for publicity and publications. A number of them were turned into postcards which were sold by the mission for fund raising. O'Ferrall (1908) must have been one of the first to employ Beattie's photographs, but they were widely used in the early decades of the twentieth century. The Beattie photographs provided the naturalistic evidence for contemporary literary accounts of missionary activities. The photographs also continue to exert a firm grip on our understanding of the relationship between missionaries and indigenous societies. The photographs were mainly of two types: topographic surveys (which might incidentally include people), and personal studies. In his publications Ivens used both types. For general survey purposes he employed images of women canoe traders and a display of large Ulawa food bowls in a village setting. Powerful individual studies were provided by Beattie's photographs. The Qarea study must have had an impressive aura — it is among the most regularly reproduced images. The picture of the Nukapu youth recalls the site of Bishop Patteson's killing on that island in 1871.

Plate 4. Young man of Nukapu, and Qarea warrior, Malaita (Ivens 1918). Courtesy of Museum of Mankind, British Museum.

Inevitably when Wench came to illustrate her book she turned to Beattie's photographs. Three of the eight illustrations were taken by Beattie: the same Qarea warrior; an action picture titled rather cautiously

"Young Melanesian hunting;" and a more topographical study "sacrificial altar, Malaita, British Solomon Islands."

Beattie's photographs thus provided visual evidence of strange customs, magnificent specimens of prowess, and the civilizing effect of the mission (the numerous studies of churches). But Beattie provided more than this; he offered a visual prompt for the development of a vivid tale. One particular image, figure 5, serves to make this point.

Plate 5. Beattie postcard. "People of Santa Cruz trading with the 'Southern Cross' 1906." Courtesy of Melanesian Mission, English Committee Records.

As Beattie (1906) recorded in his journal on the arrival of the "Southern Cross" in Graciosa Bay, Santa Cruz:

> Here we were safe in the fine harbour where the old Spaniards four hundred years ago attempted to found a colony but failed, and were "wiped out" by the warlike savages that swarmed around them. The descendants of these very savages were now becoming evident, coming out to the ship in their canoes, and in a very few hours time the ship was surrounded by a fleet of these canoes manned by a horde of yelling Cruzians, wanting to trade, with rings in their noses and hugh [sic.] bunches of rings in their ears, their arms and wrists covered with bangles of shell, and their whole appearance looking uncanny (Beattie 1906: 15).

After providing this snapshot Beattie sets the picture in motion: "The ship was swarming with native Cruzians, and their noise was perfectly terrific [sic]. We shut up the cabin doors as they are adroit thieves" (Beattie 1906: 16). What is most remarkable about this description is not so much the visual detail (the account later develops a cinematic quality when he describes the Cruzians diving for tobacco sticks thrown from the ship), but the inclusion of stock elements. These surface again and again in Melanesian Missionary accounts. O'Ferrall's account echoes the significant elements:

> When the ship comes to anchor, or even before, if a rope is thrown to them, the natives clamber up her sides, and the decks are soon covered with a merry, noisy crowd, who press their wares upon you and will scarcely take a refusal. All cabin doors are locked and port holes closed, for the Cruzians are all born thieves and exceedingly clever ones (O'Ferrall 1908: n.p.)

Ivens' version is more "colorful" and dramatic although not substantially different:

> They pester everyone to buy, thrusting their wares into one's face and muttering *tambaika* (tobacco). ... Great hands are laid on one's arm; huge mouths red with areca nut and lime are thrust in one's face; the scent of strong-smelling herbs worn in the shell armlets almost overpowers one; clothes are marked with stains of yellow ocher; an unmistakable odor of natives pervades everything, and keen eyes follow every movement; great heads bleached with lime or wrapped up in bark cloth are thrust into the windows; everything moveable has to be put out of reach, and portholes have to be shut (Ivens 1918: 241–242).

Thus as the standard account evolved it was embellished to such an extent that it came to include not only the invasion of the ship and potential pillage, but also the vision of "giants." It is perhaps understandable, therefore, that Wench's account of landing at another island in the group contains all the stock elements:

> As soon as the "Southern Cross" dropped anchor, dozens of gaily painted canoes shot through a gap in the barrier reef and fetched up alongside. When the men in them dropped their paddles and began to clamber on board, most of us swiftly dived below and fastened all port holes, for we had been given to understand that the average Tikopian believed he had a right to anything he might see. Two or three of our more timorous colleagues stayed in the saloon, but I went to my position at the rail and inspected our visitors more closely. The Tikopians were huge men, towering a good head and shoulders above those members of our crew who were standing around and making me feel only half my normal size (Wench 1961: 104–105).

This reminiscence relates to the same period of time Ivens discussed because Wench visited Tikopia in 1915. The stories by Ivens (1914, 1918, 1927), Wench (1961), Beattie (1906), and O'Ferrall (1908) elaborate a common core of expectations which constitutes a prism through which their observations were refracted. Wench's version might be described as the most manipulative emotionally. Not only are we invited to thrill at the implicit danger, but also to identify with the "plucky little English-woman," not content to cower below decks, who must employ her moral stature to undertake the review of the troops despite (or perhaps because of) her physical frailty. The structure of her account suggests a narrative that has been fashioned and honed through repeated telling, probably at many public occasions.

The logical extension of this emphasis on difference is the development of racialization. Missionary activities and exhibitions in Britain were certainly consonant with a keen sense of identity based upon skin color. The Melanesian Mission play titled "Darkness and Dawn," written for performances at exhibitions and other fund-raising activities, offered notes on the dress for native characters. The first point made was that "Melanesians are of a dark brown 'chocolate' colour. The skin may be coloured with coconut oil and brown umber. The teeth of the elders are blackened" (Ivens 1914: 6). This insistence on difference, including bio-logical difference, acted as a powerful agent in the imaginative recon-struction of South Pacific life in which objects could serve as visual cues, props, and illustrations. Wench's collection was but one of many circu-lating throughout the period of high colonialism.

Modern and postmodern ambiguities

It is tempting to see this collection as a relic of an overturned history. After all, the missionary exhibition is a pre-World War II phenomenon. In both Great Britain and Melanesia social life and art have been irre-versibly changed by the war and its aftermath. As a historian has docu-mented (Akin 1988: 1), new aesthetic forms, including eagles and other non-indigenous motifs, have entered the lexicon of carving in Melanesia. Some have come to stay. Subsequently, promoters of tourism have offered marketing advice on "suitable" motifs to sell effectively (Tickle 1987). Furthermore, we no longer think of exhibitions as naturalistic ways of getting in touch unproblematically with another time and place. We are aware that exhibitions are conscious constructions and we think of missionary exhibitions in particular as naive and self-serving.

Yet, I want to argue that our modern sense of superiority may be misplaced. Modern exhibitions still employ the ruses of the missionary exhibition. They also continue to incorporate not just the previously collected items but also their previous association with primitiveness. It could be argued that dioramas — particularly those that incorporate sophisticated technology — still suggest that objects tell a story, often an unproblematic one. We also have to face the unpleasant reality that learning with respect to one topic is not always readily transferred to another. As one teacher recently commented: "Young people seem able to hold two contradictory views simultaneously. Thus, at one moment, the students could understand that all media images are constructed while still accepting photographs of people from Third World countries at face value" (Tomlinson 1989: 20). This cognitive dissonance is not, of course, confined to the young. Images of the South Pacific continue to remain caught in "an aesthetic of difference" (Peltier 1984: 105), an ever remote world. The modern collections remain on a par with the "cabinets of curiosities" of the eighteenth century.

The advent of large-scale tourist art has led neither to a new "world tourist art" nor to a straightforward re-presentation of the old. What is frequently offered are elements of a stereotyped fantasy consistent with a stable model — in this case, of the South Pacific. Some elements can be recombined in new circumstances. The bonito, so regularly featured in traditional Melanesian carving and fable, can be incorporated in a contemporary concern for fish stocks and ecological management. As such, the old concerns can be recirculated and can contribute to a new form of the noble savage dressed in green. But other products change, such as a "basket" (a traditional term that in pidjin covers objects as diverse as purses and rucksacks), that is made of Chinese nylon fishing filament and which does not look sufficiently different from everyday objects of the "civilized" world (Graburn 1978: 52). Producers are not fully aware of the aesthetics of tourist art, nor can they predict the vagaries of fashion or always accommodate satisfactorily to tourist demand. "They aim, instead, for diversification, novelty, and external appeal" (Jules-Rosette 1984: 28). Rather than offering the panacea of income diversification, moving into the international market propels the maker towards a set of expectations that is alien and therefore further cuts the maker off from the traditions that provided the impetus for work in the first place (Dark 1990). According to a study of Trobriand carvers:

> The carver is finding himself in a cost-price squeeze where returns on carving are static or dropping, whilst prices on the items he desires are rising. The more widely travelled visitors note that equally good carvings can be obtained elsewhere in the world for much less, an indication that

elsewhere people are either more underpaid or underemployed than the Trobriands (Ranck 1980: 66).

I wish to conclude by suggesting that the stereotyped imagery that has been discovered in the missionary exhibition is consistent with modern tourist aesthetics. For example, the modern Malaitan comb combines all the exotic features of the old with modern materials. It fits within the narrow range of expectations of "exotic fantasy." This fantasy may be as powerful today as it was one hundred years ago. We may strain to retain an approach to contemporary culture that does not engage in negative stereotyping, but yet we continue not only to view the same objects, we see them through the eyes of the original collectors thanks to the advent of photography which arrived just in time to accompany the serious collectors of the mid to late-nineteenth century. It is the power of associative memory that reasserts the prior life of the object that we had hoped to banish for good. Thus, the objects resist being incorporated into a relativist or postmodern account because, somehow, they remain "talismans of primitivity" (Clifford 1988). There may be powerful contemporary reasons why this remains true. A current example of a virtual intersection might be to assert that Wallerstein's theory of economic peripheralization can be usefully applied to cultural theory (Regin – Chirot 1986). The cultures of the South Pacific remain today, as do their economies, at the maximum distance from the world's core cultures and economies. The latter retain their pre-eminence precisely by marginalizing other peoples.

Yet many attempts to reverse the trend to peripheralization may in turn have serious repercussions for cultural policy. The renaissance of nationalism in the supposedly developed world reminds us that this process does, indeed, involve the creation of "imagined communities" (Anderson 1991). The process includes the incorporation of peripheral elements of the state into national identity. On both sides of the 141st parallel of New Guinea conflict exists over the policies of national governments to forge a sense of nationhood (Fathers 1991, 1992). But the open revolt in Bougainville against the Papua New Guinea government is perhaps the most dramatic case in point. The Indonesian government's attention to Irian Jaya also provides a cause for reflection.

The Festival of Indonesia is a high profile cultural event (Taylor – Aragon 1991: 10) which promotes world recognition of Indonesian cultures. The festival organizes large-scale exhibitions (such as "Beyond the Java Sea" that travelled to North America and Europe) which have a clear message that Indonesia embraces a wide diversity of cultures. The festival also promotes the recognition of anthropologically celebrated cultures such as the Asmat of Irian Jaya. The Asmat — who are renowned for their superb carvings — have been subject to serious anthropological study since the Second World War. Exhibitions sponsored by the Asmat Progress and Development Foundation tour the world performing traditional ceremonies and demonstrating the making of handicrafts (Schneebaum 1991a, 1991b).

It is difficult to view these performances without thinking back to missionary exhibitions. The following is a quotation from a museum label for an exhibition in Rotterdam, Holland, called *Het Hout van de Asmat*:

> Thanks to the shifts within Asmat society its art has changed not only in appearance but also in its character. It is increasingly losing its religious significance, with the result that the stringent prescriptions for its forms are being abandoned. For instance, the mission, amongst others, encourages the wood carvers to tackle new subjects and to this end organizes a big wood carving competition in Agats every year at which prizes are awarded to the best and most original works. After the prize-giving a sale is held at which the remaining carving is auctioned off. This stimulates the skill of the talented artists and keeps it up to the mark. However, with its new genre scenes Asmat art has struck out for good along a new path and its future is uncertain (Museum voor Volkenkunde, Rotterdam, 1987).

One is immediately drawn to ask who determines the criteria for the "best" and "most original" work? The new production system uncomfortably suggests Wench's "make and earn" program. However, unlike Wench's students, the Asmat are inevitably mortgaged to such craft development. First, there is an Asmat Center in Agats providing a handicraft training workshop, a performance area, a souvenir shop and tourist accommodation. Secondly, the Asmat Museum in Jakarta's Mini Indonesia Park is intended to create "the most complete Asmat museum in the world." Asmat craft is destined to remain a living and highly visible exemplar of the preservation of traditional culture as a part of Indonesian pluralism while at the same time the Asmat are being exhorted through their efforts to "develop themselves more in line with present-day progress and development."

There is at the heart of this enterprise — as in the Melanesian Mission exhibitions and displays — an unproblematic approach to the interpretation of artifacts. According to Adrian Gerbrands (1990: 51), a world authority on Irian Jaya and the Asmat in particular: "Things made by man are the picture book of his culture... All we have to do is learn how to read it." It has been the burden of this paper to suggest that this is a very large "all" which is not reducible to a simple set of learning skills. Contemporary displays of "folk cultures" run the risk of ignoring the complexity of such reading in the same way as missionary pageants.

When considering any collection, whether the work of Christian missionaries or museum curators, it may help to think of it as the locus of psychic transactions between objects and viewers. In a passage about the ideal aesthetic experience, Csikszentmihalyi and Rochberg-Halton (1981: 173–196) identify three elements in such transactions: the way aesthetic encounters can encourage the emergence of new experience, the intrinsically rewarding flow of psychic energy between objects and the person appraising them, and the fact that artifacts may shape or reinforce notions of ultimate and meaningful goals. The authors comment:

> As the cluster of objects one values solidifies, so do the meanings one derives from experiences with them. Different selves emerge around goals embedded in cherished belongings through habitual interactions. The possessions one selects to endow with special meaning out of the total environment of artifacts are both models of the self as well as templates for further development (Csikszentmihalyi – Rochberg-Halton 1981: 188–189).

Such a distinction between present and future selves helps situate the different interpretative possibilities that Wench's collection provides, whether considered according to Kopytoff's biographical approach which asserts that the elements of transactions change over time, or according to Clifford's more literary approach in which the items in the collection jostle together to provide elements of rival narratives. The notion of "transactions" – that is the influence of actual encounters with artifacts in which every encounter will be to some extent different – provides a first step away from the cast-iron stereotyped meanings of artifacts. Moreover, the notion encourages a broader range of possible understandings of the mentality which shaped missionary collections and which shapes contemporary responses to such collections. The basic Melanesian aesthetic system, particularly in the design and decoration of domestic items, becomes recognizable in a complex way when the items in the collection are considered together. "Charms," that psychic center of force, retain a power despite their insinuation into a new museum context. The associative totals of the elements provide for both an historic and contemporary range of accounts that save us as well as the objects from a unilinear existence. The goals of the collectors remain as varied as their motives. Wench and the missionary presence become one large and symbolically charged element in our understanding of the collection and its history. This understanding remains, at best, provisional as we recognize that the values we bring to our viewing are more akin to those held a century ago than we care to admit. On the other hand, artifacts retain some independence from context; we find ourselves trying to break free from the assumptions of our forbears. It is worth charting how we fare and what devices we employ in our attempts to break free in order to avoid recreating modern courts of actors condemned to an unchanging and meaningless performance.

Acknowledgements

I gratefully acknowledge permission to cite material from the Auckland Institute and Museum; Birmingham City Museums and Art Gallery; The British Museum, Department of Ethnography, London; The Church Missionary Society Papers, University Library, Birmingham; The Melanesian Mission English Committee Records, Harpsden, Oxfordshire; The Pitt Rivers Museum, University of Oxford; St. John's College Library, Auckland; The Society for the Propagation of the Faith Papers, Rhodes House Library, University of Oxford; The Tasmanian Museum, Hobart. I would also like to thank the following individuals for their assistance: Ms. Jill Hâssell, Ethnography Department, British Museum; Mrs. Jenny Pinder and Rev. John Pinder, formerly of the Melanesian Mission English Committee; Rev. David Salt, General Secretary, Melanesian Mission English Committee; Mr. John Stacpoole, Provincial Archives Committee, Diocese of Auckland. Finally, I would like to thank Stephen Harold Riggins for his patience and assistance in editing this chapter.

References

Akin, David
    1988   "World War Two and the evolution of Pacific art," *Pacific Art News*,
           1.
Anderson, Benedict
    1991   *Imagined communities*. London: Verso.

Anglican Church in New Zealand
1917   *Church gazette*. Auckland, New Zealand.
1926   *Church gazette*. Auckland, New Zealand.
Appadurai, Arjun (ed.)
1986   *The social life of things: Commodities in cultural perspective.* Cambridge: Cambridge University Press.
Asmat Progress and Development Foundation
N. D.   *Asmat.* Jakarta: Asmat Progress and Development Foundation.
Beattie, John Watt
1906   "Journal of a voyage to the western Pacific in the Melanesian Mission yacht Southern Cross, 25 August to 10 November." Royal Society of Tasmania. Tasmanian Museum and Art Gallery. Hobart, Tasmania, Australia. Manuscript RS. 29/3.
Boutilier, James
1978   "Missions, administration, and education in the Solomon Islands, 1893–1942," in: James A. Boutilier – Daniel T. Hughes – Sharon W. Tiffany (eds.), 139–161.
Boutilier, James A. – Daniel T. Hughes – Sharon W. Tiffany (eds.)
1978   *Mission, church and sect in Oceania.* Ann Arbor: University of Michigan Press.
Church Missionary Society
1928   "Africa and the East." Exhibition. CMS Archive, University of Birmingham Library, H H30E 1D/E.
Clifford, James
1988   *The predicament of culture: Twentieth-century ethnography, literature, and art.* Harvard: Harvard University Press.
Codrington, Robert H.
1891 [1969] *The Melanesians: Studies in their anthropology and folk-lore.* Oxford: Clarendon Press.
Csikszentmihalyi, Mihaly
1975   *Beyond boredom and anxiety: The experience of play in work and games.* San Francisco: Jossey-Bass.
Csikszentmihalyi, Mihaly – Eugene Rochberg-Halton
1981   *The meaning of things: Domestic symbols and the self.* Cambridge: Cambridge University Press.
Dark, Philip C.
1990   "Tomorrow's heritage is today's art, and yesterday's identities," in: Douglas G. Pearce (ed.), 55–68.
Fathers, Michael
1991   "Revolution in paradise," *Independent on Sunday.* 21 July, 8–10.
1992   "A tropical gangland," *Independent Magazine.* 25 January, 22–25.
Gerbrands, Adrian A.
1990   "Made by man: cultural anthropological reflections on the theme of ethnocommunication," in: Pieter ter Keurs – Dirk Smidt (eds.), 45–74.

Gilborn, Craig
1982   "Pop pedagogy: Looking at the Coke bottle," in: Thomas J. Schlereth (ed.), 183–191.
Graburn, Nelson H.
1978   "'I like things to look more different than that stuff did': An experiment in cross-cultural art appreciation," in: Michael Greenhalgh – Vincent Megaw (eds.), 51–70.
Greenhalgh, Michael – Vincent Megaw (eds.)
1978   *Art in society: Studies in style, culture and aesthetics.* London: Duckworth.
Hanson, F. Allan – Louise Hanson (eds.)
1990   *Art and identity in Oceania.* Honolulu: University of Hawaii Press.
Hastings, Douglas (compiler)
1891   *Official record of the New Zealand and South Seas exhibition.* Wellington.
Hesseltine, William B.
1982   "The challenge of the artifact," in: Thomas J. Schlereth (ed.), 93–100.
Hornsby, Jim (ed.)
1989   *Photography: Towards a multicultural approach.* Tunbridge Wells: South East Arts.
Ivens, Rev. Walter
1914   *Darkness and dawn: A missionary play descriptive of the work of the Melanesian mission.* London: The Melanesian Mission.
1918   *Dictionary and grammar of the language of Sa'a and Ulawa, Solomon Islands with appendices.* Washington: Carnegie Institution.
1927   *Melanesians of the south east Solomons.* London: Kegan Paul.
Jules-Rosette, Bennetta
1984   *The messages of tourist art: An African semiotic system in perspective.* New York: Plenum Press.
Karp, Ivan – Steven D. Lavine
1991   *Exhibiting cultures: The poetics and politics of museum display.* Washington: Smithsonian Institution Press.
Keurs, Pieter ter – Dirk Smidt (eds.)
1990   *The language of things: Studies in ethno-communication.* Leiden: Rijksmuseum voor Volkenkunde.
Kirshenblatt-Gimblett, Barbara
1991   "Objects of ethnography," in: Ivan Karp – Steven Lavine, 386–443.
Kopytoff, Igor
1986   "The cultural biography of things: Commoditization as process," in: Arjun Appadurai (ed.), 64–91.
Marcus, George E. – Michael M. Fischer
1986   *Anthropology as cultural critique: An experimental moment in the human sciences.* Chicago: University of Chicago Press.

Museum voor Volkenkunde
1987   *Het hout van de Asmat.* Exhibition. Rotterdam, The Netherlands.
New Zealand South Seas Exhibition 1889–1890
1889.   *Official Catalogue.* Dunedin.
O'Ferrall, W. C.
1908   *Santa Cruz and the Reef Islands.* Westminster: The Melanesian Mission.
Pearce, Douglas G. (ed.)
1980   *Tourism in the South Pacific: The contribution of research to planning.* Christchurch, New Zealand: University of Canterbury for UNESCO.
Pearce, Susan M.
1986   "Thinking about things: Approaches to the study of artefacts," *Museums Journal* 85(4), 198–201.
Peltier, Philippe
1984   "From Oceania," in: W. Rubin (ed.), 90–116.
Pocius, Gerald (ed.)
1991   *Living in a material world: Canadian and American approaches to material culture.* St. John's, Nfld.: Institute of Social and Economic Research.
Prown, Jules D.
1991   "On the 'art' in artifacts," in: Gerald Pocius (ed.), 144–155.
Ranck, Steven
1980   "The socio-economic impact of recreational tourism on Papua New Guinea," in: Douglas G. Pearce (ed.), 55–68.
Regin, Charles – Daniel Chirot
1986   "The world system of Immanuel Wallerstein," in: Theda Skocpol (ed.), 276–312.
Ross, Ruth
1983   *Melanesians at Mission Bay: A history of the Melanesian mission in Auckland.* Auckland: New Zealand Historic Places Trust.
N. D.   Ruth M. Ross Papers. Auckland Institute Library. Auckland, New Zealand. MS 1442.
Royal Anthropological Institute, Section H Committee (ed.)
1929   *Notes and queries on anthropology,* 5th ed. London: British Association for the Advancement of Science.
Rubin, William
1984   *Primitivism in twentieth century art: Affinity of the tribal and the modern.* New York: Museum of Modern Art.
Schlereth, Thomas J. (ed.)
1982   *Material culture studies in America.* Nashville, TN: American Association for State and Local History.
Schneebaum, Tobias (ed.)
1991a.   "Asmat event," *Pacific Arts* 4: 33–34.

1991b.   *The Asmat.* Jakarta: Asmat Progress and Development Foundation.
Shuh, John H.
    1982   "Teaching yourself to teach with objects," [Nova Scotia] *Journal of Education* 7, 8 – 15.
Skocpol, Theda (ed.)
    1986   *Vision and method in historical sociology.* Cambridge: Cambridge University Press.
Society for the Propagation of the Faith
    1909   *Official handbook to the missionary exhibition.* Hull: Society for the Propagation of the Faith.
Suter, Rev. W. B.
    1935   "Missionary exhibitions III," *United Mission to Central Africa Bulletin* 28.
Taylor, Paul Richard – Lorraine V. Aragon
    1991   *Beyond the Java Sea: Art of Indonesia's outer islands.* Washington, D. C.: The National Museum of Natural History.
Thomas, Og (ed.)
    1983   *Teaching with overseas artifacts.* Wheatley, Oxford: Oxford Polytechnic.
Tickle, Les
    1987   "'Something/nothing?' Significant meanings and cultural artefacts in the Solomon Islands and England," *Museum Ethnographers Group Newsletter* 21, 20 – 21.
Tomlinson, Philip
    1989   "Questioning ethnocentric attitudes: A fifth and third year project," in: Jim Hornsby (ed.), 20 – 22.
Wench, Ida Clara
    1961   *Mission to Melanesia.* London: Paul Elek.

**Part II
The built environment and the political ecology of artifacts**

The logic of the mall

Rob Shields

Shopping centers and malls rarely present themselves as artifacts except in the globalizing, objectifying view of city planners and architects.[1] Only when one looks down from a tall building like Toronto's CN Tower or New York's World Trade Center at a mall and its wider urban context of streets, empty lots, parking areas, and buildings do most people experience such an omniscient and objectifying view. One leaves behind the involved sense of being a participant in or even author of the everyday enactments and interactions in the city. The enclosed shopping mall with its street-like gallerias and multi-level atria is a micro-city. De Certeau argues that from such a literal and literary height:

> Icarus can ignore the tricks of Daedalus in his shifting and endless laby-rinths. His altitude transforms him into a voyeur. It places him at a distance. It changes an enchanting world into a text. It allows him to read it; to become a solar Eye, a god's regard. The exaltation of a scopic or gnostic drive. Just to be this seeing point creates the fiction of knowledge. Must one then redescend into the sombre space through which crowds of people move about, crowds that, visible from above, cannot see there below! The fall of Icarus (De Certeau 1985: 123).

Most of the time, a large shopping mall is known from within. This is also true of the city which is experienced by movement through it. Most often we are users of the mall, not observers. The social construction of objects requires a view from the standpoint of a Daedalus. Such ensembles of objects are not artifacts in the traditional sense but are *environments* which, once entered, enfold and engulf us in their ordering time-space logic of interior spaces and store opening hours. Hence the caution displayed here: I am reticent to engage in an objectification of the mall, reifying it as a certain type of object or even a certain class of spatiotemporal environment. "Science" is no justification for the loss of the object. For at the end of such a project, the peculiar specificity of the shopping center or mall would have been lost: its ambiguous status as both object and super-object: a place and environment. Further, the extent to which users' everyday sociosemiotic relationship to the mall and its objects alters its and their object-statuses would also be lost.

Seeing any "thing" as an object implies a certain critical distance, a perspectival space in which a subject can size up an object independently of his or her own relationship with it. Such critical distance is epistemological as well as merely a question of geometry and physical distance. Outside of the mall, knowledge and memory of its complexity continues to affect our understanding of it as not an object or artifact, but a place which is the site of both objects and events, of the "social life of things" (Appadurai 1986) and the things of social life.

This chapter considers shopping centers and malls as objects, places, and as a commodifying and objectifying environment for both objects and persons. This ambiguity will be illustrated using examples from North American and European shopping centers. My concern is with malls as part of the class of artifacts which cross ontological boundaries to be ambiguously both objects which can be appreciated for their total design (Gropius 1962) and also super-objects, which cannot be treated in an abstract, "distant" manner. These sites are stage settings for other objects and for social actions. They are environments which overpower us. They frustrate our attempts at objectivity and defy our assumptions of ontological superiority. I wish to highlight the difficult status of built objects which cross taxonomic and semantic boundaries between object, place and environment; or of commodities which synthesize use, exchange and symbolic values; and even of persons who vacillate between conceiving themselves as subjects and as objects on display, like the merchandise.

Mall artifacts

Shopping malls include different types of shops along interior galleries (shop-lined passages which may be multi-level, glass-covered axes of space but which are sometimes not much more than corridors) which usually terminate at a large department store, an interior courtyard or some other attraction. The Toronto Eaton's Centre is one example where a grand galleria in the style of Milan's nineteenth-century Galleria Vittorio Emmanuelle extends one city block from the Eaton's department store to the old Simpson's department store, almost replacing the main shopping street which runs parallel, just outside (Shields 1991).

The department stores are poles of attraction at either end of the galleria, which architects believe motivate pedestrian flows so that people circulate from one end to the other end of the mall, attracted by the sound of a fountain or a glimpsed splash of sunlight at the far end of a galleria. To this basic arrangement, parking facilities, office towers, conference centers, hotels, museums and public transportation facilities (bus-only streets, subways) have been added to make a complex building type. While developed and policed as a private facility, shopping malls are open to the average consumer, presenting themselves as "public spaces" in the tradition of the nineteenth century European shopping arcades, bazaars or markets (Geist 1983). In some cases events and exhibitions are put on to attract people.

The Rideau Centre in Ottawa illustrates the complexity of such urban projects from the 1980s on (Ploegaerts − Momer 1989) and their distance from the first malls in the 1950s (Dawson − Lord 1983) which were simple axes of shops between two large "anchor" department stores, surrounded by acres of parking in a suburban location. Built in the city core, the Rideau Centre is typical of the North American malls built in the last dozen years to consolidate the ailing market position of large department stores which attempted to reorganize the downtown facilities they owned, increasing them by assembling the surrounding land or negotiating with municipalities to enclose public streets. Grand public atria and galleria lined with shops and restaurants, hotels, and conference centers connect existing and newly added department stores. These continue established pedestrian routes on the site but often labyrinthine twists are introduced. As such there is little unusual about the Rideau Centre which conforms to those shopping centers like the West Edmonton mall more widely described in the literature (*Canadian Geographer* 1990). Its interior finishes run the range of banal surfaces and standard commercial building finishes: inch-thick marble panels hide bare concrete from view; tile, mirror and "contract plants" (installed, maintained, and replaced by a local horticultural company for a set annual fee) round off the decor. This banality complements the merchandise on display and the mass-character of both the consumption experience proffered and the controlled, even staged, social events which can be experienced. One might say that the standardized decor and color schemes of such malls are discrete attempts not to up-stage the mass-produced merchandise. Nonetheless, the mall is stratified on its three levels, the lowest being dedicated to an economy-minded "mix" of service stores (photographic processing, pharmacies, food-stores, a health spa, opticians, a pet store and so on) and discount clothing retailers. On the upper level, rents and prices are higher. It is more light-filled because of skylights, the natural light lending a sense of openness. Here the focus is on "high-end" jewellers, shoe stores, more expensive clothing retailers and chic specialty boutiques.

In its use of diversionary strategies, the mall is the epitome of artifice. Like any artifact, a term which etymologically unites notions of skill (*ars*) and making (*facere*), even the most banal aspects of the mall are made with the same cunning and skill as the commodities within it.

Walking the mall

And so into the heart of the mall, where we may at least gain a comprehensive knowledge of what kind of environment this is and the range of artifacts it contains. Malls are environments which enfold and engulf us in their spatial logic of interior shopping streets, multi-level atria and switch-back stairs and escalators linking the floors. They have the power to guide but also to deny human will, as in the case of the rigid enforced temporal rhythms of opening and closing hours. Knowledge of the interior is also gained on terms prescribed by the designers, display artists and operators of the shopping center.

To return to the example of the Rideau Centre, its most striking features are in the plan in which the gallerias are laid out in a triangle, defying newcomers' assumptions that, like most commercial developments, the Rideau Centre must be arranged on a right-angled grid. In section the labyrinthine effect continues due to a sloping site where one enters on the third level at the apex of the triangular plan while exiting at the first level on the base of the triangle. At the apex on one side of the development is one set of key bus-stops while along the base at the opposite side is another key node in the urban transportation system where most bus routes intersect. More than 70% of the patrons of the Rideau Centre travel by public transport (Anderson 1992: 3). The conjunction of commercial shopping center and public transportation functions is typical of 1980s developments, not only in North America, but also in, for example, France. While the figures are not strictly comparable, independent studies of suburban Parisian shopping malls, such as Creteil Soleil, record that over 30% of their "mall traffic" actually consists of people taking shortcuts to and from metro and bus stations which are integrated in the commercial areas of the malls (Moise 1983).

Many of these people may only cut through the Centre from one bus to another; along the way they are diverted by being forced to walk through gallerias which are oriented at an angle to the direct path (Roderick 1991). North American shopping malls are generally constructed to at least appear to facilitate pedestrian shortcuts (if only to waylay the walker by diverting the person past countless shopfronts in gallerias without exits). Again, the figure of Daedalus may be counterposed to the wilful Icarus. The interior plan is labyrinthine (Moles 1982) and one is often forced to take a circuitous path. Architectonic elements such as stairways and escalators often lead in other directions, away from a chosen and rationalized, direct path. One often circles banks of escalators to find those that move in the desired downward or upward direction (Fig. 1 − 3). The non-Cartesian spatial flow frustrates our attempts at objectivity and denies our ontological superiority. One may abandon oneself to the switchback flow of these "peoplemovers," double back to end up in one's desired location, or race against the machine to climb up the "down" stair at double its speed. No matter what choice, we are thrown into the itinerary of the classic *flâneur*. By plan, this imposed *flânerie* overwhelms our rationalized, modernist usage of space which emphasizes instrumentality and utility.[2]

This wandering itinerary of the flâneur − the stroller and prowler made famous by Benjamin (1989) − is a practice which implies a leisurely comportment and activities, such as browsing. It is a type of appreciation often classed as shopping, yet quite different from other forms of shopping which might include shoplifting as much as purchasing (Shields 1992). Browsing is one of several forms of the social relation to objects (Simmel 1950). As a practice, wandering from side to side along a mall, drawn by goods, displays, and promises leads to other practices (trying on, trying out, purchasing and so on). Where the cunning of alluring displays and the visual promise of a "SALE!" sign fails to distract us away from our bee-line path, a railing or shift of floors accomplishes the same effect. We are animated into agitated motion by the commodities and the architectonic features of the mall. No longer quite in control, one becomes a drifting "mall-walker," one's body is drawn by nonverbalized desires and attracted by curiosity as much as directed by a rational goal-oriented project.

The Situationist' project of *dérive*, or "drifting" (Debord 1958), was intended to reveal the emotional structure of the city, in an attempt to

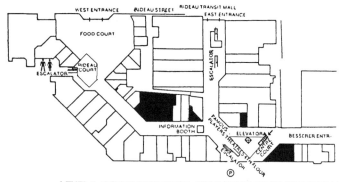

LEVEL 1 (NORTH ENTRANCE: RIDEAU STREET TRANSIT MALL)

Figure 1. Rideau Centre, Ottawa, Ontario, Canada. Level 1. North entrance: Rideau Street Transit Mall.

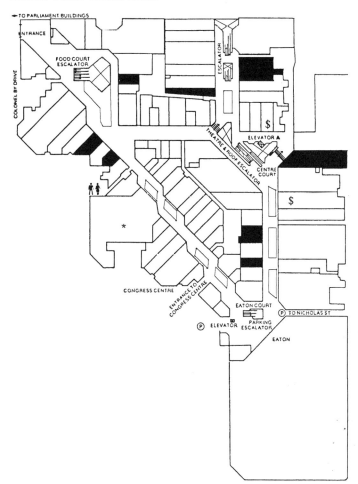

LEVEL 2 (NORTH WEST ENTRANCE: COLONEL BY DRIVE)

Figure 2. Rideau Centre, Ottawa, Ontario, Canada. Level 2. North West Entrance: Colonel By Drive.

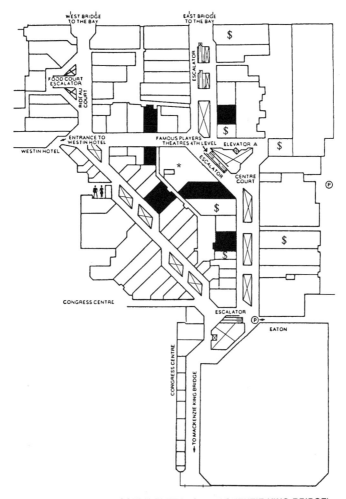

LEVEL 3 (SOUTH ENTRANCE: MACKENZIE KING BRIDGE)

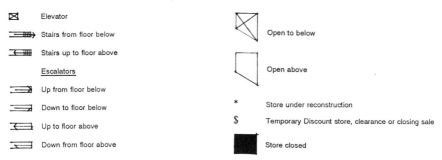

Figure 3. Rideau Centre, Ottawa, Ontario, Canada. Level 3. South Entrance: Mackenzie King Bridge.

displace or outflank the regimes of rationality governing everyday life.[3] Much more "purposeless" than Benjamin's idea of *flânerie*, *dérive* is the organizing principle of the consumer's movement between a mall's "points of interest" and the goods on display. It is the cultural form of the appropriation of the mall as an environment by the user, whose wandering footsteps trace out a narrative path, actualizing the mall as a social space (De Certeau 1985) of not only commodity exchange and consumption but of *flânerie*, browsing and *dérive*.

The itinerary of *flânerie* and *dérive* is just one example of how the person is overwhelmed by the mall and caught up in its spatial logic of pedestrian flows, places for pausing at mezzanine railings, and store displays which may spill out into the galleria spaces and places for stopping, sitting on benches and in food courts where competing vendors sell a variety of foods concocted from the cuisines of foreign cultures or distant lands. Like fish in an aquarium, it is difficult to distance ourselves physically or conceptually. One is tempted to redefine the mall as a collection of artifacts in a space of display, but this would be to omit the aspect of commodity exchange, the movement of people browsing, hunting for bargains, purchasing. Another temptation would be to reduce the analysis of the mall to a semiotic smokescreen over unequal exchange relations, but this would be to omit the non-economic activities of people (Gottdiener 1985), their *passive resistance* and non-compliance with the indexes and norms urging consumption, their focus instead on the consumption of space (Lefebvre 1981) and the elaboration of everyday life. The goods on display — all artifacts — play a key organizing role in the individual's zigzagging path through the mall. But the processes of commodity consumption (browsing, trying on, purchasing, being seen with and so on) are the pretext and the normative purpose of a person's presence in the mall. This is augmented by the significant number who "frivolously" concentrate on the tactile participation in the crowd of others (Maffesoli 1988; Nava 1987; Shields 1991) or a sensual enjoyment of the display (Haug 1986:16–18).

Michel De Certeau's (1984: xvii) maxim lies at the center of peoples' socio-semiotic relation to the mall: "An unalienated everyday life invents itself by *poaching* in countless ways on the property of others." It is thus essential to notice the complexity of the relation between the user and the mall environment (and ultimately its designers and administrators). This multiplicity is rivalled only by the changeability of the hierarchy in which these relations might be ranked. In some cases the economic transcends the social, in others, the semiotic is raised to extreme heights and the economic remains viable only as an epiphenomenon. "Thick description" is essential (Geertz 1966). These are not just questions of alternate ideological interpretations but also arise from use and appropriation, whereby each person is a locus where countless relational determinations intersect.

Consider again the Rideau Centre. Ottawa has a large population of refugee Somalis, most of whom are caught for months in the limbo of Immigration Office red tape, forbidden to work but receiving welfare payments. Against the predominantly racist and anti-minority practices of mall security documented in the Ontario Attorney General's *Task Force Report* (Anand 1985), this group of users was able to appropriate part of the private mall space as a Somali community space for gathering, securing a privileged status as loiterers in the cafes and food courts of the Rideau Centre. The primary (unconscious) tactic was to quietly dress the part of better-off mall users and to enact a chic European cafe culture in the lower, more popular, "teen-oriented" areas and levels of the mall. Dress, poise, and comportment were silently deployed. This visually enriched the atmosphere of the Rideau Centre as a public space. This tactic led to the unanticipated consequence of the appropriation of space for several months. As a silent tactic, this was certainly outside the experience of security guards. The Somalis' long presence in groups of two and three (mostly male but not always) over drawn-out cups of coffee stabilized the sometimes boisterous, younger shoppers attracted to the jean shops and hunting knife boutiques.[4] The mall management followed by demanding increased rent from the lower-level food outlets the Somalis frequented, which led to their closure. This process continues at a new "hangout" on the other side of the main atrium. Appearance triumphed over reality, even for those with a knowledge of the receipts. In some cases it is more important to engage in a semiotics of apparent consumption, rather than its actual practice.

Mall objects

Artifacts may be defined as things which are shaped through the application of human labor (Miller 1987: 112). This may not necessarily involve construction or manufacture, privileged in the work of Marx (1973). Simply the repositioning of a set of stones to endow them with the symbolic value and significance of markers may be enough to constitute objects as artifacts.

And the artifact is yet more complex. Despite the attempt through the 1970s and 1980s to produce an architectural (Broadbent 1981) or an object semiotics based on linguistic models of semiosis (Krampen 1979; see also the extensive survey of French work by Gottdiener and Lagopoulos 1986), this has been confounded. Miller notes that "divisions which may appear important in language and ideology may be absent from object differentiation, while distinctions within the domain of artefacts may constitute important divisions which would elsewhere be ignored or denied" (Miller 1987: 115). Thus gifts have a commodity-like character (Sahlins 1974: 149−162) and vice versa (Appadurai 1986: 12−13). Everyday objects constantly cross imposed analytical divisions. They are simultaneously symbols and material forces in our lives. "The use of [an] artefact as [a] symbol does not in any way detract from its significance as tool, material worked, or environment experienced" (Miller 1987: 105). Barthes (1964) pointed out that through "transfunctionalization" (as when a shovel becomes not just a tool but also a symbol of manual labor) objects can be simultaneously signifiers (as symbols or indexes of events, feelings or places) and signifieds and hence are at the center of social conflict over classification and meaning in everyday life. Similarly, artifacts are produced and yet act back dialectically on their producers as both sets of tools and even contexts of social action (Lefebvre 1981). The use of an artifact often involves turning it into something different, something "actually useful" (De Certeau 1984). In the process the intended "designed meaning" of objects may be subverted intentionally as in a word-play or pun; or unintentionally as in a serendipitous slip of the tongue. Such "object-puns" to coin a phrase may disrupt the status of the artifact. This transformation is ontologically hostile to a fixed view of the sociosemiotic status of artifacts: things change from being objects to extensions of peoples' bodies or expansions of the envelope of peoples' body-spaces. This hidden production manifests itself only in appropriation and use, may involve single individuals, or may involve both the coordinated and/or uncoordinated "habitual" efforts of many people.

Despite the analytical definition of an artifact, and the possibility indicated at the beginning of at least imagining a mall as a singular object set off in its particularity from the surrounding city, the classification of large built complexes (such as a shopping mall, a temple complex or an entire suburb) as artifacts runs counter to the Cartesian sense of the term "artifact," which demands that it be framed or mediated in such a way as to appear to be not only a discrete object but an undividable, irreducible and absolute whole. The shopping mall is like a folderol doll which comes apart to reveal that it is only a fragile shell containing a universe of entities which challenge the logicality of defining the outer shell as an artifact, when it is so clearly an environment which contains a collection of artifacts. The problem of buildings' super-human scale further confounds the analysis of such artifacts.

Inside-outside

Where we do allow even the pretence of coming to appreciate the mall as an artifact, it is usually not from an aerial vantage point but via another mediating space, such as television, where the mall is represented in a framed and edited, simulacral context (Baudrillard 1972; Bauman 1988) where we can create the illusion of separating ourselves from such an immense construction. Televisual and photographic images can reduce scale to postcard size and may present a bird's-eye view or a travelling sequence around the mall or juxtapose various views to build up an idea of the totality of the mall. Yet, while proffering an overall vision of the mall, quite different televisual effects and camera technics are required to convey a sense of the complexity and polyphony of commodities, events, persons, and sensations within the mall (Williamson 1992).[5] Even from the exterior, it is difficult to get an overall view of most shopping malls. And if we can find a commanding vantage point, this exterior view tells us little about the obsessively-internal character of the shopping mall, which defines itself by its interior decoration and not its exterior architecture. From the outside, a sprawling, windowless complex turns inward, scarcely even marking its entrances.

There are exceptions. In the giant West Edmonton Mall a model complete with little cars and plastic people summarizes the expanse of the complex of indoor wavepool, hotel, skating rink, air conditioned lake and interior "Fantasyland" fun fair. This architect's model is an incongruity, and unusual. It allows the user of the mall to appreciate the vision of the West Edmonton Mall's private developers, the Ghermazian brothers (Shields 1989). One may imagine a mise-en-abyme of a tiny plastic "you" hidden inside staring at a yet smaller model containing yet another simulated self... However, even the model which eschews realism in favor of the architects' convention of crisp white plastic and cardboard, reminds us of the artificiality of this fantasy.

When we do encounter the mall as an artifact, it is often the self-presentation of the shopping center in media advertisements. But even here, we meet a simulation which models the shopping mall, not a direct and realistic representation. Most malls do not have the architecture to make an advertising feature of it: above and beyond all else, malls are consumer-oriented "people spaces." In advertisements attention is usually once again focused back on the interior action and possibilities the mall offers as a setting and environment. Clowns, buskers, and "happy shoppers" suggest a vibrant cultural "scene," or a carnivalesque Festive Market."[6] The essence of the mall is thus not its constructed physicality but its interior contents. That this is the focus of such advertisements serves to remind us that the social is also the heart of the mall's artifice.

Within, the mall space is characterized by its juxtaposition of objects, persons, crowds, and functions. These are organized according to a logic of display which we might call the meta-code organizing even the presentation of bodies and the turns of one's path. This logic is emphasized by the architectonic provision of mezzanines which allow one to appreciate in one breathtaking glance what Victor Hugo once called the "chant of commodities" on many floors at once. This is to argue that many of the latest shopping malls are not designed primarily as public spaces on the model of the town market despite their incorporation of the norms of "sidewalk behavior." A logic of display is increasingly foremost in the design process through the 1980s. It is the appropriation and reworking of the mall space by its users that transforms the mall into a de facto public space.

A contemporary assessment of mall artifacts — whether commodities or not — must therefore recognize the importance of context and display:

> Even if each individual object can be viewed as being endowed with intrinsic qualities, it should not be forgotten that objects are never perceived in isolation. It is therefore necessary to set forth a second category of dimensions of objects: that of *display syntax* or how objects are displayed in relation to each other. Goffman (1959: 123) certainly understood that the meaning of objects is influenced by other surrounding objects ... but he never formalized this insight (Riggins 1990: 354).

There are various precedents for the analysis of the distribution of elements in space and the form of their arrangements (Krier 1979). Miller (1987: 109–130) emphasizes the impossibility of analysing artifacts in isolation from their context. In the case of domestic displays, Riggins

(1990) proposes that objects be analyzed not only in terms of their intrinsic qualities but in contextual qualities of their display, which can be broken down for analytical purposes into co-location, the placement of objects in the same space, and two display technics. First highlighting, where the visual emphasis on some objects through their lighting or placement at eyelevel introduces a hierarchy relative to understated objects. Second, dispersing and scattering objects in a relatively large space, or clustering juxtaposed objects in close proximity (Riggins 1990: 355–356).

The effect of clustering is not only imposed through shelf space or the confines of a cabinet or display window but may be a matter of relative distribution in a large area. Clustering objects accomplishes the specific effect of making clear the shared status of the objects as parts of what I will call a collection. With this concept, we move from content (the objects) to form (Simmel 1950). As a totality, a collection serves as a representation, amongst other purposes. In the specific case of the shopping mall, the commodities on display in individual stores are presented as collections which as subsamples of the store's stock not only indicate the wares available in a booth or shop space but indicate the total "gestalt" or flavor (Riggins 1990: 358) of the shop. A similar logic guides the grouping and "mix" of shops in any given mall or mall area, as seen in the case of the Rideau Centre, which seeks to develop an image based on the type, price or quality of goods made available. The luxury of a focus on an object in isolation from the distracting colors and enticing textures of other objects is thus deceptive. The shopping mall environment further accentuates the collective impact of artifacts: mirrors and views from mezzanines extend the visibility of objects and pile up sights and visions of goods and other people. It is necessary to reassert this interaction between people and objects. For, as will be argued below, in some respects, the form of the crowds (Simmel 1950) and the mode of social behavior of these "persons" are also artifacts of the mall. The scope of the mall's collection, its experience via the perambulating footsteps of the "mall walker," *flâneur* or frustrated errand-runner in a hurry, only further complicate the analysis of the mall and its objects.

Formally, the contents of a typical shopping mall may be broken down into three classes of "mall objects," all of which are directed either to people (commodities for sale, public facilities, infrastructural equipment, crowd control); to the display of goods; or to the control of other, undesirable foreign objects. Although an exhaustive typology is not intended here, mall artifacts include equipment such as shopping carts, cash registers and the strange paraphernalia of fitting things to the body which includes shoe-store gauges to measure foot-size and hinged mirrors giving one an all-round view of one's object-like and even commodity-like appearance when dressed in commodities or interacting with them. Many mall artifacts are understated objects whose presence can sometimes even distract from the highlighted commodities. There is also the "street furniture" of the mall such as benches, artificial trees and ashtrays; in some sense many of these objects are extensions of the architecture itself, such as railings and safety equipment including fire extinguishers, hoses, and so on. Much of this equipment is heavily regulated by state building codes (Gordon 1991) so that the requirements of the placement of such equipment determines the design and specific dimensions of washrooms, exits, stairways, parking areas and lobby areas. Similarly, the policies of near-monopoly service corporations, such as telephone companies, structure the form installations of public telephones take. People-moving equipment, such as escalators and elevators, have been much remarked upon recently (Jameson 1984) while the design of signage has become a separate specialty of semiotics and ergonomics. The most understated and dispersed of objects are garbage and various refuse receptacles which remind us that the struggle for control over artifacts and the ordering of objects and people is the major aspect of the day-to-day management of stores and shopping malls. The brightly printed plastic shopping bag is an accessory in its own class; and lastly there are the commodities for sale which are only temporarily resident in the mall.

Commodities, collections and frames

In his uncompleted project on the nineteenth-century shopping arcades of Paris, Walter Benjamin foregrounds the importance of that special class of artifacts, commodities, to capitalism and to the new urban spaces of nineteenth-century Europe, the shopping arcades and department stores. But unlike Marx, whose passages on the fetish character of commodities Benjamin approvingly cites in his notes (Benjamin 1989: 665−684), his primary interest was not on the exchange of commodities but on the "commodity-on-display" (Buck-Morss 1989: 81). On display, goods for sale are even further separated from the context of their production. Long before Baudrillard's metaphysics of the object (Baudrillard 1972), Benjamin observed the importance of the symbolic value of objects over and above their use value (they were unneeded luxuries) (Lewis 1975: 374) and their exchange value (the discounting of which has driven many a bourgeois to bankruptcy) (Saisselin 1985: 33−41). Commodities are the ultimate "object puns," but just whom the joke is on is never predictable in advance.[7] Haug notes that in its contemporary mode, the commodity is "aestheticized":

> the sensual appearance and the conception of its use-value becomes detached from the object itself. Appearance becomes just as important – and practically more so – than the commodity's being itself. Something that is simply useful but does not appear to be so, will not sell, while something that seems to be useful, will sell. Within the system of selling and buying, the aesthetic illusion – the commodity's promise of use-value – enters the arena as an independent function in selling (Haug 1986: 17).

Buck-Morss (1989: 181) draws attention to Benjamin's citation of Marx to the effect that "if one considers the concept of value, then the actual object is regarded only as a sign; it counts not as itself but as what it is worth." In the mall, however, only commodities are commonly considered to be artifacts. Any other artifacts become mute objects which might "interpellate" but must not distract the user of the mall. It is for this reason that mall managers consider researchers' and journalists' fascination with mall decors "perverse." The stress on appearance also appears to be a stress on classification. The usefulness of objects, their intrinsic applicability in everyday life as tools suffers a loss of legitimacy. To walk through a shopping mall looking for the "most useful" artifact might be a search which would lead to an ill-concealed firefighting hose or to the toilets. Alternately, children in shopping malls continually remind one that the litter on the floor can be as fascinating as the goods on display, if one keeps an open mind. Refuse is normatively treated in contemporary malls as part of an undifferentiated category of pollution (Douglas 1982). This is correlated with its complex status. Responsibility for refuse crosses and blurs public and private divisions of responsibility, jurisdiction, and power (see Table 1). Such objects are the "background noise" which should unobtrusively facilitate the reign of the merchandise for sale. By contrast, the ambiguous liminal status of commodities, betwixt and between object and image, tool and symbol, is foregrounded. It is commodities that are to fascinate the mall user (see Table 1) rather than to horrify him or her, as they did Marx.

> If the social value (hence the meaning) of commodities is their price, this does not prevent them from being appropriated by consumers as wish images within the emblem books of their private dreamworld. For this to occur, estrangement of the commodities from their initial meaning as use-values produced by human labour is in fact the prerequisite. It is, after all, the nature of the allegorical object that once the initial hollowing out of

meaning has occurred ... this meaning 'can at any time be removed in favour of any other' (Benjamin, as quoted in Buck-Morss 1989: 181 – 182).

However, the commodities' shifting identities, their beautifully illusory appearances and dubious essences are not acknowledged as central to the nature of all artifacts which transgress the divisions of signifier and signified, symbol and index, including the mall itself as both object and enveloping environment. In such a selectively focused environment, the artifacts which are on display are privileged and thus may reach new glories and new independence when their phantasmagoric identity is legitimized by their status as commodities before the gaze of consumers. This situation is summarized in Table 1.

Table 1. Summary of the Status of some Mall Artifacts

Type of objects
1. Comfort, health, and safety infrastructure
2. Display and sales
3. Cleaning and garbage disposal
4. Physical structure and finishes of mall

Oriented toward
1. People
2. Commodities
3. Foreign and used objects
4. Contents include people

Regulation
1. State
2. Mall management
3. State and management
4. State and management

Provision
1. Public
2. Private
3. Public-private
4. Private

Conventional status
1. Tools
2. Artifacts
3. Pollution
4. Environment

Beyond being a display space, then, the mall is a complete environment. But the relationship of the built fabric of a shopping mall to the commodities for sale inside is even more specific than that of a general environment. Consider that the difficulty of assessing the malls built recently is their architectural humility. Very often, as argued concerning the Rideau Centre, there is little architecturally innovative or noteworthy (these problems are exemplified in the *American Institute of Architects Journal* 1979 issue on Canadian malls). More often than not, the built fabric of a mall vanishes behind floor-to-ceiling mirrors which double the crowd of people and merchandise. Mall interiors are thus understated, especially in comparison to the architectural features of late nineteenth-century shopping arcades, the contemporary shopping malls explicit prototype. Furthermore, the very ubiquity of the building contributes to a sense of dispersion. This counter-intuitive effect is achieved through the emphasis placed on framing the collections of commodities and crowds of people. Gombrich, in his study of design (1979) distinguishes between works of art and their well-designed frames (see also Goffman 1975). Miller expands on the definition of a good frame as exactly the opposite of a work of art. The frame:

> should be immediately absorbed without any period of consideration and, rather than being the focus of attention in itself, should direct our attention to the object within it ... the frame's anonymous and modest presence belies its significance for the appreciation of the work of art. It might be suggested that it is only through the presence of the frame that we recognize the work of art for what it is, perceiving it and responding to it in the appropriate way. In short, it is the frame rather than the picture which establishes the mode of appreciation we know as art (Miller 1987: 101).

The applicability of this statement to the shopping mall is clear. Among other functions, the shopping mall, like a giant curio cabinet must frame a collection in which commodities are juxtaposed against each other and are highlighted in contrast to supporting objects which are downplayed. These objects are co-present together in a mediating space which is experienced through the movement of the shopper. Sight lines from floor to floor and across the length and breadth of a particular mall allow panoramas of commodities to be glimpsed from many separate viewpoints. Vistas unfold, presenting possible routes along which commodities may be examined in more detail and which will reveal further juxtapositions of items and vistas of yet more commodities. Like an elaborate frame which reinforces the value of the work it encloses, the more luxurious a mall, the more "up-scale" the stores and goods are presumed to be and the higher the prices. The shopping mall thus functions as an index of the collection of commodity-artifacts within.

The internal spatial arrangement along the malls — from the provision of open sight lines to the openness of store fronts, the primacy granted to display cabinets and the conventions of placing "grab bins" and display tables at the front of the store, or allowing merchandise to spill out an allotted distance into the mall — all "suggest" a set of "directions for use" even if users often resist. This physical and visual "address" to the potential consumer is: grab something, "pick me up." Touching and examining articles is held to stir desire for and affinity with the object. Regardless of the commodity nature of the mall artifacts, the tactility of the shopping mall experience sets it apart from other institutions such as the museum which are characterized by a similar interaction with artifacts but in the form of appreciation. Museums increasingly mix exhibits and booths selling reproductions and souvenirs, making them only one end of a continuum which extends unbroken to the malls which also host popular exhibits, fashion and art shows and demonstrations of craft-making. The frame of the mall thus may also have the effect of closing off the interior shopping spaces from the outside world to create a privileged space of spontaneous purchase and consumption based not on use, usefulness, or applicability to everyday life "outside" but based on appearance, aura and framed relevance to mall-reality.

The mall necessitates a particular "shoppers comportment." Assured of a flat clean floor surface one may walk while looking left or right, scanning for bargains, the desired object on sale at a lower price than at the shop one planned to patronize. The visual experience is of one long travelling shot in which object succeeds object (Williamson 1992). The overwhelming number and contrast of objects on display breaks up the individual's rational control over his or her gaze. As opposed to a rationalized experience, the shopping mall, like any human environment, is a sensual place, experienced through a veil of distraction where multiple events and many objects which may be related only by their proximity compete for attention all at once. Objects elicit memories, bringing the past directly into the present (Weiner 1983: 210). Objects evoke desires and wishes linked to the depths of our construction of selfhood.

The mall subject or persona

This brings us to the final point, which concerns the sociosemiotics of "mall subjects" as much as "mall objects." We have observed that the shopping mall is a mediating space which allows subjects and objects to come into new material and symbolic relations. Furthermore, in the mall there appears to be a similarity of things and people: nowhere else in contemporary social life are we as clearly both subjects (for ourselves) and objects (of others' gaze). There are few places where one can as easily come into a relation to oneself as an object of the consuming gazes of others. While it is easy to overstate this, the argument being made here is that shopping malls allow an augmentation of the modes of subjectivity by foregrounding the objectivizing gaze of people watching each other and looking at goods on display (Nixon 1992; Shields 1992; Ferguson 1992). The result is a qualitative change in the psychology of the mall as well as in the social ethos of the mass of shoppers and service workers.

This is to say that even individuals are "worked over," digested, and reduced into self-conscious objects. Bodies are forced and lured into particular paths. But beyond this elementary observation the ontology of the body is respatialized or "re-understood" to privilege its superficial, exterior appearance − its surface rather than its deep, intimate, self-spaces (compare Ferguson 1990; see Shields 1991 ch. 6). Rather than a careful, Goffmanesque self-presentation (Riggins 1990), one is re-presented by the setting itself through the provision of novel viewing angles. Wyse argues that malls are "negative" spaces for women, who discover with a shock that they are seen by voyeurs who exploit the immodest angles offered by open stairs in mall atria. Onlooking children gaze down from balconies making a game out of counting the bald. A simple ascent from floor to floor on an escalator or glassed-in elevator allows one to pan across the crowd from at first below and later from above. Yet Meagan Morris argues that Australian (single storey) malls offer a protected, secure space for women with young children (Morris 1988). This may allow them a rare present-day opportunity to act out the domestic role of mother in a public space.

But is this a motherhood with depth, or merely the display of the capacity to act in one of many roles? Shopfloors and gallerias are architectural platters for the pantomime "presentation of self" by people and commodities. The artificiality of people and things is here the basis of an aestheticized ethos (Maffesoli 1988) suggested above. The mall has the curious effect of turning everything and everyone that enters through its doors into an artifact, an object whose enhanced "aura" (in Baudrillard's sense of richness of intertextuality and symbolic reference rather than Benjamin's sense of symbolic originality and uniqueness) is derived from the skill and cunning with which it has been fabricated. People acting roles thus engage in a subtle play with their identity-positions further complicating any sociosemiotic analysis. It is a small step from acting roles to donning masks: to assuming what Maffesoli has called a more plural subjectivity, a *dramatis personae* in which mask-like superficial identities suit the multiple roles and contexts of contemporary life.

As a hypothesis one might therefore venture that in the mall, people are interpellated in a manner quite different from Althusser's understanding of the hailing of subjects who are "brought into individuality" and consciousness. In the mall, people are interpellated not just as subjects, but also as objects. As such, they are no longer the rational individual *per se* glorified by modernist notions of the bourgeois, the citizen, and of public man (Maffesoli 1988; Ferguson 1990; Shields 1992).

The person who participates in the carnival of objects, sights and other people undergoes a process similar to commodification. There is no question of a simple carnivalesque or liminal upheaval of categories of identity. However, the allegorical slippage introduced by mask and symbolism introduce a sense of uncertainty, of ludic "play" and cultural possibility which are often forgotten in the hasty economic reduction of commodity exchange. Like the commodity, the person finds himself or herself objectified, reified, so that s/he can be interpellated as one object among all the others. Do people envy the status and framing they see being given to commodities? In the mall, the persona is relatively anonymous, separated from one's rootedness in community and kin. It is in this sense that one is estranged from an identity rooted in one's economic function (job), social structure or one's roots. This opens up possibilities for "play" with self-identity which may or may not be indulged in by the denizens of the mall. The essentialist self is "hollowed-out" just like the commodity is an object whose naturalized "use-value" has been suppressed in favor of symbolic and indexical meanings. The way is opened for identity to become an allegorical mask, disrupting the naturalistic notion of an essential personal identity.

A unique sense of self founds the rational ideal of the individual. By contrast, the work of Maffesoli suggests that the etymology of "person" in *persona* hints at the mask-like character of identity at other historical times and in other cultures. Persona is the truth of the idiomatic saying that "a person wears many hats." This is thus neither a new nor dramatic shift, only a recognition of the layered, relative and mask-like nature of identity obscured by nineteenth-century reifications of the self (Cadava et al. 1991; Maffesoli 1988; Shields 1992).

The persona is an artifact of the mall. The self is "hollowed-out" like the commodity form and shares the ephemeral nature of the commodity on display. It is a self on display but which suffers the instability of the changeable nature of identity as a *dramatis personae*. Trying on clothes and self-presentations, one becomes a persona who literally "wears many hats." The confounding essence of the commodity — as with most other objects, as we have noted above — is its capacity to take on various meanings. This equivocality also typifies the walkers and shoppers, hangers-out and passers-through in the mall. Benjamin anticipates the notion of persona in his study of Baudelaire — a paragon of mimesis. The indulgent persona is a form of self-alienation from a true and transhistorical humanity, the "hollowing out of inner life" (Benjamin, as quoted in Buck-Morss 1989: 188).[8] The persona thus enters into the experience of the commodity, the allegorical object par excellence, "from the inside" (Benjamin, as quoted in Buck-Morss 1989: 188) which is to say that experience itself is commodified. Ignoring the dialectical potential of this self-affirmation in negation, Benjamin condemns the everyday urban experience of modernity: "Allegories stand for what the commodity has made out of the experiences that people in this century have" (Benjamin, as quoted in Buck-Morss 1989: 188). However, the users of the mall have made a virtue out of ambiguity, and the taking of moralizing positions at this juncture advances neither analysis nor understanding.

Concluding transgression

Despite what has been argued to be its clearly artifactual nature, the shopping mall exceeds and transgresses the framework of object typologies. Although they are separate spaces, apart from the surrounding world, shopping malls lack the status of the undividable totalities which are conventionally treated as objects. Yet to speak of a mall as an environment is only to begin to establish the complex interrelation between highlighted commodities on display and de-emphasized, understated objects which frame or support the theater of merchandise and patrons. Without the necessary critical distance only abstract analysis can confer, one falls back to the viewpoint of the mall user — Daedalus within the labyrinth. This has been adopted as a legitimate stance from which to discuss the status of objects within malls and the modes of social relation which can be established with them.

Central to the logic of the mall is a struggle to classify artifacts which is social. But commodities are given a privileged, ambiguous status between object and symbol which corresponds to the transgressive status of the persona, both subject and object interpellated into the circulation of personae, of goods and of capital. The persona takes on the same relationship to subjectivity as the commodity has to the simple tool. Like the commodity form, the persona is a crafted work, artfully constructed: a union of *ars* and *facere*. Furthermore, each momentary mask, each passing identification is tradeable and subject to commodification. The mall is not only a privileged space of commodified artifacts organized according to a logic of display; the persona is an artifact of such a space.

Yet it is important to resist concluding that the mall is a curio cabinet framing commodities and persons. Despite countless physical barriers and semiotic indicators or "directions for use," the mall is subject to constant reappropriation by its users' sophisticated spatial and appearential ruses such as that of the Somalis' silent tactic of good European taste. Mall users' artifice of superficial identities is a kind of protective armour against taking the mall too seriously. Clandestine practices push the economic ordering of commodities and bodies into a personally-managed schema of museum-like displays, on the one hand, and on the other hand, goods to be tried on, flirted with or in (in the case of clothes) and then dumped or stuffed down a pantleg. Make-shift spatial practices turn the mall into a public space for encounter and gathering, without which the mall as an economic institution would be socially empty and economically bankrupt.

Notes

1. I would like to record my thanks to Stephen Riggins for his comments and patient persuasion over the course of writing this paper.
2. I use the term *flânerie* here in its popular sense. *Flânerie* is more strictly a specific type of "prowling," not "wandering" the street (Shields forthcoming). The *flâneur* as understood by Benjamin (1989) is a fore-runner of the detective who exerts a high degree of self control over his (gender intended) image or persona while pursuing a covert, personal investigation of the urban.

3. *Dérive* in this sense implies a host of idiomatically well-known and precisely expressed ideas which are undertheorized. *Dérive* is thus "drifting with the current," "floating along," "going with the flow," and more importantly, allowing oneself to be diverted to leeward or towards the lights, bustle and activity of one place or another — "Where will we go tonight?" *Dérive* is, then, a form of automatist urban *flânerie* in which one allows oneself to be diverted by the "solicitations of architecture and one's desires." Substantively without any objective, the formal purpose of *dérive* is to find out where one ends up, to know what "will have happened."

4. In this on-going research I am indebted to my research assistant Ardith Stoute.

5. See Janice Williamson's 18-minute video. *A Pedestrian Feminist Reading of West Edmonton Mall*. Video Pool Inc. 300 – 100 Arthur St., Winnipeg, Manitoba R3B 1H3.

6. The name of the redevelopment of McWhirter's department store in downtown Brisbane, discussed by Gail Reekie (1992).

7. Saisselin quotes Zola's description of the seductiveness of commodities: "It was woman the department stores fought over for their business, woman they continually entrapped by their bargains, after having made them dizzy by their displays. They had awakened in her flesh new desires and had become an immense temptation to which they fatally succumbed, yielding first to the purchases of a good and careful housewife, then won over by coquetry, finally devoured. By increasing sales, by democratizing luxury, the stores became a terrible agency of spending, creating havoc in homes, working up women to the madness of fashion which was ever dearer and dearer" (Zola 1883: 83, as cited in Saisselin 1985: 39).

8. Buck-Morss (1989: 187) all but makes this same point as she assembles Benjamin's notes on Baudelaire: "On the physiognomy of Baudelaire as that of a mime: Courbet [who was painting the poet's portrait] reported that he looked different every day." Baudelaire was "his own impresario," displaying himself in different identities — now *flâneur*, now whore; now ragpicker, now dandy..." Baudelaire "played the role of a poet..." He wrote of "bracing his nerves to play a hero's part." Note the importance of the theatrical imagery, the manipulation of different identities which nonetheless are only mask-like vehicles for the display of a fragmented but still enduring self.

References

American Institute of Architects
1979 *American Institute of Architects Journal*, special issue: Canadian spaces (December).

Anand, Raj
  1985   *Report of the task force on the law concerning trespass to publicly-used property as it affects youth and minorities.* Toronto: Office of the Attorney General of Ontario.
Anderson, Mark
  1991   "Council writes off enclosures as Rideau Street's bad dream," *Ottawa Business News*, Aug. 8−21, 1, 3.
Appadurai, Arjun
  1986   "Introduction: Commodities and the politics of value," in: Arjun Appadurai (ed.), 3−63.
Appadurai, Arjun (ed.)
  1986   *The social life of things: Commodities in cultural perspective.* Cambridge: Cambridge University Press.
Barthes, Roland
  1964   "Eléments de sémiologie," *Communications* 4: 91−135.
Baudrillard, Jean
  1972   *Pour une critique de l'économie politique du signe.* Paris: Gallimard.
Bauman, Zygmunt
  1988   "Strangers: The social construction of universality and particularity," *Telos* 78: 1−42.
Benjamin, Walter
  1985   "Central Park," *New German Critique* 34: 1−27.
  1989   *Paris, capitale du XIXe siècle: Le livre des passages.* J. Lacoste trans. Paris: Editions du CERF.
Blonsky, Marshall (ed.)
  1985   *On signs.* Oxford: Basil Blackwell.
Broadbent, Geoffrey
  1981   *Signs, symbols and architecture.* Cambridge, MA: MIT Press.
Buck-Morss, Susan
  1989   *The dialectics of seeing: Walter Benjamin and the arcades project.* Cambridge, MA: MIT Press.
Cadava, Eduardo − Peter Connor − Jean-Luc Nancy
  1991   *Who comes after the subject.* London: Routledge.
Canadian Geographer
  1991   Special issue on the West Edmonton Mall, 35(3).
Csikszentmihalyi, Mihaly − Eugene Rochberg-Halton
  1981   *The meaning of things: Domestic symbols and the self.* New York: Cambridge University Press.
Dawson, John and Lord, J. Dennis
  1983   *Shopping centre development.* New York: Longman.
Debord, Guy
  1958   "Théorie de la dérive," *Internationale Situationniste* 2: 19−23.
De Certeau, Michel
  1984   *The practice of everyday life.* S. Rendall trans. Berkeley: University of California Press.

1985   "Practices of space," in: Marshall Blonsky (ed.), 122 – 149.
Douglas, Mary
1982   *Essays in the sociology of perception.* London: Routledge.
Ferguson, Harvey
1990   *The science of pleasure.* London: Routledge.
1992   "Watching the world go round: Atrium culture and the psychology of shopping," in: Rob Shields (ed.), 21 – 39.
Geist, Johann-Friedrich
1983   *Arcades.* Cambridge, MA: MIT Press.
Gilles, Ivain
1958   "Formulaire pour un urbanisme nouveau," *Internationale Situationn-iste* 1: 15 – 20.
Goffman, Erving
1959   *The Presentation of self in everyday life.* Garden City, NY: Doubleday.
1975   *Frame analysis.* Harmondsworth, UK: Penguin.
Gombrich, E. H.
1979   *The sense of order.* London: Phaidon.
Gordon, Charles
1991   "Beyond risk: Issues of political economy and building safety," *Safety Science* 14: 155 – 166.
Gottdiener, Mark
1985   "Hegemony and mass culture: A semiotic approach," *American Journal of Sociology* 90: 979 – 1001.
Gottdiener, Mark — Lagopoulos, A.-Ph. (eds.)
1986   *The city and the sign.* New York: Columbia University Press.
Grön, Ole — Ericka Engelstad — Inge Lindblom (eds.)
1991   *Social space: Human spatial behaviour in dwellings and settlements.* Odense: Odense University Press.
Gropius, Walter
1962   *Scope of total architecture.* New York: Collier Books.
Haug, Wolfgang Fritz
1986   *Critique of commodity aesthetics: Appearance, sexuality and advertising in capitalist society.* Minneapolis, MI: Minnesota University Press.
Jameson, Frederic
1984   "Postmodernism, or the cultural logic of late capitalism," *New Left Review* 146: 53 – 92.
Khatib, Abdelhafid
1958   "Essai de description psychogéographique des Halles," *Internationale Situationniste* 2: 13 – 17.
Krampen, Martin
1979   *Meaning in the urban environment.* London: Pion.
Krier, Rob
1979   *Urban space.* London: Academy Editions.

Leach, Jerry W. — E. R. Leach (eds.)
1983   *Kula: New perspectives on Massim exchange*. Cambridge: Cambridge University Press.
Lefebvre, Henri
1981   *La production de l'espace*. Paris: Anthropos.
Lewis, R. W. B.
1975   *Edith Wharton: A biography*. New York: Harper and Row.
Maffesoli, Michel
1988   *Le temps de tribus*. Paris: Méridiens Klinckseick.
Moise, P. et al.
1983   *Attractivité des centres commerciaux regionaux le samedi: Les cas de Rosny II et de Créteil-Soleil*. Paris: Institut d'Amenagement et d'Urbanisme de la Region d'Ile-de-France.
Moles, Abraham
1972   *Théorie des objects*. Paris: Editions Universitaires.
1982   *Labyrinthes du vécu. L'espace: matière d'actions*. Paris: Méridiens Klinckseick.
Marx, Karl
1973   *Grundrisse*. Martin Nicolaus, trans. New York: Vintage.
Miller, Daniel
1987   *Material culture and mass consumption*. Oxford: Basil Blackwell.
Morris, Meaghan
1988   "Things to do with shopping centres," WPI Centre for Twentieth Century Studies, University of Wisconsin-Milwaukee.
Nava, Mica
1987   "Consumerism and its contradictions," *Cultural Studies* 1: 204–210.
Nixon, Sean
1992   "Have you got the look? Masculinity and shopping spectacle," in: Rob Shields (ed.), 149–169.
Ploegaerts, Luc — Momer, Bernard
1989   "L'appropriation des espaces commerciaux par les personnes agées," *Metropolis* 87: 31–42.
Reekie, Gail
1992   "Changes in the adamless eden: The spatial and sexual transformation of a Brisbane department store 1930–1990," in: Rob Shields (ed.), 170–194.
Riggins, Stephen Harold
1990   "The power of things: The role of domestic objects in the presentation of self," in: Stephen Harold Riggins (ed.), 341–367.
Riggins, Stephen Harold (ed.)
1990   *Beyond Goffman: Studies on communication, institution, and social interaction*. Berlin: Mouton de Gruyter.
Roderick, Ian
1991   "An ethnography of the bus mall." Unpublished Ms. Department of sociology and anthropology, Carleton University, Ottawa, Canada.

Sahlins, Marshal
1974   *Stone age economics.* London: Tavistock.
Saisselin, Rémy
1985   *Bricabracomania: The bourgeois and the bibelot.* London: Thames and Hudson.
Shields, Rob
.1989   "Social spatialisation and the built environment: the West Edmonton Mall," *Environment and Planning D*: Society and Space 7: 147 – 164.
Forthcoming   "Fancy footwork: Walter Benjamin's notes on flânerie," in: Keith Tester (ed.).
Shields, Rob (ed.)
1992   *Lifestyle shopping: The subject of consumption.* London: Routledge.
Simmel, Georg
1950   "Sociability: An example of formal sociology," *The Sociology of Georg Simmel.* New York: Free Press, 40 – 57.
Tester, Keith
Forthcoming   *The flâneur.* London: Routledge.
Tomlinson, Alan
1990   "Introduction: Consumer culture and the aura of the commodity," *Consumption, identity and style.* London: Routledge, 1 – 35.
Weiner, Annette
1983   "'A world of made is not a world of born': Doing kula in Kiriwina," in: J. Leach – E. Leach (eds.), 147 – 170.
Williamson, Janice
1992   "Notes from storyville north: The West Edmonton Mall," in: Rob Shields (ed.), 216 – 232.
Zola, Emile
1883   *Au bonheur des dames.* Paris: Charpentier.

The ideological commodification of culture: Architectural heritage and domestic tourism in Japan

Adolf Ehrentraut

Introduction

The architectural heritage of many countries annually attracts millions of visitors as a major expression of contemporary mass tourism. Adventurous as they might be, most tourists rely in some measure on their guidebooks both for recommended itineraries and for authoritative interpretations of heritage sights. This chapter explores the sociopolitical significance of this pattern in Japan, focusing specifically on the relation between vernacular heritage architecture, its popularization through cultural guidebooks, and the social construction of political ideologies.

The chapter is organized into five sections. The first two respectively address certain theoretical issues shaping the analysis and describe the data sources on which the analysis is based. The third section concentrates on the selectivity and content of architectural heritage entries in two cultural guidebook series, the political implications of which are then pursued in the next section. The final section draws the preceding themes together in the context of domestic tourism and makes some concluding comments about the comparative significance of the findings.

Theoretical perspectives on heritage conservation

Architectural heritage involves the selective preservation of the built environment. The philosophical premises of this activity have been promulgated in a number of international declarations which affirm, for example, that "[t]he past as embodied in the architectural heritage provides the sort of environment indispensable for a balanced and complete life" and that this heritage "is a capital of irreplaceable spiritual, cultural, social and economic value" (Council of Europe 1976: 31 – 32).

The criteria governing the preservation of heritage architecture have also been enunciated in a set of principles commonly known as the Venice Charter (Keune 1984: 40 – 41), to which Japan among many other countries is signatory. Within the Charter's broad parameters, the professional architectural and museological literature continues to debate principles of conservation and presentation, focusing here particularly on the issue of didactic authenticity, whether pertaining to the accuracy of restorations (Phillipot 1976) or the animation of exhibits (Angotti 1982). Less frequently are concerns expressed over the disproportionate preservation of elite architecture, which threatens with historic oblivion equally the "architectural traditions of the proletariat" in Gdansk (Stankiewicz 1977: 14) and the "dwellings of the rural poor" in Wales (William 1988), for example.

In this light the issues of authenticity and representativeness can be approached from broader perspectives concerned with the nature of social order and the process of social stratification. From a functionalist perspective, heritage architecture thus illustrates the cognitive legitimization of value orientations and the expressive and integrative symbolism of collectivities (Parsons 1951: 348 – 398), a position which need not deny that the pattern maintained involves profound inequalities among its constituent social elements. From a radical perspective committed to the articulation of these inequalities, architecture as such is a visual ideology which itself "constitutes a particular form of the overall ideology of a social class" (Hadjinicolaou 1973: 95).

It follows that in its designation as heritage, scheduled architecture expresses the worldview of a dominant class and, consequently, constitutes a cultural reproduction of class relations in a given society. Under such circumstances, the elevation of domestic vernacular architecture to heritage status, be it worker houses or farmhand cottages, theoretically involves an appropriation of the cultural codes of subordinate strata that still serves the interests of the dominant stratum. In specifically political terms, heritage buildings can thus be conceptualized as symbols of collective myths of descent (Smith 1984) and as elements in the social construction of peoplehood (Wallerstein 1987), with the pattern of preservation itself shaped by the class structure of the respective society, as shown, for example, by Barthel (1989).

Whether heritage architecture is now argued to comprise collective symbols of solidarity or cultural reproductions of class relations, any analysis of its authenticity or representativeness is predicated on the characteristics of the heritage ideology, the processes involved in its social construction, and the mechanisms of its dissemination. One promising approach to the last issue lies in the interdisciplinary perspectives on mass tourism.

A central proposition among theories of tourism sees the average tourist engaged in a secular pilgrimage through the cultural landscape in search of experiential authenticity (MacCannell 1976). Although competing models have argued for more differentiated conceptions of tourist motivation and behavior (Cohen 1979; Redfoot 1984), in the present context the pilgrimage proposition has obvious relevance: the designation of a structure as architectural heritage is a form of sight sacralization that assures the visitor of the authenticity of his or her experiences and therefore of the validity of the individual and collective identities constructed on their basis.

In turn, the sheer expanse and complexity of regional and national landscapes make tourist dependence on landscape markers inevitable. Yet given the theoretical considerations above, the resultant guidebooks are not mere compilations of landscape markers but also vehicles for heritage ideologies that, in their selection and description of architectural monuments, actively shape the construction of heritage meanings. It follows that their entry patterns for heritage architecture provide a useful data base for the analysis of the above processes, particularly with respect to domestic vernacular architecture, which casts the issues of appropriation and representativeness into the sharpest relief.

Architectural heritage conservation and popularization

In Japan the practice of architectural heritage conservation dates back to 1897, when the first legislation for the protection of shrines and temples was enacted. Subsequent legislation, which had expanded the number of heritage categories piecemeal, was revised and combined in 1950 into the Law for the Protection of Cultural Properties that established a new heritage authority within the Ministry of Education, the Agency of Cultural Affairs (Bunkachô), mandated to protect Japan's cultural heritage on the national, prefectural and municipal levels. The Agency quickly developed a comprehensive administrative structure, embarked on an extensive program of restoration, and undertook frequent investigations into unscheduled structures for possible inclusion in the inventory. By 1985 this inventory comprised 3438 buildings, amounting to 31 percent of all the tangible cultural assets scheduled on the national level (Bunkachô 1987: 166).

The majority of heritage structures are shrines and temples not infrequently scheduled since the turn of the century. In 1983, for example, such structures made up 79 percent of the inventory, with vernacular domestic architecture accounting only for 17 percent and the remainder comprising exemplars of western architecture (Bunkachô 1983: 4). As discussed in detail elsewhere (Ehrentraut 1989a), the conservation of *minka* architecture, the residential architecture of commoners in town and countryside, is essentially a postwar development characterized by a major research program, a rapid increase in scheduled houses, and a wave of restoration projects that began in the late 1960s. A measure of the continued importance assigned to this heritage category is the amount of funds allocated for its restoration program for 1985, for example, which involved 29 projects and consumed 20 percent of the year's total restoration budget of three billion Yen (Bunkachô 1987: 206−207). Thus, while lacking the romance of feudal castles or the numinosity of major shrines, farmhouses are obviously considered by the political authorities to be a significant component of the nation's architectural heritage.

For practical reasons, the research on this architecture and its popularization reported here was limited to the Kantô region, which includes the seven prefectures of Ibaraki, Tochigi, Gumma, Saitama, Chiba, Tokyo and Kanagawa. Together these prefectures cover an area of 33 thousand square kilometers, have over 35 million inhabitants and possess an architectural heritage inventory of nationally scheduled structures amounting in 1985 to 385 exemplars (Bunkachô 1987: 166). As suggested by reliability checks in some other areas as well as by the general restoration pattern of nationally scheduled farmhouses across all prefectures (Ehrentraut 1989a), the data obtained for the Kantô region are, for present theoretical purposes, reasonably representative of the country as a whole.

As already mentioned, one of the major mechanisms for the popularization of heritage inventories are tourist guidebooks. These exist in Japan in remarkable abundance and sophistication both for major regions and for every prefecture of the country. Their format ranges from catholic publications on heritage to more populist guides that leaven the serious pursuit of high culture with eating and shopping tips and the diversions of amusement parks and holiday resorts.

Probably the two most authoritative prefectural series devoted nearly exclusively to cultural antiquities are those published by the Jimbun and Yamakawa companies respectively. The former are compiled internally, the latter by prefectural historical and cultural societies composed of high school teachers and a sprinkling of school board and museum officials. As of 1985, the Jimbun volumes for the Kantô region were in their seventh to tenth printing of revised editions since their original publication between 1967 and 1968; the Yamakawa volumes initially appeared between 1973 and 1977 and were now in their fifth to fourteenth printing of both original and revised editions, with the first completely revised volumes for Ibaraki and Kanagawa Prefectures being issued in a new series format in 1985. In short, both publications are indeed widely purchased and, presumably, widely used.

A reasonable impression of the cultural landscapes which these guidebooks popularize is already conveyed through their indexes. In the case of Ibaraki Prefecture, for example, the Jimbun index, which is divided into convenient subject headings in conformity with the series format, lists 95 temples, 38 shrines, 23 castle ruins, 13 mountains, six coastal cliffs and one waterfall. There are as well various parks and museums, assorted historic sites ranging from battlefields and cemeteries to the birthplace of famous men, 22 hot springs, and 43 golf and country clubs. In comparison, the undifferentiated index of the Yamakawa guide includes 164 temples, 75 shrines, 56 castle ruins, 19 mountains, two waterfalls, no coastal cliffs and a similar assortment of historic sites, scenic places and cultural institutions. There are no entries for golf and country clubs.

This pattern is representative of the other volumes. Although differing additionally in such aspects as thematic emphases, organization of material, use of illustrations and length of entries, all describe richly textured cultural landscapes for their respective prefectures. In each of these landscapes there are also markers for residential homes, identified by family name and the term *jûtaku* or residence, and very occasionally, the more honorific term *yashiki* or mansion. Connoting essentially vernacular domestic architecture, the terms are clearly distinct from various appellations reserved for the elite residences of the samurai and their feudal overlords, the *daimyô*. These *jûtaku* entries constitute the focus of the subsequent analysis.

The guidebook entry pattern for heritage houses

In the Kantô region there were a total of 82 residences officially designated as heritage structures by the early 1980s, 46 on the national level of administration and 36 on the prefectural level. As Tables 1 and 2 show, however, a heritage designation by no means ensured inclusion in either of the two cultural guidebook series: among the nationally scheduled structures, 84.8 percent are listed in the Jimbun guides and 47.8 percent in the Yamakawa guides, with only 41.3 percent included in both. Even more pronounced is the selectivity on the prefectural level, where the former lists 41.6 percent of the designated houses, the latter 36.1 percent and only 19.4 percent are included in both publications. Houses scheduled by municipalities seem excluded on principle and have therefore been disregarded in the following analysis.

Table 1. Guidebook entries of national heritage houses

Prefecture	Official heritage inventory	Guidebook entry Jimbun & Yamakawa	Jimbun only	Yamakawa only
Ibaraki	9	7	2	—
Tochigi	5	3	2	—
Gumma	6	—	2	2
Saitama	7	2	5	—
Chiba	5	3	1	1
Tokyo	4	—	3	—
Kanagawa	10	4	5	—
Totals	46	19	20	3
(%)	(100)	(41.3)	(43.5)	(6.5)

A second area of selectivity is the prefecture itself. For example, the Jimbun series lists for Ibaraki Prefecture all nine of its national heritage houses but for Gumma only two out of its inventory of five. The Yamakawa guides, on the other hand, mention two different houses from the Gumma inventory but not a single structure from five other prefectures which collectively have 35 heritage houses. As shown by Table 2, variations in the treatment of prefectural inventories are even more pronounced. This selectivity has obvious implications for any hegemonic

Table 2. Guidebook entries of prefectural heritage houses

Prefecture	Official heritage inventory	Guidebook entry Jimbun & Yamakawa	Jimbun only	Yamakawa only
Ibaraki	9	–	–	4
Tochigi	–	–	–	–
Gumma	4	3	–	1
Saitama	1	1	–	–
Chiba	7	–	2	–
Tokyo	7	3	3	–
Kanagawa	8	–	3	1
Totals	36	7	8	6
(%)	(100)	(19.4)	(22.2)	(16.7)

construction of heritage meanings and will be discussed subsequently, after the entries themselves have been examined.

The entries basically assume two formats. While some heritage houses are simply identified by name and location as elements of the cultural landscape without further comment, the majority of entries provides data on the *kakaku*, the social status of the family lineage during the Edô period, when the country was ruled by the Tokugawa shogunate (1603 – 1867). Table 3 presents frequency distributions across several family status categories both as reported in the guidebooks and as established through the national restoration reports on individual structures, the official heritage inventories of the seven prefectures and the odd entry in the guidebook series themselves. The status categories are extracted from these materials and form an ordinal scale of decreasing specificity that ranges from administrative rank to social stratum and lineage antiquity, with subcategories ordered by prestige into the same direction. Cases are assigned to a given category on the basis of the most specific applicable criterion.

Table 3 shows that, as was the case with the inventories, the guidebooks do not invariably report the status information obviously available to their compilers, as indicated by the references included in bibliographies of the individual volumes. Thus the Jimbun guides collectively report the known status in only 60.4 percent of their entries, while in the Yamakawa volumes this figure drops to 39.6 percent. The very selectivity, however, arguably increases the significance of the information which the volumes present as attributes or dimensions of architectural heritage.

Table 3. Reported status of lineages of heritage houses

Status category	Actual status[a]	Reported by Jimbun	Yamakawa
Official rank			
District magistrate	1	1	1
Village headman	31	22	10
Lower village official	2	–	2
Social stratum			
Rich farmer	4	1	2
Rich merchant	6	2	4
Lineage history			
Samurai descent	3	1	2
Founding settler family	1	–	–
Old local family	5	5	–
Totals	53	32	21
(%)	(100)	(60.4)	(39.6)

[a] 19 ordinary lineages and 10 lineages for which no reliable status data were available have been deleted from the tabulation.

Apart from the 19 houses owned by ordinary farmers and the 10 for which no reliable lineage data were obtained, all excluded from the tabulation, there are 53 houses that belonged to lineages whose status is considered worthy of note. Among these, 31 belonged to lineages who served as village headmen during the Tokugawa period, and this too is the status reported most frequently by both publications. Regionally called *shôya* or *nanushi*, the headman position constituted the administrative link between village and fief bureaucracy, with its incumbent "held responsible in one way or another for the execution and enforcement of all laws, regulations, and edicts affecting the village" (Befu 1966: 25). Reporting upwards to the *daikan*, the district magistrate, and assisted by such lower village officials as the *kumigashira*, the leaders of five- and ten-man neighborhood groups, the headman held his position as hereditary right or in limited rotation with the heads of other prominent local lineages, together with whom he and his lineage formed the upper stratum of rural society below the samurai overlords of the castle towns. The rank of village headman consequently implies in various combinations most of the other status criteria given in the table.

Aside from the obvious criterion of wealth, accumulated either as farmer or merchant, there are three further criteria that pertain to the ancestry and antiquity of the lineage. The first of these is descent from samurai ancestors who, having fought on the losing side of the 16th century wars of unification, returned to the land to become farmers; the second is pioneer status (*kaihatsu*) as original settlers of their district during the general agricultural development of the Kantô region; and the third, obviously implicit in the others but often invoked in the absence of more noteworthy facts, is the appellation of *kyûka* or *chihô no kyûka*, of an old family deeply rooted in the district.

While Table 3 provides an overview of these status attributes, it does not convey the qualitative character of their diverse combination into entries that range from terse observations to veritable cameo hagiographies. An illustration of the former format is the entry for the Hananoi residence (Plate 1), a national heritage house in Chiba Prefecture:

> *Konjôin no niômon mae o sarani iku to, Edô jidai no tenkeitekina minka ga aru. Arayamashi Maegasaki de daidai nanushi o tsutometa kyû Hananoike no omoya (jûbun) de, Kambun nenkan (1661–72) ni taterareta mono o ichiku shita.* [Also situated before the guardian gate of the Konjô temple is a typical house of the Edô period. The main house (cultural property) of the old Hananoi family, which served for generations as village headmen in the Maegasaki district of Arayama City, it was built in the Kambun era (1661–72) and has been relocated to its present site and completely restored] (Chibaken kôkôgakkô kyôiku kenkyûkai rekishibukai 1981: 71).

Among the best examples of the more fulsome format is the entry for the Uchida residence (Plate 2), a nationally scheduled heritage residence in Saitama Prefecture. The entry has eighteen lines: the first thirteen describe the construction history of the house and its various architectural characteristics, the remaining five are devoted to the family lineage:

> *Nao Uchidake wa, Hachigattajô no karôshoku o tsutometa iegara de, Edô jidai ni wa daidai seshû de Makuda no nanushi o tsutome, ôku no meishi o haishutsu shi, kono chihô no kaihatsu ni ôkina kôseki o nokoshita.* [The Uchida family, who served as castellans of Hachigatta castle [which fell in 1590], during the Edô period became the hereditary headman lineage of Makuda village, there successively bringing forth men of ability who rendered highly meritorious service in the development of the region] (Jimbunsha kankô to tabi henshûbu 1981a: 219).

Other instances of this format identify lineages as erstwhile "*Fukaya jôshu, Uesugishi no kashin* [vassals of the Uesugi clan, lords of Fukaya castle]" (Plate 3) (Jimbunsha kankô to tabi henshûbu 1981a: 186), as "*Numata han no yakushu goyôtashi o tsutometa gôsô* [rich merchants who

Plate 1. The Hananoi Residence, moved to a municipal park and restored as an architectural exhibit.

Plate 2. The Uchida Residence, still occupied in its original location.

Plate 3. The Hirayama Residence, restored in its original location as an architectural exhibit, with the modern family residence in the left foreground.

were official purveyors of medicines to the Numata domain]" (Gumma bunka no kai 1980: 199) and as "*kôtai nanushi o tsutome, tonya mo kanete*" [alternate village headmen as well as wholesale merchants] (Jimbunsha kankô to tabi henshûbu 1981b: 175). As in the case of an innkeeper and headman lineage of samurai descent, such entries may additionally note that the Emperor Meiji had stayed in the family establishment in the ninth month of the eleventh year of his reign, or, as in the case of a senior headman lineage responsible for seven villages, that the family had bred falcons for the shogun and held the honor of annual presentation at the shogunal court (Jimbunsha kankô to tabi henshûbu 1981c: 114, 148).

In summation, then, the conception of heritage presented in the guidebooks is premised not merely on the architectural characteristics of the scheduled buildings but also on the lineage status of the generations that inhabited these buildings during the Tokugawa period. Although the guidebooks repeatedly omit lineage information readily available to their authors, both series on the whole reflect a scheduling pattern in which village elites are over-represented and headman lineages preeminent, and both provide lineage particulars that evoke a multidimensional image of prominence in local affairs as well as respectability in the wider stratification system of Tokugawa society as such. While the entries thus acknowledge that the heritage structures are technically farmhouses rather than samurai mansions or *daimyô* castles, they also ensure that their erstwhile occupants, as well as any contemporary descendants, are thereby not mistaken for common peasant stock but recognized as lineages of substance and influence. The symbolic meanings conferred upon a structure by virtue of its architectural features are thus compounded by the social prominence of its inhabitants, a prominence which the handful of unexceptional lineages simply throws into sharper relief.

In this context the selectivity exercised through the inclusion pattern does not detract from the basic thrust of the pattern of entry content. As Tables 1 and 2 make obvious, the pattern complies with the official distinction between national and prefectural heritage categories by including a far larger proportion of exemplars from the former than from the latter category and, of course, by disregarding mere municipal heritage structures entirely. Similarly, while the variance in the frequency distributions of reported lineage data is pronounced both between the two series and among their respective individual volumes, the basic pattern of the content remains the same: where architectural information is complemented by social information, it is the lineage status, and especially its administrative rank, which strikes the compilers as worthy of inclusion in the entry. The selectivity on both counts therefore underscores a conception of architectural heritage that makes these houses not just monuments to the vernacular architectural tradition of a bygone age but to a major component of its social order as well, namely, the upper stratum of Tokugawa village society.

The political significance of the entry pattern

The inclusion of this conception of heritage in the cultural guidebooks has political implications on both community and national levels of analysis. In the former context, these implications arise from the agrarian reforms which the American occupation authorities implemented as a major legislative program in their restructuring of postwar Japanese society. Ideologically opposed to the concentration of landownership in a small landlord class and the resultant condition of tenancy for the general rural population, the reformers instituted a massive redistribution of land that essentially eliminated the traditional economic dependencies and attenuated, at the very least, an entire range of other hierarchical relations which these dependencies had reinforced. For landlord families, this frequently meant a painful readjustment to new social and political realities in which people were inclined to question the relevance of traditional status criteria and to withhold the automatic conferral of political powers predicated on them (Dore 1959: 364—387).

Under these circumstances, the national or prefectural designation of the ancestral home as heritage, whether still in private possession or publicly administered, transforms the structure into a visual reproduction of feudal relations that legitimizes contemporary claims to authority and political office through generations of community service now enshrined, so to speak, as heritage. Given that the municipal political arena involves constituencies of several thousand inhabitants even in the case of villages, the popularization of heritage home and ancestral lineage status through cultural guidebooks heightens the visibility of the politician and underscores the legitimacy of his or her candidacy and incumbency. Heritage is thus good public relations, as is also evident from the composition of the official committees responsible for the restoration of scheduled heritage shrines, temples and farmhouses, which primarily draw on the local political and administrative establishments (Ehrentraut 1988, 1989a). Indeed, one may well wonder in this connection whether the sudden surge of farmhouse designation and restoration in the 1960s is entirely coincidental.

For voters with socialist inclinations, of course, be they descendants of local tenant lineages or industrial workers commuting from the suburbs, the heritage designation of headman residences may well be ideologically objectionable and headman ancestry consequently grounds for disqualifying a candidate out of hand. Yet here it must be emphasized that headmen lineages cannot simply be reduced to specimens in some marxist bestiary. Although historically such lineages were indeed frequently the immediate target of peasant insurrections, they were also village benefactors and protectors who in times of famine, for example, provided food from their own storehouses and petitioned the domain authorities for communal tax reductions and exemptions (Hashimoto 1982: 156). Probably the most famous illustration of such leadership is the case of Sakura Sôgorô (1597—1645), headman in a domain which its *daimyô* was exploiting with exceptional enthusiasm and venality. Bypassing the domain administration on behalf of the domain's more than one hundred villages, Sôgorô succeeded in presenting a petition directly to the Shogun Iemitsu, whose reprimand to the *daimyô* eventually reduced feudal predation in the domain to more normal proportions. For the impertinence of his illegal petition, however, Sôgorô and his wife were crucified and their three children beheaded (Edmunds 1974[1934]: 584–587).

Given this duality in the historical role of village elites, the average conservative voter may therefore indeed see in headman ancestry a proper pedigree for political office in Japan's traditional "patron-client democracy," a form of democracy "based on a value system that stresses community solidarity, repression of internal dissent, deference to community leaders, conformity to group decisions, and resignation to the way things are" (Flanagan – Steiner – Kraus 1980: 428). This interpretation is reinforced by more general considerations.

From a societal perspective, heritage farmhouses are visual expressions of an agrarian ideology which transfigures the feudal realities of peasant existence into a romanticized vision of rustic simplicity and harmony (Ehrentraut 1989a). Encapsulated in the emotive concept of *furusato*, of native home and village, this vision is otherwise celebrated in such cultural productions as the annual village festivals and the folkloristic performances of heritage songs and dances. But the ideology is not simply another illustration of the commodification of culture: for the past hundred years, it has been one of the central themes of the political process on all levels of Japanese society.

During the rapid transformation of Japanese society at the turn of the century, some of the modernizing ideologues of the Meiji oligarchy developed what Gluck has called the "agrarian myth" (1985: 178–204), in which the putative virtues of the vanishing rural order served as ethical counterpoints to the evils bred by industrialization and urbanization. In later years this constellation of beliefs and values, centering on the loyalty and harmony, the cooperation, diligence and frugality identified as primordial Japanese virtues, served as one of the ideological premises for the institutionalization of *jichi* or rural self-government, conceptualized by Yamagata Aritomo, then prime minister, as the very "foundation of the state" (quoted in Gluck 1985: 192). The actual carriers of this doctrine were the local elites, consisting not only of lineages which modernization had raised from obscurity but also of ancient lineages prominent in their districts for centuries, in short, the very type characteristic of the present heritage homes (Smethurst 1980: 232ff). When in the 1930s this agrarian ideology became crystallized in the militarization of rural society, the established families continued to perform this function through leadership of the reservists and youth associations and similar patriotic organizations

(Smethurst 1974: 100–114). The young men who served in these organizations and survived the war years are now themselves the generation that provides the contemporary leadership of the conservative party.

It is in this larger context that the dissemination of heritage information through the tourist guidebooks contributes to the social construction of a political culture in which the agrarian themes of the past are not negated but affirmed and perpetuated. The cultural landscape they define is not marked by monuments critical of past social relations and the ideologies in which these are embedded, as is the function of heritage buildings in socialist societies where, for example, the kulaks are pilloried (Matvienko 1982), but a landscape that clearly serves the political interests of the dominant strata of Japanese society by legitimating fundamental continuities in the social stratification system and anchoring their symbolism in the collective symbolism of national identity.

Before concluding that the guidebooks are simply state organs of social control that ensure its hegemonic definition of the ideological universe, it is advisable to recall that the guides did not include every lineage status and not even every heritage house. As argued elsewhere (Ehrentraut 1989b) in connection with the heritage designation of certain Shinto shrines in the Kantô region, this selectivity by a mass medium is in part an expression of the organizational and occupational filters which edit and transform official heritage messages in the process of their transmission. While the very inclusion of heritage structures in such guidebooks reflects the broad parameters of the ideological premises underlying their heritage designation, publishing companies are not mere extensions of governmental heritage agencies but, as businesses engaged in the commodification of culture, subject to various forces that range from market considerations to the parochial convictions of individual contributors. From the perspective of mainstream organization theory, these forces make ministry departments and mass media companies loosely coupled organizations at best (Hall 1987: 232–260), which obviously permits the latter to disregard a substantial number of heritage monuments in the very prefectures their volumes seek to publicize. In this sense, the selectivity illustrates Althusser's (1971: 135–149) concept of ideological state apparatuses, wherein an element of negotiation shapes the essentially hegemonic decoding of the dominant cultural discourse. The entry patterns are therefore also useful illustrations of the complexity of the processes involved in the construction of heritage symbols and the difficulties inherent in exercising effective political control over the social production of culture in a democratic society.

Heritage houses and domestic tourism

A final perspective on the guidebooks is provided by their function in Japanese domestic tourism as such. In this connection Graburn (1983: 63) has postulated that a major objective of Japanese tourists is the "nostalgic confirmation of their cultural landscape," which more generally can be conceptualized as an expression of Tuan's (1976) notion of geopiety. Modern Japanese domestic tourism in this light is not some new development associated with westernization and urbanization but has roots in the religious pilgrimages permitted even under the severe travel restrictions imposed by the Tokugawa shogunate. These pilgrimages are best exemplified by the circuit of the 88 designated Buddhist temples on Shikoku that has retained its popularity to the present day (Tanaka 1989). The contemporary pursuit of similar touristic activities, including secular pilgrimages to assorted scenic and historic locales (Kitagawa 1987: 127−136), is significantly shaped by various markers of the cultural landscape, and while Japanese dependence on such markers can be overstated, the tourist literature available in the ubiquitous book stores is, as already mentioned, indeed voluminous and certainly more detailed than in many other countries (Moeran 1983).

In this context, the official designation of buildings as architectural heritage creates within the built environment a hierarchy of symbolic significance, a hierarchy that defines for the visitor both importance and correct interpretation of the symbol and therefore also the authenticity of the experience it is intended to evoke. In turn, the inclusion of such sacralized sights among guidebook entries not only disseminates knowledge about their markers but recommends as well the appropriate itinerary for their visitation. Embedded among the shrines and temples, among castle ruins, battlefields and scenic sites, the heritage farmhouses thus become integral elements of the cultural landscape which designation and dissemination have constructed.

Given the ideological content of this heritage as outlined above, domestic tourism is more than the recreational consumption of cultural productions by a mass audience in its leisure hours: it becomes a process of political socialization through which a conservative worldview is transmitted. The markers define the sight: a headman residence symbolizes not generations of parasitic greed and exploitation but dedicated leadership and community service. In this light, domestic tourism serves as another institutionalized mechanism through which dominant class interests shape the social construction of an ideological universe within which the legitimacy of their interest remains paramount.

However, neither the construction nor dissemination of an ideology implies its acceptance, particularly when a measure of consonance and interdependence among institutional elements becomes fragmented along various occupational and organizational dimensions and when the very exposure to the ideological message remains relatively voluntary. Whether the audiences are now students on obligatory field trips, employees on company tours, housewife associations on outings in the countryside or simply individual families intent on their weekend leisure, their reactions to the heritage message remain a matter of further research.

From a comparative perspective, both the heritage architecture and the cultural guidebooks of Japan are obviously unique in many specific respects. In terms of their basic institutional configuration, however, there are equally obvious parallels to the conservation and popularization of architectural heritage in other developed societies. The Britain of the National Trust, for example, hardly mirrors either the historical or contemporary realities of its working class nor are the Knaur guides to the cultural monuments of Austria or West Germany any more sensitive to the daily lot of their average visitor and his or her ancestors. These guidebooks, too, disseminate symbol systems that serve as building blocks for collective identities ranging from parochial attachments to the broad labels of ethnicity, race and nation. In this light the Japanese findings suggest useful avenues for comparative research into the processes involved in the construction of such symbols.

References

Althusser, Louis
  1971   *Lenin and philosophy and other essays*. London: NLB.
Angotti, Thomas
  1982   "Planning the open-air museum and teaching urban history: The United States in the world context," *Museum* XXXIV(3): 179 – 188.
Barthel, Diane
  1989   "Historic preservation: A comparative analysis," *Sociological Forum* 4(1): 87 – 105.
Befu, Harumi
  1966   "Duty, reward, sanction and power: Four-cornered office of the Tokugawa village headman," in: Bernard S. Silverman – H. D. Harootunian (eds.), 167 – 189.

Bunkachô
1987   *Bunkachô nempo: Shôwa 59 nendo* [Annual report of the Agency for Cultural Affairs: Fiscal year 1984]. Tôkyô: Bunkachô.
1983   "Shin shitei no bunkazai" [Newly scheduled cultural properties], *Bunkazai* [Cultural Property] 5: 4 – 25.
Chibaken kôkôgakkô kyôiku kenyûkai rekishibukai
1981   *Chibaken no rekishi sanpô* [A stroll through the history of Chiba prefecture]. Tôkyô: Yamakawa Shuppansha.
Cohen, Erik
1979   "A phenomenology of tourist experiences," *Sociology* 13(2): 179 – 201.
Council of Europe
1976   *A future for our past: European architectural heritage.* The Hague: Government Printing Office.
Dore, Ronald
1959   *Land reform in Japan.* London: Oxford University Press.
Edmunds, Will H.
1974 [1934] *Pointers and clues to the subjects of Chinese and Japanese art.* London: Sampson, Low, Marston. [Reprinted Genève: Minkoff Reprint].
Ehrentraut, Adolf
1988   "Symbols of heritage: The restoration of Shinto shrines in Japan," *Tsukuba Journal of Sociology* 13: 61 – 73.
1989a   "The visual definition of heritage: The restoration of domestic rural architecture in Japan," *Visual Anthropology* 2(2): 135 – 161.
1989b   "The social construction of architectural heritage in Japan," in: Jean M. Guiot – Joseph M. Green (eds.), 61 – 73.
Flanagan, Scott C. – Kurt Steiner – Ellis S. Kraus
1980   "The partisan politicization of local government: Causes and consequences," in: Kurt Steiner – Ellis S. Kraus – Scott C. Flanagan (eds.), 427 – 469.
Gluck, Carol
1985   *Japan's modern myths: Ideology in the late Meiji period.* Princeton: Princeton University Press.
Graburn, Nelson
1983   *To pray, pay and play: The cultural structure of Japanese domestic tourism.* Aix-en-Provence: Centre des Hautes Etudes Touristiques.
Guiot, Jean M. – Joseph G. Green (eds.)
1990   *From orchestras to apartheid: Selected papers from the 15th Annual Conference on Social Theory, Politics, and the Arts.* North York: Captus University Publications.
Gumma bunka no kai
1980   *Gummaken no rekishi sanpô* [A stroll through the history of Gumma prefecture]. Tôkyô: Yamakawa Shuppansha.

Hadjinicolaou, Nicos
1978   *Art history and class struggle*. London: Pluto Press.
Hall, Richard H.
1987   *Organizations: Structures, processes, and outcomes*. Englewood Cliffs, NJ: Prentice-Hall.
Hashimoto, Mitsuru
1982   "The social background of peasant uprisings in Tokugawa Japan," in: Tetsuo Najita — J. Victor Koschmann (eds.), 145—163.
Jimbunsha kankô to tabi henshûbu
1981a   *Kyôdo shiryô jiten: Saitamaken kankô to tabi* [Home prefecture encyclopedia: Sightseeing and travel in Saitama prefecture]. Tôkyô: Jimbunsha.
1981b   *Kyôdo shiryô jiten: Tochigiken kankô to tabi* [Home prefecture encyclopedia: Sightseeing and travel in Tochigi prefecture]. Tôkyô: Jimbunsha.
1981c   *Kyôdo shiryô jiten: Gummaken kankô to tabi* [Home prefecture encyclopedia: Sightseeing and travel in Gumma prefecture]. Tôkyô: Jimbunsha.
Keune, Russel V. (ed.)
1984   *The historic preservation yearbook*. Bethesda, MD: Adler and Adler.
Kitagawa, Joseph M.
1987   *On understanding Japanese religion*. Princeton: Princeton University Press.
Lowenthal, David — Martyn J. Bowden (eds.)
1976   *Geographies of the mind: Essays in geosophy*. New York: Oxford University Press.
MacCannell, Dean
1976   *The tourist: A new theory of the leisure class*. New York: Schocken.
Matvienko, Anatole Vassilievitch
1982   "The museum of folk life and architecture," *Museum* XXXIV (3): 162—166.
Moeran, Brian
1983   "The language of Japanese tourism," *Annals of Tourism Research* 10: 93—108.
Najita, Tetsuo — J. Victor Koschmann (eds.)
1982   *Conflict in modern Japanese history: The neglected tradition*. Princeton: Princeton University Press.
Parsons, Talcott
1951   *The social system*. New York: The Free Press.
Phillipot, Paul
1976   "Historic preservation: Philosophy, criteria, guidelines," in Sharon Timmons (ed.), 367—382.
Redfoot, Donald L.
1984   "Touristic authenticity, tourist angst, and modern reality," *Qualitative Sociology* 7(4): 291—309.

Silverman, Bernard S. — H. D. Harootunian (eds.)
1966   *Modern Japanese leadership: Transition and change.* Tucson: University of Arizona Press.
Smethurst, Richard J.
1974   *A social basis for prewar Japanese militarism.* Berkeley: University of California Press.
1980   *Agricultural development and tenancy disputes in Japan.* Princeton: Princeton University Press.
Smith, Anthony D.
1984   "Ethnic myths and ethnic revivals," *European Journal of Sociology* XXV: 283–305.
Stankiewicz, Jerzy
1977   "The conservation of working-class buildings in Gdansk," *Monumentum* XV-XVI: 105–107.
Steiner, Kurt — Ellis S. Kraus — Scott C. Flanagan (eds.)
1980   *Political opposition and local politics in Japan.* Princeton: Princeton University Press.
Tanaka, Hiroshi
1989   "Japanese pilgrimage places: Tradition and modernization," Paper, Japan Social Sciences Association of Canada, Annual Meeting, Toronto.
Timmons, Sharon (ed.)
1976   *Preservation and conservation: Principles and practices.* Washington, DC: Preservation Press.
Tuan, Yi-Fu
1976   "Geopiety: A theme in man's attachment to nature and place," in: David Lowenthal — Martyn J. Bowden (eds.), 11–39.
Wallerstein, Immanuel
1987   "The construction of peoplehood: Racism, nationalism, ethnicity," *Sociological Forum* 2(2): 373–389.
William, Eurwyn
1988   *Home-made homes: Dwellings of the rural poor in Wales.* Cardiff: National Museum of Wales.

"Take home Canada": Representations of aboriginal peoples as tourist souvenirs

Valda Blundell

This paper considers those inexpensive mass-produced objects which international tourists frequently purchase as mementos of their trips to Canada.[1] A visit to virtually any souvenir shop in Canada will reveal that many of these objects represent aboriginal Indians and Inuit. At such sites/sights, travellers find display cases filled with miniature tepees and totem poles as well as small carvings of northern animals and native hunting scenes. Also available are various lines of Indian dolls and items such as t-shirts, towels and postcards with pictures on them of natives or native cultural forms (see Plate 1).

Such mass-produced "native-type" objects are not the only representations of aboriginal Canadians that tourists can buy. There are, for example, shops in Canada that specialize in the more expensive hand-made or limited edition arts and crafts, and some shops sell both mass-produced forms and those that are hand-made. The focus of this chapter is on objects that are produced and displayed *not* primarily as representations of aboriginal cultures, nor as mementos of some experience of contemporary aboriginal life, but as keepsakes of the country itself, as *souvenirs* that can be thought of as distinctly *Canadian*.[2] They are objects like those I came across in an Ottawa shopping mall where Indian dolls dressed in buckskin had been placed in the display window of a gift shop beneath a sign urging shoppers to "Take Home Canada."

My goals in this chapter are to indicate the signifying practices employed in producing and marketing such mass-produced souvenir forms and to determine some of the consequences of these practices. In particular, I review challenges to the ways in which these "native-type" forms are marketed, including claims by aboriginal peoples that current marketing practices work against their own cultural and economic interests. I then consider how the federal state is responding to these challenges, and in the process I argue that Canada's current tourism policy encourages the very practices that are now under fire. Finally, I identify points

Plate 1. Souvenir dolls on sale at the Ottawa International Airport. Photograph by the author.

of potential transformation in the souvenir trade by suggesting what alternative forms of souvenirs might look like.

My point of departure for this analysis is the observation that the cultural artifacts of colonized aboriginal peoples have been used by colonizing groups in processes of nation building. Often such artifacts have become national symbols and treasured components of a country's national heritage. According to the anthropologist Nelson Graburn (1986: 5), this has been the case because colonial nations have had "special difficulties in establishing a national identity and in promoting the symbols to convey it." For example, nations such as Canada, the United States, Australia, and New Zealand have had to differentiate themselves from the mother country and also from one another. Given the shared background of the colonizing peoples of these countries, they have looked for a source of national identity within the colonized country itself.

For Canada, Graburn (1986: 5) suggests that "the domain with the greatest potential" has been the natural landscape and the native peoples, "both of which have figured prominently in Canadian art history." Indeed, aboriginal cultural forms have become part of what he calls Canada's "borrowed" identity (Graburn 1976a). Countries such as Australia and New Zealand have also borrowed the cultural forms of indig-

enous aboriginal peoples in processes of constructing their national identities. Such locally derived signs allow these countries to differentiate
themselves from one another at the same time that they serve as quickly
recognized signs of the nation itself. As such, they are especially useful
in promotional materials designed to attract tourists from abroad.

For example, bark paintings and boomerangs appear in travel advertisements for Australia and Maori artifacts in advertisements for New
Zealand. In the case of Canada, travel advertisements often depict objects
made by native Indians, such as the distinctive masks and totem poles
of Northwest Coast cultures. Advertisements promoting travel to Canada
also depict Inuit-produced soapstone carvings, which of all the Canadian
native-produced cultural forms, have become most widely recognized
internationally as distinctively Canadian works of art (Graburn 1986;
Muehlen 1990/91: 39). Not surprisingly, when tourists travel in these
countries they are offered mass-produced representations of aboriginal
forms as mementos of their trips.

Plate 2. Souvenirs obtained by the author between 1988 and 1990. Back row:
plastic wallet, two plastic "Indian" dolls dressed in leather, plastic "brave" doll,
plastic "mountie" doll. Front row: mould-made "Wolf" carving with its booklet-
style tag, plastic totem pole, metal bottle opener, beaded key chain, mould-made
refrigerator magnets sculpted as Indian man and Inuit girl, "marble" kayak.
Photograph by John McQuarrie.

Currently available objects

Mass-produced replicas of aboriginal objects: A vast array of mass-produced native-type forms are currently being sold as souvenirs of Canada (see Plate 2).[3] These include replicas of familiar Indian and Inuit artifacts and art forms, many no doubt purchased for children: drums, rattles, tomahawks, and feather head-dresses. Plastic totem poles, which come in a range of sizes, are sold in virtually every souvenir shop in Canada. Also offered are small boxes, decorated in the Northwest Coast style. Especially ubiquitous are plastic, ceramic, or "cast stone" objects that depict Inuit hunting scenes and animals found in the north. These figures are reminiscent of soapstone carvings made by Inuit, both in their style and subject matter.

Representations of aboriginal peoples: A second category of objects consists of representations of aboriginal peoples themselves, for example, plastic dolls dressed in (sometimes imitation) leather with fringes and beads, headbands and feathers. Some come with drums, bows, or spears to add that extra "native touch" (cf. Macaulay 1989).

Plate 3. Postcards representing Inuit girls. Left, from the "Canada" series produced by the Postcard Factory of Toronto. Right, reproduced by permission of Nortext Iqaluit, Northwest Territories. Original photograph by Nick Newbery.

Functional objects: A vast array of "functional" items either replicate aboriginal forms or in some way depict aboriginal peoples. My own collection of such souvenirs includes a bank and bottle opener in the shape of totem poles, refrigerator magnets sculpted as the heads of an Inuit girl and a befeathered Indian man, a plastic wallet that is simulated to resemble birch bark and has an appliqued image on its cover of a young Indian girl, a cup in the shape of an Indian, towels with pictures on them of Indian artifacts, and a beaded key chain with a miniature Indian doll as its handle. In addition, tourists collect postcards as souvenirs and send them to their friends and relatives back home, many of which represent native peoples and native cultural forms (see Plate 3).

Conventions for signifying forms as souvenirs of Canada

Producers and retailers use several conventions to identify these objects as signs of Canada.[4] For example, native-type objects are displayed in shops alongside printed messages that inscribe them as "souvenirs." Invariably, these signs are printed in red and white so that they are color coded to match the Canadian flag (see Plate 4).

The word "Canada" (or a regional designation) is often written on the object itself, as is the case for the little "brave" doll in Plate 2, where "Peterborough Canada" is written on its base, and the bottle opener in the shape of a totem pole in Plate 2 where "Canada" is embossed at its opening end. Many postcards also have "Canada" as their caption, or the name of one of the country's regions, as can be seen in Plate 3. Retailers report that many tourists prefer a keepsake with "Canada" written on it.[5]

Furthermore, these native-type souvenirs are located in shops in display cases or on open shelves along with other handy signs of the nation, including miniature Canadian flags (or images of them), as is shown in Plate 4, and small figures of scarlet-coated mounties. Some companies produce both the native-type and these other forms of souvenirs. For example, the company located in St. Tite, Quebec, "Indien Art Eskimo Inc.," makes both the "mountie" doll and the "Peterborough Canada" Indian doll illustrated in Plate 2.

In the case of items classified as functional, native images also co-occur with these other common signs of Canada. For instance, the postcards in the "Canada" series produced by the Postcard Factory of

Plate 4. Souvenir totem poles on sale at the Ottawa International Airport. Photograph by author.

Toronto include in their cast of Canadian signifiers pictures of "traditional" Inuit hunters; befeathered Indian Chiefs; and Canada's official totem, the beaver. Viewers encounter these postcards together as a set on specialized display racks in gift shops.

Finally, many objects have labels or tags attached to them which inscribe them as "souvenirs of Canada" by means of a written text, and at the same time claim that they are "authentic." The tags attached to the dolls seen in Plate 1 and to the "brave" doll seen in Plate 2 read in part an "authentic souvenir."

Souvenirs and the production of meanings

Souvenirs are not merely capitalist commodities with exchange values. They also come to have meanings for the travellers who buy them. Indeed, as Jonathan Culler (1981: 281) observes, tourists are the "accomplices of semiotics." All over the world "tourists are engaged in semiotic projects, reading cities, landscapes and cultures as sign systems."

Such readings also take place in the souvenir shops of Canada when tourists encounter mass-produced representations of native Indian and Inuit cultural forms. It is at such sites/sights that tourists link meanings about natives with meanings about travel in order to mark their experience of visiting Canada.[6] However, these meaningfully connected meanings do not simply emerge in the souvenir shop itself.[7] Tourists leave home with beliefs about natives and about travel that are deeply entrenched in their own cultures. When they encounter souvenirs they draw upon this bricolage of culturally constructed beliefs, this historical grammar of stock metaphors, in order to make sense of what they see (Johnson 1986, 1986/87; Overton 1980: 22–23; Uzzell 1984; Williamson 1978; Wolff 1981: 95–116).

Producers and retailers tap into these same widely held beliefs to make souvenirs attractive to buyers. Through processes of commodity aesthetics, they encourage tourists to translate one system of meaning into another, so that objects come to stand for tourists' values, desires, and other feelings. What is possibly unattainable becomes (seemingly) attainable (Vestergaard – Schroder 1985: 155; Williamson 1978: 31).

Ideas about aboriginal peoples and about travel

In offering native-type souvenirs to tourists, entrepreneurs draw upon ideas that are widely held among tourists, especially those from western nations. In particular, entrepreneurs draw upon the tendentious, but nonetheless pervasive, belief that the aboriginal peoples of advanced industrial states are "primitives" who have failed to evolve or "progress" as have the peoples of the West.[8] They tap into ideas that construct Indians and Inuit as exotic children of nature who preserve (although vestigially and anachronistically) an Eden-like past when life was somehow more free, indeed more "authentic," than life in the "modern world."[9]

These same ideas construct aboriginal expressive forms as "primitive art," privileged loci of mythical, transcendent essences. Because they can evoke this sense of authenticity, aboriginal forms are especially appealing as signs of Canada. Not only do they lend a distinct identity to the country, their own privileged authenticity rubs off on Canada, so that Canada itself seems real (cf. Vestergaard – Schroder 1985: 155).

Aboriginal forms are additionally appealing to tourists as signs of Canada because ideas about aboriginal peoples and ideas about travel can be linked. Given the presumption that authenticity is now missing in the modern industrialized world but persists in other places (in particular among so-called "primitive" peoples and among certain peasant, ethnic, and rural folk), travel becomes a way of reclaiming this lost authenticity (cf. McKay 1988; Overton 1980; Williams 1973). Indeed the argument that many tourists are seeking authentic experiences of other cultures is now widely advanced by both academic and market researchers, although for different reasons.

In his seminal book, *The Tourist*, Dean MacCannell argues that modern international sightseers are primarily middle-class individuals from Western nation states, and that for many of them touring is a search for authentic experiences which can counter the mundane, indeed alienating, conditions of their post-industrial lives. Along with other critical scholars, MacCannell (1989: 1) analyzes touristic behavior as a model or symptom of a unifying post-industrial consciousness in the face of a globalizing modernity that depends for its progress on a "sense of instability and inauthenticity" (1989: 3). "For moderns," MacCannell alleges, "reality and authenticity are thought to be elsewhere: in other historical periods and other cultures, in purer, simpler life-styles" (1989: 3).[10]

For David Uzzell, tourism offers opportunities to act out fantasies, time out from the routines of life back home, as well as the relaxation of social constraints. Given their deeply engrained Calvinist attitudes, however, Western tourists can feel guilty about having so much fun. But they can "atone for their guilt" by having authentic encounters in other cultures, by experiencing the "'real' life of the country they are visiting... Pleasure is not easily won," Uzzell (1984: 94) continues, "there is a cost to be borne, and the currency is culture."

Critical scholars challenge constructions of tourism that locate authenticity outside tourists' own everyday lives (e.g., Hewison 1987; MacCannell 1984, 1989; Taylor 1989). They argue that too often tourist attractions developed and promoted as the loci of authentic experiences are designed to provoke nostalgia rather than critical thought. As contrived simulacra that romanticize and sanitize the past, they work to hide from visitors current social inequalities and their real historical sources. Critics, such as MacCannell, worry that when tourism is promoted as a kind of time-travel into a past-preserved-in-the-present, aboriginal (and also ethnic and rural) peoples become recruited to act as traditional societies for others. They also worry that cultural forms commoditized for tourist markets will replace those that express peoples' own current views of the world, indeed that people may be enticed to produce quaint, exotic-looking forms that conform to the false presumption that they are premoderns. And they fear that individuals or groups that fail to so conform will be accused of having lost their own cultural identity (cf. Berger 1979).

However, despite these concerns of critical scholars, the tourist industry has embraced the idea that leisure travel can be promoted as a way of providing affluent Western tourists with authentic experiences of other cultures.[11] Advertisements commissioned by businesses involved in tourism therefore represent aboriginal forms not only to convey the distinctiveness of Canada, but to convey the availability in Canada of authentic experiences of other cultures. When aboriginal forms are depicted in such travel advertisements, however, they are rarely used to promote actual encounters with contemporary aboriginal peoples. Instead, they serve as signs of a promised, but indeterminate, authenticity to be found in Canada. It is "authenticity" itself which becomes the promoted tourist attraction/commodity.

One such use of aboriginal forms can be seen in a travel advertisement in the inflight magazine of Canadian Airlines (February 1989) which promotes travel to the Northwest Territories. The visual format of this advertisement includes the silhouetted figure of an individual paddling a kayak (a widely recognized Inuit object) across water in the glowing light of the "midnight sun" (Plate 5). The figure itself is an indeterminate sign, readable as an Inuit, but also as the visiting tourist. To the right of this inviting shot, as a kind of signature tag, is a picture of an Inuit woman's knife (an ulu) depicted as an isolated object. In this advertisement, images of Inuit objects are used to present this destination as attractively mysterious, a kind of Eden in the north. Indeed, the written caption to the advertisement, "Canada's Northwest Territories — Within Reach, Yet Beyond Belief," also works to establish the north as a mythical, dreamlike place.

In such travel advertisements, aboriginal images serve as handy signs of Canada (or a region such as Canada's West Coast or Far North), and

Plate 5. Advertisement for travel to the Northwest Territories.

they also help to construct Canada as a place where authentic experiences can be had. When souvenir producers offer tourists similar native-type forms to mark their visits to Canada, such forms can be thought of as typically Canadian since their own privileged authenticity rubs off on Canada. Furthermore, as souvenirs such artifacts serve as a sign of an individual's own experience as a traveller. For example, to tourists in Canada who buy such objects, they may signify that "Canada was just how we pictured it" as the tourist-directed sweat shirt in Plate 6 proclaims, while offering up a humorous pastiche of handy Canadian cliches: a flag-holding, moose-riding mountie; a beaver; the national parliament buildings; and an Inuit with dog sled and igloo.

In other words, when tourists buy a souvenir, it is not only meaningful as a typical sign of Canada. It also comes to have yet another meaning, which is the meaning of a souvenir itself. As a souvenir, the object

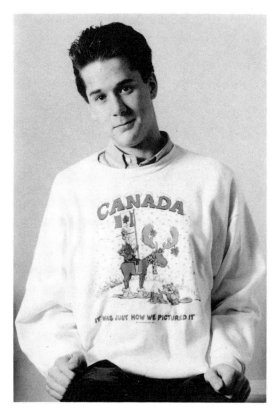

Plate 6. Author's son wearing souvenir sweatshirt purchased at the Ottawa International Airport. Photograph by John McQuarrie.

signifies not only the place visited but also the tourist's own experience there. It enters into a relationship with other cultural units in another discourse, not a discourse regarding travel, but a personal discourse about the individual's own experience of "otherness."[12] This argument is developed by Susan Stewart (1984) in her insightful book, *On Longing*, in which she writes that souvenirs retain their "signifying capacity only in a generalized sense, losing [their] specific referent[s] and eventually pointing to an abstracted otherness that describes the possessor" (Stewart 1984: 148). An exotic looking native-type form is an ideal choice as a sign of a tourist's own experience because of widespread ideas about aboriginal peoples: "Removed from its context, the exotic souvenir is a sign of survival — not its own survival, but the survival of the possessor outside his or her own context of familiarity. Its otherness speaks to the possessor's capacity for otherness" (Stewart 1984: 148).

As Stewart also argues, the metaphor in operation here is one of taming, as in the case of most native dolls, which serve as cute little primitives who possess an attractive but nonthreatening exoticism (cf. Macaulay 1989). What is accomplished through such semiosis is a simultaneous distancing to a premodern time of aboriginal peoples and a rapprochement to the tourist's time which takes place, of course, within the terms of the dominant discourse about aboriginal peoples. Furthermore, it is through such semiosis that personal memories come to reflect and perpetuate these widespread, though contested, beliefs about aboriginal peoples and travel.

To summarize thus far, I am arguing that three mutually complicit levels of semiosis can come into play when tourists see native type forms in souvenir shops in Canada. Such forms can be read: *firstly*, as distinctly Canadian; *secondly*, as privileged sites/sights of an authentic otherness (presumed missing in the tourist's own everyday life); and/or *thirdly*, as signs of the authentic nature of the tourist's own experience in (and of) Canada.

Native-type forms and authenticity

For native-type forms to do this semiotic work, however, their own "authenticity" must somehow be conveyed. This is why entrepreneurs offer objects that conform to the expectation that the native is a "primitive," not the irredeemable savage on the darker side of the stereotypic coin, but the noble savage, the romantic "child of nature," who remains isolated from the "modern" world and preserves a timeless, more genuine way of life.

Entrepreneurs do not advance such messages directly, but convey them — with varying degrees of subtlety — through representational conventions specific to tourism and to advertising, including those that are visual in nature. Albers and James (1988) argue that postcards are a particularly good source for examining such historically specific conventions. In the case of most postcards, and also most travel advertisements, aboriginal forms are not obviously "fabricated" — what seem to be ethnographic or archeological objects are shown along with real people who pose with them. Furthermore, the common use of photographs provides the appearance of a reflected naturalism, making their images seem real to viewers. However, as Albers and James also show, photographed native forms convey the same ideological meanings about aboriginal peoples and about travel noted above. Such meanings are produced through dehistoricizing and nostalgia-provoking conventions that depict aboriginal peoples and their cultural forms without reference to any lived context. Objects or people are often romantically lit at sunset or sunrise, thus locating "primitive" cultures at both the dawn of humanity, and at the same signifying moment, evoking their demise — at dusk. Other dehistoricizing conventions locate aboriginal cultures in an eternal past-in-the-present by portraying only the forms assumed to have existed in the past and joining them with others unmistakably from the past. Conventions also contribute to the indeterminate nature of native signs, for example through understated captions that homogenize aboriginal cultures, masking their variability in time and space, as in many cryptic captions on postcards (e.g., "Indian Chief," "Igloo," "Eskimo Hunter," etc.). For example, one widely available postcard in the "Canada" series produced by the Postcard Factory of Toronto poses befeathered Indians with red-coated mounties in front of a colonial stagecoach.

But what about the inexpensive, mass-produced souvenirs which lack the reflected naturalism that makes postcards and travel advertisements seem "real?" Tourists encounter multiple copies of souvenirs that are often crudely made, and so they may wonder in what sense these objects can be considered genuine. Indeed, while ideas about what constitutes authenticity, like those about aboriginal peoples and tourism, are historically specific and socially variable, one widely held view in the West is that authentic objects are those that are hand-made by the people they depict (cf. Appadurai 1986a: 45).

Claims made by authenticity tags

Through authenticity tags on souvenirs imitating native forms producers attempt to advance ideas about authenticity that are broader than the more conservative ones noted above. They advance vague claims in an imprecise language that permits, indeed encourages, tourists to interpret objects as genuine in a number of ways.[13]

First, tourists may consider an object's authenticity to derive merely from the fact that it is "hand crafted in Canada" as the tag on the tallest doll in Plate 2 claims. For many dolls, such claims are true only for the clothing of the doll itself, as their bodies are mass-produced, and some (including the tallest doll in Plate 2) sit on white plastic stands stamped "Made in Hong Kong." Generally the claim that an object is made in Canada is the only one printed on the cheapest native drums, rattles, or feather headdresses.

Second, tourists may consider an object to be authentic if it represents people, places or objects found only in Canada, as suggested by booklet-style tags. The tag on the dolls in Plate 1 and the mountie doll in Plate 2 produced by Indien Art Eskimo Inc. reads: "Historical themes, people and customs of our country have inspired our artisans in the creation of this valuable doll. We certify the doll you buy is authentic, entirely designed and crafted in our workshop in St. Tite, Quebec, Canada."

Third, tourists may understand authenticity to exist if the object conforms to their own notions of what is properly "native," even if the object is entirely and obviously made abroad. This may be the case for figures of animals or hunters because they may be thought to represent the reality of aboriginal life in the north.

Fourth, authenticity tags may also suggest an ethnographic status for an object, so that tourists may consider its authenticity to derive from its conformity to an ethnographic original. This idea is promoted in tags attached to objects by a Vancouver-based company called "Boma" which mass-produces totem poles and figures reminiscent of Inuit carvings. Boma's booklet-style tags (with trilingual texts in English, French, and Japanese) provide ethnographic information about totem poles and Indian cosmology written in the past tense.

Finally, tourists may consider an object's authenticity to derive from its being native-made, a reading that the name of an object's producer(s) may convey. For example, a line of small, mass-produced carvings reminiscent of Inuit soapstone carvings have tags claiming each to be a "Wolf Original" (see Plate 2). One salesperson at Ottawa's airport gift shop told me that some buyers believe these "Wolf Originals" to be made by a native person, and some consider them to be Inuit soapstone carvings, although critics report that neither of these interpretations is correct. This particular salesperson expressed concern that tourists might be misled, stating that a "real" soapstone carving would cost at least $500.00. However, at the time of this interview there was no written material in the shop indicating that "Wolf" is not a native person. At about the same time and at another Ottawa shop (Hudson's Bay in the Rideau Centre), display cards on shelves with "Wolf" carvings stated that they were "patterned after Eskimo culture" and that the "artist" had "studied Eskimo culture."[14] This message could be interpreted as evidence that these objects are ethnographic replicas, and therefore authentic in this sense.

According to some observers, many tourists are prepared to accept such broadly conceived ideas about authenticity. As Erik Cohen has argued regarding commoditized touristic forms, "most tourists [already] entertain concepts of 'authenticity' which are much looser than those entertained by intellectuals and experts, such as curators and anthropologists." And thus:

> ... tourists are prepared to accept such a product, even if transformed through commoditization ... as "authentic," insofar as some at least of its traits are perceived as "authentic." Such traits can be taken to authenticate, metonymically, the product as a whole (Cohen 1988: 383).

Cohen also states that ludic behaviors enter into touristic interpretations. For many tourists:

> ... tourism is a form of play ... which like all play, has profound roots in reality, but for the success of which a great deal of make-believe, on part of both performers and audience, is necessary. They willingly, even if often unconsciously, participate playfully in a game of "as if," pretending that a contrived product is authentic, even if deep down they are not convinced of its authenticity (Cohen 1988: 383).

Tags currently attached to souvenirs imitating native forms allow several meanings to be read, including several ways of interpreting these objects as authentic. Furthermore, whatever their messages are taken to be, the presence of tags seems to add to the attractiveness of the object itself. Based on comments by shopkeepers to my students and me, it would seem that many tourists consider the various tags now found on native-type forms to be critical components of the souvenirs they select. One shopkeeper told us that the native-type souvenirs are difficult to sell if they do not have such tags.

Challenges to current uses of authenticity tags

Souvenir shops are not just places where entrepreneurs represent native forms as souvenirs of Canada. They are also sites/sights where the practices used to produce and sell such objects are now being contested, especially by Canada's aboriginal peoples. For example, over the past several years, articles regarding this issue have appeared in the native magazine *Windspeaker* (Desjarlais 1987; McDougal 1988; O'Farrell 1989) as well as in the consumer magazine *Protect Yourself* (Palik 1985) and in Canada's national news magazine, *Maclean's* (Van Dusen 1983).

Critics argue that consumers are frequently misled into thinking that currently offered forms are made by aboriginal producers, or that their sale in some way benefits native peoples. In point of fact, they continue, mass-produced souvenirs (as well as many examples of more expensive hand-made items) are rarely produced by natives or by businesses that employ them. Instead, non-natives offer stereotypic objects that reinforce distorting meanings about aboriginal peoples. Furthermore, given the dominance of such mass-produced objects in the market, it is difficult for aboriginal producers to sell their own generally hand-crafted items (Shanks n.d.: 10). Some souvenir shops carry nothing that is native-made (Macaulay 1985: 10). Recently, the gift shop at the Ottawa Airport, for instance, did not display a single native-made item.

Among the challenges to current marketing practices are those regarding authenticity tags, which are accused of misleading buyers. Labelling practices used to market objects imitating native forms have been the subject of two reports by Ottawa attorney Mark Denhez. The first of these was commissioned in 1983 by the national political organization of the Inuit, the Inuit Tapirisat. A second report, completed in December of 1990, was commissioned by the Department of Indian Affairs and Northern Development (DIAND), the Government of the Northwest Territories, and Arctic Cooperatives Limited (the central distribution agency for the Northwest Territories Inuit Cooperatives).

Denhez (1990) claims that many of the tags or labels attached to currently marketed objects not only confuse buyers but are actually illegal under various federal and provincial laws (including the National Trademark and True Labelling Act and the Competition Act), although the provisions of these acts are rarely enforced (see also O'Farrell 1989). For example, inexpensive objects labelled "hand made" or "hand crafted" are usually machine made; those labelled "originals" are often mass-produced; and those said to be of "stone" or "wood" are generally made of artificial materials.

Other labelling practices imply that a form is made or designed by an aboriginal person when this is not the case. For example, the use of words such as "Indian," "Eskimo," "Native," or some exotic, native-sounding words in the credited name of the company may incorrectly lead buyers to conclude that they are owned by aboriginal peoples (Denhez 1983: 4, 1990: 34−35; Palik 1985).[15] The "Wolf Originals" noted above are a case in point as is a line of "Little Wolf" carvings and another line of carvings credited to "Dimu." Those by Dimu are generally more expensive than those by "Wolf" or "Little Wolf," and while they are actually made from soapstone (unlike those of the "Wolfs"), they appear to be machine-tooled although their labels say they are "hand carved" (as reported by Macaulay 1989: 12). Booklet-style tags attached to some "Wolf" carvings even warn buyers to beware that carvings by others imitate "Wolf," implying the idea that − unlike others − they are authentic. Staff in souvenir shops often seem unsure about whether objects are native made. For example, Denhez (1990: 33ff) reports instances where shopkeepers have falsely confirmed that items are native-made.

Uses by non-native producers of the "Inuit style"

Another challenge to current production and marketing practices concerns the use by non-native producers of artistic styles that are generally associated with aboriginal cultures. This is considered especially problematic by Denhez in the case of several lines of mass-produced carvings, including those credited to the "Wolfs," and to "Dimu," as well as a line labelled "Images of the North by Siku," all of which depict northern animals and Inuit hunting scenes in ways that are highly reminiscent of Inuit-produced soapstone carvings. The argument advanced is that these Inuit-style carvings take advantage of the popularity of genuine Inuit carvings at the same time that they undercut production by Inuit artists. While precise figures as to the economic magnitude of Inuit-style carvings are hard to obtain, Denhez (1983: 4) estimates that "at any given time the stock of Wolf products alone on Canadian retail shelves probably approaches the million dollar mark."

Palik (1985: 56) reports that Inuit artists and dealers in Inuit-produced art have been angered by the labels used by the makers of imitations: "they believe the wording on many labels, at best, takes advantage of the popularity of Inuit carvings and, at worst, leads buyers to think they are purchasing individually crafted works by Inuit artists." Denhez (1990: 93ff) also concludes that "allusions to native style may very well lead some consumers to believe that some level of native participation existed" in the making of such mass-produced carvings. Given this potential for consumer deception, Denhez concludes that such practices are illegal under several acts, including the Trade-marks Act which has the intent of preventing consumers from being misled, as well as the Business Practices Act and the Industrial Design Act.

In the case of a mass-produced object that replicates the original work of a known artist or a functional item that in some way incorporates a depiction of such a work the "moral rights" provision of the Canadian Copyright Act, enacted in 1988, may well apply. This act states that an artist's right of integrity is infringed if the work is "... to the prejudice of the honour or reputation of the author, distorted, mutilated, or otherwise modified; or used in association with a product, service, cause or institution" (as quoted in Agnew 1990: 27).

For many mass-produced items, including functional ones, however, it is not the use of a particular work of art that is at issue but rather the use of motifs or styles generally associated with aboriginal cultural forms, for example, the Northwest Coast style characteristic of mass-produced totem poles and small boxes. In some instances, manufacturers produce such commodities under license from aboriginal producers. However, these products, along with those made by native peoples, must compete with others that purport to be based on native designs but in fact are neither native made nor authorized by any aboriginal producer or cultural group (Denhez 1990: 40). As is also true of Inuit-style carvings, it is argued that any unauthorized borrowing of aboriginal motifs constitutes unfair competition. (For similar critiques regarding Australian aboriginal culture, see Anderson 1990.)

These challenges to the unauthorized uses by non-native producers of aesthetic styles associated with aboriginal cultures are part of a broader concern now being voiced by aboriginal peoples regarding what constitutes acceptable appropriation of the expressive forms of one cultural group by members of another. Accusations of unacceptable appropriation have recently been made by aboriginal critics with regard to non-native produced museum exhibits (e.g., Ames 1986, 1987; Blundell – Grant 1989; Myers 1988; MUSE 1988) and with regard to portrayals of aboriginal cultures by non-natives in fine art, film, and literature (e.g., Cardinal-Schubert 1990; Doolittle et al. 1987; Todd 1990).

Such challenges clearly indicate that natives are advancing a conception of authenticity that is very much at odds with the conception being advanced by many non-native entrepreneurs. That is to say, while many entrepreneurs of native-type souvenirs encourage broadly conceived, even playful, notions of authenticity, critics are sceptical. Too often, they argue, such practices benefit non-native entrepreneurs at the expense of aboriginal producers. To be authentic, they say, native-type objects must be produced by aboriginal peoples or replicated by others only with their consent.

In his report, Denhez (1990: 97) recommends two forms of action that would promote a conception of authenticity more in line with native interests. These recommendations are aimed at eliminating what are considered to be unfair marketing practices. The first recommendation is that the government intervene to ban labelling which, in the words of the Competition Act, leaves "a general impression conveyed which is erroneous." This form of action is considered a "purely negative disposition" and Denhez notes that manufactures might decide to put nothing at all on their products. Therefore, a second recommendation is that further action be taken to require "full disclosure" on labels so that consumers are told what their product is as well as what it is *not*. In other words, the argument is that non-native made objects carry a label indicating that they are "imitations."

To date, government agencies have not acted on calls by critics for greater regulation of Canada's souvenir trade. Few cases have been brought before the courts. In the 1960s the state did introduce so-called "igloo tags" for Inuit-produced art forms, which are meant to certify that such objects are Inuit-made. According to some critics, however, igloo tags were not introduced primarily to protect Inuit producers from imitators but to permit carvings to pass easily through American customs. Furthermore, the federally supported igloo tag program identifies Inuit-made products "but it in no way curtails misrepresentation in imitation products (except imitation of the tags themselves)" (Denhez 1990: 50). In fact, Denhez (1983: 1) suggests that promoting the igloo tag as the way to counter misleading claims on non-native made forms is "like permitting margarine producers to call their product 'butter' and Consumer and Corporate Affairs responding with a 'cow tag' campaign."[16]

Federal tourism policy

The role of the Canadian state is, in fact, a contradictory one. Through its policy of multiculturalism (and the entrenchment of aboriginal rights in the repatriated Canadian constitution) the federal government espouses equal opportunities for aboriginal peoples, including (one might reasonably conclude) rights to retain and shape their own cultural forms. At the same time, however, the state is involved in promoting Canada to foreign tourists as a culturally distinct destination because it sees this as a way to increase Canada's share of world tourism receipts and improve the nation's economy.[17] To support this strategy, government officials cite the results of market studies commissioned by the relevant federal agency, Tourism Canada. For example, a highly influential study of target markets in the United States, which is the largest source of foreign travellers to Canada, suggested that Americans will visit Canada not so much for its spectacular outdoor scenery but because it can provide them with a culturally different encounter (Tourism Canada 1986). Of late, government officials have even begun to speak of "border magic," that special experience tourists will have when they cross over into culturally different Canada (Tourism Canada n.d.: 9).

While Canada can offer neither the spectacular cultural sights of Europe nor the peasant peoples of third-world countries, according to state tourism texts it does have a rich multicultural heritage and the presence of native peoples which can be promoted for cultural tourism. Indeed, in recent state publications on tourism, multiculturalism as a formula for national unity through cultural retention and sharing has become muted in favor of multiculturalism as good for the tourist business (Blundell – Harp 1989).

In order to promote Canada as culturally distinct, Tourism Canada sponsors expensive magazine and television campaigns in the United States (and also in several overseas countries). As do others in the business of tourism, in some instances these advertisements represent aboriginal peoples as "surviving primitives" (and also certain other ethnic and rural folks as premodern) in ways designed to provoke nostalgia for an authentic cultural experience. In this way, the state itself encourages potential visitors to presume that the native is a primitive, and to mark their visits to Canada with (expected) native-style artifacts.[18]

Consider, for example, the magazine advertisement reproduced in Plate 7 which was produced for Tourism Canada and directed towards American audiences in 1988. Here the images of an Inuit soapstone carving and an Inuit girl with a child on her back along with their written captions work to signify Canada's Far North as a place where visitors can experience a timeless, primitive otherness. It is not the North's spatial remoteness that is signified here, but its remoteness in time; it is, as the

Plate 7. Tourism Canada advertisement placed in American magazines in 1988. Reproduced by permission of Tourism Canada, Industry, Science and Technology Canada.

advertisement's main caption proclaims, "A Land of Legends," not a land where an alternative culture is currently being lived.

Note that the stone carving is photographed like an object in an art museum, in isolation, decontextualized from any concrete, historically lived context. Readers are told that Inuit carvings are "age-old stories told in stone," an inscription that locates these contemporary productions in the same time-frame as Inuit myths and legends. (They, like Inuit, are of the past.) Indeed, the use of the term "stone" in the caption is not innocent, recalling as it does a "Stone Age" culture persisting from the past and the notion of a static, immutability (as in the common English expression "carved in stone"). The implication that Inuit carvings are "primitive" forms of art is of course misleading, given their contemporary nature. In fact, the production of these carvings is quite recent (post World War II) and, furthermore, their style and content have been heavily influenced by the tastes of a southern market (Graburn 1967, 1976b; Trott 1982).

A humorous and strategically placed caption in the advertisement also constructs the north as a place where tourists can (temporarily) imitate the native (that is, be authentic), when the written text "Backpacking on

Baffin Island" serves as the caption for photographs of both the Inuit girl carrying a child on her back (another decontextualized image) and the photo of tourists hiking in the mountains with their rucksacks. Note also that readers of the advertisement do not see what they as tourists will see, but they view themselves as tourists being seen, having the promised experience. Indeed, another example from this same generation of American-directed magazine advertisements also offers a native artifact to connect with the idea that tourists desire ("fancy") to walk in another person's shoes, that is (as Susan Stewart might say) to take on the capacity for otherness. This message is subtly conveyed in an advertisement for the Western Prairie provinces by a photograph of beaded moccasins and its caption "Fancy footwork."

The state also has a role in the marketing of native-style souvenirs because such forms are widely sold at duty-free shops in airports and at shops in national and provincial parks (cf. O'Farrell 1989). At some public institutions most objects offered are non-native made. This was the case for souvenirs sold at the Canadian Pavilion at Expo 86 and at other public institutions funded by the governments of New Brunswick and Ontario. This included the products at the shop at Upper Canada Village, operated by the St. Lawrence Parks Commission of the government of Ontario, which is said to be the largest retailer of arts and crafts in eastern Ontario (Denhez 1990: 32). A similar situation exists at a store near Niagara Falls managed by the Niagara Parks Commission, also part of the Government of Ontario.

> The building itself is overwhelmed by a large provincial coat of arms above the name of the Commission. The large sign at the door displays the Commission's logo, and announces "Indian Handicrafts/Eskimo Art." The contents on the shelves, however, are mostly fake [i. e. not native-produced] ... [and so] ... a purchaser could be legitimately forgiven for concluding that his purchase had a tacit, if not overt, warranty of authenticity from the public sector (Denhez 1990: 32).

Federal policies for aboriginal economic development

There are other ways in which the Canadian state acts in a contradictory manner with respect to the production of cultural forms by or about aboriginal Canadians. Consider state policies and programs that promote the production by aboriginal peoples of arts and crafts as a means of economic development. The native production of arts and crafts is one of the few economic activities encouraged by state agencies, and there is a long history in Canada of government programs designed to encourage such activities (Muehlen 1990/91; Nicks 1990). For example, this has been the case for Inuit soapstone carving in the north, where government involvement in its inception and subsequent development and promotion have often meant that other economic strategies favored by some local Inuit have not been encouraged by the Canadian state (see, e.g., Brody 1975: 104–106, 133–134; Levine 1976).

Not surprisingly, arts and crafts production is now of major economic importance to many aboriginal peoples and to many reserve economies. One government source reports that 40,000 Inuit and Indians are actively engaged in arts and crafts production (Tourism Canada 1989: 9). Denhez (1990: 41–42) reports that for several northern communities, the making of arts and crafts supplements the income of over fifty percent of the adult population and that in view of the activities of the international anti-fur lobby (Wenzel 1991) Denhez expects the importance of the arts and crafts industry in local economies will grow.[19]

Given government support of aboriginal arts and crafts production as an economic strategy, it is surely anomalous that the government has failed to enforce existing laws or support additional labelling legislation that would improve the ability of native producers to compete with non-natives, particularly with the makers of the mass-produced native-style souvenirs that have been the focus of this paper.[20] This is no small matter for aboriginal producers, since the souvenir trade in Canada constitutes a multi-million dollar business annually (although precise figures are hard to obtain).[21] Indeed, the government seems reluctant to fund research that would outline strategies for remedial measures to correct inequities in marketing practices (e.g., how to encourage less ambiguous labels) as well as studies that would provide more precise information regarding the economic dimensions of the souvenir trade in Canada, including the extent to which mass-produced non-native made items encroach on those of native producers.

> Over a two year period, the national Indian Arts and Crafts Corporation (with the support of Arctic Cooperatives Limited, the Professional Art Dealers Association of Canada, and Canadian artists representation) requested funding from the federal government's Native Economic Development Programme to research this issue. After numerous postponements, the request was ultimately declined (Denhez 1990: 4).

The disparate views of federal agencies

Indeed, when it comes to issues regarding cultural expression by or about aboriginal Canadians, different federal agencies seem to work at cross purposes. For example, despite the reluctance of the Department of Indian Affairs and Northern Development (DIAND) to fund research regarding the extent of aboriginal arts and crafts production, Denhez (1990: 49) reports that DIAND has generally been "broadly supportive of stricter controls of labelling and more intervention pertinent to fakes" [i. e., non-native produced commodities]. Denhez (1990: 59) further reports that DIAND's response to his 1983 report was that "government intervention against native fakelore was desirable." However, in the mid-1980s the Department of Consumer and Corporate Affairs took a very different position, responding "... that governmental intervention on behalf of native arts and crafts was a phenomenon to be seen in Third World countries, and that intervention presupposed a preoccupation with 'ethnicity' which bordered on the repugnant" (Denhez 1990: 59).

Paradoxically, this view was being advanced by Consumer and Corporate Affairs at the same time that another government agency, Tourism Canada, was more than willing to promote "ethnicity" in order to increase Canada's tourism revenues. For instance, in a document titled "The Challenges in Tourism Product Development" (prepared by Tourism Canada for presentation to the 1988 annual meeting between federal and provincial/territorial tourism officials) it is argued that "Canada has a rich native and multicultural heritage ... with great appeal to domestic and international visitors," which is not being adequately "highlighted or showcased" for potential tourists (Tourism Canada 1988b: 24–25).

Conclusions

Entrepreneurs tap into widely held ideas about aboriginal peoples and about travel in order to make objects attractive to tourists. They consequently advance a contentious discourse regarding what constitutes an authentic souvenir of Canada. In advancing their own versions of authenticity, entrepreneurs both perpetuate mystifying ideas about travel and remove aboriginal cultural expressions from aboriginal control, treating them as national resources to be borrowed at will. As aboriginal

peoples themselves protest, the result is that their own cultural productions are frequently devalued, both economically and symbolically, for
the profit of non-native others. Paradoxically, while the state promotes
aboriginal cultural expression as a component of its tourism and economic
development policies, it does little to protect aboriginal producers from
what must be considered unfair types of competition.

The signifying practices now employed to produce and market native-
type souvenirs of Canada therefore work to seal aboriginal peoples into
existing relations of dependence (cf. Johnson 1986/87: 52). They work
against the economic interests of aboriginal producers at the same time
that they convey damaging meanings about them. Indeed, they rework,
yet again, the idea that aboriginal peoples belong properly in the past
along with the other heritage forms of the nation, an idea that does not
promote the equal and active involvement of aboriginal Canadians in
political processes that affect their own contemporary lives.

However, tourists are not necessarily passive consumers of such promoted meanings. Consequently, ongoing scholarly research can determine
the conditions under which such meanings are, or are not, read. As
practitioners of semiotics, we can thus act as the accomplices of tourists
and of aboriginal Canadians by identifying points of possible transformation and resistance in the souvenir trade. Objects now offered are not
likely to provoke critiques by tourists of damaging misconceptions about
aboriginal peoples.

Now it can be argued that aboriginal producers themselves sometimes
cater to tourists' expectations; in fact many protest that their productions
are difficult to sell if they do not do so. But it is also the case that when
aboriginal producers represent themselves they often challenge the views
of others, for example through irony and parody.[22] And they make objects
that more accurately reflect the lived conditions of their contemporary
lives, as is the case with the postcard shown in Plate 3 (on the right)
which was produced in the north with input from locally resident Inuit
people.[23] This postcard depicts two Inuit girls in their own everydayness.
But this particular object is not widely sold in the souvenir shops of
Canada.

To the extent that the souvenir business is a closed shop as far as
aboriginal producers are concerned, tourists who visit souvenir stands
will not see representations of aboriginal Canadians as they actually live
today. Instead, confronted with Indian dolls dressed in buckskin or
replicas of totem poles and tomahawks, they will find little that is
unexpected, and so their own preconceptions will not be challenged.

Some tourists will visit museums and art galleries where native-produced objects are exhibited or marketed, and in this way they may gain
some sense of the world as aboriginal Canadians experience it. And a
few adventurous travellers may even visit aboriginal peoples in the settings
of their own everyday life, although few tourists stop at aboriginal
reserves. But I suspect that many visitors to Canada experience Indians
and Inuit entirely through the imaged and imaginary forms of mass
culture, including those they encounter in souvenir shops. When these
are the primary ways in which tourists encounter aboriginal peoples, they
will no doubt remain alienated from the true meanings of what they see
(cf. MacCannell 1989: 68). Indeed, through their purchases — playful as
they may be — they will facilitate current inequities between aboriginal
and non-aboriginal peoples in Canada. But these consequences are hidden
from tourists by mystifying ideas about aboriginal peoples and about
travel that locate authenticity outside their own everyday lives back home.

Notes

1. This paper, presented in an earlier version at the international conference on
   the Socio-semiotics of Objects: The Role of Artifacts in Social Symbolic
   Processes, at the University of Toronto, is one result of research within
   Carleton University's Centre for Research on Culture and Society. I am
   indebted to John Harp, Michèle Kérisit, Laurence Grant, Sheila Young Evans,
   and Simon Brascoupe for their contributions to our unit's ongoing work on
   tourism. My thanks also to my students at Carleton for collecting information
   about tourist souvenirs, in particular David Macaulay, Les Voakes, Kay
   Whitton, and Franca Boag.
2. Cf. Mathieson and Wall (1982: 169) who argue that "... most tourist purchases are not stimulated by a genuine interest in the host culture, but are
   acquired as a memento of the visit and as a sign to peers of the extent of the
   buyer's travel experience."
3. In Canada the vast majority of these mass-produced native-type souvenirs
   retail for under $30.00 Canadian.
4. Johnson (1986/1987: 67) notes: "context determines meanings ... as much as
   the form itself..." Therefore, one can compare typical native-style souvenirs
   sold in souvenir shops with those in specialty shops where one finds similar
   commodities, but without the same degree of emphasis on their Canadianness,
   nor are they offered within a single category as Indian or Eskimo/Inuit
   objects.
5. The *Ottawa Citizen* (May 27, 1990) reported that souvenir-seeking tourists
   to the nation's capital prefer a keepsake with "Canada" or "Ottawa" written

on it. Interviews by me and my students of salespeople confirm this view (cf. Brennan 1988).

6. I use the terms "to mark" and "marker" as does MacCannell (1989: 41) who defines a tourist attraction as "an empirical relationship between a *tourist*, a *sight* and a *marker* (a piece of information about a sight). ... Markers may take many different forms: guidebooks, informational tablets, slide shows, travelogues, souvenir matchbooks, etc."

7. Along with Gottdiener (1986: 991), I draw here upon Eco (1976: 27) who distinguished five separate ways in which any object can be considered, viz. "(a) physically, as a material object; (b) mechanically, as an instrument or tool that performs a function, that is, possesses use value; (c) economically, as possessing exchange value; (d) socially, as a sign of some status, and (e) semantically, as a cultural unit that can enter into relationships with other cultural units in a discourse..." The focus in this chapter is on the semantic approach and on how native-type souvenirs enter into various discourses, including those about travel.

8. Numerous studies have shown that such beliefs are widespread in the West (e.g., Bataille − Silet 1980; Berkhofer 1978; Chamberlin 1975; Cooke 1984; Hirschfelder 1982; Price 1978; Stedman 1982).

9. While aboriginal peoples are romanticized as "noble savages," they are also thought to be a "dying race," with a deficient culture that must inevitably fall before that of the West. Berkhofer (1978) argued that these views reflect contradictory ideas in the West about the essence of human nature and of civilized society itself (cf. White 1978). Nonetheless, such opinions distort both the past and current conditions of aboriginal life. They are persistently reproduced in a range of textual forms which direct audiences in western countries toward these privileged meanings. For example, whether inscribed as noble or ignoble, aboriginal peoples are persistently represented through time-distancing practices that construct them as "primitives" or "traditionals," as people who belong to another time and are anachronistic in the contemporary world (Blundell 1989b).

10. MacCannell (1989: 3) continues: "... the concern of moderns for 'naturalness,' their nostalgia and their search for authenticity are not merely casual and somewhat decadent, though harmless, attachments to the souvenirs of destroyed cultures and dead epochs. They are also components of the conquering spirit of modernity − the grounds of its unifying consciousness." He does not label this emergent consciousness as postmodern, but assumes that the postmodernism of critical theorists is in itself an aspect of a globalizing modernism. For MacCannell (1989: xi), those forms often referred to as postmodern "... are more a repression and denial necessary to the dirty work of modernity so it can continue to elaborate its forms while seeming to have passed out of existence or to have changed into something 'new' and 'different.'" The similarity between tourism and a postmodern outlook is also

noted: "... the need to be postmodern can thus be read as the same as the desire to be a tourist: both seek to empower modern culture and its conscience by neutralizing everything that might destroy it from within" (MacCannell 1989: xiii).

11. In 1989 the first International Conference on Cultural Tourism was held in Miami, Florida. One conference participant, Lars-Eric Lindblad, president of Lindblad Travel which is said to be one of the pioneers in culture-related tourism, articulated one view of the economic significance of native cultural expressions, arguing that cultural tourism can help preserve a country's cultural heritage, but "for those who are less interested in culture than in the so-called bottom line... I would like to say that there is money in those ruins. There is money in those crazy costumes that natives wear and the songs and music that is being performed" (as quoted in *Travel Weekly*, May 18, 1989: 16).

12. Native-type forms can be considered semantically as units in discourses on cultural tourism and also in discourses about an individual's personal travel experiences. Stewart (1984: 136) notes that the souvenir can never stand alone, but enters into the personal discourse of its possessor: "It will not function without the supplementary narrative discourse that both attaches to its origins and creates a myth with regard to those origins."

13. Cf. the discussion in Mathieson and Wall (1982: 169) who consider the "misrepresentation" of the age or authenticity of objects to be a common effect of production for tourists.

14. Reported by Kay Whitton.

15. The term "Eskimo" rather than "Inuit" for the aboriginal peoples of the Far North is more common outside Canada, especially in the United States.

16. People who market hand-made Inuit crafts are now using their own labels. Various aboriginal producers have also devised labels to assert their claim that objects are genuine because they are native-made. One could argue, however, that the proliferation of labels confuses buyers by creating the impression that all labels attached to objects by or about aboriginal people are somehow authenticating.

17. Tourism is of major importance to the Canadian economy. It accounts for some 600,000 direct jobs, 60,000 business firms depend on tourists, and the industry is Canada's third highest foreign exchange earner (after motor vehicles and automobile parts). Foreign visitors spend over $6 billion annually. Domestic travellers add another $15.5 billion (Tourism Canada 1988a: 7−8). However, more money leaves Canada through tourism than enters the country, resulting in annual travel deficits which reached $3.5 billion Canadian in 1989 (Tourism Canada 1990: 8).

18. Recent policies go further promoting as well representations of natives as actual tourist attractions, for example museum exhibits or reconstructed heritage sites. But here again, what is being promoted is not some experience

of aboriginal life as it is lived today, but the idea that natives preserve the past, that authenticity resides in this surviving past-in-the-present, and that tourists can access it.

19. Arts and crafts production is also important to aboriginal peoples because "it can be carried out even in the most isolated communities, using traditional skills which are to be found in countless native communities. Furthermore, the materials tend to be community-based: native clothing, for example, often relies upon the hunting and trapping industry" (Denhez 1990: 41).

20. Denhez (1990) provides a chronology of the federal government's failure to respond to repeated calls for such enforcement.

21. Denhez (personal communication) estimates that native type items made by non-native producers generate between four and sixteen million dollars annually in Canada (see also O'Farrell 1989).

22. I have made this case elsewhere regarding the contemporary powwow (1985/ 86, 1989a) as does Ryan (1989) regarding contemporary native-produced artifacts.

23. The photograph used on this postcard and others in this series were taken by Nick Newbery, a local non-Inuit school teacher living in the North, and selected by the staff of the Nortext Publishing company in Iqaluit which includes Inuit individuals (as reported by Michael Roberts, an owner of Nortext).

References

Agnew, Ella M.
  1990   "Who owns what? A lawyer interprets the new Canadian Copyright Act for artists, collectors, and galleries," *Inuit Art Quarterly* 5(2): 24–29.
Albers, Patricia C. – William R. James
  1988   "Travel photography: A methodological approach," *Annals of Tourism Research* 15: 134–158.
Ames, Michael
  1986   *Museums, the public and anthropology: A study in the anthropology of anthropology*. Vancouver: University of British Columbia Press.
  1987   "Free Indians from their ethnological fate," *Muse* V(2): 14–19.
Anderson, Peter
  1990   "Aboriginal imagery: Influences, appropriation, theft?" *Eyeline*, 12 (winter): 8–11.
Appadurai, Arjun
  1986a   "Introduction: Commodities and the politics of value," in: Arjun Appadurai (ed.), 3–63.

Appadurai, Arjun (ed.)
1986b   *The social life of things: Commodities in cultural perspective.* Cambridge: Cambridge University Press.
Bataille, Gretchen M − Charles L. P. Silet (eds.)
1980   *The pretend Indians: Images of native Americans in the movies.* Ames: Iowa State University Press.
Berger, Thomas R.
1979   "Native rights in the new world: A glance at history." Ottawa, Ontario: *National Museum of Man Mercury Series,* No. 78.
Berkhofer, Robert F., Jr.
1978   *The white man's Indian: Images of American Indians from Columbus to the present.* New York: Vintage Books.
Blundell, Valda
1985/86   "Une approche sémiologique du powwow canadien contemporain," *Researches amérindiennes au Québec* XV(4): 53 − 66.
1989a   "The tourist and the native," in Bruce Cox et al. (eds.), 49 − 58.
1989b   "Speaking the art of Canada's native peoples: Anthropological discourse and the media," *Australian-Canadian Studies* 7(1 − 2): 23 − 43.
Blundell, Valda − Laurence Grant
1989   "Preserving our heritage: Getting beyond boycotts and demonstrations," *Inuit Art Quarterly* 4(1): 12 − 16.
Blundell, Valda − John Harp
1989   "The new Canadian Museum of Civilization: Tapping the Disney World approach to success," *Inuit Art Quarterly* 4(3): 38 − 39.
Brennan, Pat
1988   "Tourists are willing to spend big bucks on today's souvenirs," *Toronto Star,* February 15.
Brody, Hugh
1975   *The peoples' land: Whites and the eastern Arctic.* Markham, Ontario: Penguin Books.
Cardinal-Schubert, Joane
1990   "In the red," *Artscraft,* Spring: 4 − 11.
Chamberlin, J. Edward
1975   *The harrowing of eden: White attitudes toward North American natives.* Toronto: Fitzhenry and Whiteside.
Cohen, Erik
1988   "Authenticity and commoditization in tourism," *Annals of Tourism Research* 15: 371 − 386.
Cooke, Katie
1984   *Images of Indians held by non-Indians: A review of current Canadian research.* Ottawa: Research Branch, Indian and Northern Affairs Canada.

Cox, Bruce — Jacques Chevalier — Valda Blundell (eds.)
1989   *A different drummer: Readings in anthropology with a Canadian perspective.* Ottawa: Carleton University Anthropology Caucus and Carleton University Press.
Culler, Jonathan
1981   "Semiotics of tourism," *American Journal of Semiotics* 1(1–2): 117–140.
Denhez, Marc (B. C. L)
1983   "Regulation of fake Inuit art: Some legislative options in the light of international developments." MS.
1990   "The labelling of imitation native art: Proposal for notification and enforcement of existing legislation." MS.
Desjarlais, Dwayne
1987   "Native crafts or crap?" *Windspeaker,* 12 (June): 31.
Doolittle, Lisa — Heather Elton — Mary-Beth Laviolette
1987   "Appropriation: When does borrowing become stealing?" *Last Issue* 5(l): 20–33.
Eco, Umberto
1976   *A theory of semiotics.* Bloomington: Indiana University Press.
Gottdiener, Mark
1985   "Hegemony and mass culture: A semiotic approach," *American Journal of Sociology* 90(5): 979–1001.
Graburn, Nelson
1967   "The Eskimos and 'airport art,'" *Transaction,* October: 28–33.
1976a   "Introduction: Arts of the fourth world," in: Nelson Graburn (ed.), 1–32.
1976b   "Eskimo art: The eastern Canadian Arctic," in: Nelson Graburn (ed.), 39–55.
1986   "Inuit art and Canadian nationalism: Why Eskimos? Why Canada?," *Inuit Art Quarterly* 2(3): 5–7.
Graburn, Nelson (ed.)
1976   *Ethnic and tourist arts: Cultural expression from the fourth world.* Berkeley: University of California Press.
Hewison, Robert
1987   *The heritage industry: Britain in a climate of decline.* London: Methuen.
Hirschfelder, Arlene
1982   *American Indian stereotypes in the world of culture: A reader and bibliography.* Metuchen, NJ: Scarecrow Press.
Johnson, Richard
1986   "The story so far: And further transformations?," in David Punter (ed.), 277–313.
1986/87 "What is cultural studies anyway?" *Social text: Theory/culture/ideology* 16: 38–80.

Levine, Les
1976   "We are still alive," *May Day* 2: 9–19. Vancouver.
Macaulay, David
1989   "The representation of Canadian native peoples and their cultures in souvenirs and tourist art." Ottawa: Carleton University. Department of Sociology and Anthropology. MS.
Mathieson, Alister — Geoffrey Wall
1982   *Tourism: Economic, physical, and social impacts.* New York: John Wiley and Sons.
MacCannell, Dean
1984   "Reconstructed ethnicity: Tourism and cultural identity in third world communities," *Annals of Tourism Research* 11: 375–391.
1989   *The tourist: A new theory of the leisure class.* New York: Schocken Books.
McDougal, Gina
1988   "Native craft imitators — beware," *Windspeaker*, July 22: 25.
McKay, Ian
1988   "Twilight at Peggy's Cove: Towards a genealogy of maritimicity in Nova Scotia," *Borderlines* 12: 28–37.
Muehlen, Maria
1990/91 "Government activity in Inuit arts and crafts," *Inuit Art World* (special issue of *Inuit Art Quarterly*) 5(4): 38–42.
Myers, Marybelle
1988   "The Glenbow affair," *Inuit Art Quarterly* 3(l): 12–16.
Nicks, Trudy
1990   "Marketing of an image," *Artscraft* 2(3): 4–8.
O'Farrell, Elaine
1989   "Imitators harm artisans," *Windspeaker*, February 17: 12.
Overton, James
1980   "Promoting'the real Newfoundland:' Culture as tourist commodity," *Studies in Political Economy* 4: 115–137.
Palik, Betty
1985   "Inuit carvings: Do you know the real thing?," *Protect Yourself*, December: 55–59.
Price, John
1978   *Native studies: American and Canadian Indians.* Toronto: McGraw-Hill Ryerson.
Punter, David (ed.)
1986   *Introduction to contemporary cultural studies.* London: Longman.
Ryan, Allan J.
1989   "Indian art: How ironic!" Paper presented at the annual meetings of the Canadian Anthropology Society, Ottawa.
Shanks, David
N. D.   "Marketing strategy." National Indian Arts and Crafts Corporation. MS.

Stedman, Raymond William
1982 *Shadows of the Indian: Stereotypes in American culture.* Norman: University of Oklahoma Press.

Stewart, Susan
1984 *On longing: Narratives of the miniature, the gigantic, the souvenir, the collection.* Baltimore, MD: Johns Hopkins University Press.

Taylor, Ian
1989 "A private game: Canadian heritage professionals and the protection of archaeological and cultural property," *Australian-Canadian Studies* 7(1–2): 5–21.

Todd, Loretta
1990 "Notes on appropriation," *Parallelogramme* 16(1): 24–33.

Tourism Canada
1986 *U. S. pleasure travel market: Canadian potential.* Main report. Ottawa, Ontario.
1988a *Canadian tourism facts.* Ottawa, Ontario.
1988b *The challenges of tourism product development.* Ottawa, Ontario.
1989 *Native tourism products.* Draft. Products and Services Division. Ottawa, Ontario.
1990 *Tourism on the threshold.* Industry, Science and Technology Canada. Ottawa, Ontario.
N. D. *Changing opinions: The marketing of "Canada, the world next door."* Industry, Science and Technology Canada. Ottawa, Ontario.

Trott, Christopher
1982 "The semiotics of Inuit sculpture: Art and *Sananguat*," *Recherches Sémiotiques/Semiotic Inquiry* 2(4): 336–359.

Uzzell, David
1984 "An alternative structuralist approach to the psychology of tourism marketing," *Annals of Tourism Research* 11: 79–99.

Van Dusen, Julie
1983 "The war on fake carvings," *Maclean's*, May 16: 47.

Vestergaard, Torben – Kim Schroder
1985 *The language of advertising.* New York, Basil Blackwell.

Wenzel, George
1991 *Animal rights, human rights: Ecology, economy and ideology in the Canadian Arctic.* Toronto: University of Toronto Press.

White, Hayden
1978 *Tropics of discourse: Essays in cultural criticism.* Baltimore: The Johns Hopkins University Press.

Williams, Raymond
1973 *The country and the city.* London: Granada Publishing.

Williamson, Judith
    1978   *Decoding advertisements: Ideology and meaning in advertising.* London: Marion Boyars.
Wolff, Janet
    1981   *The social production of art.* London: Macmillan.

Objects, texts, and practices:
The refrigerator in consumer discourses between the wars

Peter R. Grahame

Objects in a consumer society

Commentators agree that life in a consumer society is marked by an abundance, even a surfeit, of objects.[1] Yet there seems to be little agreement concerning how to approach these objects analytically. What do they mean? Are they vehicles of domination (Horkheimer — Adorno 1972) or resources for resistance (Hall 1976; Fiske 1989)? In spite of surface disagreements, diverse investigations have employed a common strategy: a range of objects is examined in order to show how they signify an underlying pattern of meaning. For example, an assortment of household appliances may be viewed as: (a) components of a "standard package" of middle class possessions (Riesman 1964), (b) technologies which have failed to liberate women from domestic drudgery (Cowan 1983), or (c) quasi-religious icons of modernity (Marchand 1985). This approach, which foregrounds the unifying significance assigned to the assortment, carries with it the risk that each specific object becomes one-dimensional, simply one in a succession of elements within a larger commentary. In this way, each appliance is profiled solely with regard to how it illustrates a pattern which has been pre-selected in the light of some broader purpose.[2] I suggest that in so far as the treatment of ordinary objects in consumer culture has taken this form, the analyses produced have been opportunistic in character. When objects are assembled into lists, assortments, or collections to document a pattern, the constitution of each object within a specific complex of texts and practices tends to be downplayed or neglected. In this paper, I propose to adopt an alternative strategy which directs attention to how a single appliance — the refrigerator — emerged within a discursive complex linking objects, texts, and practices.

My initial reason for examining the refrigerator was simply that it came to my attention as one product which received substantial attention in consumer-oriented publications of the 1920s and 1930s, a key period in the formation of what is now called the "consumer culture" (Grahame 1989). In treating the refrigerator as a discursive object, I plan to ask what presence it had in some of the popular literature of the period, and what manner of persistence it had within the broader discourse. Was the refrigerator a simple entity, a unitary "thing," or was it complex both in its imagery and its material underpinnings? I consider several discourses that were made available to sectors of the public who might acquire refrigerators, including both advertisements and articles in women's magazines, as well as product test reports in key consumer movement publications during the interwar years.

Proceeding in this way, I ask not what was *the* meaning of the refrigerator, but rather what understandings were textually supported during this period? To anticipate: what we consider here is not just the introduction of the refrigerator, but the transition to refrigerator-based provisioning, culinary, and dining practices. And this transition is, in certain ways, textually organized on a variety of fronts.

Texts and social organization

The larger aim of the present study is to develop an approach to analyzing consumer culture which does not simply indulge in cultural criticism (i. e., evaluative commentary). The approach which I take focuses on the social organization of knowledge in everyday life, with particular attention to how practical knowledge is mediated through talk and text (Garfinkel 1967; Giddens 1987; Grahame 1991; Smith 1984; Woolgar 1988). This approach as I understand it avoids two pitfalls: (1) treating the text as an epiphenomenon, and (2) treating the text (and more generally, language) as the privileged model for this analysis of other phenomena.

Mechling (1975) in his paper "Advice to Historians on Advice to Mothers" warns against confusing published advice to women with women's actual behavior during a given period: what was recommended was not necessarily what was done. The author recommends treating advice manuals as objects of study in their own right, but then focuses narrowly on the social conditions of their production and use (social class as determinant). The result is a refined version of the initial impulse: treat the text as an index of behavior. In effect, the analyst must "get behind" the text to find out what is going on.

In *More Work for Mother*, Cowan (1983) examines the production history of the mechanical refrigerator in order to show that the dominance of the electric compressor version since the 1920s owes more to market manipulation than to superior technical design. This arbitrary triumph underscores her larger claim that the proliferation of domestic appliances involved a false claim of liberation under the guise of efficiency. As interesting as this revelation is, analytically it amounts to a strategy for reading around the texts rather than an examination of the discourses which surrounded the introduction of the mechanical refrigerator.

The view taken here is that the analysis of textual phenomena should not be made to depend on an invidious contrast with "actual behavior," face-to-face interaction, what is "beyond the text," etc. The textual order is to be treated as an organized phenomenon in its own right, a specific ordering of the social world. For example, one may ask, what kinds of active readings does the text support, in terms of the resources which it provides or invokes? What kinds of practical knowledge are taken for granted, and what kinds must be assembled via the text?

Investigating the social organizational dimensions of discourse is not just a question of extracting the rules which govern meanings. The approach of Marchand in his characterization of the refrigerator tableau in advertising seems too limiting. Consider the following:

> Within a single decade, beginning about 1920, one visual image became familiar to nearly all Americans through the efforts of advertising alone. This was the tableau of the small group clustered reverentially around the open door of the new refrigerator. In their symbolic power and their zeal to inspire reverence in the viewer, the cliched refrigerator tableaux generated a pattern of secular iconography (Marchand 1985: 269).

> Convention dictated that in such tableaux no adult except the salesman could gaze in a direction other than at the icon itself. Convention also prohibited a husband from appearing in the company of a refrigerator without the presence of his wife (Marchand 1985: 271).

Even a limited examination of refrigerator advertisements during the 1920s will show that Marchand's claims hold only for a subset of advertisements. It is not hard to find advertisements with husband present, wife absent, or with other adults turning their gaze from "the icon," while still other advertisements show only the appliance itself.[3] The idea of the refrigerator as a secular icon tends too much towards an approach which diverts attention towards a favored model of language while giving insufficient attention to the social embededness of discursive practices. Carrying the impulse further, one may want to say that the refrigerator is a "signifying element" in the "language of modernity." In a similar vein, another writer has proposed that we can treat shopping malls and beaches as texts (Fiske 1989). Yet the result is more metaphor than analysis, since it extends the notion of text to include anything that can be subjected to decoding practices. The text should be seen as part of the social world, rather than elevated as a model or stand-in for that world (world as "text").

Socio-semiotics is sometimes conceived as a field of analysis which investigates relations between two orders, the linguistic and the social.[4] The text (linguistic order) signifies family life, capitalist society, etc. (social order) while remaining somehow distinct from them. In my view, this conception splits apart the very phenomenon whose workings await discovery. I follow Smith (1984, 1990) in striving to treat texts as *constituents* of social organization. The study of advertisements, consumer advice, and so on, involves the examination of specific forms of textually-mediated social organization. Such texts are not just "about" the world, they are active ingredients of it.

Introducing the mechanical refrigerator

In this section I propose to explore the diversity one encounters when examining the popular discourse of refrigeration which appeared during roughly the mid-1920s to mid-1930s. In particular, I will examine three sectors of this discourse: (a) advertisements in women's magazines, (b) articles in women's magazines, and (c) product test reports in consumer product testing magazines. In particular, advertisements and articles appearing in the same magazine, *Good Housekeeping*, will be examined, while product test reports from two magazines, *Consumers' Research Bulletin* and *Consumers Union Reports* will be considered.[5] Obviously what appears in these materials does not encompass the whole discourse of refrigeration during this period, but it can be viewed as a useful place to begin for at least two reasons. First, these sectors of the discourse include the promotion, explanation, and criticism of mechanical refrigeration as these were presented to popular audiences. Second, it is reasonable to suppose that at least some consumers were practically acquainted with all three sectors since, as an editorial in *Consumers Union Reports* pointed out, some of their readers also read *Good Housekeeping*. (See note five.)

Advertisements

Advertisements appearing in *Good Housekeeping* between the mid-1920s and mid-1930s show significant variations in how they depict the refrigerator as an object of knowledge and desire. The remarks which follow are based on a close examination of advertisements for three brands which were promoted regularly in the pages of *Good Housekeeping*: Kelvinator and Frigidaire advertisements, which show many similarities, and General Electric advertisements, which are distinct from both of the former in some key respects.

During the early part of this period (chiefly between 1924 and 1926), Kelvinator and Frigidaire advertisements dramatized the benefits of electric refrigeration and emphasized its difference from the conventional iced refrigerator (or "ice box").[6] Both brands placed emphasis on the power of electric refrigeration to transform foods and make possible the introduction of new kinds of food. Frigidaire advertisements explained that chilled foods became more appetizing, while Kelvinator copy went further and proclaimed the advantages of "Kelvinated" foods:

> Kelvinated foods just fairly coax midsummer appetites. Taken from the cold frosty air of a Kelvinator-chilled refrigerator they are irresistible.
> Think of sliced oranges, served ice-cold; — of cantaloupe or grapefruit; chilled through and through; or of home-canned fruits, served cold in their rich juices. Think of the cream for your cereals cold and refreshing (*Good Housekeeping* 9/25: 114).

The novelty of an abundance of chilled foods was paramount. Another Kelvinator advertisement linked this novelty with entertaining:

> Kelvinator Electric Refrigeration will help you make *your* parties events to be remembered. Kelvinated foods are unusual.
> Think of being able to serve dainty *chilled* salads instead of ordinary ones. Think of cooling your beverages with cubes of sparkling *colored ice* rather than plain cracked ice. Imagine sherbets, frappes and other frozen delicacies, prepared without ice (*Good Housekeeping* 10/25: 317).

Indeed, ice cubes and frozen desserts were invariably mentioned in Frigidaire and Kelvinator advertisements as benefits of owning a mechanical refrigerator.

While receiving prominent mention in their own right, these references to special foods form part of a larger picture: the early advertisements for Kelvinator and Frigidaire focused on the ways in which mechanical refrigeration differed from reliance on ice. Both brands repeatedly cited the inconvenience of relying on an ice supply which required continuous replenishment. For example, an early Kelvinator advertisement could remind the reader that in many localities, ice delivery was unavailable on Sunday: "After a summer Sunday − when Monday morning dawns sunny and hot − what do you find in your refrigerator to *tempt* breakfast appetites?" The owner of a Kelvinator could "*Start the Week Smiling with a Refreshing Breakfast of* KELVINATED FOODS." Since Kelvinator provides refrigeration which is "just as frosty and cold after a week-end as at any other time," the user is freed from worry about "ice melting over Sunday" (*Good Housekeeping* 9/2: 114). During the mid-1920s, a recurrent theme of advertisements for both brands was that ice delivery was inconvenient and uncertain.

Even more prominent, however, was the idea that electric refrigeration produced a chilling effect which was qualitatively and quantitatively different from that achieved through using ice. An early Frigidaire advertisement showed a hand wielding a refrigerating unit as if it were an ice block, with the legend, "Put this in your Refrigerator instead of Ice" (*Good Housekeeping* 9/24: 184), and at the end of this phrase a Kelvinator advertisement still challenged, "Make Ice − don't melt it!" (*Good Housekeeping* 7/27: 151). Frigidaire advertisements repeated that its frost coil was colder than ice, and kept foods colder. Kelvinator advertisements presented a more embellished version of the same claim, proclaiming a "wonder-working Zone of Kelvination" between 40 degrees and 50 degrees (*Good Housekeeping* 12/24: 208). The ability to maintain a temperature below 50 degrees Fahrenheit was, in fact, a standard which was frequently cited in discussions of refrigeration, and it was associated with the view that what counted as correct refrigeration could be specified scientifically and ruled upon by authorities (a point discussed further below). In addition to referring to science, experts, and authorities (this tendency was especially strong in Kelvinator advertisements), advertisements for both brands announced the ability of their units to produce a "uniform" and "dry" cold. The qualities touted in these early advertisements − being colder, more uniform, and drier − implied a common axis of comparison: electric refrigeration was something whose desirability was to be demonstrated by contrasting it with iced refrigeration. In a similar way, many of these same advertisements emphasized foods (frozen desserts and salads, ice cubes) which could not be produced in the iced refrigerator since their preparation depended on the ability to generate below-freezing temperatures.

As if to underscore the idea that the commodity being introduced during this period was not the refrigerator per se, but rather electric refrigeration, Kelvinator and Frigidaire advertisements repeatedly proposed that their refrigeration units could be installed in the refrigerator cabinet which the reader already possessed. As the early Frigidaire advertisement cited above put it, "Put this [the frost coil] in your Refrigerator instead of ice." A Kelvinator advertisement proclaimed "FITS your REFRIGERATOR. You needn't buy a new one to enjoy Kelvinator" (*Good Housekeeping* 12/26: 151). Another Frigidaire advertisement explained, "Your present ice-box can be converted into a Frigidaire electric refrigerator" (*Good Housekeeping* 10/25: 121). Details of the conversion process were not generally provided, but early Frigidaire advertisements showed that the frost coil would be placed in the refrigerator's ice compartment, while the compressor mechanism would be located in the basement below the refrigerator. The availability of suitable basement space was thus presupposed. To be sure, Kelvinator and Frigidaire units could be bought installed in their own brand-name cabinets, yet from 1924 through 1926, the offer to install the refrigerating mechanism in the buyer's present fridge was a recurrent feature of advertisements for these brands. Note that in these advertisements the emphasis is on a new technology rather than a wholly new kind of appliance. They celebrated a new type of equipment which could go to work in a variety of cabinet designs; thus the new technology was not at this point completely severed either symbolically or materially from the older iced refrigerator.

Against this background, General Electric advertisements which began to appear in 1927 represented a significant departure. They announced the creation of a "simpler and different electric refrigerator" (*Good Housekeeping* 7/27: 113). These advertisements emphasized the unique design of the General Electric while dispensing, in most cases, with any account of the general benefits of electric refrigeration. The General Electric design included several elements which could be demonstrated vividly. Readers could be invited to "do their own investigating" of this fridge, since certain aspects of its design were readily observable. The most prominent element was the placement of a sealed compressor mechanism on top of the cabinet (it was later dubbed the "Monitor Top"). The cabinet (which appeared to be metal-clad) was mounted on legs, a fact which offered both practical convenience and potent symbolism, since it afforded the reader an opportunity to make a significant discovery:

> Look under the cabinet. With the General Electric Refrigerator you'll notice at once that all the models are up-on-legs. This makes it easy to clean under them. But, more important, it means that *all* the machinery is safely sealed away in the air-tight steel casing which you see on top of the cabinet (*Good Housekeeping* 6/28: 133).

The distinct monitor top and legs helped to indicate that this fridge was to be contrasted with other mechanical refrigerators, not with the old-fashioned ice type. Introductory advertisements included the observation that this new, simpler kind of refrigerator could be located anywhere, since installing it was simply a matter of plugging it into an electrical outlet. While a 1927 advertisement explicitly stated that no part of the mechanism was below the box or in the basement, the same point was suggested more subtly in the 1928 advertisement which invited the reader to "look under the cabinet." A further innovation was the introduction in 1929 of the all-steel cabinet (by contrast, the Frigidaire models depicted in 1925 advertisements quite evidently featured wooden cabinets which resembled the older iced refrigerators). The point to be emphasized here is that the General Electric design involved elements which were *demonstrably* different (their comparative effectiveness was another issue). This permitted a kind of advertising copy which focused on uniqueness of design as a reason to buy, and which suggested that the reader was competent to judge the design elements which were so distinctively displayed.

These design-centered General Electric advertisements differed from the early Kelvinator and Frigidaire advertisements in other ways. They made no reference to iced refrigeration: there were no comments about the inconvenience and uncertainty of ice delivery, and no claims about the colder temperatures achieved. Nor were there any references to special foods such as iced desserts, ice cubes, and chilled salads.[7] These advertisements treated electric refrigeration as an established amenity which no longer needed to be introduced; it was no longer necessary to dramatize the special benefits of a new kind of cold. The focus, instead, was on the General Electric as a distinctive appliance resulting from "fifteen years of intensive research" (*Good Housekeeping* 7/27: 113). The notion of installing a refrigeration unit in a separately acquired cabinet was completely absent; cabinet and unit now appeared *only* as an integrated appliance.

During this second phase of electric refrigerator advertising (roughly 1927 to 1930), Kelvinator and Frigidaire advertisements began to place more emphasis on the refrigerator as an appliance with an integrated design, but they continued to stress the transformation of foods as a reason for acquiring an electric refrigerator. By 1930, all references to iced refrigeration had disappeared, and the electric refrigerator appeared only in the form of an integrated appliance (mechanism and cabinet joined as a self-contained unit). During the mid-1930s, the focus shifted to the bewildering arrays of gadgets, ridiculed in consumer product test reports, which distinguished one brand from another, and each brand's models from each other.

During the first decade of their appearance, electric refrigerator advertisements did not follow a single pattern or formula. Only a few advantages were mentioned recurrently in advertisements for all three brands considered here: these refrigerators were all routinely described as "automatic" and, of course, "electric." A recitation of the foods to be enjoyed was common to Kelvinator and Frigidaire, but missing from General Electric advertisements. Health was often mentioned in Frigidaire advertisements (a June 1928 advertisement focusing on "baby's health" is a striking example), while Kelvinator advertisements tended to construct a scientistic mystique around refrigeration (the "Zone of Kelvination"). Individual advertisements might mention how the refrigerator would alter shopping or entertaining practices (only an early Kelvinator advertisement mentioned the former, while the latter theme appeared occasionally in both Kelvinator and Frigidaire advertisements). General Electric stressed the scientific research behind their product, an angle which Kelvinator also began to pursue in the late 1920s. The insulation of refrigerators was hardly ever mentioned; I was able to locate only one instance of this, in a June 1929 Frigidaire advertisement.

With respect to visual imagery, most, but not all, advertisements showed the refrigerator, often open but sometimes closed, usually in the presence of users or buyers, but sometimes standing by itself. There is no single rule or pattern in these verbal and visual materials, but rather a diverse set of possibilities. The larger discourse of refrigeration provided a set of resources for making sense of the refrigerator as a knowable and desirable object. The presence or absence of a single theme or topic worked in relation to this larger background. For example, absence of mention could mean different things. The General Electric advertisements would scarcely have been intelligible to a reader who did not already know what a fridge was, since no mention was made of what refrigeration can do or what its benefits were. The absence of any mention of ice cubes, for example, is striking, given their prominence in advertisements for other brands (cf. Frigidaire's promise of a "constant and ample supply of sparkling ice cubes" (*Good Housekeeping* 8/26: 127). Presumably, the advertisements which focused on General Electric's unique design could indirectly invoke what the reader already knew (that electric refrigerators make ice cubes, etc.); thus they depended on the reader's prior exposure to a popular discourse of refrigeration. The omission of any mention of insulation was presumably less noticeable in individual advertisements, since information about this crucial performance feature was generally absent from promotional accounts of mechanical refrigerators.

Magazine articles

The articles which appeared in women's magazines during the 1920s and 1930s instructed readers in the everyday practices of domestic refrigeration. The refrigerator, in its changing guises, was presented as the object at the center of a sphere of conduct which was itself undergoing change and redefinition. Descriptions of proper refrigerator use were linked to both changes in refrigerator design and to the changing background of temperature control practices within which refrigerator use occurred. This is evident, for example, in advice about the location of the refrigerator in the home. Articles appearing in *Good Housekeeping* towards the beginning and end of the 1920s warned against placing the refrigerator on the back porch. This practice involved taking advantage of the cooler, unheated condition of the porch to help the refrigerator stay cooler (and thus save ice), but the dampness associated with this location caused warping in the wooden cabinets of refrigerators sold during the early and mid-1920s. Locating the refrigerator in the basement was proscribed for the same reason. In the mid-1920s, however, articles appeared which backtracked on this point. An article appearing in 1926 noted that a hot kitchen would result in increased ice or power consumption, and allowed that the problem might be controlled "by placing the cabinet in a cool back entry convenient to the kitchen, but not exposed to the weather" (*Good Housekeeping* 7/26: 205). Another article appearing in 1927 treated the cool back entry as a normal location for the refrigerator (*Good Housekeeping* 7/27: 181), but articles appearing in 1929 were emphatic that the back porch was no place for a mechanical refrigerator. As one article pointed out, their mechanisms were designed to operate at room temperature (*Good Housekeeping* 9/29: 94 – 99) and would produce erratic results when the surrounding temperatures were much lower (*Good Housekeeping* 9/29: 94 – 95).

The idea that the proper location of the refrigerator was in the kitchen was connected with a broader movement away from reliance on local, seasonal conditions for cool storage. Assorted traditional practices which capitalized on such conditions were condemned as outmoded, as is evident in the following passage:

> In a climate such as ours, perishable foods should not be stored during the winter months in window-boxes or cold rooms which depend upon outdoor temperatures for their refrigeration. During the winter season there are few days throughout when suitable refrigerating temperatures prevail. For a part of the day it is apt to be either too warm for proper food preservation or too cold, with consequent food spoilage from freezing. Because of these variations in temperature, it is also unwise to store food in a refrigerator that is not iced during winter months and which is kept in a cool place where the temperature depends upon the weather (*Good Housekeeping* 6/29: 94).

The temperature variations associated with the older techniques of cooling were now regarded as intolerable, and the use of a refrigerator was pronounced a year-round necessity. As an article in the September 1929 *Good Housekeeping* put it:

> At this season there may be some who still feel that they will need refrigerator service only as long as the warm days last. As a matter of fact, we are increasingly dependent upon good refrigeration all the year round. It is by no means a seasonal service ... the heated houses of today do not offer any safe or satisfactory place for the storage of the perishable food supply outside a good refrigerator at any season (*Good Housekeeping* 9/29: 94).

During this period, refrigeration had come to be regarded as a standardized condition to be sustained year-round in a fixed location, rather than as a loose ensemble of cold storage practices.

The idea of a scientific standard for adequate refrigeration received attention from the mid-1920s onward. A 1924 article on iced refrigerators announced the Good Housekeeping Institute's own standard of adequate refrigeration:

> ... with a room temperature of 75 degrees F. the average food compartment temperature must not exceed 50.5 degrees F. At a room temperature of 85 degrees F. the average food compartment temperature must not exceed 57 degrees F. (*Good Housekeeping* 7/24: 84).

Other definitions were more stringent. A Frigidaire advertisement appearing in the same year promised a "uniform cold — always below 50 degrees," (*Good Housekeeping* 9/24: 157) and the "Zone of Kelvination" specified "below 50 degrees — above 40 degrees" (*Good Housekeeping* 12/26: 151). By 1929, *Good Housekeeping* articles were citing a standard which appeared throughout the refrigeration discourse:

> Laboratory tests indicate the desirability of storing perishable foods at temperatures as low as 45 degrees or 50 degrees F., which can be maintained in the coldest part of the food compartment of a good refrigerator at ordinary room temperatures when kept well iced, or in a mechanical refrigerator which automatically maintains excellent refrigerating temperatures (*Good Housekeeping* 6/29: 94).

By the early 1930s, when magazine articles treated the mechanical or "automatic" refrigerator as the predominant form, adequate refrigeration was routinely defined as the ability to sustain uniform temperatures below 50 degrees F. As soon as this standard was established, older techniques and devices could be regarded as relics. Apart from the refrigerator in its various forms, the cooling device most often referred to was the window box, but others mentioned in the broader refrigeration discourse included the cold cellar and the spring house (*Pictorial Review*, March 1933: 36), the buttery or refrigerator annex (an architectural feature which promoted cooling via air circulation, *Ladies' Home Journal*, January 1922: 86), and devices based on water evaporation (*Consumers' Research Handbook of Buying* VII(1), March 1932: 25; *Pictorial Review*, March 1933: 36). None of these could sustain a uniform temperature below 50 degrees F.

The older arts of cool storage involved taking advantage of transient local conditions. With the ability to produce standardized refrigeration increasingly secured, the arts of cool storage migrated to the inside of the refrigerator. Articles on refrigeration almost always included instruction in the placement of foods with regard to temperature variations in the refrigerator. Both iced and mechanical refrigerators were noted to have different temperatures in different parts of the cabinet, depending upon design. Readers were repeatedly advised to place "milk, butter, uncooked meat or fish, and soup stock in the coldest part of the food compartment" (*Good Housekeeping* 6/28: 92), while other types of foods all had their own designated locations. In effect, the micro-climates inside the refrigerator were to be treated as standardized sites for different types of food handling. The introduction of modern equipment could not obliterate the variation of temperatures within the cabinet or the varying storage requirements of different foods, but it fostered a new attitude towards variation, which was now to be handled in the light of a general orientation to a standardized refrigeration environment.

The mechanical refrigerator contributed to establishing the scientific standard for adequate refrigeration as a norm for everyday practice. What the iced refrigerator might achieve under ideal conditions, the mechanical refrigerator could do virtually all of the time; it could even furnish effective refrigeration during the hot weather when it was most desired. With the increasing dominance of mechanical refrigeration, there was a notable shift in how the benefits of refrigeration were described. Earlier articles stressed health and the safe storage of foods, while later articles gave increasing attention to ice cubes, frozen desserts, and meal-planning practices which made heavy demands on the chilling power of the fridge.

The growing prominence of the mechanical refrigerator also intensified attention to a question which had already arisen in connection with using the iced refrigerator: cost of operation. Articles began to respond to reader concerns about how much power would be consumed in operating a mechanical refrigerator, yet the answers remained vague. The following advice was typical:

> The first essential for good refrigeration is a correctly-designed, well-insulated box of good construction, otherwise satisfactory temperatures and economical operation are not possible... Unfortunately the purchaser can not determine the efficiency of the insulation until the box is in actual use, and then only approximately by keeping, for a given period, a record of temperatures and of ice or power consumption. The Institute therefore advises buyers to use our Seal of Approval as a guide in this respect (*Good Housekeeping* 7/26: 97).

Although magazine articles guided readers in a variety of aspects of refrigerator selection, attention was directed to features which consumers could judge themselves: size, external finish, internal linings, configuration of the food cabinet, shelf arrangements, accessories, etc. It had to be admitted that the crucial features affecting performance, especially insulation, were beyond the consumer's power to detect or judge. Readers were advised, however, that frequent opening of the refrigerator door would have a drastic effect on cost of operation; here the solution was simple enough. Interestingly, in apparently unrelated remarks, articles repeatedly counselled readers not to worry about "sweating" on the outside of the refrigerator:

> This is the season when the Institute begins to get letters from careful housekeepers who are much disturbed by so-called "sweating" on the

outside of their refrigerator, and they often attribute this to some defect in their particular box. Our answer to such a question is that the condensation of moisture on a well-made refrigerator is a natural phenomenon... The amount of sweating depends to a large extent upon climatic conditions... (*Good Housekeeping* 7/27: 81).

For an account of the relation between sweating and insulation, readers would have to turn to the product testing literature (see below).

From the early 1920s to the mid-1930s, articles in magazines like *Good Housekeeping* oriented readers to a sphere of refrigeration practice which was increasingly standardized. Reliance on the refrigerator displaced an assortment of older practices, and adequate refrigeration was increasingly defined in terms of a standard which only mechanical refrigerators could achieve at all consistently. These articles introduced the mechanical refrigerator, but offered only superficial guidance in the selection of a satisfactory model.

Consumer product testing magazines

In the late 1920s, public interest in consumer literacy was stimulated by books such as *Your Money's Worth* (Chase — Schlink, 1927) and *Middletown* (Lynd — Lynd, 1929) which dramatized the inability of ordinary people to deal effectively with the new consumer marketplace which confronted them. While *Middletown* furnished its co-author, Robert Lynd, with a point of departure for further sociological studies of consumption (Smith 1979 – 80), *Your Money's Worth* became the basis of a practical experiment in consumer literacy (Silber 1983).[8] Co-authors Stuart Chase and Frederick Schlink proposed setting up independent testing laboratories in order to produce evaluations of brand-name products. The point was to build on the achievements of the standards and specifications movement in industry, but to make this kind of information available in a form readily usable by private individual consumers. As a result of a large public response, they founded Consumers' Research Incorporated in 1927. The product evaluation bulletins issued by Consumers' Research quickly evolved into the first product testing magazine, *Consumers' Research Bulletin*. Labor troubles at Consumers' Research in the mid-1930s led to the foundation of a rival organization, Consumers Union, in 1936. The new organization published *Consumers Union Reports*, later *Consumer Reports*, whose circulation soon overtook that of *Consumers' Re-*

search Bulletin. These publications introduced and refined a genre of popular non-fiction which directly challenged the claims and pretensions of both advertising and the advice published in popular magazines such as *Good Housekeeping.*

Unlike advertisements and women's magazine articles, the consumer product test reports which appeared in *Consumers' Research Bulletin* and *Consumers Union Reports* during the 1930s discussed specific factors affecting product performance, provided comparative data, and rated refrigerators by make and model. Advertising claims were debunked, and attention was directed to critical performance features. It was emphasized that essential information was often unavailable or even actively withheld by commercial interests. For example, the 1935 report on mechanical refrigerators in *Consumers' Research Bulletin* explained that:

> For the ordinary seeker of an efficient and durable refrigerator, the important details of construction are concealed from view, and the advertising copy of the manufacturers and the recommendations of the Good Housekeeping Institute ... cannot be relied upon to supply trustworthy, relevant information (*Consumers' Research Bulletin* 4/35: 20).

As the report pointed out, *Good Housekeeping* had approved most of the refrigerators rated "Not Recommended" in Consumers' Research's ratings. One of the important details of construction "concealed from view" was insulation, discussed below. Test reports also vigorously attacked the language of advertising. Consumers Union's 1936 report on mechanical refrigerators began:

> Conservador – Shelvador – Eject-o-Cube – Adjusto-Shelf – Foodex – Handi-bin – Touch-a-Bar... With these magic words, mechanical-refrigerator makers persuade the American public to buy their product. Yet these words have absolutely nothing to do with the essential qualities of a refrigerator (*Consumers Union Reports* 7/36: 3).

The product testing magazines thus directly addressed sectors of discourse of refrigeration in which misleading and false claims were circulated.

In addition to debunking aspects of the existing discourse, reports provided readers with new kinds of information. This often involved identifying basic factors underlying surface phenomena which seemed unrelated. For example, one property which clearly distinguished the mechanical refrigerator from ice-based refrigeration was the ability to make ice cubes and frozen desserts, as advertisements repeatedly emphasized. Responding to this "seller's tactic," Consumers' Research advised: "be sure you are not buying a mechanical refrigerator primarily because you like the nice little ice cubes or look forward to an endless procession of frozen desserts" (*Consumers' Research Bulletin* 3/32: 22). Not only was this viewed as a trivial benefit of mechanical refrigeration, but more importantly the rapid freezing which made these luxuries possible was described as a sign of poor refrigerating economy. A good refrigerator, Consumers' Research pointed out, did not require the frequent generation of the *"excess* refrigerating effect" that froze the cubes. Consumers Union's 1936 report also linked ice cube production with poor insulation:

> A refrigerator with poor insulation may impress the user as being good because it freezes ice cubes rapidly. But this is only because the freezing coils must maintain lower temperatures — at higher cost — to compensate for the poor insulation. Rapid freezing of ice cubes at customary regulator setting is cause for suspicion, not commendation (*Consumers Union Reports* 7/36: 3 − 4).

Both magazines sought to shift readers' attention from superficial characteristics of refrigerators to underlying fundamentals of good refrigeration which could be specified and used as a basis for comparison.

Consumers Union's 1936 report emphasized insulation as a key factor in refrigerator performance. It pointed out that "the most common defect of refrigerator cabinets is poor sealing against moisture." During hot, humid weather, water condensation or "sweating" would occur *inside* the walls of a poorly sealed cabinet, so that if the insulation was water-absorbent, it would become saturated, lose its insulation ability, and deteriorate. (Note that whereas *Good Housekeeping* presented sweating as a harmless phenomenon, it is linked here with improper cabinet construction and poor insulation performance.) Consumers therefore need to know about the different insulating materials available. Although cork and "Dry-Zero" (a kapok preparation) were effective against moisture, water-absorbent corrugated paper with an ineffective coating ("Thermocraft") was commonly used. The more absorbent material might work, though, if the cabinet was well sealed. Thus the consumer needed information about both the insulating material used and the effectiveness of cabinet sealing in order to obtain reasonable operating costs beyond the initial period of use. Accordingly, a table comparing estimated operating costs of popular refrigerator makes and models was offered in the article. This enabled the reader to discover, for example, that the poorly rated Coldspot 3324 would cost more than twice as much to operate as the General Electric M-6 which had the same storage capacity. The reader would then be in a better position to judge whether the Coldspot, which sold at half the price, was really a wise purchase. Such revelations of specific details regarding insulation can be contrasted with *Good Housekeeping* articles which worried over consumers' inability to judge features — such as insulation — which affected operating efficiency, but then blandly counselled reliance on their own Institute list of approved models.

The product test reports were even more emphatic than the magazine articles concerning rationalized refrigeration. They disregarded the older arts of cool storage as well as the newer arts of correctly using the varying temperatures created in the refrigerator. The single focus was the ability to maintain specified temperatures efficiently over a period of time. Good refrigeration resided in the refrigerator which could produce this result. Unlike other sectors of discourse, though, these reports dramatized the uncertainties surrounding the search for such a refrigerator.

The refrigerator as a displacement of local practice

Beneath its diversity, the popular mechanical refrigerator discourse of the 1920s and 1930s shows a variety of objects and practices to be "doing the same thing," whereas previously there existed dispersed practices organized around a producerly understanding of particular materials and opportunities for securing lowered temperatures. The cool storage of foods involved specific knowledge of, for example, milk and its ability to sour, the uses of sour milk, the cooling effect available from a well or underground spring, the storage requirements of different kinds of produce, seasonal variations in cellar temperatures, etc. This traditional knowledge was progressively effaced from the refrigeration discourse. During the 1920s and 1930s, one can see both the discursive construction of a *standard of performance*, and the commercial introduction of an array of *material devices* which could be *seen as* oriented to that standard.

If we consider the organization of knowledge at work in these sectors of the popular discourse on refrigeration, it seems evident that we are not confronted with the powerfully unified wave of propaganda imagined by some cultural critics. Indeed, we might ask whether there is anything which lends this discourse any coherence, or does it consist simply of dispersed reading positions? The advertisements and articles do not simply mirror or reinforce each other, and — for all their confrontational rhetoric — the test reports do not simply undo the advertisements or articles. There are tensions, overlaps, recurrences, contradictions. But through these a field of images and practices comes into view. What makes this discourse a coherent reading order is not on the surface (patterns of imagery — tableaux and their rules) or behind the text (the electric utility monopoly — promoting electrical solutions), but the overall direction of change which these texts helped to implement through the ways in which they broke with the local ordering of things and began to embody extra-local forms of organization (standardization, objective comparisons, relative freedom from local conditions, etc.). Indeed, they invited the reader to join in making extra-local organization incarnate.

The refrigerator, as seen through the discourse, was an object-mediated displacement within a whole field of temperature-reduction practices — the spring house, the unheated room, the vegetable cellar, the window box, the buttery, evaporation, the ice box, and so forth. These earlier practices were highly sensitive to local variations. They declined with the emergence of a new technology which was relatively insensitive to local variations (summer/winter, ice delivery schedules, etc.). Monday morning was now like other mornings. One could imagine a strawberry dessert to accompany the Christmas dinner. Furthermore, foods themselves were now to accommodate to this new technology. Tastes were to be redirected by the power of cooling: cold fruits, crisp salads, etc. The social concomitants of the older practices were displaced, too: local, time-sensitive shopping — shopping with regard for the nature of each food, frequent visits to well-known merchants, encounters with neighbors, and so on.

Cooling was no longer a local accomplishment — it became a standard condition. The refrigerator did "the same thing" in the city apartment and in the large, suburban, privately owned home. To a greater extent than other technologies, it stood free from architectural (the refrigerator annex, "outside icing" for the ice box), seasonal, and geographical variations, as well as from variations in the skill of the user.

All of the specific discursive constructions of the refrigerator considered here attest to this displacement of local practices and the emergence of a standardized version of food cooling. This refrigerator became the common medium for a range of storage and temperature control practices which were previously dispersed in space and time, while occasioning new practices (and ending others). It was not a "thing" (inert), but a medium for practices, and the site of their convergence. As an object, the mechanical refrigerator was inserted into a stream of practices, redirecting some, stifling others, provoking the initiation of still others.

Thus the object in its materially and symbolically constructed aspects is not simply a new way of doing "the same thing" as before — the field

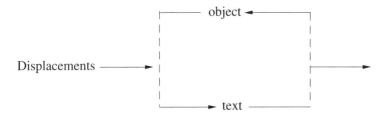

Figure 1. Field of practices.

of practice itself changes. For all contexts of utterance, the refrigerator had become a standardized environment for cold food storage. The between-40-and-50-degree standard had been generally accepted. The mechanical refrigerator produced this result more consistently, frequently bettered it, and sometimes did so more cheaply. Left behind were the diversity of practices for controlling temperatures in ways specific to the nature of different food products (cheese, fruits, etc.). A new ensemble appeared: quick freezing, long-term frozen storage, and normal cool storage.

As Csikszentmihalyi and Rochberg-Halton (1981: 14) observe, "it is quite obvious that interaction with objects alters the pattern of life; for instance, that refrigerators have revolutionized shopping and eating habits..." What I have tried to show is that in the case of the mechanical refrigerator, this alteration was supported in quite complex ways through shifts in the discursive construction of refrigeration. It is a question not only of object-mediated changes, but also textually-mediated objects: the refrigerator as we know it is not just a manufactured thing but also emerged as a written presence, a design which evolved in response to the ways in which it could be demonstrated and promoted. Having displaced other practices and solutions, the mechanical refrigerator acquired its familiar, sedimented place within the culture.[9] Must we postulate a consumer-victim (a "cultural dope") to account for what has been lost in the course of these shifts? It is not so much that consumer culture is a deception as Horkheimer and Adorno (1972) urged, but that through these reflexively tied mediations, our understandings of what we may want have undergone radically qualitative transformations. It is a striking concomitant that much of our grounding in a local knowledge of things seemed to have become effaced through this process. In this respect, the worries of cultural critics over the "politics of consumption" may yet find a justification.

Notes

1. The author would like to thank Kamini Maraj Grahame, James Heap, Katherine Moore, Dorothy E. Smith, and Marc Stern for their encouragement and support in developing aspects of this research.
2. Ethnomethodologists refer to this kind of reasoning, whereby instances are interpreted by being related to an underlying pattern, as the "documentary method of interpretation." They also point out that the relation between instance and pattern is reciprocal, so that the pattern is also assembled out of its instances; each is the ground for the other. (For an account of this phenomenon, see Heritage 1984: 84 – 97.) My point here is that the assembly of the object into the pattern cuts it loose from the practical circumstances of its presence in social life.
3. For an example of each see, respectively, ads in *Good Housekeeping*, December 1929 (Frigidaire), September 1927 (General Electric), and October 1924 (Frigidaire).
4. Versions of this position can be found in Kress (1989) who distinguishes between language and social structure, and Hodge (1989) who asked how texts signify capitalist society, family life, etc. The position which they share is developed at greater length in Hodge and Kress (1988). Rather than beginning with two separate orders, I want to consider how language and imagery are at work in the accomplishment of social organization. Texts do not just signify the social — they are media of social organization.
5. Articles which appeared in *Ladies' Home Journal* and several other women's magazines were similar, except that the issue of testing — chiefly in connection with the Good Housekeeping Institute — is much more prominent in *Good Housekeeping*. I have restricted my attention to *Good Housekeeping* in order to make the comparison with other discourse sectors more manageable, but also because *Good Housekeeping*'s claims to do impartial testing were provocative. Both of the consumer product testing magazines which I consider comment on *Good Housekeeping*, treating it as a powerful, but unworthy, rival. On this, see the Consumers' Research comment on *Good Housekeeping*'s fridge tests, quoted in this chapter, and *Consumers Union Reports* (July 1936: 2): "The Good Housekeeping Institute is a fraud. With its 'Seal of Approval' and its 'scientists,' it is, indeed, one of the greatest frauds now being perpetrated on American consumers." Two consumer magazines are examined, in part because articles on refrigerators are relatively infrequent in these publications, requiring a fuller treatment of the product test genre in order to move beyond a single case analysis.
6. The scarcity of the term "ice-box" in all of these discursive sectors should be noted: there was only one occurrence among advertisements examined, none in the magazine articles, and very few in the test report literature. The term ice(d) refrigerator, or just "refrigerator," was generally preferred. The generic

term "mechanical refrigerator" was not used in these advertisements, which specifically promoted *electric* refrigeration, but it was the term of preference in product test magazines and also in women's magazines until the term "automatic refrigerator" replaced the latter in the mid-1930s. "Mechanical refrigerator" referred to several designs, including gas and kerosene powered models as well as the more prevalent electric refrigerator. (For an account of the competition between electric and gas designs, see Cowan 1983.)

7. Christmas advertisements were an exception; however, I would argue that they constituted an essentially separate genre in which the fridge appeared as a gift, as part of seasonal festivities. One other advertisement referred to food only in a general way: "Of course it keeps food wholesome, fresh, full-flavored" — as if this scarcely needed to be mentioned (*Good Housekeeping* 9/27: 103).

8. On the relations between Lynd's sociological project and Chase and Schlink's endeavors, see Grahame (1989).

9. The emerging cultural significance of mechanical refrigeration is captured vividly in a scene from Harriette Arnow's (1972: 281) fictional account of wartime America: "'Now, Max,' Mrs. Anderson said, still smiling a strange Whit-like smile, 'you're un-American — or else you don't listen to the radio. Every woman dreams of a ten-cubic-foot Icy Heart in her kitchen — Icy Heart power — Icy Heart. We must hurry up and win the war so we can all go out and buy Icy Hearts.'" I thank Katherine Moore for bringing this passage to my attention. It would be worthwhile to broaden the examination of refrigeration discourse to include fiction, cinema, and other modes of artistic expression.

References

Arnow, Harriette
    1972   *The dollmaker*. New York: Avon Books.
Chase, Stuart — Frederick Schlink
    1927   *Your money's worth*. New York: Macmillan.
Cowan, Ruth Schwartz
    1983   *More work for mother*. New York: Basic Books.
Csikszentmihalyi, Mihaly — Eugene Rochberg-Halton
    1981   *The meaning of things: Domestic symbols and the self*. Cambridge: Cambridge University Press.
Fiske, John
    1989   *Reading the popular*. Boston: Unwin Hyman.
Garfinkel, Harold
    1967   *Studies in ethnomethodology*. Englewood Cliffs, NJ: Prentice-Hall.
Giddens, Anthony
    1987   "Structuralism, post-structuralism and the production of culture," in Giddens — Turner (eds.), 195–213.

Giddens, Anthony — Jonathan Turner (eds.)
1987   *Social theory today*. Stanford, CA: Stanford University Press.
Grahame, Peter R.
1989   "The construction of a sociological consumer," in: Jaber F. Gubrium
        — David Silverman (eds.), 70–93.
1991   "Finding the reader: Early consumer activism and the project of
        consumer literacy," *Continuum, the Australian journal of media and
        culture* 5(1): 215–227.
1992   "Consumption and the sociology of culture," *Discourse and Society*
        3(4): 501–504.
Gubrium, Jaber F. — David Silverman (eds.)
1989   *The politics of field research: Sociology beyond enlightenment.* Lon-
        don: Sage.
Hall, Stuart — Tony Jefferson
1976   *Resistance through rituals: Youth subcultures in post-war Britain.* Lon-
        don: Hutchinson.
Heritage, John
1984   *Garfinkel and ethnomethodology*. Cambridge: Polity Press.
Hodge, Robert
1989   "National character and the discursive process: A study of transfor-
        mations in popular metatexts," *Journal of Pragmatics* 13: 427–444.
Hodge, Robert — Gunther Kress
1988   *Social semiotics*. Ithaca: Cornell University Press.
Horkheimer, Max — Theodor Adorno
1972   *Dialectic of enlightenment*. New York: Seabury Press.
Kress, Gunther
1989   "History and language: Towards a social account of linguistic
        change," *Journal of Pragmatics* 13: 445–466.
Lynd, Robert S. — Helen Merrell Lynd
1929   *Middletown: A study in American culture*. New York: Harcourt and
        Brace.
Marchand, Roland
1985   *Advertising the American dream*. Berkeley: University of California
        Press.
Mechling, Jay
1975   "Advice to historians on advice to mothers," *Journal of Social History*
        9: 44–63.
Riesman, David
1964   *Abundance for what? and other essays*. Garden City, NY: Doubleday.
Riesman, David with Howard Roseborough
1964   "Careers and consumer behavior, in: David Riesman, 113–137.
Silber, Norman Issac
1983   *Test and protest: The influence of Consumers Union*. New York:
        Holmes and Meier.

Smith, Dorothy E.
   1984   "Textually-mediated social organization," *International Social Science Journal* 34: 59 – 75.
   1990   *Texts, facts, and femininity*. London: Routledge.
Smith, Mark C.
   1979 – 80 "Robert Lynd and consumerism in the 1930s," *The Journal of the History of Sociology* II(I): 99 – 119.
Woolgar, Steve
   1988   *Science, the very idea*. London: Tavistock.

Communicating democracy: Or shine, perishing republic

Eugene Halton

> You making haste haste on decay: not blameworthy; life is good, be it stubbornly long or suddenly
> A mortal splendor: meteors are not needed less than mountains: shine, perishing republic.
>
> Robinson Jeffers (1987 [1924]: 14)

When one looks at recent American electoral politics, political symbolism appears to be so powerful in the United States as to have utterly annihilated politics. Not only has political discourse been gutted by hype and media sensationalism, but the very nature of the public sphere itself — including the communicative practices which constitute a public life as well as the physical places in which these take place — has been corroded by the dual materializing and etherealizing processes of megatechnic America. By examining two very different kinds of public spaces as self-representations of democracy, I hope to bring to light some of the dark tendencies which have transformed the American vision of autonomy into the dream of automatic culture and kitsch.

The commanding images of American media culture have taken on a life of their own, so that celebrity and slogan have long since replaced substance. As was clear in the election of Ronald Reagan and his continued popularity throughout the 1980s despite widespread cynicism concerning his policies, the American people love having a star — especially a "teflon president" on whom nothing bad ever sticks — and would seem to prefer entertainment to popular democracy. Yet when one contrasts a President Reagan to a President Vaclav Havel of the Czech Republic, it is clear that playwrights who can write their own scripts are to be preferred to actors.

American politics, and perhaps American culture more generally, seems to have become based on the concept of the *empty symbol*, which mirrors back to the individual only what the individual will want to see. The empty symbol, as politicians use it, is perhaps similar to a technique in psychotherapy associated with Carl Rogers, wherein the therapist repeats the patient's statements as if saying something new, thereby prompting the patient to continue without having to take the lead. Similarly, if less empathically, the empty symbolist is one who attempts to signify anything while saying nothing. This is a smiling politics, the feel-good politics of Ronald Reagan, the sound bite and flag politics of George Bush, the politics which prevented Michael Dukakis from admitting he was a liberal in the 1988 Presidential election. It is a politics of entertainment, cynicism, and kitsch.

Kitsch, as Milan Kundera (1984) reminds us in *The Unbearable Lightness of Being*, is the enemy of art, being, and democracy. It is, as he pointedly reminds us, the denial that "shit happens." In his words: "Kitsch is the absolute denial of shit, in both the literal and figurative senses of the word; kitsch excludes everything from its purview which is essentially unacceptable in human existence."

Given an atmosphere of utter kitsch and cynicism, one dominated by a television entertainment culture, it is no wonder that empty political symbols have assumed a central significance in electoral politics. This is particularly illustrated in the controversy surrounding the American flag, which also fuelled Bush's 1988 election campaign. The Supreme Court ruled that the burning of the flag is a legitimate expression of freedom of speech, guaranteed by the First Amendment to the Constitution. Instantly politicians could wrap themselves in the flag of kitsch patriotism, often knowing that it is much harder to stand up for the less immediately visible principles of the constitution.

I take these symbols of empty politics to be accurate indicators of a more widespread unravelling of the moral fiber of American culture, which in turn is part of the larger unravelling of modern life. We live, in my view, at the end of the Age of Nominalism, an age which believes that the world consists of mere things and mere words which stand for and apart from them.[1] What I hope to do here is to examine two self-representations of democracy, in order to highlight the difficulties which democracy and its communication face in the United States today. These cases also illustrate how rational bureaucratic processes and kitsch sentimentalism eat away from opposite directions at the possibility of the public realm.

Despite what I see as a dangerous withering away of the democratic fabric of American life, I would like to point out an unlikely candidate for a symbolic self-representation of democracy in the best sense. Given the combination of cynicism and kitsch, the Vietnam Veterans Memorial stands as a remarkable public symbol of democracy in the face of overwhelming odds against it. After examining the Vietnam Veterans Memorial as a self-representation of democracy, I will turn to a contemporary cult of high-tech vehicular democracy.

The Vietnam Veterans Memorial

When we remember that the Greek root *symballein* means literally "to throw together," we see how the Vietnam Veterans Memorial is perhaps the outstanding political *symbol* in America today. It not only manages to be a convincing public monument at a time when such things are difficult to realize, and for a war which produced bitter divisions in America, divisions which continued throughout the planning and realization of the Memorial, but it achieves supremely what the chief task of a "symbol" is, to bind something together through a representation.

The memorial was commissioned with four criteria in mind: it had to be imposing, reflective, include all the names of the 58,175 Americans killed in the war, and make no political statement. Given these criteria, it is all the more remarkable that the memorial stands today as a powerful and moving political symbol, which honors the dead while yet containing all of the ambiguities of the war.[2]

The memorial stands in a public park area of Washington known as "the mall," whose vistas include the principal symbols of American democracy, the Capitol Building and the White House, and a number of monuments and memorials and museums. Despite the precipitous decline of many middle-sized American cities and the public space that they afford, due to the effects of suburban shopping malls and other factors, the Washington mall area remains a visible national public space. The mall area was part of the plan of the city of Washington submitted in 1791 by the French engineer Major Pierre-Charles L'Enfant, a plan of grand Baroque proportions strangely at odds with the ideals of the newborn American democracy. Despite L'Enfant's intentions, the great static vista provided by the mall evoked the absolute despotism of centralized power and control symbolized by Versailles instead of the bounded powers of a federal republic. L'Enfant's total plan also required a larger population than Washington possessed, and a public control over land which was not achieved. Hence his plan was only partially realized, aided by an attempt to renew the plan in 1901.

The mall contains the ideal Baroque broad vista, an ideal unfortunately better suited to the tourist's eye than the inhabitant's daily use. Nevertheless, the mall provides the national public space for public demonstration and protest, and is capable of holding huge numbers of people, from those who marched on Washington during the civil rights and anti-Vietnam War movements of the 1960s to the pro-and anti-abortion groups today.

At the center of the mall stands the Washington Monument, a traditional obelisk raised to giant proportions, which dominates the downtown skyline. The cornerstone of the monument was laid on July 4, 1848, but due to a lack of funds — revealing a lack of foresight similar to that of the realization of L'Enfant's Washington city plan — the monument was not completed until 1888.

At the western end of the mall is the Lincoln Memorial, which houses a large statue of Abraham Lincoln and words from speeches in which he proclaimed the end of slavery in America. On the steps of the Lincoln Memorial, Martin Luther King delivered his most impassioned and memorable speech during the Civil Rights Movement in the early 1960s before more than half a million Americans. There are no visible physical markers at this site, yet powerful images of it remain through filmed recordings, illustrating perhaps how evanescent public speech can sometimes be more enduring than weighty public monuments.

A couple of hundred meters from the Lincoln Memorial and its visible and invisible memories stands the Vietnam Veterans Memorial, which was unveiled in 1982. The design of the Memorial was based on a national competition, which was won by a 21-year-old student at Yale University, Maya Lin. In what could only be described as fate, the student was an Asian woman, whose design of a large open wedge was to fix for the permanent record a memorial of the American men who died in the Vietnam war. If the selection of L'Enfant for the Washington city plan symbolized both the American dependence on European civilization and perhaps admiration for the French Enlightenment and thankfulness to the French for help during the revolutionary war, perhaps we can look at Lin herself as a representative symbol of the new generation of Asian Americans and women who will reshape the face of America. In an interview after her design was selected, Lin said that she did not want to make a phallic symbol. And when one visits the memorial it is clear that she did not, for it is, if anything, the opposite, a vaginal symbol. I am not, in most circumstances, a Freudian, yet it was clear to me upon visiting the memorial that it is a "gash," in the colloquial senses both of "wound" and "vagina."

There is a fantastic tension between the great erection of the Washington Monument which one can vertically ascend by foot or elevator, and the Vietnam Veterans Memorial, which one descends into by foot. The two walls of the Vietnam Veterans Memorial are intentionally aligned on a 120 degree axis with the Washington Monument and the Lincoln Memorial. When asked in 1983 whether her memorial "had a female sensibility," Lin responded, "In a world of phallic memorials that rise upwards, it certainly does. I didn't set out to conquer the earth, or overpower it, the way Western man usually does. I don't think I've made a passive piece, but neither is it a memorial to the idea of war" (as quoted in Hess 1983: 123).

Plate 1. Vietnam Veterans Memorial by Maya Lin. Washington, D. C.

The memorial was marked with controversies from the beginning, with many veteran groups resenting the abstractness of the design — for example, only the names and dates were listed — and the original design was later changed to add words stating that the names listed were veterans killed in the Vietnam War, to erect a flag over the juncture of the memorial, and to place a realistic statue by sculptor Frederick Hart of three soldiers, a Black, a White, and a Hispanic, at a distance opposite the memorial. One veteran appeared before the commission on fine arts to complain that the design was a "black gash of shame." Because of lingering controversies regarding the Vietnam War, and controversies surrounding the memorial, President Reagan did not attend the unveiling of the memorial in 1982, but did participate in the unveiling of the realistic statue in 1984 (see Wagner-Pacifici — Schwartz). It is fascinating to note that Reagan could only associate himself with the kitsch realism, not with the real monument. One sees perhaps how Reagan's "handlers" sought to associate him in the media with good news, and to distance him from the possibility of bad news.

The memorial can be described as abstract, minimalist even. Yet it somehow contains both a quiet dignity and a nonabstract tangibility through the names carved into the reflecting marble. In the controversy surrounding the Vietnam Veterans Memorial, which many Americans simply call "the wall," one sees a fascinating twist on the culture of the "empty symbol."

Again, by "empty symbol" I wish to draw attention to a curious tendency in the right-wing politics and left-wing art of the 1980s to signify no quality or content — recalling the title of Robert Musil's (1965) novel, *The Man Without Qualities* — as most fully realized politically in Ronald Reagan and artistically in minimalism. Artistic minimalism, despite its postmodernist pretensions, can be seen to continue the earlier minimal- izing tendencies of Abstract Expressionism as a "process art" in which the content does not matter, and of Pop/Op as *only* signifying content, in which the form does not matter. Lin was surrounded by the culture of artistic minimalism, but had to confront the fact of death in her funerary architecture class at Yale University. She created the empty object which reflects back the viewer's own image, which is exactly the politics of Ronald Reagan, but with opposite effect. What normally goes by the name of minimalism, what one sees in museums and hears in music, is glorified banality. Somehow, by contrast, this memorial is real and earnest; it carries death with dignity. Although deriving from mini- malism, it is clear that Maya Lin did not let the cynical and shrewd and blasé attitude so prominent in the 1980s override her attempt to make a real memorial. When one looks back at the controversy which surrounded the memorial, with the Texas millionaire and future Presidential candidate Ross Perrot flying veterans to Washington and conducting a skewed survey of prisoners of war (rather than veterans in general or families of veterans), it is also clear that Lin's memorial is a triumph over schmaltzy

Plate 2. Vietnam Veterans Memorial by Maya Lin. Washington, D. C.

sentimentalism as well as starved minimalism: it succeeds because it straightforwardly fuses the human and epic proportions of tragic war.

Yet another of the contradictions of the Vietnam Veterans Memorial is its frank acknowledgement of death. Death itself seemed to contradict the 1980s "feel good" mentality which Ronald Reagan celebrated and sold to Americans, so it is all the more remarkable that the Vietnam Veterans Memorial was able to speak so directly of the meaning and memory of death to a nation which only wanted to forget. To give one example, it seems fair to say that the significance of Memorial Day, a national holiday at the end of May intended to commemorate those killed in war, has declined in recent years. Originally began as a tribute to the soldiers of the American Civil War, Memorial Day has been celebrated in most American communities by parades and public speeches. Perhaps the best discussion of the place of Memorial Day in American life can be found in W. L. Warner's (1975) *The Living and the Dead*, the last of the five volume "Yankee City" series, where he describes the Memorial Day Parade as a ritual pilgrimage to the town cemetery, to the "city of the dead" as he calls it.

Memorial Day seems to have declined in significance, just as cemeteries have declined in significance in America. Though Americans remain a highly religious people, American culture has turned away from the commemoration of death. Whether the decline in Memorial Day is due to the denial of death syndrome, or to the fallout of the Vietnam era and its moral ambiguities, or to its less readily "marketability" in contrast to other holidays, or simply that it expresses outdated sentiments, is unclear.

It is a common practice for people at the wall to make rubbings of names, and tour guides will provide paper to make rubbings. Hence at any given walk through the memorial there will be one or more people actively making a rubbing, thereby imparting a participatory atmosphere to the quiet stone to the dead. The only comparison I can think of is perhaps the graffiti on the old Berlin Wall, which signified the ridicule of Communist absolutism and anything else imaginable. That symbol of the great divide, with exploding mines on one side and irreverent images and graffiti on the other, was, and I suspect will remain, the most powerful political symbol of twentieth-century Germany, with its "no man's land" around the remains of Hitler's bunker, where he burrowed his way back to Hell, with its barbed wire and police guards and police dogs which stood as self-representations of the so-called German Democratic Republic, and with its images in the Fall of 1989 of the concrete demise of Communist concrete. "The wall" will continue to signify, in my opinion, the battle between democracy and totalitarianism which continues to be fought in our century, even if every last piece of it is sold as a sacred tourist relic.

The wall, even more than the Kaiser Wilhelm *Gedankskirche* (a church deliberately left in partial ruins), encompasses the broadest span of twentieth-century Germany. The Vietnam Veteran's Memorial, which deliberately avoids the term "Vietnam War," also symbolizes defeat, and in the late twentieth-century, defeat is an important legacy of the modern era, an antidote to its boundless confidence and total wars. Both the Vietnam Veterans Memorial − "the wall" − and what Germans called the *Mauer* (wall) can serve as artifactual reminders of misguided national purposes.

Somehow the Vietnam Veterans Memorial manages to bind together the feelings of those who died in or believed in the war, with those who did not. It captures the ambiguity of the war and of the 1960s in its seeming refusal to acknowledge the tradition of war memorials, yet also clearly honors the dead. Despite initial opposition to it by veterans groups, its subsequent popularity has prompted a life-sized replica to be displayed in major cities around the United States, so that more people can see it, as well as permanent "mini-walls" in smaller cities and towns, which symbolize a connection to the great wall in Washington.

One of the reasons this memorial seems to work so well, it seems to me, is because it is endowed with the binding power of the feminine. How odd, that a monument to dead male soldiers is so powerfully feminine! And yet it is precisely its feminine ability to encompass and nurture that helps set it apart. The American historian, Henry Adams, suggested around the turn of the century that the modern dynamo has taken the place as the energy of modern culture, which the Virgin held for Medieval culture. Adams, and later Lewis Mumford, noted that the power of the feminine had been lost as a moving culture symbol. Yet perhaps in this powerful contemporary symbol of American democracy and its failings we see the possibility of a renewal through the feminine.

My next case will take us from a self-representation of democracy which transcends kitsch, to one which bathes in kitsch.

Airstream Amerika

Nothing, in my view, more deserved attention than the intellectual and moral associations in America. American political and industrial associations easily catch our eyes, but the others tend not to be noticed. And even if we do notice them we tend to misunderstand them, hardly ever having seen anything similar before. However we should recognize that the latter are as necessary as the former to the American people; perhaps more so.

In democratic countries knowledge of how to combine is the mother of all other forms of knowledge; on its progress depends that of all the others (Tocqueville 1969[1840]: 517).

In Italo Calvino's (1974) *Invisible Cities*, Marco Polo describes to an aging Kublai Khan the many strange and mysterious cities of Khan's empire he has seen. Fantastic in shape and frequently surreal in lifestyle, they together weave a picture of an empire in dissolution and decay. I shall describe an American association every bit as weird as some of those cities which Calvino's Polo depicts, and in some ways even more queer: an association that forms a city which, like Polo himself, is self-moving and filled with *Wanderlust*.

It is a city that defines itself through techno-leisure, and which embodies those now classic American values of rugged mass "individualism" and the automobile. Indeed, one might say that it is literally an elaborate system of auto eroticism. It is a city which can be characterized as a landscape of signs, a transitory city whose entire existence is predicated upon mobility: upward and onward mobility. In its artificiality it is perhaps only rivalled by that great American desert Mecca, Las Vegas. But where Las Vegas is a city dedicated to Mammon, in his manifestation as chance and uncertainty in gambling, the city I will describe is dedicated to hierarchical, rationalized, totemic *order*, in which the figure of Mammon is not always as immediately apparent.

If, as Durkheim (1968: 231) believed, "social life, in all its aspects and in every period of its history, is made possible only by a vast symbolism," then the contemporary cult of the *Airstream* especially serves as an indicator of American leisure culture. By exploring the strange travelling rituals of a club formed around the inventor of the Airstream travel trailer, Wally Byam, we see in actuality a group approximating an ideal of the values of leisure and retirement that are so central to the American "way of life," and a semiotic landscape that embodies these values and the larger mind that they serve: that which Lewis Mumford has termed the "megamachine."

In the airstream city we see an aggregate of anonymous possessors of Airstreams possessed by a vast power, property, prestige complex, a soulless never-never land where *things* and their ownership, not *citizens*, form the heart of the city. The airstream cult provides one small opening to a discussion of the virtual dictatorship of the automobile in contemporary Western civilization, of commodity fetishism, of the myth of classless "rugged individualism" in the context of mass society, and of the stubborn ability of objects to retain animistic qualities in seemingly rational, technocratic society.

The new world legacy

In many ways the American vision can be characterized as the journey of the individual into the community of nature. One sees this vision in the literary transcendentalists of the 1850s, such as Thoreau, Melville, Whitman, and Emerson, through the organic architecture of Louis Sullivan and Frank Lloyd Wright, through the founding of nature movements near the end of the 19th century — the Audubon Club, the Sierra Club, and others — and even somewhat later in the spread of the Boy Scout movement. Just as Frederick Jackson Turner declared the frontier closed, and just as Americans were competing the program of genocide practiced on Native Americans, White, largely Protestant, Americans could adopt the totemic outlook of the Native Americans through the

Boy Scouts (Mechling 1989). Later the automobile and professionalized sports would provide media for totemic mass cults.

One sees this vision as well in the poetry of Robinson Jeffers; the naturalistic philosophy of self and community elaborated by the philosophical pragmatists; the photography of Ansel Adams; the furniture, home, and sculpture of Wharton Esherick; the organic vision of Lewis Mumford. A common feature of this New World vision is the attempt to strip the pretensions of Western Civilization and its lusts for power and prestige by growing a new kind of individual and community, rooted in the organic environment.

Unfortunately this grand vision of organic utopia has been paved over by another America, by the one most of us are familiar with. This other America is the one Jean Baudrillard (1989) has referred to in his book *America* as the place where the lights are never turned off. Who can deny the omnipresence of this omnivorous Disneyland empire and its Disney world view? Even if, I must say, Baudrillard's tourist's-eye view of American culture runs about as deep as the view that French culture can be expressed in the law that all adult Frenchmen are required to carry baguettes under their arms at all times in public, still, it is clear that "actually existing America" is far removed from the organic vision of its greatest artists and thinkers.

The caravan

In June and July, 1984, and again in 1990, four thousand Airstreams and almost ten thousand Airstreamers, all members of the Wally Byam Caravan Club, converged on the campus of the University of Notre Dame for their annual international caravan. Shining silver Airstreams occupied every available open space surrounding the campus, to create a city of wheels in which a rich system of totemic and hierarchical symbolism predominated. The Wally Byam Caravan Club is named after the inventor of the Airstream Travel Trailer, which the Airstream club describes as the "prestige units of travel trailers." The term "caravan" evokes the nomadic life of travel and trade in the Middle East, but the Airstream club itself draws on the image of "wagon trains" of the American frontier, when settlers would travel with all of their worldly possessions in covered wagons.

Most Wally Byam Caravan Club members are retired, and a number of males are former career military men. The club is then predominantly a gerontocracy, and one in which one's rank and social standing is quite significant. Perhaps this indicates a need to recreate social roles lost through retirement, a fantasy microworld where roles are clearly delineated and where one can even dream again of "career" advancement. I was told, for example, of an electrician who found his much needed services for the caravans brought him very quickly to a position of prominence. Alexis de Tocqueville (1969[1840]: 513) was one of the first to note that "Americans of all ages, all stations in life, and all types of disposition are forever forming associations." Who knows but that the club might presage the kinds of organizations one might see developing in a demographically aging American population?

In the Wally Byam Club we see all the hallmarks of the cult of ritualized leisure and prefabricated spontaneity, all in the name of a mythic individualism. Linked by the common bond of an ability to purchase an Airstream (at an average 1990 price of $27,000 to $49,000 U. S.), the community of the elect engage in an elaborate system of totemic hierarchy. Members arrive at the international caravan, for example, wearing ribbons they have received for attending regional caravans symbolic of the greater prestige of those who are more active in the club. The membership number printed in red letters on Airstreams also signifies how long one has been a member of the Caravan club. Members with these numbers assume higher prestige than owners of Airstreams who do not join the club, and the lower one's number, the closer one is to the origin of the club and its mythologized founder: to the "good old days" or, as Mircea Eliade put it, "in illo tempore," the time of "creation."

Perhaps there is some greater need in American culture to adopt totem-like classifications as a sort of echo of the native peoples crushed by the "American Dream." One only has to turn to that greatest symbol of the American way of life, the automobile, to see the elaborate totemic naming system of largely predatory animals, such as the stingray or cobra, or of prowess, such as the mustang or bronco, or of prestige, such as the monarchs and regals, etc., to see that technology carries an animistic aura seemingly quite at odds with the modern ethos. Power, sexuality, prestige, mobility — the lethal ability to kill as many people in the United States each year as one would expect from a war — these are some of the primary values that cars carry both in America and more generally in the modern world. But how strange it is that high-tech should have such primal urges and emblems attached to it. Freud might well under-

Plate 3. Convention of the Wally Byam Caravan Club at Notre Dame University.

stand how totemic symbolism and its taboo status in modern life might
easily co-exist. Photographs of his office at Bergasse 19 in Vienna reveal
a cultic semicircle of ancient statuettes surrounding the enlightened scientist. The Airstream is one of the highest of high-tech vehicles, and is
clear from the Wally Byam Caravan Club, also a veritable social hiero-
glyph.

In the flag symbolism, which reflects the penchant for totemic emblems
of this group as well as traditional patriotism, and in the hierarchical
alignment of the high-status vehicles near the "sacred" space of the
University of Notre Dame, one sees the re-creation of the ancient concept
of *axis mundi*. Although the University of Notre Dame is a private,
Catholic university, whose religious center is the "golden dome" − the
administration building on which stands "Notre Dame du Lac" − the
university is universally known in America for its football teams, and is

regarded by many as the symbolic center of American football. A famous film about Knute Rockne, the coach of the team during its golden years in the 1920s and 1930s, featured one of the star players, George Gipp ("the Gipper") who was acted by Ronald Reagan. And Reagan drew quite consciously on the popularity of this film by retaining the nickname the "Gipper" throughout his political career. So in understanding the political symbolism of the University of Notre Dame, it is important to keep in mind how it is more of a "religio-athletic" institution than a religious university. And it is precisely the "sacred" athletic aura with which the Airstream cult chose to surround itself. Hence the highest ranking vehicles, belonging to the officers of the club, were to be found next to the football stadium which Rockne built, between it and the huge indoor basketball complex. Most of these elite Airstreams were also distinguished by the large number of flags they flew — about five per vehicle — and by their low club membership numbers. The President's Airstream on the right of Plate 4, for example, showed membership number 124. The next level, that of past presidents and officers, formed the rows slightly more removed from the stadium. Another pocket of prestige was an area reserved for the grandparents of regional "Miss Teen Stream" beauty contestants. On one perimeter of the Airstream city was

Plate 4. Airstreams from the convention of the Wally Byam Caravan Club at Notre Dame University.

a functional "neighborhood" reserved for dog owners, which was established because of prior experiences of barking dogs disturbing the peace. Both individual Airstreams and the collective city they form are paradigms of modern functionalism. When the architect and city designer Le Corbusier declared that the house is a machine, he expressed the modern dream of transforming human life into that of the machine. That dream lives in the soul of Airstream America.

The automobile, autonomy, and the automatic

> Around 1930, just when the "new capitalism" suddenly slumped down to earth, the motor car industry picked itself up by exchanging economy for style... Within the next two decades, the motor car became a status symbol, a religious icon, an erotic fetish: in short, "something out of this world," increasingly swollen and tumescent, as if on the verge of an orgasm. What words other than Madison Avenue's can adequately describe these exciting confections, glittering with chrome, pillowed in comfort, sleepy-soft to ride in, equipped with mirrors, cigarette lighters, radios, telephones, floor carpeting; (liquor bars and tape-recorders are still optional) (Mumford 1979: 369).

Although not usually associated with political symbolism, I would like to suggest that the automobile can be seen as a key anti-political symbol in contemporary American life, and more broadly, as a symbol of the mechanization of life and consequent loss of organic human purpose and sense of limitation. The 1980s began with the prospect that the home office, through the personal computer, would achieve a far greater role in the "workplace," and ended with the automobile — that master symbol of American culture — as the model office of the future. Through the cellular telephone, the fax machine, and the computer, the automobile is in the process of becoming the ideal high-tech, travelling office in the age of gridlock, as ever-increasing amounts of congested roadways reduce mobility to and from work. Taken together, all of these developments signalled an ever greater reliance on automatic, technical culture.

The term "auto" means self — hence "automobile" or self-moving — but the meanings of Ralph Waldo Emerson's (1969: 72–93) essay "Self-reliance" and contemporary "auto reliance" could not be more disparate. Consider the irony of business people sitting in stalled traffic, diligently working with all the conveniences of home and office: the auto-immobile.

Perhaps it would have been better if another term, originally applied to one of the earliest self-moving vehicles, had been adopted, the "loco-mobile." Given the increasing amounts of time Americans are spending in these "moving places," and given the effects cars have had in dominating and devitalizing cities through residential sprawl, workday congestion, and the sheer roadways themselves, and given the continuing subordination of organic human purpose and habitat to the requirements of the delocalizing, centralized machine mentality, the term "locomobile" also captures the "moving craziness" of contemporary American culture.

American culture today highlights the modern battle between autonomy and the automaton. The great dream of the modern era has been to provide for and enlarge the autonomy of humankind through technical invention and control over the necessities of life. As that dream has been realized it has all too frequently revealed itself in diabolical reversal. The vast technical culture and wealth of America have not led the way toward the good life, but instead toward the goods life, toward a reified culture centered on commodities rather than citizens, toward an ultimate goal of automatic things and away from human autonomy. This is not the necessary outcome of the development of technology, but the consequence of the withering of human purpose in the face of the "magic" of technique.

The parade of democracy

> "We're just one big happy mass of silver" (Airstreamer, cited in *New York Times*, 9/25/90).

Throughout the two weeks of the Caravan, club members engage in numerous internal political and cultural activities, as well as attending entertainment events, all centered in the huge University of Notre Dame indoor sport amphitheater. But the climax and central ritual of the entire caravan is the Fourth of July parade. Not only is the caravan timed to conclude on Independence Day, but all of the state groups devote time during the two weeks to making symbolic floats and costumes. The theme of the 1990 international caravan, for example, was the "good old days," around which a variety of images – from elderly people dressed as infants to antique automobiles – were constructed to reveal a nostalgic "history" which mirrors the self-image of the Airstreamers as friendly, fun-loving, patriotic explorers of America.

Indeed, the Airstream cult could be termed a "community of nostalgia," in contrast to what Robert Bellah and the coauthors of *Habits of the Heart* (1985) have designated as "communities of memory." A real community, according to Bellah et al., retells its past in order not to forget it. The stories and rituals through which a community's memories are made public must be more than mere positive idealizations of itself:

> A genuine community of memory will also tell painful stories of shared suffering that sometimes creates deeper identities than success... And if the community is completely honest, it will remember stories not only of suffering received but of suffering inflicted — dangerous memories, for they call the community to alter ancient evils... At some times, neighborhoods, localities, and regions have been communities in America, but that has been hard to sustain in our restless and mobile society... Where history and hope are forgotten and community means only the gathering of the similar, community degenerates into lifestyle enclave. The temptation toward that transformation is endemic in America, though the transformation is seldom complete (Bellah 1985: 153–154).

By contrast with a community of memory, the Airstream cult represents an ideal type of the opposite: all bad events are banished from its collective memory banks, and the ultra-modern vehicle that the Airstream was and purports to remain is fused with sentimental nostalgia: the "good old days." One Airstreamer told the story of a small Caravan through Mexico, and how every night the twenty or so Airstreams would form a circle as was done in the days of the pioneer wagon trains. He recalled the campfire and songs, but had virtually nothing to say about Mexico itself: his memories were made within his circle of the familiar, not from the unfamiliar world without. This was a tourism which travelled fully insulated by a bubble of American culture.

One saw, in the Airstream caravan of 1984, an ironic inversion of Orwell's *1984*. Here was no totalitarian dictatorship imposing a denial of real history while stifling dissent. Instead there was a society freely choosing to deny the real history one develops by being rooted in a community, to deny that anything might be wrong with itself. The Airstream Cult might be regarded as a collective immune system to history. It was a collective embodiment of the "feel good" and forgetful ideals of Reagan America. Though the Airstreamers like to think of themselves as friendly and open, theirs is the friendliness of mass anonymity, the "gathering of the similar."

The Fourth of July is, of course, the date of American independence from England, and so holds a patriotic significance in American "civil religion," as well as being perhaps the chief civic holiday of local communities. But there is an additional layer of symbolism beyond the obviously political: the heroic founder of the Airstream cult, Wally Byam, was born on July 4, 1898. Hence the parade also acts as a commemoration of the founding father, fusing national symbolism with the "creation myth" of the Airstream itself.

What could be a more appropriate form of ritual to signify the cult of mobility than the parade? When we examine some of the floats in the parade, the symbolic values of the airstream cult become even clearer. The Brazilian ethnographer Roberto DaMatta (1991), has studied the carnival in Rio, and shown how highly structured and authoritarian Brazilian society temporarily transforms itself into relatively nonhierarchical community in the carnival parades. Such a temporary reversal of structure illustrates the "ludic" or "liminal" phase of rituals described by ethnographer Victor Turner (1969), where normal roles are temporarily reversed. DaMatta has noted how Mardi Gras in New Orleans, where all the groups are led by a king or queen, reveals the American desire for hierarchy beneath the egalitarian, democratic facade.

Similarly, we see in the organization of the parade itself the ritual exhibition of hierarchy through the arrival of elected Airstream dignitaries to the reviewing platform in the large four-wheel-drive automobiles — known as vans, broncos, blazers, and suburbans — used to pull the Airstreams. Later, the teenage girls who are state winners of Airstream beauty contests and who are competing to become "Miss Teen Stream" arrive in Corvette Stingray automobiles rented for the occasion. Here one sees "auto eroticism" at its purest, as the sports cars symbolize the budding sexuality of youth. In this sense the ruling Airstream gerontocracy can vicariously express the blush of youthful sexuality through the girls and the potent Corvette Stingrays on which they ride.

Indeed, both the parade and the "city of wheels" is perhaps an example of what Niklas Luhmann (1990: 1 – 20) calls "autopoeisis," where system, not person, is self-generating. But where Luhmann elevates social systems to cultic status, by alienating them from the persons who comprise them, the elevation of vehicles to cultic status, both in the Airstream microcosm and American culture in general, conveys to me a more malignant dictatorship of the machine over democratic life.

Throughout the parade many of the floats fused Airstream symbolism with the symbolism of the University of Notre Dame, whose football team is widely known as the "fighting Irish." One sees this in the group of older women dressed as Leprechauns resting before the beginning of

Plate 5. Airstreamers dressed as leprechauns, Wally Byam Caravan Club.

the parade (Plate 5). The contrast between age (the sitting Leprechaun women) and beauty (the standing Miss Teen Stream contestants in the sports cars behind them) is also striking.

Similarly in the float named "Green Magic Carpet" one sees the combination of the mobile "magic carpet" of the Middle East, the land of caravans, and Irish green (Plate 6). On the front of the float is a motto used by University of Notre Dame football fans: "Irish fever. We've got it." The twin domes on the front of the float may appear to be a model of a nuclear reactor, but are in fact a representation of the university's indoor sports complex.

When it comes to the power of symbols, neither learning nor religion convey the main message of the University of Notre Dame. Rather it is the mythic power of the American sports complex, perfumed by the faint aura of religion and higher learning, which provides energies for ritual expression. Here, too, one can see American society in microcosm. Simmel (1978) observed that as the concept of God lost its mediating power as *coincidentia oppositorum* in modern culture, money arose to take its place in the hierarchy of modern values. If money represents the materialistic symbol of transcendence in the modern age, then sport, I submit, represents the materialization of religious ritual.

Plate 6. "Magic carpet" float from the Airstream parade.

When we remember that most of the modern sports, including the major American sports of football, basketball and baseball, were invented in the last decades of the 19th century (MacAloon 1980), it is possible to see the great significance of modern sport globally, with its elevation of the human body and of large-scale spectacle, as deriving from the myth of materialism. The old gods may have been dying, as Durkheim lamented in 1912 in *The Elementary Forms of the Religious Life*, but new ones were indeed being born all around him. Like sport, the automobile and the airplane were powerful emergent symbols of modern materialism and culture.

All three symbols — sport, automobiles, and airplanes — crystallized as central institutions of American culture after the Second World War. Professional football and basketball rose to the prominence of baseball in America, and Americans became enthusiastic subjects of year-round televised sporting events. Somewhat later, airports became status symbols for cities in America and throughout the world: in the age of institutionalized modernism a city without its own airport was as deficient as a city without a skyscraper. Transportation in America underwent fundamental changes in the 1950s due to policy decisions heavily influenced by oil companies and automobile makers to build a national highway system. Such decisions greatly empowered car and truck transport, while undermining mass transit systems nationwide. It was during this period of euphoria over the new interstate highway system that the Wally Byam club was formed and began to flourish, so that by 1959 – 60 it could caravan through Europe and Africa, meeting Hallie Selassie and Ugandan witch doctors. And it is precisely this 1950s spirit of "on the road" which remains the core value of the club today. In this sense the club represents the ideal realization of the mobile society, where both home and city are in continual motion.

The Airstream city of wheels is nothing less than a utopia, a contemporary mobile analogue to the earlier utopian communities of the New World, just as the development of the city itself may have been the original utopia, as Lewis Mumford suggested, concretely realized at the dawn of civilization:

> ... As Fustel de Coulanges and Bachofen pointed out a century ago, the city was primarily a religious phenomenon: it was the home of a god, and even the city wall points to this super-human origin; for Mircea Eliade is probably correct in inferring that its primary function was to hold chaos at bay and ward off inimical spirits.
>
> This cosmic orientation, these mythic-religious claims, this royal preemption of the powers and functions of the community are what transformed the mere village or town into a city: something "out of this world," the home of a god. Much of the contents of the city − houses, shrines, storage bins, ditches, irrigation works − was already in existence in smaller communities: but though these utilities were necessary antecedents of the city, the city itself was transmogrified into an ideal form − a glimpse of eternal order, a visible heaven on earth, a seat of life abundant − in other words, utopia (Mumford 1967: 13).

The ancient city wall held "chaos at bay" and warded off "inimical spirits," just as the walled medieval city, whose success may have been the initial impetus to modern capitalism, warded off potential enemies. Americans seem to have activated these ancient functions of the wall in shopping malls, which ward off that which is "undesirable." But where the ancient wall served the life of the city, the modern mall serves itself, and privatizes the life of the city into itself. Americans have increasingly chosen to spend their time and money in walled malls instead of in cities, so that by 1987 the over 30,000 U. S. shopping centers generated 586 billion dollars in sales, or 13 percent of the gross national product, while employing almost 9 million people, or 8 percent of the U. S. labor force. The ancient gods of the city and of the home have not been dispelled by modern materialism, but have been reinstated in the ever-tightening cult of American consumerism. In this new monotheism, the organic seasons of nature have metamorphosed into extended indoor shopping seasons, and the ancestor cult transformed from an act of propitiation into a declaration of consumptive independence.

Malls represent a vision of utopia in contemporary American society, promising to free Americans from crime, urban blight, and uncertainty. But they do this by alienating people from spontaneous conduct, from voluntary association other than that of a consumer, and ultimately from a public life. As privatized public spaces they rigidly enforce the new American code of controlled and monitored behavior, the "culture of control" (Gehm 1990). They are not only *controlled*, but also *controlling* environments. Malls promise that the good life is to be found in the life of goods, but their reality is that they are literal embodiments of the dark side of Thomas More's ambiguous term "utopia," which suggests both *eutopia* — the "good place" — and *ou topos*, literally "no place." They give ample testimony to the benumbed confusion in America that capitalism and democracy are synonymous, and to the continued atrophy of vital democracy.

Similarly the Airstream city is a highly controlled environment: structurally it keeps poor people out, functionally it is monitored by its own security force, the "blue berets," who police the grounds on motor bikes, culturally it values the "like-minded" organization man, symbolized as much by the high numbers of retired career military personnel in the membership as by the official club songbook and "Wally Byam Creed." One sees virtually no poor, non-white, or sick Airstreamers, despite the myth of classless community which permeates the group.

The loss of public spaces to private malls, where free speech can be treated as trespassing, raises the question: just what is a city and how might the city itself symbolize democracy? As part of the larger dynamics of the modern era, American culture has transformed technique from a means to the good life to a virtual goal unto itself, with the result that Americans have increasingly seemed to be willing to sacrifice the art and practice and struggles of concrete life to the conveniences of abstract technique: to give up the active cultivation of home life to the passive consumption of television and TV dinners, to give up multipurpose centers for civic life and local commerce to self-enclosed, privatized, behavior-monitoring shopping malls, to surrender the pursuit of qualitative autonomy to the pursuit of dollars. Yet the high crime and divorce statistics, the addiction rates, the escalating political hypocrisy, the easygoing ignorance of those cultural values which are not conveniently transmitted by the media, and the widespread disparagement of serious, non-commercial, non-sporting activities, all testify to a culture in decline, not to a culture realizing enriched and rewarding lives.

Conclusion: Perishable democracy

As anyone familiar with American electoral politics and television knows, or as I hope the Airstream cult might illustrate, American culture frequently utilizes powerful symbols of democracy. Yet though these are self-representations of democracy, they virtually never *represent* democracy. Rather they are signs of the reduction of American political life to entertainment. They signify an antidemocratic mass society in which rituals of consumption, mass media, and leisure have largely replaced the cultivation of local, regional, and national public life.

The Vietnam Veterans Memorial stands as a curious exception in contemporary American life in the ways it has been able to channel powerful sentiments into the serious consideration of democratic values. It does not glorify the war, but it does call forth emotions of loss and raises, for many, the question of the purpose of the Vietnam War as well as the tangible specter of defeat. It is a symbol wedged between American kitsch sentimentalism and cynical "sound bite" politics, yet it somehow works. It grows out of an aesthetic of minimalism and postmodern "earth art," two vacuous styles which say more about the depletion of the human person in the late-20th century as the living mediator of culture than about the making of art. Yet it transcends minimalism as a powerful testimony to the significance of the human person, collective memory, and all-too-human death. As "earth art" it can be seen to resonate with, whether intended or not, the Taoist idea of the "empty container," or that which paradoxically reveals itself in fullness out of its emptiness. As a public monument it provides an uncanny and unique solution to the great difficulty we face at the end of the modern era between rational architectural forms which severely limit the expression of human feeling, and the lure of nostalgia to reduce human feeling to kitsch. Perhaps we can see in it the potential binding power of the feminine, as a welcome and needed dimension of political and cultural self-representation today.

Old-time nationalistic self-representation will no longer do: the catastrophic events of the twentieth century have repeatedly shown the dangers of political symbols which lack the capacity for self-examination and self-criticism. In the new world culture which is emerging in the American population itself, bringing the vision of America as microcosm of the world community to a new phase, we ought to go past the symbols of unquestioning national glory and private self-interest to those of self-critical and mutual responsibility. If democracy is to be anything other than a brief "mortal splendor" in the drama of American culture, it will need to undo the antidemocratic mass culture which the word "Americanism" now communicates and which thoroughly dominates American life. The great challenge which democracy has always posed in America — to create self-critical autonomous selves embedded within broader community purposes — is one whose survival in an ever more automatic America is questionable.

Notes

1. I developed this perspective in my books *Meaning and Modernity* (Chicago: University of Chicago Press, 1986) and *Bereft of Reason* (Chicago: University of Chicago Press, 1994).
2. I am especially grateful to Barry Schwartz for helpful discussions concerning his research with Wagner-Pacifici on the Vietnam Veterans Memorial (Wagner-Pacifici — Schwartz 1991).

References

Baudrillard, Jean
    1989   *America*. Trans. by Chris Turner. London: Verso Press.
Bellah, Robert — Richard Madsen — William Sullivan — Ann Swidler — Steven Tipton
    1985   *Habits of the heart*. New York: Harper and Row.
Bronner, Simon J. (ed.)
    1989   *Consuming visions: Accumulation and display of goods in America, 1880 – 1920*. New York: W. W. Norton.
Calvino, Italo
    1974   *Invisible cities*. Trans. by William Weaver. New York: Harcourt, Brace, Jovanovich.
DaMatta, Roberto
    1991   *Carnival*. Notre Dame, IN: Notre Dame University Press.
Durkheim, Emile
    1968 [1912] *The elementary forms of the religious life*. London: George Allen and Unwin.

Emerson, Ralph Waldo
1961 [1841] *Selected prose and poetry*. New York: Holt, Rinehart, and Winston.
Gehm, John
1990   *The culture of control: Electronic monitoring of probationers*. Unpublished Ph.D. dissertation. University of Notre Dame.
Hess, Elizabeth
1983   "A tale of two monuments," *Art in America*, April: 120–127.
1985   "America remembers," *National Geographic* 67: 552–573.
Jeffers, Robinson
1987 [1924] *Rock and hawk: A selection of shorter poems by Robinson Jeffers*. New York: Random House.
Kundera, Milan
1984   *The unbearable lightness of being*. Trans. by Michael Heim. New York: Harper and Row.
Luhmann, Niklas
1990   *Essays on self-reliance*. New York: Columbia University Press.
MacAloon, John
1980   *This great symbol: Coubertin and the founding of the modern olympic games*. Chicago: University of Chicago Press.
Mechling, Jay
1989   "The collecting self and American youth movements," in: Simon J. Bronner (ed.), 255–285.
More, Thomas
1964 [1516] *Utopia*. New Haven, CN: Yale University Press.
Mumford, Lewis
1967   "Utopia, the city, and the machine," in: Frank E. Manuel (ed.) *Utopias and utopian thought*. Boston: Beacon Press, 3–24.
1979   "The American way of death." In: *Interpretations and forecasts, 1922–1972*. New York: Harcourt, Brace, Jovanovich.
Musil, Robert
1965   *The man without qualities*. Trans. by Eithne Wilkins and Ernst Kaiser. New York: Capricorn Books.
Rochberg-Halton, Eugene
1986   *Meaning and modernity*. Chicago: University of Chicago Press.
Simmel, Georg
1978 [1907] *The philosophy of money*. London: Routledge.
Tocqueville, Alexis de
1969 [1840] *Democracy in America*. New York: Doubleday Anchor Books.
Turner, Victor
1969   *The ritual process*. New York: Aldine Press.
Wagner-Pacifici, Robin – Barry Schwartz
1991   "The Vietnam veterans memorial: Commemorating a difficult past," *American Journal of Sociology* 97(2): 376–420.
Warner, W. Lloyd
1959   *The living and the dead: A study of the symbolic life of Americans*. New Haven: Yale University Press.

Part III
Clothing and adornment: The skin of culture

Are artifacts texts? Lithuanian woven sashes as social and cosmic transactions

Joan M. Vastokas

Towards a new theory of the artifact

Five essential points of theory arise from a consideration of artifacts in a socio-semiotic perspective: (1) the meaning of artifacts, including works of visual "art," is constituted in the life of the objects themselves, not in words or texts *about* them; (2) the artifact is not an inert, passive object, but an interactive agent in sociocultural life and cognition; (3) the signification of the artifact resides in both the object as a self-enclosed material fact and in its performative, "gestural" patterns of behavior in relation to space, time, and society; (4) the processes, materials, and products of technology, especially those of a society's dominant technology, function as cultural metaphors at many levels and in many sociocultural domains; and (5) theoretical insights derive, not from theorizing in the abstract, but from direct observation and experience of the phenomenal world of nature and culture.

Interpretation of cultures as "texts," which may be "read" like a system of linguistic signs, is now being questioned as fanciful and irrelevant to "the real humans who live out their lives through them" (Keesing 1987: 169). The prevalent use of linguistic models of analysis to interpret material artifacts, a category which includes works of visual art, is especially inappropriate (Vastokas 1978: 244). This questioning of culture as "text," however, does not find its major support among social scientists and cultural critics who, for the most part, remain mesmerized by the privileged status that language and text have enjoyed in Western society since at least the late Middle Ages. The pre-eminence accorded language and especially the written word is in itself a cultural symptom. It is to be explained, of course, in terms of the origins of writing as "secret," "sacred," or "privileged" knowledge, the preserve of shaman-priests in the case of the pictorial forerunners of writing in native North America; of temple administrators in ancient Mesopotamia; or of monks from noble families in the Medieval monasteries which gradually evolved into the modern university, the last available to non-elites only in the twentieth century.

The notion of language as the chief determinant in our conceptualization of the world was given scholarly sanction by anthropological linguistics in the "Sapir-Whorf hypothesis" (Sapir 1951; Whorf 1956). But extension of linguistic models to the analysis and interpretation of other cultural domains (art, myth, literature) begins mainly in Europe. Inspired most immediately by the work of Ferdinand de Saussure, Claude Lévi-Strauss (1963) and Roland Barthes (1957, 1967) have been mainly responsible for cementing the tradition of language and text as pre-eminent modes of human cognition and communication. It is not an unrelated fact that the *practice* of art history, which purports to be the study of architectural, sculptural, and pictorial artifacts, has laid methodological emphasis upon the written document (Vastokas 1986 – 1987). The idea of the work of art itself as *the* essential document is often submerged in a preoccupation with texts surrounding the production and reception of art works. As Donald Preziosi states so clearly, art history in practice is not a clearly defined discipline in itself, but a "subset" of history (Preziosi 1989: 165 – 166).

This pre-eminence of language and text remains true for even more recent interpretation theorists. Michel Foucault (1972) recognizes and acknowledges the essential gap between words and things (see Tilley 1990: 282 – 283), but persists in concerning himself not with things or the word, but with "discourses" *about* things. The "episteme" (more familiarly, paradigm) within which he himself operates functions as a blind spot, that is, the assumption that the discourse constitutes the "reality" and not what the discourse is about.

In the most recent publication on material culture interpretation at this time of writing, Christopher Tilley positions himself squarely within Foucault's perspective. For Tilley, the meaning of artifacts resides in the texts written about them. There is no meaning in the artifact itself. Instead it is to be found both "in the text's organization and syntax and in the relation of the text to the world" (Tilley 1990: 332). He persists in promoting the idea of the artifact as a "discursive object," which "is formed through language acting on the world." Moreover, "we are never dealing with the artifact... Our knowledge and understanding comes through a linguistic, textual medium... Writing material culture is producing material culture ... the *meaning* of material culture is created in the text" (Tilley 1990: 332). Because for Tilley, meaning resides in the discourses surrounding the artifact and not in the artifact itself, he concludes we can never come to an understanding of prehistoric societies such as the Upper Palaeolithic:

> There is no such thing ... as human nature. The subject is thoroughly constructed and *the only thing* [emphasis added] which we are likely to have in common with a palaeolithic social actor is the possession of a physical body of more or less the same kind. The men and women of the past did not just think or conceive the world differently from us, they *were* totally different (Tilley 1990: 340).

But it is precisely that *only thing* we share with prehistoric and with other men and women — our physical bodies — that permits us a way out of the "prison house" of language, a release from the tyranny of the text and from mentalistic irrelevancies. Recent work in the field of cognitive psychology supports the direct know-ability of the world and implies the communicability of that knowledge between and among humans who, in many ways, *are all the same*. This is so, because our perceptions and responses to the phenomenal world are grounded in and processed by the neuro-physiology of our bodies, in our brains, and our nervous systems, and they are conditioned by the architecture and to-pography of the brain, by its specialized functions, including the differ-ential functioning of the two hemispheres, by areas of specialization within the cerebral cortex, and by the specialization of individual brain cells (see Ornstein 1986 and especially Barlow et al. 1990). Words are but secondary "translations" of thought and feeling processes, which originate in direct sense experience of the phenomenal world. Even written texts, before they are language, are *images*, pictorial signs (Gelb 1963: 7). The real challenge now is not to force fashionable models of verbal analysis upon visual and concrete artifacts. What is needed instead is a new theory and method of interpretation grounded in the realities of the physically existing object as it is actually made, used, and interpreted within the complexities of its full sociocultural and environmental context.

A number of scholars have recently called for a semiotics of material culture "without reference," as Roland Fletcher (1989: 37) expresses it, "to the meaning, categories, taxonomies or explanations applicable to verbal expression and human action understood in terms of these verbal meanings." But even earlier, the American philosopher John Dewey, unfortunately neglected by social and cultural theoreticians, proclaimed clearly against the tyranny of the text. For Dewey, there are non-verbal meanings "that present themselves directly as possessions of objects which are experienced" (Dewey 1958: 83). To date, however, the majority of those calling for and seeking to initiate a more appropriate and more fully rounded semiotics of the object have done so in a reductionist manner. Still laboring under the methodological conditioning of linguistic analytical procedures, their preoccupation is with the artifact as a static, self-contained, noncontextualized object, or as a document whose internally structured design motifs constitute signs to be interpreted and read. In a recent example of the persistence of this static structuralist perspective, Donald Rubinstein (1978: 67) analyzes the "visual syntax" of the motifs in Micronesian textiles, seeking "to illustrate how their structural arrangement is replicated in other art and architectural forms." Such structuralist studies of the mirroring of one material cultural genre in other kinds of artifacts and of their mutual reflection in "underlying cultural principles of social and spatial order" (Rubinstein 1978: 67) are by now a commonplace and perhaps redundant endeavor. This is so, because the resultant interpretations are primarily descriptive rather than explanatory, grounded as they are in the artifact as an inert object, merely a reflection or mirror of cultural "patterns" and not as an active agent in a creative, ongoing and dynamic system.

One exception to this static, structuralist approach has been the orientation of archeological theorist, Ian Hodder. For Hodder, artifacts play a vital performative role in cultural process. Artifacts are interactive; they are "symbols in action," to use Hodder's phrase, agents in social and economic relations (Hodder 1982). Most importantly, he questions the concept of artifacts as "'documents' of a kind which can be read or decoded by the outside observer" (Hodder 1982: xiv). However, Hodder himself lapses into the linguistic sideroad in a more recent publication (1986: 122), wherein he says that "we can consider the archaeological record as a 'text' to be read." He need not have succumbed to fashion, since, in his own more perceptive account, the archeological "context" is most closely linked etymologically and phenomenologically with "the Latin *contexere*, meaning to weave, join together, connect" and that: "This interweaving, or connecting, of things in their historical particularity has been ... evident in many branches of archaeology" (Hodder 1986: 119).

But Hodder's analysis does not go far enough. The potential for a fully developed semiotics of objects falls short, mainly because Hodder fails to recognize and to exploit all the signs available in both the artifact itself and its actual performance in social and cultural life. However, it is not entirely his fault. It is the fault of the modernist Western conception of the artifact which accounts for this limited perspective of the object.

Since the emergence of the Renaissance and the rise of materialist and positivist values, both artifacts and works of visual art have been perceived and interpreted as isolated, discontinuous objects, divorced physically and meaningfully from both social life and from the surrounding environment. Most recently, they have become mere commodities, with primarily economic exchange value (Vastokas 1990). Great effort is now required to make a radical paradigm shift, in this case from the point of view of the artifact as inert object to the artifact as an actor in the narrative drama of daily cultural life.

In order to construct a more valid, more meaningful, and eventually more explanatory theory and method of material culture process and its interpretation, we need to develop a semiotics of visual phenomena. Such a theory would take into account the full spatial, temporal, and gestural dimensionality of the artifact. Although bounded within the frame of its own material existence, it is neither static nor isolated. To borrow a phrase from art critic Rosalind Krauss (1989), the artifact operates in "an expanded field."

The concept of culture as live and continually creative "performance," rather than static "text" or "document," provides a theoretical perspective for a more valid semiotics of the artifact. Advanced mainly by Victor Turner (1985; see also Wagner 1981), the performance concept calls for a phenomenological approach to the description and analysis of social behavior, including what may be termed the "behavior of artifacts." Every manufactured object has a life and a life-history of its own. In the process of its production, whether by hand or machine, the artifact is born, stamped with the conscious intentions and unconscious expressions of its creator(s). Then the artifact lives out a life in time and space of greater or lesser duration, both as a meaningful and expressive object in itself, and as a ritual performer in social and cultural life. Finally, it dies, passes out of use, destroyed or deposited in the garbage dump or in a museum.

From the point of view of the artifact as actor, then, the object may be observed at rest or in motion. It may even exhibit gestural behavior patterns in relation to space (location, direction, arrest and movement), to time (calendric, ritual, social), and to other physical phenomena (persons, animals, objects, waterfalls, caves, and buildings). This narrative concept of the artifact as an active agent, extends as well to easel painting and other kinds of "pictures" which, before they are "works of art," are artifacts in a performative context (see also Turner 1984: 20), capable of mobility within a spatial, temporal, and social universe. Paintings are material artifacts of various dimensions in themselves and are constructed of frame, canvas, and pigment. They move around from artist's studio, to gallery or private dwelling, to museum or office building. These moves occur in the context of meaningful social events. Even in the relatively "passive" case of easel paintings, we have them "on display," which is their particular kind of "action," at public gallery openings, exhibitions, or in private meditations. In the case of other kinds of artifacts, such as Kwakiutl Indian transformation masks, which split open at critical junctures in ceremonial dances to reveal an alternate identity, the object can play *the* pivotal dramatic role in narrative performance (see Hawthorn 1967: 59).

Signification of the artifact, then, is not limited to its internal structural and formal characteristics, but extends as well into space and time where it interacts dialogically with other phenomena. The patterns of the artifact's movements (direction, rhythm, pace), including its stops and stopping points, constitute essential, if not *the* most essential, signs of its signification and serve to inform and to augment the meanings of both social and ceremonial action. This is most readily apparent in the case of Northwest Coast Indian architecture, wherein the movements in space and time of performances and ritual paraphernalia of the various dancing societies provide the most significant clues to the latent symbolic meanings of architectural space and structure (see Vastokas 1966: 177 – 179, 1978: 253 – 254). For a new theory and method of artifact interpretation, then, we need to redefine the dimensionality of objects, to recognize their relationality in form and meaning, to acknowledge their spatial and temporal extensions beyond the limits of their physical contours or "frames." Artifacts function and signify in an expanded social and environmental space-time. To observe the artifact as a multi-dimensional phenomenon in the context of cultural performance is to experience its full reality and, ultimately, to achieve more valid interpretations and explanations.

Another related position taken here is that the phenomenal world impacts directly upon the human imagination, by-passing verbal language and linguistic processes entirely. Gestalt psychologist Rudolf Arnheim has long held the view that thinking is primarily a visual process; for him "visual perception is visual thinking" (Arnheim 1969: 14). Arnheim's position is reinforced by recent studies of the brain and its processes and parallels the observations of not only visual artists, but also those of scientists and engineers. Georgia O'Keeffe saw "shapes that were clearly in [her] mind" (O'Keeffe 1976: No. 15), while practising engineers report the precedence of visual imaging in their work (Ferguson 1977: 827–836).

Now technology — its processes as well as its products — looms very large in the phenomenal "lifeworld" of any culture.[1] A corollary of this and another presupposition here is that cultural ways — including moral and aesthetic values, art forms, social and ritual performances, as well as social structural patterns and relationships — are affected to a high degree by the dominant technological system. The revolution in material culture studies since the 1960s has resulted in the recognition that artifacts are culturally expressive, symbolic objects. While most attention these past three decades has been paid to the meaning of the artifact in itself, there is increasing recognition that the dynamics of the technical processes in themselves play an important cognitive role in the social and ideational life of cultural systems. There is general acknowledgement now, of technology as ideology in the broadest sense, that technological metaphors serve as models or "gestalts" for knowledge and for understanding the world. Numerous studies have appeared recently, demonstrating an equation between technology and culture (for example, Bush 1975; Macey 1980; Rivière 1969; Trachtenberg 1965). The dominant materials and technical processes as well as the artifact itself are shown to figure into cultural patterns and ideology at many levels and in many domains, such as cosmology, ritual, social relations, literature, philosophy, dance, and visual art. The philosopher of technology Donald Ihde (1990) has recently argued that abstract thought originates in technological processes. Taking inspiration from the phenomenologists Edmund Husserl, Martin Heidegger, and Maurice Merleau-Ponty, Ihde cites Husserl's observation that the processes and products of carpentry, for example, gave rise directly to geometrical thought without the intervention of language. Husserl sees a direct continuity between body, mind, and world wherein carpentry constitutes a "geometrical praxis" (Ihde 1990: 28–29). This is confirmed ethnographically among the Northwest Coast Indians, for whom the universe is a carpentered world (Vastokas 1969: 19–20). In this culture, the practice of woodworking and true carpentry in the construction of rectangular plank houses resulted in a configuration of the cosmos itself as rectangular, which was strikingly unlike the circular and open-edged worlds of interior North American tribes whose technologies were dominated by the sewing and lashing of flexible hides, bark, and poles.

The case of the Lithuanian woven sash

In the case of the preindustrial folk society of Lithuania, from the sixteenth to the end of the nineteenth centuries, a feudal system of agriculture was the major means of economic subsistence. However, textile production and usage provided the dominant metaphors and models for group identity, social interaction, and for expressive culture in the form of folk song, dance, folk art, and cosmology. These metaphors — visual and verbal — were derived not only from the finished products themselves, but from the tools, the materials, the processes, and the actual performance of the textile artifacts in the social network (Vastokas 1989). Spinning and weaving constituted the "praxis for cognition" in much of Lithuanian folk culture.

Above all other textile products, however, the woven or braided sash (*juosta*) served and continues to serve as a "key symbol" (Ortner 1973) in Lithuanian society. The sash ranges in size from relatively thin, twisted cords to woven bands, several inches wide, and up to fifteen feet in length. Most examples average about six to nine feet. Not all sashes were patterned, but those that were, were the most highly regarded and it is these patterned sashes in particular that play a dominant role in social and ceremonial life. The form of the sash — its size, the techniques used in its production, and its decorative motifs — was related to its specific utilitarian and symbolic function. The sash is most familiar as an item in Lithuanian folk costume, worn as a belt by both men and women, as a headpiece for women, and, in narrower width, as a necktie for men. Woven originally from homespun linen, hemp, and wool, cotton was introduced by the end of the nineteenth century and, today, factory-spun threads and synthetic yarns are produced, colored no longer with vegetable, but with chemical dyes (Tamošaitis — Tamošaitis 1988: 11).

The sash is the "prototype of all forms of Lithuanian folk weaving" and stands above all textiles: "the place of honour belonged to the weaver of sashes," as Lithuanian ethnographer Antanas Tamošaitis writes, "no other form of Lithuanian folk art had such a rich variety of meaning, of associated traditions and rituals, such aesthetic uniqueness in its designs, symbolism, and colour combinations" (Tamošaitis — Tamošaitis 1988: 10, 17). The sash is so important that it persists even today — albeit in transformation — both in immigrant Lithuanian communities in the West as well as in Lithuania itself as a symbol of ethnic and national identity.[2]

Although sash-making for traditional use declined within Lithuanian village culture at the end of the nineteenth century, sashes have continued

Plate 1. Vilnius, Lithuania, July, 1989. A demonstration of spinning by a young girl at the city's annual folk festival. Photograph by the author.

in production both within Lithuanian society and as a form of tourist art, for sale in *Dolerines* ("dollar shops") located in Intourist hotels where only foreigners with "hard currency" may also acquire such commodities as chocolate, scotch whiskey, picture books, and amber jewelry. Woven most often now on mechanical looms and increasingly mass-produced for the tourist market, the sash has been transformed and has acquired new forms and functions, particularly in the context of political aspirations for liberation from the Soviet Union. Initially, it was during the years of independence from the Russian Empire (1918–1940), that the sash first acquired its current status as a major symbol of Lithuanian national identity. In that period of cultural revitalization, sash-making was revived and adapted to such new uses as bookmarks, ties, watch

bands, pillow cases, place mats, and other forms of household paraphernalia (Tamošaitis — Tamošaitis 1988: 60). In Lithuanian homes today
one may often see several sashes hanging together in entrance ways, like
icons, to which are also attached such other emblems and signs of national
identity as the tricolor Lithuanian flag (yellow, green, red) and souvenir
pins representing national heroes or historically significant architectural
monuments. The earlier custom of occasionally weaving words, phrases,
and greetings into the sash, has been adapted in the twentieth century to
the making of political statements. As early as 1913, for example, the
Lithuanian sculptor Petras Rimša, who had learned to make sashes during
that first wave of independent national aspiration, wove into a long wide
sash the following statement: "In 1864 the Russian authorities banned
our press. We published books and newspapers beyond the border and
secretly smuggled them in and read them. The authorities persecuted us
because of this and punished us severely. Finally they gave in and lifted
the ban in 1904" (cited and translated in Tamošaitis — Tamošaitis 1988:
42).

An examination of the traditional Lithuanian sash, from the perspective of its material, form, social function, and associated metaphoric
meanings grounded in myth and folklore as well as past and present
cultural performance, gives support to the theoretical contention of this
paper that, as far as objects are concerned, verbal language and linguistic
models and methods of interpretive analysis cannot tell the whole story.

Until recently, however, very little interpretation of any kind of the
function and meaning of the Lithuanian sash had even been attempted.
The most recent study to appear examines the symbolism of a single
geometric motif, the *rožėlė* ("rosette"), which commonly appears in the
design of sashes (Tumėnas 1989). Although interesting and important as
a system of signs, our purpose at this time is not a semiotics of Lithuanian
sash motifs, but of the sash itself as a whole artifact, as a visual configuration, in its total performative context within Lithuanian folk society.

On the surface level, each kind of sash, and there are at least some
fourteen different types (Tamošaitis 1976: 66), had its own particular role
and its own meaning within social custom. The ethnography of these
roles in Lithuanian village culture has been most fully described by
Antanas Tamošaitis, a pioneer in folk art collection and research in
Lithuania and an informant in his own right. He was the first to make
a systematic collection of Lithuanian folk textiles and the first to engage
in a rigorous analysis and description. His fieldwork dates largely from
the 1920s to the 1930s, but the results have only recently been published

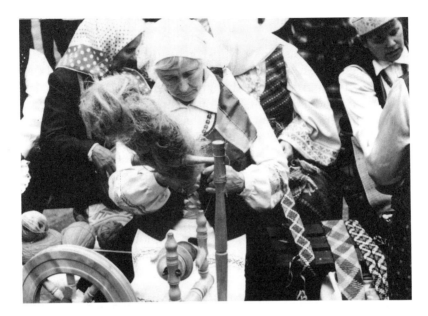

Plate 2. Vilnius, Lithuania, July 1989. Woman spinning, with braided sashes to her left. Photograph by the author.

owing to the disruptions of World War II, the Soviet occupation of Lithuania, and Tamošaitis' emigration to Canada in the early 1940s. The formal aspects of the sashes themselves are described by his wife, Anastazija Tamošaitis, a fiber artist and expert weaver of traditional Lithuanian clothing. Her account (Tamošaitis — Tamošaitis 1988: 231–282) details the technical production of the sashes, the preparation and dyeing of linen and wool fibers, the various kinds of looms and other instruments employed, the different weaving and braiding techniques, and the regional style areas throughout the countryside.

The oldest extant sashes date only from the eighteenth century, but archeological and linguistic investigations indicate that textiles in general were likely an important technology and ideological factor in Lithuanian culture from an early period. Textile production in Lithuania dates most likely as far back as the pre-Indo-European Neolithic, the period of initial food production and its associated ceramic and textile crafts in the Baltic area *circa* 4000–3500 BC (Gimbutas 1989: 334).

As a branch of the Indo-European language family, however, Lithuanian along with Latvian and the now-extinct East Prussian, are grouped under the designation "Baltic Languages" which separated from Proto-

Indo-European around 1500 BC (Mallory 1989: 89) and, by 1300 BC, a distinctive culture appears to have emerged on the eastern shores of the Baltic Sea. Many aspects of this prehistoric culture persisted in rural Lithuanian village culture well into the nineteenth and early twentieth centuries. For purposes of ethnographic analogy, that is, for helping to interpret the hidden meanings of Lithuanian sashes by using comparative cultural material, it is not unimportant that Lithuanian exhibits a considerable retention of Proto-Indo-European forms (Mallory 1989: 157) and a close linguistic relationship with Sanskrit, the language of Vedic India (Gimbutas 1963: 37, 40—42). There is also reason to suspect that cultural affinities between prehistoric Baltic culture and that of the ancient Hindus extend more widely than language, into mythology, cosmology, religion, and even material culture, a subject requiring further exploration (see also Gimbutas 1963: 43).[3] For the semiotics of the Lithuanian sash in particular, ancient Indian thought exhibits many parallels and clues for interpretation, as indicated below.

Plate 3. Vilnius, Lithuania, July, 1989. Woman shown braiding a sash. Photograph by the author.

At the same time, however, archeologist and linguist Marija Gimbutas demonstrates convincingly the coexistence in Lithuania, as in other parts of Europe, of "two different symbol systems:" the more familiar patriarchal and hierarchical Indo-European cultural pattern, as championed by Georges Dumézil, and a previously unacknowledged "matristic-gylanic" system wherein elements have survived mainly through the female line, of a pre-Indo-European, "Old European" culture and mythological system.[4] This Old European Neolithic dates from 6500 to 3500 BC in southeastern Europe and from 4500 to 2500 BC in western Europe. It was neither hierarchical nor militaristic, but cooperative and concerned primarily in myth, ritual, and religion with "the mystery of birth and death and the renewal of life, not only human but all life on earth and indeed the whole cosmos" (Gimbutas 1989: xvii-xix). Gimbutas' richly documented argument that the Indo-European system did not replace, but was superimposed upon and merged with the pre-existing matristic Neolithic culture (Gimbutas 1989: 318), exemplifies in itself, the more sophisticated, integrative, and pluralistic perspective of post-structuralist archeological and cultural interpretation theory. Most importantly here, as we shall see, her distinction helps to account for the different ideal and actual roles of men and women in traditional Lithuanian folk culture, in particular, the role of women in relation to the complex of associations attached to textile production and the role of men in defense, warfare, trade, and in their dealings with foreign landowners.[5]

Archeological evidence indicates that Lithuanian women were making sashes as early as the ninth century AD. Fragments of sashes as well as weaving tools have been discovered in birch bark boxes buried with deceased women. The earliest written sources describing sashes date only from the seventeenth century, not surprisingly, considering that Lithuanian was an entirely oral language until the first books appeared in the sixteenth century (Mallory 1989: 82). Whatever its time of origin, sash weaving reached an aesthetic and technical peak in the district of Dzūkija, a culturally and dialectically distinct region, noted also for the richness of the traditional Lithuanian folk song. This relationship of sashes and songs is not fortuitous, given that it was customary for girls and women to sing and weave sashes at the same time. Tamošaitis reports that "Dzūkian (sic.) women can not only sing hundreds of songs by heart, but they are most creative designers of patterned sashes... Songs and sashes are the two most characteristic forms of creativity among the Dzūkians" (Tamošaitis – Tamošaitis 1988: 56, 271).

As is the case in most cultures, weaving and sash making were crafts traditionally practised by girls and women. And, while sashes are known in many cultures, the Hopi of the American Southwest, for example (Aitken 1949; Kent 1939), by comparison they are especially prominent artifacts in Lithuanian material culture. Nowhere else are sashes woven and used in such great abundance and variety, nor with such great persistence, even into the late-twentieth century. The centrality of the sash for Lithuanians seems to demand an interpretation and explanation.

Girls learned to weave sashes first and only later, cloth, from their mothers, grandmothers, or older sisters. A daughter would be warned on occasions that she resisted, that it would be better to live without a shirt to wear, than to be without a stock of sashes to give away as presents. Heirloom sashes kept in mother's or grandmother's dowry chests were employed as examples in the teaching process. As she proceeded in her lessons, the young girl was instructed in the meaning of specific motifs. It seems that sashes were made primarily in the evenings, when families gathered to engage in conversation, singing, and the production of various simple crafts.

Dienos darbeliai	[The finest linens
Plonos drobelės.	Are the work of the day.
Nakties darbeliai	Many patterned sashes
Margos juostelės	Are the work of the night]

(Tamošaitis — Tamošaitis 1988: 29).

By the time of her marriage, a girl's dowry chest would contain "at least twenty or thirty wide sashes and numerous narrow ones" (Tamošaitis — Tamošaitis 1988: 10).

In traditional Lithuanian culture, sashes were woven primarily as gifts. Finely made wide sashes were given to the elites: to pastors when visiting parishioners on their Christmas rounds; to physicians when tending the village sick; and to school teachers. They were presented, Tamošaitis reports, "not so much as objects of material value but as symbolic artistic creations in expression of gratitude, respect, friendship, good-will, devotion, or kinship" (Tamošaitis — Tamošaitis 1988: 23, 29 – 30). But gifts of sashes were most important in the contexts of weddings. Young girls and women wove sashes in preparation for their wedding day from as early as six years of age. These were intended as gifts not only for her new husband, but also for the husband's family, the matchmaker, the matron of honor, and for all the wedding guests. Stored away for years in the bride's dowry chest, the sashes served as witnesses to her talent and to her ability to work hard, two highly important values in traditional Lithuanian culture.

On such occasions, the sashes were distributed "in a ritualistic manner," the precise gestures of which are not described by Tamošaitis. The first to receive a sash was the *Kvieslys*, the young man who had summoned the wedding guests on horseback a week or two before the wedding. Several wide sashes would be tied diagonally over his shoulders and chest and narrow ones would be tied to his ceremonial staff, *maršakelė*. During the marriage ceremony, bride and groom stood before the altar on a carpet made of sashes sewn together. Each day of the week long traditional wedding festivities required different rituals, songs, and gift-giving behavior. Everyone in attendance received a sash "with great ceremony," including young children who received miniature sashes known as *pakiliukės*.

Sashes were employed in every conceivable way during the wedding celebrations. On the first day, the bride tied a sash to the gate of the family homestead. Sashes covered the bread and cakes at the wedding feast. The first to ask the bride to dance received a sash and sashes were the bridesmaids' gifts to the bridegrooms.

Upon arrival at her mother-in-law's home, where she was to live with her husband, a special sash (*pripečkinė*) was tossed onto the stove and another tied to the flail. On making her first trip to the well, the bride tied a small sash to the shadoof. At a homestead spring, she would leave a sash "so that the water would never cease flowing and would always be pure." Narrow sashes were also placed on the fence around the granary, on its doorknob, and on the manger, "so that the cows would be healthy and produce much milk." Sashes were tied around fruit trees, to a wayside chapel or cross in the garden, in the orchard, "all holy gifts to the ancestral spirits of (the) farmstead." This was done because it was once believed that "coloured sashes, and especially patterned ones, would ward off evil spirits and cause good deities to bring happiness and good fortune." The Dzūkians, in particular, considered "that such sash patterns are symbolic and that certain colours, especially red, possess magical power" (Tamošaitis – Tamošaitis 1988: 24–25).

Sashes were also significant in connection with agricultural practices. They were tied to cattle being taken to graze in the forest. As they were being led to pasture for the first time in spring, the herdsman wore a narrow sash. At first ploughing of the fields, the plough was decorated with a sash. At harvest, the first sheaf of rye was tied with a wide sash. Upon completion of the harvest, a ceremonial wreath was tied with a sash and "presented with great ceremony" to the landowner (Tamošaitis – Tamošaitis 1988: 10).

The sash presented by the bride to her new husband was not simply handed over, but was tied around his waist, perhaps three times. The bride's custom of tying the sash around her husband's waist visualizes dramatically the notion of binding another to oneself in a new social relationship. The phenomena of tying, binding, knotting, it has been suggested, is especially characteristic of Indo-European ideology, wherein a "binding complex" has been identified by Georges Dumézil. While motifs and gestures of binding, tying, and knotting are present in many cultures throughout the world, Mircea Eliade finds that in Indo-European speaking cultures, "binding" or "tying" constitutes a particularly coherent system of metaphoric thought, manifest in ritual behavior, mythology, and ideology (Eliade 1961: 123). Dumézil parallels the Lithuanian deity Bentis, the "god who binds," with Varuna of the Hindus, who is often represented with a cord in his hand. On the social level, Eliade sees the situation of humans in the world as expressive of "the ideas of bondage, shackling, attachment" and, in Hindu thought, the goal is to free oneself from these "bonds" (Eliade 1961: 116−117). But knots and bonds and tying also function to signify healing and protection, since, in many cultures, Eliade notes, "power" resides in every act of tying. Thus, the custom is widespread, he writes, "of protecting oneself against illness and evil spirits by means of knots, strings, and cords, especially during ... childbirth" (Eliade 1961: 112). It appears that in the Indo-European symbol system "the ties that bind" are perceived in a negative light, as signifying undesirable relationship to persons, things, or life itself. This would contrast with the symbolic value system proposed by Gimbutas for the pre-Indo-European matristic-gylanic system wherein attachment, ties, relationships are given positive, life-enhancing value.

In addition to their importance as wedding gifts, functioning to rein-force and to cement new social ties within the community, sashes were also given at childbirth, baptism, and played an important role in burial rites. A sash was given to the new born child by its godmother to protect it from harm and to ensure its future happiness (Tamošaitis − Tamošaitis 1988: 32). In this connection, the sash performs a magical function. Sashes were once believed to ward off evil spirits. At funerals, sashes were used to lower the coffin into the depths of the grave. In Lithuania Minor, a particular kind of sash, *šimtaraštė*, was woven for use in funeral rites. This sash was some fifteen feet long and every design motif was different. Sashes were also used as property markers for sacks of grain going to the mill, and around the waists of travellers embarking on long journeys. Sashes are still being given as gifts to travellers today, both within the country and to visitors from abroad.

Thus from birth to death, woven sashes played and continue to play the role of a life-metaphor, signifying continuity and connection, well-being and protection. The sash had power in itself as well as in its woven patterns. As such, sashes were used not only at every critical juncture in the narrative of individual and social life, not only in "rites of social passage" from one status to another (birth, baptism, marriage, death), but also in "rites of territorial passage," for travellers, at thresholds, and at vital places around the farmstead such as boundaries separating one's neighbor's fields, at gateways, barn doors, and door knobs.[6] As a "locational marker," sashes were thrown into stoves, wells and springs and tied to fruit trees. Sashes were never bought or sold, but were given as gifts and passed either across generations or down from one generation to another and cherished as family heirlooms (Tamošaitis 1976: 66; Tamošaitis — Tamošaitis 1988: 277). Sashes thus weave symbolically, the social, spatial, and temporal dimensions of the world together in traditional Lithuanian culture, and this "weaveworld" is made manifest semiotically, not at the level of particular utilitarian and social functions, but at the level of their total phenomenal integration.[7]

The spatial, temporal, and social junctures at which sashes are employed symbolically to connect, to bind, to protect, and to signify the relationality and the continuity of all life, are the indices of the latent meaning of Lithuanian sashes. Tamošaitis cites a passage from a Lithuanian writer of the nineteenth century, Eduard Gisevius, which provides an important clue to the place and the meaning of the sash in Lithuanian mythology: "... from the moment of birth the Spinner begins to spin for each child the thread of his fate, which extends out to a star; when death steals this person away, his thread is broken and the star, burning out, falls to earth" (Tamošaitis — Tamošaitis 1988: 32). In Lithuanian oral tradition, Laima, goddess of luck and fate, is the cosmic spinner.

> Deivė Laima nauja gimiui ištiesė jo gyvenimo Laimės juosta.
> [The goddess Laima has spread out the newborn's lifetime sash of happiness and good fortune] (Tamošaitis — Tamošaitis 1988: 31).

It becomes clear, then, that the sash is a "thread" and signifies the "thread of life," the "tie that binds" both society and the universe together, as well as the life of individuals to that cosmic whole.

This clear-cut association of the sash with the goddess Laima indicates that the socio-semiotics of the sash in Lithuanian folk society is founded originally in the pre-Indo-European, Neolithic symbol-system of the "Goddess religion" proposed by Marija Gimbutas, a symbol-system which seems to exhibit continuities even with the Upper Paleolithic (Gimbutas 1989: xix, xxii). The Lithuanian goddess of fate, Laima, is associated by Gimbutas with other European deities, for example, with the Basque Andrea Mari, Ireland's St. Brigit, the East Slavic Mokosh/ Paraskeva-Pyatnitsa, and the Romanian Sfinta Vineri. "Twisting, spinning, weaving, and sewing," she writes, "are common to the Greek Athena, Roman Minerva, and the goddesses still alive in European folk beliefs" (Gimbutas 1989: 68).

In her various manifestations from the Upper Paleolithic onwards, the "great Goddess" was associated with birth, death, and the renewal of life, "not only human but all life on earth and indeed the whole cosmos" (Gimbutas 1989: xix). This is the core complex of ideas underlying the symbol system of the "great Goddess" and its visual and material symbols as they survived even into nineteenth-century European folk societies. Furthermore, "... the Goddess religion and its symbols survive as an undercurrent in many areas. Actually, many of these symbols are still present as images in our art and literature, powerful motifs in our myths and archetypes in our dreams" (Gimbutas 1989: xix).

However, in addition to the main themes of Goddess symbolism as enunciated by Gimbutas, and encompassing them all in a single unifying concept, lies an even deeper level of semiotic significance. The most fundamental underlying theme of the matristic Goddess complex, it might be suggested, is that of *continuity* (which can also be read as connectedness, relationality, cooperation, gender-harmony, and so forth). This theme is in opposition to what could be identified similarly as the core, bottom-line theme of the Indo-European ideational complex, *discontinuity* (read also: hierarchy, ranking, dividing, patriarchy, conflict, social-, gender-, and cosmic-disharmony, and so on). These fundamental thematic distinctions underlie our reading of the Neolithic symbol system as reconstructed by Gimbutas in comparison with that of the Indo-European mythological and cultural construct as interpreted in the work of Georges Dumézil (see Littleton 1973a, 1973b). Continuity and discontinuity are fundamental ideational themes made manifest in the two distinct mythological, social, iconographic, and artifactual domains of the Old European culture and that of the late Indo-European.

This fundamental dichotomy is signified metaphorically and actually in the dominant technologies innovated in these two cultural systems: the pliable and plastic technologies of textiles and ceramics of the Neolithic, crafts requiring manual skill and patience and practised by women, and the bronze metallurgy of the Indo-Europeans, pre-eminently devoted to the production of weapons and decorative ornaments for an elite social class. Implicated herein, too, is the notion of power, the production of bronze artifacts requiring access by trade, if not conquest, to mines and alloys in foreign territories. Considered phenomenologically, textiles and ceramic technologies are geared to the production of artifacts which contain, shield, protect, and nurture. They are life-enhancing objects. In contrast, the Indo-European bronze artifacts are life-destroying. They are masculine crafts, intended primarily for military purposes, their production restricted to craft specialists and their distribution limited to elites. Bronze artifacts functioned either for sumptuous display, in the case of ornaments, or, more significantly in the case of weapons, for dismemberment, cutting, stabbing, for piercing and for killing.

Yet the Lithuanian sash also exhibits connections with Indo-European ideology. For the Vedas of the ancient Hindus, too, all things in the universe are strung together on cosmic threads, in a vast textile fabric.[8] The Vedic universe itself is conceived as a macrocosmic textile in which all things — human destiny, stars, planets, and nature — are woven together on threads and cords in a harmonious and wonderfully patterned cloth. The "macrocosmic warp and woof" is thought of as a veil or garment "comparable to the tissues woven on human looms" (Coomaraswamy 1977, I: 82).

Although "the weaving of fate" is a key concept in European thought, it is likely rooted in even more ancient systems of thought than the Indo-European. For, as Richard B. Onians indicates, even the Koryaks of Northeast Asia held to the notion of a human soul connected by a strap to the cross-beams of the Supreme Being's house: "... and as is the length of a soul's strap so will be the length of his life when he is reborn into the world" (Onians 1988: 349).

The cognitive association between the sash as a material "gestalt" and the concepts of continuity and the "cosmic thread" in Neolithic and Indo-European traditions is manifested in Lithuanian folk society as socio-cultural practice. The sash figuratively and semiotically fuses the symbol system and lifeworld of the "great Goddess" with that of the Indo-European. In its Neolithic aspects, the sash functions consistently as an offering at locations and on occasions significant to agricultural and human fertility and survival: at weddings, births, baptisms, funerals; at springs, wells, hearths; in orchards and fields; and on cattle. As such, the sash exhibits its phenomenological orientation to the earth. In its Indo-European aspect, the sash signifies "ties" to the larger cosmos, to the stars in the sky, to the world beyond the grave. But the sash seems only superficially associated with the Indo-European system. The semiotic context of the Lithuanian woven sash is rooted primarily and more thoroughly in the Neolithic symbol system of Old Europe.

In traditional Lithuanian culture, then, it can be said that women enacted figuratively and actually, the role of the goddess Laima, spinning, weaving, and, especially, distributing sashes throughout the social network. By giving sashes to other persons, places, and things, the Lithuanian woman weaves the social, artifactual, and natural universe into a single "fabric."

Latent in this pattern of the social, spatial, and temporal distribution of sashes is their passage, not only horizontally across the social network and across territorial space (wefts), but vertically up and down the generations and into the graveworld beyond (warps). As a performative, interactive agent at many levels and in many dimensions, the sash constitutes the fundamental cognitive gestalt for social and universal order and relationships in traditional Lithuanian society.

This gestural performance of the sash also manifests phenomenally the visual thinking induced in the processes and products of spinning and weaving. It is these processes that provide an underlying dynamic gestalt for the social and ideational life of Lithuanian society. And, also, it is the integrative, slow and repetitious, but steady and regular rhythm of textile production that characterizes the narrative role of women in Lithuanian socio-cultural life. Through the spinning and weaving process, begun so early in life with sash making, the female self is constructed. As noted by Benjamin Lee and Greg Urban (1989: 5) "... the semiotic point of view suggests that the self may be a precipitate of the dialogue with other selves." These other "selves," however, can also be objects. And in traditional Lithuanian folk society, where Indo-European discontinuities and more recent Western individualism did not prevail, even *things* functioned interactively as part of the social universe.

The sash as a seemingly modest domestic artifact, then, played a most significant socio-semiotic role in Lithuanian cultural life. As well, it articulates the role of women in the fabrication and maintenance of social and cosmic order. Women's sphere, it would seem, was that of creation and "culture," of rhythmic regularity, and of maintaining threads of continuity. Men's role, in contrast, as a consequence of economic, political, and historical conditions, was to cope with "chaos," discontinuity, and destruction, that is, with the outside world of foreign landowners and unpredictable invasions.

Acknowledgements

The author is most grateful to several persons in the preparation of this paper. Above all to Antanas Tamošaitis, Anastazija Tamošaitis, and Aldona Veselka of Gananoque, Ontario, so much is owned in terms of friendship and inspiration. For reading original versions of this manuscript and for making suggestions for its improvement thanks also to Gediminas Lankauskas of Peterborough, Ontario.

Notes

1. "Lifeworld" is a term coined in 1936 by Edmund Husserl and employed by Don Ihde in his exploration of the impact of technology as ideology in contemporary culture (Ihde 1990: 21). I choose it as one more appropriate to a semiotic theory of artifacts than, say, "worldview," since "lifeworld" incorporates the more dynamic and phenomenal notion of "lived experience."
2. As in Gandhi's India (Bayly 1986; Bean 1989), traditional folk textiles in general loomed large as an expression of national identity and the striving for independence from imperial powers.
3. Georges Dumézil's analysis of the ideological and mythological correspondences among Indo-European speaking traditions (Littleton 1973) postulates a proto-Indo-European cultural and ideological foundation of great relevance for further investigation along these lines.
4. Gimbutas (1989: xx) employs the terms "gylany" and "matristic" rather than "matriarchy" and "matrilineal" to describe the social order of Old Europe, wherein both sexes were equal, even though a matrilineal system of descent prevailed and women as heads of clans or "queen-priestesses played a central part."
5. As in the case of most histories to date, Lithuanian historical narratives almost entirely exclude the activities of women. From their first appearance in the fifteenth century, they focus upon "the origins of the Lithuanian nation and state, the genealogy of the [male] rulers, their military campaigns and relations with neighbours." Topics of concern remained throughout: the activities of military heroes, aristocratic families, clergy, and intellectual elites, the characteristic hierarchic social structure of the Indo-Europeans. See "Historiography" in the *Encyclopedia Lituanica* (1974, II: 423–431).
6. In the development of any semiotic theory of visual phenomena (whether artifact, painting, textile, automobile, or temple), Arnold Van Gennep's 1908 (1960) publication, *Les Rites de Passage*, would provide useful concepts of dimensionality within space and time, including the all-important notion of liminality.

7. My use of the term "weaveworld" in the context of the function and meaning of Lithuanian sashes is inspired by the title of the amazing novel by Clive Barker (1987).
8. Perhaps it is not irrelevant that the latest discovery of theoretical physics is that the universe is connected by "cosmic strings," that is, by "invisible threads ... sparsely spread, like an unravelled skein of yarn, across the length and breadth of the cosmos" (Bartusiak 1988: 61; see also Davies — Brown 1988).

References

Aitken, Barbara
   1949   "A note on Pueblo belt-weaving," *Man* 49: 37 and plate E.
Anonymous
   1974   "Historiography," *Encyclopedia Lituanica*. South Boston, MA: Juozas Kapočius Publisher 2: 423 – 431.
Appadurai, Arjun (ed.)
   1986   *The social life of things: Commodities in cultural perspective.* Cambridge: Cambridge University Press.
Arnheim, Rudolf
   1969   *Visual thinking.* Berkeley: University of California Press.
Barker, Clive
   1987   *Weaveworld.* Toronto: Collins.
Barlow, Horace — Colin Blakemore — Miranda Weston-Smith (eds.)
   1990   *Images and understanding: Thoughts about images, ideas about understanding.* Cambridge: Cambridge University Press.
Barthes, Roland
   1957   *Mythologies.* Paris: Editions du Seuil.
   1977   *Image. Music. Text.* London: Fontana Press.
Bartusiak, Marcia
   1988   "If you like black holes, you'll love cosmic strings," *Discover* 9(4): 60 – 68.
Bayly, C. A.
   1986   "The origins of swadeshi (home industry): Cloth and Indian society, 1770 – 1930," in: Arjun Appadurai (ed.), 285 – 321.
Bean, Susan S.
   1980   "Gandhi and khadi, the fabric of Indian independence," in: Annette B. Weiner — Jane Schneider (eds.), 355 – 376.
Bush, Donald J.
   1975   *The streamlined decade.* New York: Braziller.
Coomaraswamy, Ananda K.
   1977   *Selected papers: Traditional art and symbolism.* Vol. 1. Roger Lipsey (ed.). Princeton: Princeton University Press.

Davies, P. C. W. – Julian Brown (eds.)
1988   *Superstrings: A theory of everything.* Cambridge: Cambridge University Press.
Dewey, John
1958   *Art as experience.* New York: Capricorn Books.
Dumézil, Georges
1973   *Gods of the ancient northmen.* Einer Hagen (ed.). Berkeley: University of California Press.
Eliade, Mircea
1961   *Images and symbols.* New York: Sheed and Ward.
Ferguson, Eugene S.
1977   "The mind's eye: Non-verbal thought in technology," *Science* 197 (4306): 827–836.
Fletcher, Roland
1989   "The messages of material behaviour: A preliminary discussion of non-verbal meaning," in: Ian Hodder (ed.), 33–40.
Foster, Hal (ed.)
1983   *The anti-aesthetic: Essays on postmodern culture.* Port Townsend, WA: Bay Press.
Foucault, Michel
1972   *The archaeology of knowledge.* London: Tavistock.
Gelb, Ignace J.
1963   *A study of writing.* Chicago: University of Chicago Press.
Gimbutas, Marija
1958   *Ancient symbolism in Lithuanian folk art.* Philadelphia: American Folklore Society.
1963   *The Balts.* London: Thames and Hudson.
1989   *The language of the goddess.* San Francisco: Harper and Row.
Greenhalgh, Michael – Vincent Megaw (eds.)
1978   *Art in society.* London: Duckworth.
Hawthorn, Audrey
1967   *Art of the Kwakiutl Indians and other Northwest Coast tribes.* Seattle: University of Washington Press.
Hodder, Ian
1982   *Symbols in action: Ethnoarchaeological studies of material culture.* Cambridge: Cambridge University Press.
1986   *Reading the past: Current approaches to interpretation in archaeology.* Cambridge: Cambridge University Press.
Hodder, Ian (ed.)
1989   *The meanings of things: Material culture and symbolic expression.* London: Unwin Hyman.
Ihde, Don
1990   *Technology and the lifeworld: From garden to earth.* Bloomington: Indiana University Press.

Ingersoll, Daniel W., Jr. — Gordon Bronitsky (eds.)
1987   *Mirror and metaphor: Material and social constructions of reality.*
        Boston: University Press of America.
Keesing, Roger M.
1987   "Anthropology as interpretive quest," *Current Anthropology* 28(2):
        161—176.
Kent, Kate Peck
1939   "The braiding of a Hopi wedding sash," *Plateau* 12(1): 46—52.
Krauss, Rosalind
1983   "Sculpture in the expanded field," in: Hal Foster (ed.), 31—42.
Lee, Benjamin — Greg Urban (eds.)
1989   *Semiotics, self, and society.* Berlin: Mouton de Gruyter.
Littleton, C. Scott
1973a   "Introduction, part I," in: Georges Dumézil, ix—xvii.
1973b   *The new comparative mythology: An anthropological assessment of the
        theories of Georges Dumézil.* Berkeley: University of California Press.
MacAloon, John J. (ed.)
1984   *Rite, drama, festival, spectacle: Rehearsals toward a theory of per-
        formance.* Philadelphia: Institute for the Study of Human Issues.
Macey, Samuel L.
1980   *Clocks and cosmos: Time in Western life and thought.* Hamden, CN:
        Archon Books.
Mallory, J. P.
1989   *In search of the Indo-Europeans: Language, archaeology, and myth*
        London: Thames and Hudson.
O'Keeffe, Georgia
1976   *Georgia O'Keeffe.* New York: The Viking Press.
Onians, Richard B.
1988   *The origins of European thought: About the body, the mind, the soul,
        the world, time and fate.* Cambridge: Cambridge University Press.
Ornstein, Robert
1986   *The psychology of consciousness.* Harmondsworth: Penguin Books.
Ortner, Sherry B.
1973   "On key symbols," *American Anthropologist* 75: 1338—1346.
Preziosi, Donald
1989   *Rethinking art history: Meditations on a coy science.* New Haven:
        Yale University Press.
Rivière, P. G.
1969   "Myth and material culture: Some symbolic interrelations," in: Rob-
        ert F. Spencer (ed.), 151—166.
Rubinstein, Donald H.
1987   "The social fabric: Micronesian textile patterns as an embodiment
        of social order," in: Daniel W. Ingersoll — Gordon Bronitsky (eds.),
        63—82.

Sapir, Edward
1951   *Selected writings of Edward Sapir.* David Mandelbaum (ed.). Berkeley: University of California Press.
Spencer, Robert F. (ed.)
1969   *Forms of symbolic action.* Seattle: American Ethnological Society.
Sužiedėlis, Simas
1970   "Agriculture in history," *Encyclopedia Lituanica.* South Boston, MA: Juozas Kapočius 1: 32 – 35.
Tamošaitis, Antanas
1976   *"Juosta"* (sash), *Encyclopedia Lituanica.* South Boston, MA: Juozas Kapočius 5: 65 – 67.
Tamošaitis, Antanas — Anastazija Tamošaitis
1988   *Lithuanian sashes.* Toronto: The Lithuanian Folk Art Institute.
Tilley, Christopher
1990   "Michel Foucault: Towards an archaeology of archaeology," in: Christopher Tilley (ed.), 281 – 347.
Tilley, Christopher (ed.)
1990   *Reading material culture: Structuralism, hermeneutics and post-structuralism.* Oxford: Basil Blackwell.
Trachtenberg, Alan
1965   *Brooklyn bridge: Fact and symbol.* Chicago: University of Chicago Press.
Tumėnas, Vytautas
1989   "'Rožėlės' ornamento simbolika" [symbolism of the 'rosette' motif], *Krantai: meno kultūros žurnalas* 12: 14 – 21.
Turner, Edith L. B. (ed.)
1985   *The edge of the bush: Anthropology as experience.* Tucson: University of Arizona Press.
Turner, Victor
1984   "Liminality and the performance genres," in: John J. MacAloon (ed.), 19 – 41.
1985   "The anthropology of performance," in: Edith L. B. Turner (ed.), 177 – 204.
Van Gennep, Arnold
1960   *The rites of passage* Chicago: University of Chicago Press.
Vastokas, Joan M.
1966   *Architecture of the Northwest Coast Indians of America.* Ann Arbor, MI: University Microfilms.
1969   "Architecture and environment: The importance of the forest to the Northwest Coast Indians," *Forest History* 13(3): 12 – 21.
1978   "Cognitive aspects of Northwest Coast art," in: Michael Greenhalgh — Vincent Megaw (eds.), 243 – 259.
1986 – 1987   "Native art as art history: Meaning and time from unwritten sources," *Journal of Canadian Studies/Revue d'études canadiennes* 21(4): 7 – 36.

1989   "Technology as metaphor: Spinning, weaving, and textiles in Lithuanian folk culture." The Graham Goddard Lecture, Dept. of Anthropology, University of Waterloo, Ontario.

1992   *Beyond the artifact: Native art as performance.* The Fifth Robarts Lecture, York University. North York, Ontario.

Wagner, Roy
1981   *The invention of culture.* Chicago: University of Chicago Press.

Weiner, Annette B. — Jane Schneider (eds.)
1989   *Cloth and human experience.* Washington, DC: Smithsonian Institution Press.

Whorf, Benjamin Lee
1956   *Language, thought, and reality: Selected writings of Benjamin Lee Whorf.* John B. Carroll (ed.). Cambridge, MA: Massachusetts Institute of Technology Press.

Feathers and fringes: A semiotic approach to powwow dancers' regalia

Michèle Kérisit

In the contemporary understanding of the term, a powwow is a secular celebration featuring the performance of native North American songs and dances.[1] Since World War II, native communities in Canada and the United States have witnessed a spectacular development of the powwow. The event is usually held during a two or three day weekend and features competitions between dancers organized according to gender, types of dancing styles, and regalia. Male and female dancers' regalia are spectacular and elaborate outfits made of embroidered and beaded cloth and buckskin, feathers, furs, and shells. These regalia constitute one of the contemporary native cultural forms through which native cultural and political empowerment is signified. As a public display of "Indian" manhood and womanhood, powwows are part of ironic counter-discursive practices about native-white relationships and legitimize an "Indian difference" through a discourse on native tradition.

This paper proposes a semiotic analysis of one component of the male regalia, the feather ornament called the bustle, which is a semicircle of feathers attached at the center to a beaded rosette, a mirror, or in one type of male regalia, to the upper part or the head of a predatory animal (see Plate 1). My analysis focuses on this particular ornament because it is paradigmatic of the construction of an "Indian heritage, intricate with motion and meaning, legendary as well as historical, personal as well as cultural" (Momaday 1969: 4). It is a cultural form that embodies a discourse on what it is to be a North American native man or woman in the late-twentieth century. Its shape and composition are indicative of the constant reworking of contradictions that play on the larger context of social relations between native communities and the dominant non-native society.

Bustles, as well as the rest of the regalia, are also saying something about the dancers' desires to be loved, looked at, and admired by others. As systems of (re)presentation of self, they are enmeshed in a dramaturgy of seduction where signs of masculinity and femininity are publicly constructed. Their meaning emerges from an interplay of gendered metaphors, intricate with historical (re)interpretations of a collective identity. It is from this conjunction between a language of desire and a language of political empowerment that they draw their vitality as constantly evolving cultural practices.

Before engaging in a semiotic analysis of the bustle, however, it is important to sketch the specific ethnographic background within which powwow regalia become meaningful: summer competitive powwows held in the province of Ontario, Canada. This will be done in the first part of the chapter. The second part will concentrate on the bustles themselves and the multiple dimensions of their signification.

Plate 1. Male Fancy Dancer (left) and male Traditional Dancer (right) at an Ontario powwow in 1983. Photograph by John Flanders.

Contemporary Ontario summer powwows

There are, broadly speaking, two kinds of powwows in Ontario: the *competitive summer powwow,* held outdoors during summer weekends, in which dancers and singers receive prizes for the quality of their performances, and the *traditional powwow*, which rejects the competitive aspect of the first in favor of activities devoted to education (elders conferences, story telling or workshops). Whereas summer competitive powwows attract large crowds of peoples from surrounding communities and distant places, "traditional" powwows tend to be publicized less and to draw their audiences from a smaller geographical area. The four powwows where the following observations were made in 1987 and 1989 belong to the first "genre," competitive summer powwows: the Odawa Powwow held in Ottawa, the Grand River's Champion of Champions' Powwow on the Six Nations Indian Reserve near Ohsweken, the Wikwimikong Powwow on Manitoulin Island, and the Walpole Island Powwow.

Besides the competitive dancing and drumming that takes place at a summer powwow, the event also features a number of festive occasions such as communal meals taken by dancers, drummers, powwow organizers, invited elders or members of other native communities and reserves. Religious ceremonies are sometimes held at sunrise and sunset. Baseball games and canoe races frequently precede afternoons and evenings devoted to dance and music.

The powwow is a time of enjoyment and laughter, of "feeling good." It is a time of intense social interaction, drawing crowds from near and distant native communities (sometimes thousands of miles away), when native peoples from the city visit their home reserve and keep in touch with their families and friends. Powwow time is also a time when the festive mood of the day is prolonged during the balmy summer nights in the camping site adjacent to the powwow ground, especially among youth.

The celebration is organized around a few spatial features that show a great regularity all over North America (Young 1981; Rynkiewich 1980; Corrigan 1970). Participants dance in a ring, the powwow ground, that circles around a drum arbor where groups of singers and drums are gathered. This circle has, on its periphery, a platform where the master of ceremonies announces and explains the course of the powwow. It is from there that speeches made by elders and powwow organizers, giveaway announcements, and opening prayers are delivered. Dancers always enter the "powwow ground" from an opening in the railing at the east of the circle. Alcohol and drugs are explicitly forbidden within this circle.

Bleachers are usually put up for the spectators around the powwow ground. Adjacent to this circle, or around it, there are booths where crafts and food are sold to participants and visitors. In the immediate vicinity of the powwow ground a place is reserved for the communal meals eaten by dancers, singers, organizers, and elders participating in the powwow. This setting is part of a broader locale that includes the camping grounds where people pitch their tents for the night and the parking lot for day visitors. At night the community surrounding the powwow field is filled with visitors who have attended the performances during the day or the evening. Thus, the circle of the powwow ground is the inner ring of a series of concentric circles that attract the attention and the action of a whole community during powwow days.

The course of a powwow is formally organized around the competition between dancers. The prizes at the powwows I attended ranged from $400 to $800, which is not an insignificant incentive to participate in powwows, although "gamesmanship and acute competition, especially among dancers, are strongly discouraged" (Dyck 1979: 94).

Each afternoon and evening dancing session is preceded by the grand entry, the ceremonial entry of dancers onto the powwow ground. Following a number of veteran flag bearers, the dancers circle the ground four times until the flags are finally set up around the drum arbor. Each dancing session ends with the same procession when the flags are removed from the ground, except in the evening when they have to be taken away before sunset. Dancing sessions are punctuated by ceremonies and speeches given by respected elders or community leaders. The most popular ceremony, however, is the give-away, which honors a participant of the powwow.[2]

Powwows are open to the general public, native and non-native alike. Most powwows attract bus loads of tourists eager to spend a few hours watching native dancers and buying crafts and souvenirs. Powwows are part of a "tourist circuit," which, it should be added, is an attraction as much to non-native as to native tourists themselves. The place of pow-wows in tourism circuits is not recent. In fact, powwows are, and have been in the past, one of the rare places where native and non-native peoples come into contact in large numbers. It is presently the only place where non-natives come into contact with contemporary native-per-formed art forms. Most tourists "know" native arts and crafts through shops that dot the countryside of Ontario and/or through museums, but they usually have not been in contact with live performances. I would suggest that this aspect of the powwow as locus of contact between contemporary native cultures and non-native spectators has been and is still instrumental in the evolution of cultural forms displayed during powwows, especially feather ornaments. The latter have been elaborated, transformed, and made meaningful under the watchful gaze of a public.

The discourse on tradition

Powwows as such have rarely attracted the attention of anthropologists, but when they have been the focus of research, powwows have been analyzed as sites where meanings are generated as "coping mechanisms" either for the assimilation of native peoples into the dominant and non-native society of North America or for their noncontroversial affirmation of difference.

Except for Valda Blundell (1985), who takes the actual display of costumes and dances as a system of significations where meanings are negotiated, most studies of powwows focus on the function of the pow-wow as an integrating event within the domain of native politics and economy (Frideres 1983; Dyck 1983; Lurie 1971; Campisi 1975) or as a mediatory event between native society and white society (Corrigan 1970; Young 1981). The descriptions given by these authors deal with the chronology of events, the spatial setting of the powwow, the social and tribal distribution of the people participating in the celebration, and with the social organization of the powwow.

A few studies have been conducted on the origins of specific powwows, the most extensive ones being Gloria Young's (1981) doctoral dissertation on the Tulsa Powwow in Oklahoma and Loretta Fowler's (1987) analysis of the different powwows taking place on the Belknap Reservation in northern Montana. Studying an urban powwow, Young (1981: 393) sees in the Tulsa Powwow an event which simultaneously asserts the ethnic identity of urbanized native peoples and moves "Indian people and Indian culture in the United States from the isolation of tribalism to full societal participation." Fowler's analysis, on the other hand, focuses on the dynamics of political conflicts within the Belknap Reservation in order to understand the role played by the different powwows held on the reservation.

Fowler's study, which takes into account "symbols of identity" during powwows (but not powwow regalia), deals with a specific cultural and political milieu (Montana, Gros-Ventres, Assiniboine, United States). Although the premises of an analysis of ethnic and cultural identity based on negotiating processes and conflicts are of utmost theoretical impor-tance, Canadian powwows have not been analyzed in these terms.

A framework for the study of contemporary native cultural politics in the subarctic and arctic regions of Canada has been suggested by Usher (1982). Although the focus of his paper is the Canadian north, his perspective is applicable to Canada as a whole. Current state policies concerning native cultural life have to be analyzed according to Usher in the context of a capitalist and ideologically dominant definition of the word "culture," a definition which dissociates culture from mode of production. For Usher (1982: 4), a definition of culture as the "material and artistic expression of ethnicity" accompanied by vague notions of "tradition and heritage" masks the real relations of domination between the capitalistic "southern" society and the native population of the North. These struggles over the definition of culture are echoed by native organizations that are caught in a double-bind between an approach that emphasizes the importance of the material base of their culture and the increasing encroachment of the "overarching societal project of industrialization" promoting a definition of culture as "heritage" detached from its material base (Usher 1982: 11). In the North, this double bind might be alleviated by a radically different perspective that emphasizes the importance of an adapted "traditional" mode of production that would generate and keep a culture that has not yet "disappeared."

There is no doubt that powwows belong to the on-going debate — grounded in a very real material situation — whereby native peoples have to define their claims to sovereignty by a discourse that legitimizes their cultural "heritage." In a very real sense, as shown in numerous court cases, native peoples have had to demonstrate the continuity of their traditions since precontact times, responding to the dominant legal system (*lex loci, lex in memoriam*). Given the "encapsulation" of the political structures of native communities and their economic instability, one of the strategies of native peoples to retain their distinctiveness (which is a question of community survival) has been to emphasize the ideological component of their relationship with the dominant white society, especially in southern Ontario. As Tanner puts it:

> Outside the more isolated northern areas, where Indians are still predominantly following a hunting way of life, the integrity of a distinct Indian value system is now in some doubt, but a major gap with the majority society is nevertheless evident (Tanner 1983: 31).

This gap is often formulated in ideological terms implying a different reading of the past and an appeal to the government and the public to fulfill their moral responsibilities:

> For all these reasons, Indians must spend what is, even for politicians, an extraordinary amount of their energy in creating, discussing and communicating a distinct Indian reality, both to each other as well as to non-

indians. This activity can be called "ideological production" (Tanner 1983: 34 – 35).

In other words, as cultural celebrations of the "Indian difference," pow-wows belong to the wider movement that attempts to provide a cultural grounding for the legitimation of political, economic, and cultural rights of aboriginal peoples in Canada. For this reason a discourse on an "Indian" collective identity is held that simultaneously unites the group defining itself as native while separating it from other groups. This does not mean, however, that we should look at a powwow and the cultural forms that it fosters as "collectively noncontroversial" (Dyck 1979: 92).

This chapter argues that the discourse about what it means to be an "Indian" in the late-twentieth century is, in fact, far from being consensual because it is permeated by contradictions that stem from different read-ings of the past. This questioning is often expressed through the uneasiness felt in front of the stagy or commercial character of competition dancing which is seen as not true to specific tribal traditions or as born in a "Hollywood" stereotyped imagery of feathered Indians. On the other hand, powwows are also taken as places where "traditional" values, meanings, and behaviors which are truly aboriginal, are displayed.

For instance, the Odawa powwow was presented in a 1987 flyer in the following manner:

> Tribal memory tells us that the land now known as Ottawa was neutral ground and was the site of many inter-tribal gatherings where friends and traditional enemies came together in peaceful coexistence. This was a time of trading, sharing, and renewal.

One of the organizers of the Six Nations Powwow explained how difficult it was to convince others to hold a powwow. Many peoples objected that the competitive nature of the summer powwow and the "intertribal" nature of the celebration ran contrary to the traditions of the Iroquois which stressed equality and tribal specificity. In fact, the question was decided on the ground that, because people from the Six Nations partic-ipated in many powwows and sometimes received prizes, the Six Nations had to do the same to return in kind, if not more. Organizing a powwow was therefore an act of reciprocity that conformed with former Iroquois traditions.

Speaking of "tradition" or "Indianness" or of "traditional" regalia does not therefore call for a number of fixed "qualities" or features that can be posited unproblematically. Rather, it consists in analyzing the semiosis at work in social reproduction through the representation of self and the composition of a visual code that can be read in powwow regalia.

Powwow regalia

As already mentioned, dancers are organized in competing categories defined by gender, by dance types with distinctive powwow regalia, and by age. Prizes are won according to the category to which one belongs. In Ontario (as in many other regions of North America), there are three categories of dancers for both men and women. I will now indicate the main characteristics of each category, adopting in my presentation the order in which they appear on the powwow ground during the Grand Entry.

Plate 2. Bustle of a dancer belonging to the men's traditional category (eagle feathers, wolf head, and bells). Manitoulin Island, Ontario, 1987.

Men Traditional Dancers

Over a basic garment consisting of shorts and shirt, men Traditional Dancers wear a profusion of highly individualized ornaments which most generally consist of undyed feathers worn as a headdress and in a single bustle, otter fur worn as turban and necklaces or bandoliers. Belts, bandoliers and arm bands are carefully beaded. Shells (or bone and plastic facsimile) are worn as breastplates and pendants. Leggings attached to the belt are made of buckskin and decorated at knee and ankle level with bands of bells. Beaded moccasins complete the outfit. Men's traditional regalia are characterized by the presence of non-dyed, eagle and hawk, "natural" feathers worn as a headdress or as body ornaments and decorated with parts of predatory animals (head and claws). Plate 2 shows a "traditional" large bustle made of eagle feathers attached at its center to the head of a wolf.

Grass Dancers

Grass dancers wear an outfit made of long multicolored wool yarn that swirls during the very fast steps of their choreography. They rarely wear headdresses, except roaches or "springers" (an antenna shaped headdress made of two wrapped wires surmounted by white fluffies). Whereas male Traditional and Fancy Dancers wear elaborately beaded moccasins, Grass Dancers wear undecorated moccasins or tennis shoes. This category of dancer does not wear feathers at body level.

Men Fancy Dancers

Men Fancy Dancers wear, over their bare chest, elaborately beaded "harnesses" that match their large beaded belts. Fixed at the nape and lower back levels are two bustles made of brightly dyed "hackle" feathers (the long shiny feathers of the domestic cock, peacock, turkey) ornamented with down feathers called "fluffies" (Plate 4). They also wear beaded aprons and "goats" (white angora fur anklets attached by a band of bells below the knee). Their moccasins are intricately beaded. The male Fancy Dancers' choreography is a series of very rapid twirling steps, obeying very strict rules.

Women Traditional Dancers

Women Traditional Dancers (Plate 5) wear buckskin or shroud dresses. Many of these are ornamented by intricate beadwork, ribbon appliqué

Plate 3. Grass Dancer. Manitoulin Island, Ontario, 1987.

(for dresses made of cloth), or decorated with shells or elk teeth. Over their dress most dancers wear a breastplate similar to those of male Traditional Dancers except that it is vertically arranged, adding to the swaying movement of the dress when dancing. This movement is enhanced by the great number of fringes that decorate the dress as well as the shawl that all women Traditional Dancers carry folded on the arm. This shawl constitutes the common characteristic of this category.

Jingle Dress Dancers

This type of dancer wears a non-shiny dress of a solid color, decorated with metal cones arranged in V shapes. Jingle Dress Dancers do not wear

Plate 4. Back bustle of a male Fancy Dancer (hackle feathers, fluffies, and beaded rosette with turtle motive). Manitoulin Island, Ontario, 1987.

Plate 5. Group of women Traditional Dancers. Manitoulin Island, Ontario, 1987.

a shawl. There is a dearth of information on the history of this outfit. It seems that the metallic cones that decorate the dress are modern replicas or substitutes for the dewclaws that used to ornament women's dresses. The conical metal jinglers are sometimes made of the lid of tobacco cans as shown by inscriptions on the cones themselves. For most women's regalia, data on the signification of ornaments are few and scattered.

Female Fancy Dancers

This type of dancer wears a dress of shiny and colorful material. Their main ornament, however, is a long shawl worn on the shoulders. This shawl is fringed and embroidered with different motives, most of them stylized feathers of ribbon appliqué.

Plate 6. Female Fancy Dancer during a competition (shawl with ribbon appliqué and beaded cape). Manitoulin Island, Ontario, 1989.

Turning now to the gendered organization of powwow feather ornaments, we note that feathers establish boundaries between different groups of male dancers: natural eagle and hawk feathers (men's Traditional), dyed hackle feathers (male Fancy Dancers), and no feathers at all (Grass Dancers). Women's categories are defined by the treatment of the shawl (folded, open and decorated, or no shawl at all). Women's shawls thus seem to function as structural opposites of feathers in the male outfits.

Furthermore, female dancers never wear feathers as body ornaments. Hatton (1986: 210) mentions the "intermittent occurrence" of the participation of women as male dancers during powwows. He concludes, however, that "nothing in these references suggests a trend, scattered as they are through two decades over the entire plains." This is confirmed by other observations made by Howard (1955: 217).

The bustle is an exclusively male ornament although one category of male dancer does not wear it at all (the Grass Dancer). The latter's outfit, with its long wool yarn swirling at every step of the dance is much more reminiscent of the women's Traditional and female Fancy Dancers' ex-

Plate 7. Grass Dancer (foreground) and female Fancy Dancer (center). Walpole Island Powwow, Ontario, 1989.

clusively "female" ornament, the shawl (Plate 7). On the other hand, female Fancy Dancers' shawls are very often decorated with ribbon appliqué of stylized feathers. One can therefore conclude that the structure constituted by feather ornaments (bustles) and shawls does not differentiate between the sexes in an oppositional manner. In fact, it creates echoes and parallels between male and female dancers.

As stated earlier, categories also enter into a hierarchical ordering that puts male dancers first and female dancers second. Men Traditional Dancers come first, Grass Dancers second, Fancy Dancers third. Women Traditional Dancers are next; then Jingle Dress Dancers; and last, female Fancy Dancers. Only male Traditional Dancers are entitled to dance the ceremonial dances that punctuate the competition. These ceremonial dances are performed when an eagle feather has fallen from the outfit of a dancer, usually belonging to the men's traditional category. The dance is carried out by four veterans, not necessarily participating in the competition. When it takes place, spectators and participants must stand and take off their hats. No photograph can be taken, underlining the solemnity of the ceremony.

It is these gendered oppositions, echoes, and hierarchies that structure the set of aesthetic practices observable in powwow regalia. However, they have changed in the course of history and it is through these changes that the "gendered" discourse of tradition is constituted which, in my opinion, is at the heart of the dynamics of the powwow as a popular art form. I will now focus on the history of the bustle, a history that parallels the evolution of the powwow itself, as well as examine the contradictory messages conveyed about the meanings of tradition.

The bustle

Two of the earliest forms of the bustle are the raven belt of Plains Siouan-speaking peoples (Hewitt 1987: 6; Laubin − Laubin 1976: 435−437; Catlin 1973: plate 287 and 289) and the Pawnee *iruska* belt depicted by Murie (1981: 464). Birds such as the turkey and prairie chicken also "furnished an abundance of plumage for decorative purposes" (Koch 1977: 7). It is possible to imagine that before the nineteenth century feathers entered into a symbolic system much more indicative of "man's relationship with nature" (Brasser 1987: 115). Nineteenth-century ethnographies offer us some insight into the intricate myths and legends pertaining to birds.[3]

By the 1850s, however, feathers entered into a military heraldry that glorified the role of men as warriors and hunters. In the nineteenth century, the belt was used as a war-honor decoration by Omaha warriors in their War Dance Society, the *Hethushka*. The ornament was a "hanging flat bustle" consisting of rows of eagle feathers sewn on a piece of cloth or buckskin and decorated by a crow skin and a wolf tail and surmounted by two upright arrows (Fletcher — Laflesche 1970[1911]: 441). These "Omaha bustles" were linked to a complex symbolic system of hunting and warfare. The eagle was:

> associated with war and with the destructive powers of the thunder and the attendant storms. The wolf had a mythical relation to the office of "soldiers," the designation given to certain men on the annual tribal hunt, who acted as marshals and kept the people and the hunters in order during the surrounding of the herd (Fletcher — Laflesche 1970 [1911]: 442).

During the Indian Wars and shortly after the colonization of the North American West (the final quarter of the nineteenth century), the bustle was used in dances called "Grass Dance," "Omaha Dance," or "War Dance," the parent forms of which were the dances of the Omaha *Hethushka* (Wissler 1916: 855; Hatton 1986: 198 – 199; Hewitt 1987: 6). These dances were part of a large complex of dances that spread from the Sioux to the rest of the Northern Plains, reaching the Blackfoot in western Canada in the 1880s (Hatton 1986: 202 – 203). A different type of bustle, called the "crow belt," was used during these social dances. It is described by Mooney (1965[1896]: 901) who observed a dance held after the ghost dance ceremony among the Arapaho and Cheyenne nations. It was a bustle made of "vary-colored feathers" and did not have a crow skin as ornament, despite its name. Mooney emphasizes the social and fashionable aspect of this dance, popular among young dancers displaying great agility in their choreography.

A second type of bustle was found among the Menominee, Winnebago, and Ojibwa in the Great Lakes region (Densmore 1973[1913]: 68) and was worn by some members of the Dream Dance Society. This "single, or sometimes double panel bustle may have [had] a layered wheel present. A large beaded rosette [was] a common feature" (Hewitt 1987: 8).

The "Sioux" bustle, worn during War Dances, in contrast to the "Omaha" bustle, had a "wheel" as well as "trailers." A good example of such a bustle has been described by Howard (1972: 2 – 6) who came in possession of a Teton Dakota dance outfit which belonged to a man named Firecloud at the beginning of this century. It consisted of a trailer, a full circle made of stacked layers of feathers, surmounted by two uprights decorated also with feathers. The feathers were dyed in bright colors and came from eagles, hawks, and screech owls, mixed with goose and turkey feathers, also dyed and decorated with red fluffies. A neck bustle duplicated the waist bustle. Other bustles show the use of pheasant feathers in their decoration.

When this new War Dance was spreading to the Plains and to the Woodlands, the various societies that had given rise to the dance had already begun to break down, although in some instances the wearing of the belt was considered a great honor, especially during the Dream Dance of the Woodlands (Hewitt 1987: 8). On the Plains, however, it was often worn out of context and became an ornament that did not seem to bear any relation to the activities of warfare and hunting.

The white gaze

At the beginning of the twentieth century, native men were also engaged in another set of events, popular not only among native nations but also among the growing number of settlers and city dwellers of the frontier. These were Indian shows which toured the United States, accompanying rodeo shows, circuses, and fairs. They employed many young native dancers who danced "for the entertainment of the curious" (Cox 1989). Native men put on dances in which they competed with each other in a manner similar to rodeo champions. They also developed a new type of dancing outfit that became the Fancy Dancer's regalia.

We know that the Fancy Dancer became a specific category at the Ponca Fair and Powwow in Oklahoma in the 1920s. It was characterized by neck, waist, and arm bustles and a "feather crest (nicknamed 'Zulu hat' by the critical Dakota [which] replaced the roach headdress" (Thiel 1982: 7). The outfit itself can be traced to a few individuals who initiated a new fashion among the dancers. It was initially and intentionally a joke (Young 1981: 275). The use of brightly dyed turkey and chicken feathers was systematized (Powers 1966: 8; Thiel 1982: 11). Fluffies (brightly dyed downy feathers) were multiplied.

Many studies have focused on the manipulation of the stereotyped imagery of the "feathered Indian" in American mythology (Berkhofer 1979; Pakes 1985) and on the importance of new technologies such as photography in the process (Stedman 1982; Scherer 1975; Albers — James 1983; Albers — James 1988). The fascination of white audiences for North American native life and art, in particular dancing regalia, is explained mostly in terms of a quest by the dominant society for a past untouched by the evils of "civilization" which contains both the threatening "savage look" and the more amiable look of the exotic Indian born in the Age of Enlightenment. Albers and Medicine contend that it is only when Indians and their cultures were "fetishized" that the symbolic meanings of their artifacts came to be effectively manipulated by alien interests.

Nonetheless, the "romantic" discourse on Indians was not the only one that was advanced at the time. In order to justify the organization of Indian dances, white promoters of pageants and fairs put forward the serious character of Indian exhibition dancing which was taken as "serious ethnological exhibition" (Young 1981: 189). The romantic aesthetization of the past, the ethnographic ("scientific") quest for exotic customs, and the political colonial discourse of Indian Agencies are explicit (and sometimes contradictory) discursive practices that shaped the ways Indian male performers were perceived by the colonizers.

Tourism was also a burgeoning industry in the western American states in the 1920s. Adler (1989: 24) traces modern tourism to a "style of travel performance which privileged the eye for comprehensive inventory" that "served as one of the rituals through which European cultural and intellectual elites sought to take title to the 'whole world' then coming into view." The appropriation of the world through the gaze of the European tourist was accompanied by the collection of "curiosities" which later became the fodder of anthropological museums. At the beginning of the twentieth century, "cultural and intellectual elites" were not the only ones to experience any longer the titillation of the exotic through their encounter with "others." Tourism was becoming available to a middle class seeking exotic frissons in safe places. The staged dances offered to the gaze of tourists afforded both settlers and tourists "sentimental and vicarious links with the symbolic Indian, noble warrior or child of nature" (Albers — Medicine 1983: 147). Child of nature or cruel Indians killing pathetic pioneers entered the American mythology through the new technologies of visual representation and the specular pleasure of American and European onlookers.

To base analyses of the encapsulation of native imagery on the yearning for a "golden age" or a curiosity for the "primitive" by artists and anthropologists does not, however, give the full extent of the disempow-

ering "dialogue" that went on at that time. Such analyses do not account
for the fact that it was native *men* and their outfits that became the
fetishized image of the "Indian," nor do they account for the ways native
dancers responded to the omnipresent gaze of spectators, tourists, photographers, and film makers.

Reports of the time give us some insight into the dynamics of native
resistance to the encroaching presence of spectators. As one agent of
Indian shows said, Indians participating in his show "taught that savagery
has market value and is worth retaining" (Thiel 1982: 19). With the loss
of their traditional roles as warriors and hunters that still dominated the
imagery of their parent cultures, young men sought a different path to
acquire prestige through theatrical performances (Wrone — Nelson 1973:
452; Radin 1920: 24—25).

This meant that the effect produced on the spectator by the outfit
(and the bustles) of the dancer was defined in *visual* terms, responding
to a white audience's gaze in demand for a "fetishized" image of the
Indian (Albers — James 1988: 136). Concluding his paper on prairie
pageants in the Canadian West, Bruce Cox (1989: 37) asserts that "the
true significance of the prairie pageants is not only Indian defiance
[against policies of the Department of Indian Affairs], but white complicity." One might wonder about the nature of this white complicity.
Among all the evils that were said to be caused by these first "powwows"
by the Indian Affairs officials of the time (they were also said to distract
Indians from their work and promote meetings in which "old" religious
customs were kept alive), the fact that Indians appeared decked in "war
paints and feathers" (Cox 1989: 36) worried Indian agents who feared
for Canada's international image and for the morality of the spectators.
One of the Indian Inspectors reported that:

> for some years past, almost every village town and city has persistently
> coaxed Indians to leave their homes and work to give exhibitions of old
> time customs, i. e., male Indians in almost nude attire, parading streets and
> other public places, giving so called war and other dances for the edification
> of wives and daughters of people who claimed to be civilized and refined
> (as quoted in Cox 1989: 37).

The white public at large reacted positively to what was perceived as a
display of "savages," to the dismay of Indian Agents and clergy responsible for the "moral" advancement of the new frontier. Yet, in the
interstices of the moral condemnation, an implicit statement is made: the
white spectators found a specular pleasure in the display of "male Indians
in almost nude attire." This phenomenon was not confined to the Ca-

nadian West at the beginning of the century. It could certainly be argued that the popularity of "Indian shows" in the American West had at least the same sexual underpinnings. A journalist reviewing a dance held on the Cheyenne and Arapaho Reservation in the Indian Territory in 1902 depicts the performers as "bucks" who were "gaily dressed with feather and headgear" (Young 1981: 191). Pakes (1985: 8) quotes a similar "typical" comment that compares the "Indian warrior dressed in all his finery" to "the peacock, the stag, and almost all animals where the male is lavishly decorated while the female is plain and unadorned."

Therefore, to explain the settlers' fascination for Indian shows in terms of the dominant ideology calls for an analysis of the "ways of seeing" developed in the non-native world towards Indians. The voyeuristic activities of the onlooker froze the image of Indian men and gave the ubiquitous feather the status of marker of an Indian identity. In his study of postcards taken by French colonizers of Algerian women (and their phantasmagoric place, the Harem), Alloula (1986: 13) writes what can also be said of the "white gaze" cast upon Indian dancers of the time: "Colonialism is, among other things, the perfect expression of the violence of the gaze, and not only in the metaphorical sense of the term."

The seduction of the exotic dancer

The presence of this insistent gaze affected native cultural forms and dancing regalia in particular. It also affected the ways native dancers represented themselves to others and to themselves. Not only did the omnipotent presence of the other's eye impose a stereotyped, Hollywood, pan-Indian look to dancers' regalia but the "violence of the gaze" also met with a resistance that is clearly stated in the way the "conservative" Dakota responded to the new Fancy outfit. This resistance is still, I believe, expressed during contemporary powwows: it is forbidden to photograph or film the most ceremonial moments (the grand entry and the retrieval dance of the eagle feather). The native sensitivity to the "white gaze" leads to an attempt to control what is being shown as native for public consumption.

In *La chambre claire*, Roland Barthes (1980) analyses the effect of photography on the perception he has of himself. He conducts a phenomenological micro-analysis of the photographed that, I believe, should be extended to a macro-sociological analysis which needs to be done systematically: the role of the photographic apparatus in the act of colonization. For Barthes, being photographed means that the representation of self is marred by the other's gaze. "L'avénement de moi-même comme autre ... une dissociation retorse de la conscience d'identité" [It is the birth of oneself as Other ... a sly dissociation of ones' conscious identity] (Barthes 1980: 28). The photographed subject is "transformed into an object and caught in the circle of self-imitation and lack of authenticity and sometimes imposture" (Barthes 1980: 28)). The emergence of the Fancy Dancer in the 1920s is part and parcel of this long attempt by native dancers to re-appropriate for themselves their own image that has been "stolen" by the colonizer's gaze. Done as a parody, it made a joke of both the former military heraldry of the nineteenth-century bustle and was the ironic response to the "white gaze."

The modifications in the nature of the feathers used to make a bustle were gradually accompanied by a reshaping of the former bustles. The two uprights sticking up from the bustle disappeared. The former full circle of feathers of the Sioux bustle or the hanging trailer of the Omaha bustle became the half-circular, fan-shaped bustle that exists today (Plate 4). This reshaping of the ornament is much more reminiscent of the fan-shaped tail of turkeys, peacocks, and other gallinaceous birds. Turkey feathers, hackle feathers, and fluffies were used in over-abundance to give the bustle the appearance it has now.

In order to be understood, irony and parody require a recognition of the underlying meanings of the objects used in the construction of the outfit. Meanings associated with the courtship display of gallinaceous birds signified this parody. On the one hand, dancers transformed themselves into beautiful "exotic" birds for the entertainment of the curious. They became "exotic dancers." At the same time, the use of the imagery of the peacock, the gobbler, and the rooster displayed a male identity that was not any longer defined in terms of the labor of hunting and warfare but in terms of the "labor of seduction." The bustle of the Fancy Dancer reformulated and translated the former military heraldry that glorified the role of the men as warriors and hunters in terms of sexual conquest. The gobbler, the rooster, and the prairie chicken are the forms on which the contemporary bustle is constructed, expressing the seductive display of masculinity. However, by displaying the signs of male birds, Fancy Dancers also display the sign of their disappropriation by the other's gaze. It is this contradiction that reshaped, in my opinion, the so-called traditional bustle.

The "traditional" bustle

While in the 1930s and 1940s the feather costume of the Fancy Dancer became very elaborate (Powers 1966: 7–8), the "older style" worn mostly in the Northern Plains by the Sioux gradually became more individualized. By the 1950s, traditional dancers had adopted the U-shaped bustle that is now the standard feather ornament of the male Traditional Dancer (Powers 1966: 6). This bustle, made of dark eagle and hawk feathers, was reworked in the light of the Fancy bustle, although a simpler interpretation would make it the direct heir of the ceremonial bustle described earlier. The Traditional Dancer's bustle marks the tension that exists between former meanings that were signified by the eagle/hawk feather and its military heraldry and contemporary meanings that emerged in the "powwow culture."

The shape and appearance of bustles worn by male Traditional Dancers are very individualized and their explicit meanings still refer to the symbolic eagle that I described. Yet, there is, in the making of the ornament, a deliberate accumulation of eagle feathers which verges on parody. Or, as one of the dancers said to me, he decorated his outfit and his bustle in order to make it "nearly ridiculous" while at the same time trying not to "go overboard." This parodic mood, often concealed under the seriousness of the eagle's imagery, is very similar to the parodic nature of the Fancy Dancer's regalia when it emerged as a category in the Oklahoma Powwows of the 1920s. The reshaping of the bustle shows the gradual adoption of features similar to the Fancy Dancer's bustle (Plate 7). The "wheel," which did not exist in the historical bustles, or was circular in the Sioux bustles of the early 1900s, has become semi-circular, in the Fancy fashion, adopting a shape similar to that of gallinaceous birds. In fact, explicit references are sometimes made to one species of bird that possesses an elaborate courtship display, similar in many ways to the gobbler and rooster of the Fancy bustle: the prairie chicken.

Whereas, in the nineteenth century, the warrior could wear at the same time turkey, crow, and eagle feathers, the contemporary "warrior" can not wear these feathers together. The supremacy of the ultimate hunter/ warrior, the eagle, is then signified by the hierarchical ordering of dancers and its ceremonial power, which parallels the position of the eagle and gallinaceous birds in the ecological chain: eagles prey on ground birds. Therefore, if there were a "mix of feathers," the proper distance between the conquered and the conqueror would not be maintained. Hence, I would suggest, a display of signs on the traditional bustles that asserts the importance of the "traditional" and denotes a will to dissociate oneself from the "fancy," which is too "seductive" and involved in a "dangerous joke" of disappropriation.

This distinction, operating from within the code of feathers, shows a radical split between what is considered "straight" (another name for the "men's Traditional" category) and what is considered "fancy." Here it is argued that this dissociation was not inherent in a sexual ethic akin to the Judeo-Christian discourse on sexual purity but to the relative position of Indian males in the whole context in which their regalia was constructed after the conquest. The male Traditional Dancer's accumulation of male and military insignia on his bustle has to be understood in the light of a history that disempowered native men in general. It is then no wonder that the fiercest attacks against the stereotypes of native peoples bear on the most universal of the signifier of Indianness, the unqualified "feather," because it is also the signifier of a (possible) male defeat.[4] However, the reshaping of eagle feather ornaments according to the Fancy Dancer's bustle attests to the contradictions within the political discourse conveyed by the male Traditional Dancer. The definition of masculinity in terms of sexual conquest is not the prerogative of the Fancy Dancer. The male Traditional Dancer also speaks a language of desire but is caught in a double bind. He is both "awesome" and at the limit of parody.

Furthermore, the central position of the eagle feather is contested by the presence of other male dancers and the emergence of the Grass Dancer outfit in the past few years indicates that it is challenged. The recent development of the Grass Dancer's outfit is, in my view, a place where the feather as symbol of Indianness is questioned. The name "Grass Dancer" itself, which is a revival of the name given to the ceremonial dance at the origin of the powwow, confers to this category an authority and prestige that the Fancy Dancer lacks. Its place as second to the Traditional Dancer during grand entry also indicates its role as a possible challenger to the political economy of signs within the feather code.[5]

A new tradition?

In contrast with the profusion of feathers worn by Fancy and Traditional Dancers, the Grass Dancer only wears downy feathers at the tip of his headdress. His outfit consists of long yarn fringes that swirl and whirl like the shawl of the women Fancy Dancer (which are also fringed with yarn or chainette). I would suggest that the growing popularity of this recent regalia challenges the predominance of the Traditional Dancer by adopting the aesthetic forms predominant in the women's costume. The contemporary Grass Dancer has the name of the former ceremonial dance that is considered to be at the origin of the powwow. The name itself comes from the bunch of grass that Omaha Dancers (who did not all wear a bustle) stuck in their belt to represent the scalps that they had taken during a battle (Fletcher – Laflesche 1970[1911]: 461). These scalps were the property of their female relatives to whom they were given upon the warriors' return. Omaha and Plains warriors' garments were decorated by strands of hair, furnished by their female relatives (Fletcher – Laflesche 1970[1911]: 448). The contemporary costume of the Grass Dancer bears the traces of its association with femininity, although it is not made of "grass" or hair any longer. But its long yarns of wool echo the long fringes of the dresses of women and the shawls they wear.

As mentioned earlier, the structural opposite of the bustles of male outfits is the shawl that women wear either folded (women Traditional) or open on the shoulders (Women Fancy Dancers). Thiel (1982: 8) notes that Eastern Plains women's outfits included "shawl of wool rainbow selvage, trade cloth decorated with abstract floral bead embroidery or ribbon applique." In old photographs of "Round Dances" (i. e., the social dances in which women participated at the turn of the century), women wore very large shawls that look like trade blankets.[6] Shawls were trade items in the nineteenth century (Koch 1977: 81 – 82). I would thus suggest that the shawls of women's regalia are trade items with which was associated the role of women as "producers of durable goods" in a society where the division of labor between the sexes defined gendered meanings as much as sexual identity (Whitehead 1981: 96).

Although it would be possible to associate the wearing of shawls with a more universal symbolism of the womb and of the house or tent which were the property of women, no semantic evidence confirms this view. Rather, in my opinion, it is precisely their place as trade items that makes them signs of femininity. They constituted the rewards of female labor and brought prestige to women who did not acquire prestige and glory in warfare and hunting but as skilled craftswomen (Whitehead 1981; Klein 1983; Schneider 1983). Shawls were signs of female prestige as feathers have been of male prestige. The involvement of men and women in the powwow reworked the wearing of shawls within the female costume. The open shawl of the female Fancy Dancer is seductive and can bear the signs of sexual mediation whereas the shawl of the female Traditional Dancer shawl is worn folded and plain, signifying its parallel position to the eagle feather.

The male grass outfit that bears the signs of a new mediation between genders, to the point of dispossessing itself of all signs of masculinity, is the aesthetic form that literally "defeathers" the Indian. It could be seen as the sign of a new discourse on tradition that does not rely any longer on military heraldry and the metaphor of the conquered and the conqueror, the hunter and the hunted, but on processes of signification that take into account (or reappropriate) the place of women in the legitimation of an Indian difference.

The position taken in this chapter is that far from being a place where all participants agree on meanings displayed during the event, the powwow and its aesthetic forms are, on the contrary, a place of constant questioning and reinterpretation. To see dancers' regalia in the light of a pristine tradition, generally fixed in the narrow span of the "ethnographic present" (1840−1890 for North American Indians), is, of course, to miss the point. In fact the regalia and their feather ornaments were reworked according to new aesthetic conventions and practices which emerged in the 1920s and have been evolving ever since. Powwow regalia are to be understood in the context of general discursive practices concerning the role of tradition in the cultural and political spheres.

Aesthetic conventions displayed in dancers' regalia rely on a code structured by the different ornamental objects that are used in the making of the regalia. Powwow regalia rely heavily on the use of feathers, furs, shells, dewclaws, and other ornaments related to animals. Many ornaments and dresses are also made of cloth, embroidered, fringed or plain. These ornaments made of animal or textile elements constitute a web of oppositions and analogies that should be depicted in order for us to understand the intricate play from which emerges the signification of the regalia, opposed to other kinds of feathers, hackle feathers, down feathers or fluffies. As feathers, they are also opposed to furs, beads, shells, and objects made of cloth. Furthermore, they belong to a system of signification opposing the head and the lower part of the body which itself parallels a distinction between different types of eagle feathers (the brown feathers of the mature Golden Bald Eagles as opposed to the black and white tail feathers of the immature Golden Eagle).

Eagle feathers that are a major ornament of powwow dancers' regalia become meaningful because they are placed on a paradigmatic axis (i. e., opposed to other feathers and other ornamental objects) and on a syntagmatic axis (as positioned on the body of the wearer and according to the gender of the body wearing it). The "Indianness" of the eagle feather is not due to a symbolic apparatus amenable to a unilinear exegesis but is generated by a number of signifiers which are momentarily fixed in specific codes according to their own structural configuration and the power they confer to their users at a specific point in history.

Furthermore, powwow regalia are not political statements per se. They engage the body of the dancer, clothing it. As we have seen, they are organized along gender lines that both oppose and echo one another. The gendered structure of the categories in which men and women participate is of utmost importance for our understanding of the multifaceted signification of ornaments because it inscribes the ornaments in a language of desire that differentiates between the sexes and mediates between them. The social dramaturgy displayed through powwow regalia is echoed by another dramaturgy, that of seduction. Signs of femininity and signs of masculinity are constitutive of a language, historically defined, consciously and unconsciously, in which each gendered individual takes position, defines his/her position in the discursive gendered practices of her/his time. At the same time, they are lived through a "fundamental irrationality: the extent to which will or agency is constantly subverted by desire, and the extent to which we behave and experience ourselves in ways that are often contradictory" (Henriques et al. 1984: 205).

Notes

1. I wish to thank Valda Blundell for her unfailing assistance without which this paper could not have been written. For a history of the meaning of the word "powwow" see Kurath (1966) and Young (1981: 192).
2. Corrigan (1970: 263) describes the give-away in the following manner: "The procedure of donations is simple: an honor song is sung and the donor and his kinsmen dance very briefly. The donor then stands at the front of the tent by the master of ceremonies who calls out the donees. Each donee steps up to the donor as his or her name is called, shakes his hand, receives his gift and returns to his place in the audience." Ontario give-aways follow the same pattern, except that the honor song takes place once the gifts have been distributed. The donees generally do not go back to their seats but stand in line at the side of the donor on the powwow ground.
3. The Pawnee *Hako*, described by Fletcher (1901: 23–24), is a good example of the intricate Plains symbolism surrounding the use of birds and their feathers in the nineteenth century. As an old informant said to Alice Fletcher: "We take up the Hako in the spring when birds are mating, or in the summer when

birds are nesting and caring for their young, or in the fall when the birds are flocking, but not in winter when all things are asleep."

4. Examples abound of this constant attack on feathers as "universal" symbols of native identity. For instance, Emma LaRocque, a Metis from northeastern Alberta, fighting the pervasive cliches marring Canadian perception of "Indians," titled her book *Defeathering the Indian* (1975). The contrast between the rejection by many native peoples of the use of feathers as markers of native identity and its overwhelming use in powwow regalia is striking. One of the aims of this chapter has been to analyze this apparent paradox.

5. There is little information on the historical transformation of the Jingle Dress Dancer's outfit. The only papers on the history of the contemporary Grass Dancer's outfit are Howard's study of the northern style Grass Dance costume (1960) and Johnson's (1972) paper on the Cree Grass Dance costume. Since then the Grass Dancer's regalia has changed considerably. For Howard (1960: 18), the Grass Dance outfit of the Plains "became the dress of the young active dancers, rather than the one utilizing the crow belt and shoulder bustle... It is more or less the equivalent of the Oklahoma Fancy Dancer." In a leaflet advertising the 1987 powwow of Saddle Lake, Alberta, the Grass Dancer comes first, before the men's Traditional category.

6. Due to the lack of historical knowledge about the female dancers' outfit, it is difficult to assess how women's categories emerged during the history of the powwow. It seems, however, that the participation of women in Round Dances at the beginning of the twentieth century gradually led to their participation in competition dancing after World War II, when men's categories (Traditional and Fancy) were already in place.

References

Adler, Judith
   1989   "Origins of sight seeing," *Annals of Tourism Research* 16(1): 7–29.
Albers, Patricia – William James
   1983   "Tourism and the changing image of the Great Lakes Indian," *Annals of Tourism Research* 10(1): 128–138.
   1988   "Travel photography, a methodological approach," *Annals of Tourism Research* 15(1): 134–158.
Albers, Patricia – Beatrice Medicine (eds.)
   1983   *The hidden half: Studies of Plains Indian women.* Lanham, NY: University Press of America.
Alloula, Malek
   1986   *The colonial harem.* Minneapolis: University of Minnesota Press.
Barthes, Roland
   1980   *La chambre claire: Notes sur la photographie.* Paris: Gallimard-Seuil.

Berkhofer, Robert, Jr.
1979   *The white man's Indian.* New York: Vintage Books.
Blundell, Valda
1985   "Une approche sémiologique du powwow canadien contemporain,"
        Recherches Amérindiennes au Québec 15(4): 53 – 65.
Brasser, Ted
1987   "By the power of their dreams: Artistic traditions of the northern
        plains," in: Julia D. Harrison (ed.), 93 – 133.
Campisi, Jack
1975   "Powwow: a study of ethnic boundary maintenance," *Man in the
        Northeast* 9: 33 – 46.
Catlin, George
1973   *Letters and notes on the manner and condition of the North American
        Indians, written during eight years travel (1832 – 1839) among the
        wildest tribes of North America.* Vol. 2. New York: Dover
        Publications.
Chevalier, Jacques — Valda Blundell — Bruce Cox (eds.).
1989   *A different drummer: Readings in anthropology with a Canadian per-
        spective.* Ottawa: Carleton University Press.
Corrigan, Samuel W.
1970   "The plains Indian pow wow: Cultural integration in Manitoba and
        Saskatchewan," *Anthropologica* 12: 253 – 277.
Cox, Bruce A.
1989   "Historical anthropology," in: Jacques Chevalier — Valda Blundell
        — Bruce Cox (eds.), 31 – 38.
Densmore, Frances
1913   *Chippewa music.* Washington, D. C.: Bureau of American Ethnology,
        Smithsonian Institution. Bulletin 53.
[1973] [Reprinted: Minneapolis: Ross and Haines.]
Dyck, Noel
1979   "Powwow and the expression of community in western Canada,"
        Ethnos 44(1/2): 78 – 98.
1983   "Political powwow: The rise and fall of an urban native festival," in:
        Frank Manning (ed.), 165 – 184.
Fletcher, Alice C.
1900 – 1901 *The hako: A Pawnee ceremony.* Washington, D. C.: Bureau of
        American Ethnology, Smithsonian Institution. 22nd annual report,
        part II.
Fletcher, Alice C. — Francis Laflesche
1911   *The Omaha tribe.* Washington, D. C.: Bureau of American Ethnology,
        Smithsonian Institution. 27th annual report.
[1970] [Reprinted. New York: Johnson Corporation.]
Fowler, Loretta
1987   *Shared symbols, contested meanings: Gros Ventres culture and history,
        1778 – 1984.* Ithaca: Cornell University Press.

Frideres, James S.
1983   *Native people in Canada: Contemporary conflicts.* Scarborough, Ont.: Prentice-Hall Canada.
Harrison, Julia D. (ed.)
1987   *The spirit sings: Artistic traditions of Canada's first peoples.* Toronto: McClelland and Stewart.
Hatton, Orin T.
1986   "In the tradition: Grass Dance musical style and female pow-wow singers," *Ethnomusicology* 30 (2): 197–221.
Henriques, Julian – Wendy Holloway – Cathy Urwin – Couze Wenn – Valerie Walkerdine
1984   *Changing the subject.* London: Methuen.
Hewitt, Rick
1987   "The bustle, part I: 1885–1915," *Whispering Wind* 19(6): 6–16.
Howard, James
1955   "Pan-Indian culture of Oklahoma," *Scientific Monthly* 81: 215–220.
1960   "Northern plains grass dance costume," *American Indian Hobbyist* 7(1): 18–26.
1972   "Firecloud's Omaha or grass dance costume," *American Indian Crafts and Culture* 6(2): 2–10, 6(3): 2–9.
Klein, Alan M.
1983   "The political economy of gender: A nineteenth century Plains Indians case," in: Patricia Albers – Beatrice Medicine (eds.), 143–173.
Koch, Ronald P.
1977   *Dress clothing of the Plains Indians.* Norman: University of Oklahoma Press.
Kurath, Gertrude
1966   *Michigan Indian festivals.* Ann Arbor, MI: Ann Arbor Publishers.
LaRoque, Emma
1975   *Defeathering the Indian.* Agincourt, Ont.: The Book Society of Canada.
Laubin, Reginald – Laubin, Gladys
1976   *Indian dances of North America: Their importance to Indian life.* Norman: University of Oklahoma Press.
Leacock, Eleanor B. – Nancy O. Lurie (eds.)
1971   *North American Indians in historical perspective.* New York: Random House.
Lurie, Nancy O.
1971   "The contemporary American Indian scene," in: Eleanor B. Leacock – Nancy O. Lurie (eds.), 418–480.
Manning, Frank (ed.)
1983   *The celebration of society: Perspectives on contemporary cultural performance.*

Momaday, Scott N.
  1969   *The way to the rainy mountain.* Albuquerque, NM: University of
           New Mexico Press.
Mooney, James
  1965[1896] *The ghost-dance religion and the Sioux outbreak of 1890.* Chicago:
           University of Chicago Press.
Murie, James R.
  1981   *Ceremonies of the Pawnee.* Douglas R. Parks (ed.). Lincoln: Univer-
           sity of Nebraska Press.
Ortner, Sherry — Harriet Whitehead (eds.)
  1981   *Sexual meanings.* Cambridge: Cambridge University Press.
Pakes, Fraser J.
  1985   "Seeing with the stereotypic eye: The visual image of the Plains
           Indians," *Native Studies Review* 1(2): 1–32.
Paredes, J. Anthony (ed.)
  1980   *Anishinabe: Six studies of modern Chippewa.* Tallahassee: University
           Presses of Florida.
Powers, William K.
  1966   "Feathers costume," *Powwow Trails* 3(7–8): 4–19.
Radin, Paul
  1920   *The autobiography of a Winnebago Indian.* University of California
           Press.
Rynkiewich, Michael A.
  1980   "Chippewa powwows," in: J. A. Paredes (ed.), 31–101.
Scherer, Joanna C.
  1975   "You can't believe your eyes: Inaccuracies in photographs of North
           American Indians," *Studies in the Anthropology of Visual Commu-
           nication* 2: 67–79.
Schneider, Mary Jane
  1983   "Women's work: An examination of women's roles in Plains Indian
           art and crafts," in: Patricia Albers — Beatrice Medicine (eds.),
           101–121.
Stedman, R. W.
  1982   *Shadows of the Indian: Stereotypes in American culture.* Norman:
           University of Oklahoma Press.
Tanner, Adrian (ed.)
  1983   *The politics of Indianness: Case studies of native ethnopolitics in
           Canada.* St. John's, NFLD: Institute of Social and Economic Re-
           search, Memorial University.
Thiel, Mark
  1982   "The powwow: Development of the contemporary American Indian
           celebration," *Whispering Wind* 15(2): 17–23.

Usher, Peter J.
  1982   "Are we defending a culture or a mode of production?" Paper
          presented at the Annual Meeting of the Canadian Anthropological
          Society. Ottawa, Ont.
Whitehead, Harriet
  1981   "The bow and the burden strap: A new look at institutionalized
          homosexuality in native North America," in Sherry Ortner — Harriet
          Whitehead (eds.), 81 – 115.
Wissler, Clark
  1916   "General discussion of shamanistic and dancing societies," *Anthro-
          pological Papers of the American Museum of Natural History* 11(12):
          853 – 876.
Wrone, David — Russel Nelson, Jr.
  1973   *Who's the Savage?*. Greenwich: Fawcett Publications.
Young, Gloria
  1981   *Powwow power: Perspectives on historic and contemporary intertri-
          balism*. Unpublished Ph.D. dissertation. Indiana University, Bloo-
          mington.

Navajo weaving as sacred metaphor

Kathy M'Closkey

In his *Critique of Judgment*, Kant (1951) postulated an absolute opposition between labor and art. Only art ("play") acted as mediator to reconcile the formal dichotomy between mind and body, reason and emotion. Kant's dualism is a result of the division of mental and manual labor originating in Greek philosophy — a preserve of intellectuals for intellectuals. Reconciliation of the dichotomy (via art) is itself an intellectual process. I argue in this chapter that the art/craft distinction (with its hidden rationale concerning the bifurcation of mental and manual labor implicit in Kantian aesthetics) "legitimized" the economic exploitation of native handwork. Because of the hegemony of the fine arts, Navajo weaving was perceived as craft, blankets and rugs were practical articles devoid of aesthetic expression.

According to Eric Wolf (1982: 388), "the ability to bestow meanings — to 'name' things, acts and ideas, is a source of power. Control of communication allows the managers of ideology to lay down the categories through which reality is to be perceived." As a weaver myself, I view a blank warp (the threads a weaver works upon) and a blank canvas as analogous means of creative expression, yet one has been elevated to the status of fine art and the other trivialized and demoted to craft in Western history.

Gary Witherspoon's (1987) monograph *Navajo Weaving* challenges the unquestioned assumption that because of the Anglo audience and trader influence, Navajo women wove abstract designs bereft of symbolism for more than a century. Witherspoon maps the history and meaning of three symbols central to Diné (Navajo) cosmology. All are represented in the geometric designs created in Navajo weaving. The most apparent forms and patterns have changed over time, but the underlying motifs remain distinctly Navajo because they are deeply rooted in the archetypal symbols of Navajo society and culture. But Witherspoon's interpretation typifies classic symbolic analysis. Drawing on concepts from Tony Wilden (1981) and Gregory Bateson (1972, 1988), I suggest that textile patterns are more like metaphors than cognitively produced and explicit symbols. The repetition and redundancy of recurrent patterns suggest a commonality of form in which Navajo textiles map optic expressions of fundamental formal relationships.

Historical background

During the Renaissance a division occurred between creative, non-utilitarian objects called "art," which were painted or sculpted, and functional practical items designated as "crafts." This division emerged at a time when Europeans began colonizing the rest of the world; it coincides with the birth of modern capitalism and the emergence of art as a commodity and speculative asset (Hauser 1965).

Drawing formed the focal point of the European painter's training, first within the Guilds and later the Academies (formed during the Renaissance). Only painters were capable of *designare* the ability to draw, compose and create. Painters spent years perfecting their ability to imitate nature. Their training included courses in architecture, geometry, perspective and anatomy (Pevsner 1940). Renaissance craftsmen were denied training in both mathematics (a purely intellectual activity), and drawing.

Artistic literacy was achieved through drawing. Since the Middle Ages drawing has played *the* central, historical role in the training of an artist. Its supreme importance has affected Westerners' perception concerning native production, shaped terminology, and consequently skewed an appreciation of the fundamental processes concerning the creation of "art." The concept of the artist as genius developed during this period and differs substantially from the view that a craftsperson, using only technical ability, executes the designs of either a patron or artist. Hence fine art becomes primarily an intellectual exercise whereas the essence of craft production resides in the technical excellence of the completed piece.

The creation of art since the Renaissance has occupied the attention of art critics, historians, aestheticians, academics and artists themselves. The history of craft has been shaped by its exclusion from the category of fine art. The institutional separation of art from craft reflects the duality concerning mental and manual labour enshrined in Western thought (Sohn-Rethel 1977). The modern discipline of aesthetics (beginning with Kant's *Critique of Judgement*) consecrated the art/craft distinction since it focused on beauty as expressed only in non-utilitarian objects (Gadamer 1986: 19; Kristeller 1952). Kant's famous dictum "the necessary (or functional) cannot be judged beautiful, but only right or consistent" (as quoted in Kubler 1963: 16) provided the kiss of death for crafts and denied an aesthetic dimension to nearly everything created by human beings in all parts of the globe. Thus the bifurcation between head and hands or the separation of intellectual from manual labor initiated by the early Greek philosophers and mathematicians was extended to the realm of art. The history of craft in Europe from the end of the 18th century is the history of loss of status, atomization of work, de-skilling, degeneration of the working environment, regimentation and intense competition which ensured the lowest prices for owners of productive means and less than living wages for the workers (Yeo — Thompson 1971). There is no doubt that textile production, like all other practical "crafts," was little respected as a vocation by the upper classes. As an avocation (the gentlewoman and her needlework), it was acceptable. This was the background upon which native textile production was viewed. Ultimately native handweavers could be perceived as participating in an archaic process compared to debased powerloom weavers.

Originally, one of the most fundamental divisions in anthropology concerned the separation between literate and preliterate peoples. Literacy (including mathematics) is a major hallmark of civilization. Edmund Carpenter has noted:

> When a dominant sense comes into play, the other senses become junk. Visual values became the mark of civilized man. Literacy ushered man into the world of the divided sense. Sight is the only sense that offers detachment. This detachment gave literate man enormous power over his environment, but led to a corresponding unwillingness to get involved (Carpenter 1970: N. P.).

The primacy of visual values associated with artistic imperialism inherent in Western art history and aesthetics has shaped and conditioned anthropologists' appreciation of non-Western artifacts. Until recently, textiles have been collected by museum personnel as anthropological remnants of the past. Oversized books depicting "Indian Arts" have appeared in the last thirty years, but textiles are often ignored. Pericot-Garcia et al. note in their book *Prehistoric and Primitive Art*:

> The North American Indian's most distinctive arts are those which are traditional to all great Western civilizations; sculpture, painting, and architecture. His contribution to each of these branches of expression was strong ... [t]he Indian was also a superb craftsman or technologist in such

decorative or utilitarian mediums as weaving, basketry, ceramics, and tool or weapon making (Pericot-Garcia et al. 1967: 190).

The authors' distinction represents an unconscious capitulation to the Western art/craft dichotomy. Only sculpture, painting and architecture are means of expression. Basketry and weaving involve technological expertise divorced from expressive and artistic intent.

Textiles as an art form have been ignored by nearly all anthropologists, archaeologists, aestheticians and art critics who could not reconcile the inclusion of functional textiles as fine art. Yet in non-Western societies, the individual who wove the textile almost always designed it. The exception would occur in a highly stratified society such as the Incas in which a class of weavers produced textiles designed by a master weaver for royalty. Nearly all weaving techniques currently in use today were practised in prehistoric times by various societies. Textile production in one form or another was practically a global phenomenon − surely the antithesis of the production of rare art.

Just as oral traditions were rendered invalid as permanent cultural expressions because they were unwritten, the parallel exists for native work: because the articulation of production and the medium differed dramatically from that practised in Europe, the former was deemed inferior. During the nineteenth century, crafts were described as being manually dexterous, decorative and intellectually undemanding. Realism reigned supreme in art, and all types of geometric patterns were considered inferior forms of design − they were an expression of the feminine, purely decorative spirit in art (Parker − Pollock 1981: 68). All of that changed of course, when the contemporary art world saw fit to redefine "geometric" as "abstraction" and canonize it as the dominant expression in twentieth-century art.

The irony is that many textiles prefigure major developments in twentieth-century abstract art, in some cases by more than a century. They have been ignored for so long because they were created primarily by women in a "domestic" situation for utilitarian purposes − a far cry from the professional institutionalized art world. There is no doubt that the status of an art work is directly related to the status of the maker. The fact that no notice was taken by professionals of the visual impact of many compelling textiles demonstrates the pervasiveness and power of the art/craft distinction itself. Placed on bodies or floors instead of walls, these works simply were not/could not be "seen" as art − they were located outside the frame of reference created and dominated by the art world.

The art/craft distinction remains a dominant way of categorizing hand-made objects. The bifurcation of mental versus manual labor epitomized, in Kantian aesthetics "legitimized", the economic exploitation of native peoples globally. Unfortunately anthropologists have worked within the framework of this conceptual dualism. Thus the deterioration in quality which occurred in post-contact situations when indigenous trade networks were disrupted or destroyed by colonial merchants failed to trigger a response by anthropologists and others because natives produced only "crafts." Descriptions of native "crafts" substituted for a fundamental understanding of the conceptual processes involved in their production. Influenced by Western philosophical traditions, anthropologists' intellectual endeavors superseded the necessity of learning even the rudiments of manual production.

The Navajo

A salient example of the kind of intellectual myopia concerning native creations is reflected in the treatment of Navajo weaving in the anthropological (and related) literature during the past century. The Navajo (or Diné) are the largest (175,000) indigenous group in North America and currently occupy an 18 million acre reservation in the southwest United States. They traditionally engaged in livestock raising (sheep and goats), agriculture, weaving, and (later) silversmithing. After the formation of the reservation in 1868, subsistence activities continued but their self-sufficient character was undermined because traders fostered a dependence on manufactured goods and perishable foodstuffs. Weaving and wool production were the backbone of the Navajo economy prior to the traders' appearance. Within five years weavers had stopped production of clothing and bedding for inter- and intratribal trade, and became commodity producers. Expansion of textile production in the form of rugs shipped to distant markets increasingly bound weavers to individual traders and their posts. Large accounts were drawn against weavers' production, thus assuring a continuing supply of rugs while destroying their bargaining position. For nearly 80 years the vast number of rugs were marketed by the pound. Since these were not "raw resources" but finished products often involving hundreds of hours of work, the extraction of surplus was intense. At times wool prices fluctuated so much that the Navajo received more per pound for their wool (1915—1918) than they did for their rugs (1930–1933). Merchants reaped double benefits from this two-way commodity trade, and many actively engaged in "credit saturation" facilitated by geographic isolation and territorial monopoly.

An extensive literature spanning nearly a century exists on Navajo weaving which emphasizes either technical and/or historic accounts (Amsden 1975; James 1976; Kent 1985; Pendleton 1974; Pepper 1902; Reichard 1934, 1936, 1939; Wheat 1976). Woven motifs were perceived as representing geometric renderings of their local environment, or decorative designs were reputedly borrowed from alien cultures and incorporated into their weaving. According to experts (Amsden 1975: 218; Reichard 1936: 183), weaving was a secular activity for the Navajo. More recently, Kent (1985: 111) maintained that rugs woven in this century will not "tell us anything about Navajo personality or values" because Anglo traders and markets have influenced Navajo weavers so much that any meanings or aesthetic styles which may have existed in early weavings were extinguished.

Gary Witherspoon's 1987 monograph, "Navajo Weaving: Art in its Cultural Context," provides a powerful refutation of all literature which denies any symbolism in Navajo weaving (and thus underscores the influence of traders on designs). He notes that every culture has two sets of symbols by which it codifies and communicates its concepts and meanings. The first is language, and the second is found in objective forms and actions which are imbued with symbolic meanings.

> ... cultural constructions and meanings are embodied in symbols... Symbols capture and express, frame and focus, recall and retain, synthesize and condense cultural beliefs of enormous proportions into simple symbols that are polysemic and multivocal (Witherspoon 1987: 99).

Witherspoon maintains that Navajo weaving has not lost its identity or its creative autonomy even though it underwent a period of Pueblo absorption and Spanish influence prior to the more recent appearance of Anglo traders and markets. He queries why the Navajo were neither diminished nor destroyed by more numerous, more powerful and technologically superior societies. Instead, they have endured and flourished: they have increased a hundredfold in population, their tribal unity and organization have been codified and strengthened, their technological skills and power have increased and expanded.

> They have made their way through several powerful cultural and technological onslaughts, through various bureaucratic and legislative forms of corruption, insensitivity and paternalism, and through the activities of

romantics and missionaries, do-gooders and racists, corporate officials and unscrupulous lawyers (Witherspoon 1987: 4).

He further notes that the history of the Navajo people can be followed through the evolution of their weaving. Blankets (including saddle blankets) and clothing, which they used to weave for their own use, became items to barter for tools and food in the latter decades of the nineteenth century before they became a cash producing art form in the twentieth century. "This ability to synthesize aesthetics with pragmatics, internal cultural expression with external market influence, individual creativity with universal cultural theme, is at the very heart of their vigor, vitality and adaptability as a human society. Their transformations were culturally inspired and facilitated, not materially determined" (Witherspoon 1987: 4).

According to him, only an interpretive approach to cultural explication can explain this uniqueness and this extraordinary transformation. But portions of his interpretation typify classic symbolic analysis (i. e., Turner 1967; Leach 1961) which has been soundly critiqued by Sperber (1975). First I present a precis of Witherspoon's analysis followed by a critique of his isomorphic account of what several of these key symbols "mean" and then I propose an alternative explanation incorporating concepts inspired by Sperber, Wilden (1981), and Bateson (1972, 1988).

Navajo semiotic geometry

The Navajo call themselves Diné. The term is a linguistic representation of a social, political, and military alliance. The indigenous symbols are shown in Plate 1. Both symbols have an important history and a rich set of meanings (Witherspoon 1987: 9). They also contain the basic design elements from which many of the patterns of Navajo weaving are derived. These symbols are found on sacred implements and in other locations including: (1) The staff of the Diné in the Enemyway Ritual, (2) The masks, clothing, and attire of the ritual impersonations of Born for the Water and Monster Slayer, (3) The hair buns of Changing Woman and ordinary men and women, (4) The rock walls of the area called Dinétah, sacred homeland of the Navajo: the area from which the Holy People emerged into this world, and where Changing Woman, the principal Navajo deity was found, and where her children (the Diné) first located after they were created.

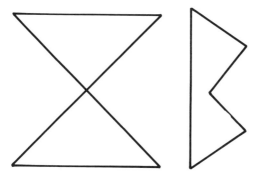

Plate 1. Symbols of "Born for the Water" and "Monster Slayer."

Four sacred mountains delineate the sacred homeland of the Navajo. If connecting lines are drawn joining them, an inexact diamond emerges. Two sacred locations lie at the centre of this diamond and it is here that a number of symbols, including Monster Slayer and Born for the Water are found on rock walls. The number four recurs frequently in Navajo mythology. The Gods and ancestors of the Navajo emerged into this world through four underworlds or previous stages of existence. There are four sacred colors (black, white, blue, and yellow), four clouds of the first world, and four seasons: spring (birth), summer (growth), fall (death), and winter (decay). Changing Woman has the power to rejuvenate each time she gets old, thus spring follows winter and initiates a new cycle (Witherspoon 1987).

Dualism is a basic pattern of classification for the Navajo, and static/active is the most fundamental dualism in the Navajo worldview. Two other basic dualisms (Witherspoon's term) are inner/outer and male/female. When dualistic categories are intersected or subdivided by another dualism, the result is a multiplication of the original dualism into four. According to the Navajo, the basic constitution of this world is found in inner and outer forms, and both inner and outer forms are paired with their opposite gender counterpart resulting in four forms (two inner and two outer forms). Generally males are associated with the static class and females with the active class. In basic dualisms such as day/night, summer/winter and alive/dead, the liminal periods of dawn/twilight, spring/fall and birth/death serve to create a four phased cycle.

Witherspoon states that the structural model of the central deities in Navajo religion also form a diagonal cross, with Changing Woman (CW) at the center. Sa'ah Naaghái (SN) and Bik'eh Hózhó (BH) are her father and mother and she is the mother of the twins Born for the Water (BW)

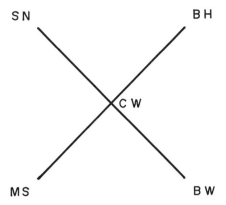

Plate 2. Paradigm of the Holy Family.

and Monster Slayer (MS). Plate 2 illustrates the "Paradigm of the Holy Family" according to Witherspoon's interpretation. He (1987: 37) notes that if outside lines are added to this structure, the line between SN and BH would reflect their linking together by marriage, the vertical lines between SN and MS and BH and BW reflect the link between grandparents and grandchildren. The horizontal line between MS and BW reflects the sibling link or bond. The result is the "Divine Family of the Navajo," or the generations of the Holy People. The term Sa'ah Naaghái refers to endless repetitions of the complete life cycle of all living beings, including the earth. The Holy Person who embodies this concept is the father of Changing Woman, and it is through him that she, as the inner form of the Earth, gets her power to rejuvenate each spring.

The symbol for Changing Woman is a diamond (a four-sided figure). These three key cultural symbols are based on the triangle, and all utilize two triangles in their construction. Born for the Water's symbol turns them "in" and puts them in opposing symmetry, while Monster Slayer's symbol turns both triangles "out" in opposite directions, giving the idea of infinite extension from a center point. According to Witherspoon's analysis, these designs represent elementary and sacred Navajo semiotic geometry which is characterized by patterns of synthesis and symmetry. The triangle represents the synthetic resolution of dualism, and the primary orientation of Navajo thought is toward synthesis (Witherspoon 1977: 195 – 202). He claims that this cultural and intellectual pattern has guided the Navajo in relating to and absorbing from alien peoples and practices: "It is at the core of their transformations through history, and

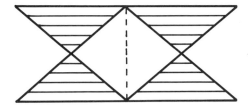

Plate 3. Basic Navajo cultural motif with divided diamond.

it is the fundamental concept that explains their adaptive and dynamic lifeways" (Witherspoon 1987: 32).

Plate 3 illustrates the basic Navajo cultural motif with divided diamond. Viewed vertically, Witherspoon claims that this symbol depicts a pairing of Born for the Water's design. Viewed horizontally, it shows two of Monster Slayer's bows pointed at each other. In the middle there are two triangles of Changing Woman paired to form a diamond. The four-sided diamond links the symbols together into a motif which can be extended infinitely. The twinning of the symbols of the Twins, and the fact that this design can be endlessly extended, either vertically or horizontally, nicely represents the notion of an endless repetition or reproduction of the life cycle of the earth and all other living creatures.

The three symbols do not appear in the Chief Blankets until the beginning of the Third Phase (around 1860 – 1880), which coincides with the appearance of the traders. In the first Phase (1800 – 1850), static and active stripes usually appear in sets of four. In the Second Phase (1820 – 1870), some rectangles appear within these stripes. In the Third Phase, diamonds, hair bun and bow designs begin to appear together (Witherspoon 1987: 46).

It is estimated that approximately 100,000 Navajo weavers have woven one million blankets, rugs, and tapestries over more than two centuries (Witherspoon 1987: 41). In many of these weavings Navajo women have woven the archetypal symbols of Monster Slayer, Born for the Water, and Changing Woman in various combinations and alternations. The manipulation, combination, multiplication, and variations of these basic elements have formed the foundation of Navajo weaving once it passed the striped-line or banded phase. These cultural motifs illustrate a pattern of organizing space that is reflected in their weaving and is fundamental to Navajo cultural and intellectual patterns. Navajo motifs stamp an identity on these textiles, express a pride, loyalty, and link with that identity. Weaving demonstrates the complexity, the power and the beauty of the Navajo imagination, and it expresses the vitality, strength and integration of Navajo society because it is built upon the symbols of their principal deities (Witherspoon 1987: 103).

But Witherspoon cautions that the overall meanings depicted in a textile should not be analyzed from a symbolic interpretation of individual design elements in the composition. Design elements take on their meanings as part of the total composition, which is a unique and abstract rendering of hózhó: "hózhó incorporates and expresses the beauty, the balance, the harmony and the order of the universe, as constructed by the Holy People in the beginning" (Witherspoon 1987: 103) and as maintained by the Diné in the present. And when this beauty and harmony is disrupted:

> Navajo rituals take them back to the Holy People for the purpose of restoring this beauty and harmony. The artistic compositions created by Navajo weavers express, accentuate and celebrate the inherent beauty and magnificence of the universe as conceived in Navajo culture (Witherspoon 1987: 103).

The holistic concept of hózhó as expressed in Navajo culture and textiles contrasts dramatically with the Western notion of "beauty" (cf. Kant's *Critique of Judgement*) and its implied separation of mind and body, mind and heart, and its fragmentation of the intellectual, emotional, and aesthetic realms. In contrast, in Navajo society:

> Art is not divorced from everyday life, for the creation of beauty and the incorporation of oneself in beauty represent the highest attainment and ultimate destiny of man... Man experiences beauty by creating it. Navajo society is one of artists (art creators) (Witherspoon 1977: 151–152).

Critique of Witherspoon's analysis

Although Witherspoon's analysis is a very powerful, persuasive, and beautifully written explication of Navajo ethos and worldview, he offers us an explanation which may be interpreted in another manner. He critiques the Cartesian dualism that pervades Western thought, yet some portions of his analysis have Cartesian overtones: (1) Adherence to a linguistic model which treats symbols as if they were encoded; this leads to confusion because the code is utilized as a set of operational rules and a dictionary of "meanings." (2) An emphasis on the notion of synthesis which belies the notion of recursiveness and disallows the recognition of metaphor as a connector of relations. This results in an incomplete notion of metaphor, which is treated as a semantic unit, and not as a formal construct mediating levels of communication. (3) Art is defined as "subjective expression in objective form" (1987: 5) which obviates the importance of process. (4) A preoccupation with *naming*. This phenomenon is critiqued by Peter Harries-Jones:

> ... Anthropology incorporates a western cultural preoccupation to interpret God, religion, and the ancestors as givers of names. Thus anthropologists exhibit their own unreflective adherence to Judeo-Christian imperatives. Such an interpretation of symbolism and metaphor is a cheap representation of what really happens... Religious unity, which incorporates the sense of the sacred, lies at an interface between the named and the unnamed (Harries-Jones 1987: 5).

Critique of the semiological view of symbolism

Dan Sperber (1975: xi) is the most vocal critic of the semiological view of symbolism which mimics the model between sound and meaning in language. He denies the validity of the association because symbols and their interpretations do not form stable pairs as signifier/signifieds do according to Saussure and others. "Symbolic elements enter not into pairing alone, but into a set of associations ... the interpretation bears not on the elements but on their configuration" (Sperber 1975: 48). Since symbols are not like language, linguistic-type analyses are inappropriate. According to Sperber, symbolism is a cognitive mechanism that is autonomous, and along with perceptual and conceptual mechanisms, it participates in the construction and organization of knowledge. He argues that there is a realm of knowledge that is tacit, not explicit. Tacit knowledge is not conscious, explicit or empirical. It is unconscious, implicit, intuitive, analogical, or even paralogical, hence it is not amenable to "de-coding." The symbolic mechanism operates as a feedback device coupled to a conceptual mechanism (Sperber 1975: 142). Sperber discusses four fundamental properties for symbolic data in contrast to linguistic properties: (1) symbolic data are not perceptually defined, (2) they are not defined by belonging to a set exclusive of other sets, (3) they never determine more than one symbolic mechanism in the same individual, and (4) the continual processing of symbolic data modifies the symbolic mechanism so that it is at once an object of learning and a process of learning (Sperber 1975: 90). Symbolic knowledge is incorporated within an individual's encyclopedic knowledge about the world, and is therefore integrated into a single complex mechanism in each individual in which acquisition is never complete — it is potentially infinite (Sperber 1975: 91). Semantic knowledge is about categories and is finite. Symbolic knowledge is knowledge *about* knowledge, a meta-encyclopedia and not, contrary to the semiological view, a meta-language in language.

Sperber views the process of gaining knowledge in which symbolism is used as involving memory. Symbolism is a punctuator of memory. Symbolism orders; memory has nothing to do with meaning but only how those meanings become part of memory. The world of symbol belongs to the world of art as practice and experience, rather than as a code. The ways in which culture is *not* like language form the foundation for Sperber's critique of the semiological view of the symbol.

Another more conventional approach to the study of symbolism is offered by John Fiske. Fiske (1982: 68–69) notes that codes emphasize the social dimension of communication — a code is equivalent to a constraint. But he also states that all codes convey meaning. Fiske confuses rules with meaning — a code cannot be both a set of rules *and* a semantic unit. A semantic unit is not equivalent to a set of rules; therefore, it is not the code which generates meaning. Communication is always made up of levels. We cannot speak of a communicative act at a single level (Wilden 1981). Fiske also confuses the level of syntactics with semantics.

However, Fiske's discussion of redundancy is very useful. Redundancy is a vital clue to patterning; it involves convention, habit, repetition, and practice. Rather than being a universe of symbols (cf. Turner), redundancy implies an ordering process. The structure of society expresses order in practice, but not as a matrix of symbols which then reads a culture as "text." The recursiveness extant in Navajo society implies a high degree of integration, which accelerated via textile production to counteract the disorder impinging upon them. The forms that Witherspoon claims are symbols which "mean" Changing Woman are *icons* — Plate 3 "goes" Changing Woman. Navajo weavers sought to reestablish order to correct the imbalances that increasingly afflicted them during the past century.

It is possible that Witherspoon's semiological approach, or analysis of symbol/meaning as isomorphisms is a result of the paramount importance of language and speech for the Navajo because:

the world was transformed from knowledge, organized in thought, patterned in language and realized in speech (symbolic action). The symbol
was not created as a means of representing reality ... reality was created
or transformed as a manifestation of symbolic form (Witherspoon 1977:
34).

Witherspoon's attachment to a linguistics model is reflected in the
following quote excerpted from one of his earliest publications:

it may be that some of the problems of symbolic analysis in terms of
evaluating and verifying the meanings contained in symbols could be
resolved by coordinating and comparing the analysis of non-linguistic
symbols to that of linguistic symbols, and vice versa (Witherspoon 1974:
45).

Another approach is provided by Wilden (1981: 10): "language is one
type of communication and one type of semiotic activity. Although the
analysis of languages provides us with insights into communication, it is
generally agreed that language cannot legitimately serve as a general
model of communication or semiotics." Wilden proposes an alternative
explanation utilizing metaphor and topology.

As mentioned earlier, Witherspoon claims that the primary metaphys-
ical assumption upon which the Navajo worldview is built is the opposition between static and active phases of phenomena. This dualism
pervades all Navajo art. Energy, activity and motion constantly rccur in
Navajo sandpaintings, ritual music, and weaving. Rather than viewing
their meanings as isomorphic to the symbols displayed, I suggest that
they are instead an elaboration on the root metaphor which Witherspoon
defines as a dualism: the passive and active principles central to Navajo
cosmology. According to Wilden (1981), root metaphors are often models
of basic aspects of reality, and critical analysis of such metaphors opens
up a whole nexus of statements representative of deeply rooted social
values. The Navajo dualism which I choose to call a root metaphor is
commutative in Navajo thought; therefore it is not (covertly) hierarchical
as are the examples described by Wilden (1981) such as yin and yang, or
the art/craft distinction discussed above. According to Wilden (1981: 6)
and Whitbeck (1989: 70), yang ultimately dominates yin although the
distinction is postulated as a binary opposition. Instead, the binary
opposition or dualism (Witherspoon's term) is balanced by the maintenance of hòzhò. For in the Navajo world, the male principle is passive,
and men are responsible for maintaining hòzhò via ritual and sand
painting activities. The female principle imbues activity because of wom-
en's productive and reproductive roles. Navajo women do not seem to

perform public rituals, although they do participate in them (Witherspoon 1977: 160). I suggest that the forms depicted in Plates 1, 2, and 3 are icons utilized metonymically to elaborate on Navajo cosmology as expressed in song, ritual, petroglyphs, and weavings.

Brenda Beck (1978: 84) notes that a metaphor points to the existence of a given set of abstract relationships hidden within some immediately graspable image. The mental set shared by members of a group must continually adapt to changing ecological, economic, and social conditions. Thus, metaphor is one of the simplest and most important mechanisms by which such a shared mental framework can be kept in touch with what lies "out there." Beck (1978: 84) summarizes several processes that characterize metaphoric thought: "(1) a movement from abstract concept to a concrete image, (2) a movement that entails a reference to affect and/or to perceptual experience, (3) a movement that bridges logical gaps, (4) a movement that relates a part to some larger whole, (5) a movement that helps to map out a nonverbal phenomenon or behaviour." A metaphor is also a process of turning from one domain to another in order to accomplish a "creative transcendence." All of these processes characterize and can be related to elements in Navajo society and reaffirm the importance of movement which is central to Navajo thought. Witherspoon (1977: 48 – 49) notes that the dominant verb in the Navajo language is the verb "to go" (not "to be") and that there are a very large number of possible conjugations. These conjugations all apply to the ways in which humans normally "go." If all the verbs relating "to move" as well as "to go" (such as in walking or running) were included, the number of possible conjugations would be astronomical. "Movement and life seem to be inseparably related ... movement is the basis of life, and life is exemplified by movement" (1977: 53).

Metaphors are "go-betweens." They provide for movement between partial and abstract principles employed on a verbal plane and concrete sensual holistic images that thrive on a non-verbal one. Metaphors are thus mediators between these two modes of thought. They are not syntactical; they belong to relations between a system cut up and constrained in different dimensions.

Wilden (1981: 1) notes that "communication begins everywhere, it mediates all our relationships, and as long as life exists it has no end." He distinguishes between digital and analogic information. The former is made up of discrete units and is discontinuous; the latter involves information whose coding is continuously variable and is labelled "difference." Iconic information is a selection and combination of both analog continuity and digital discontinuity. Wilden then describes the creation of iconic forms which may be appropriately applied to the forms created by Navajo weavers:

> In a figure-ground perception, for example, we turn certain differences into distinctions by the boundary we insert between figure and ground. This digitalization of difference creates the icon of the figure, which consists of a potential infinity of analogue information, punctuated by a digital boundary (Wilden 1981: 20).

This is an apt description of the various "geometric" configurations that appear in a multitude of combinations in Navajo textiles. The digital patterns in the textiles *are* discrete units. The digitalization of difference (analogue) creates a number of icons which serve by analogy to validate Navajo cosmology and society in space and time.

The Navajo provide us with a very interesting example of the way in which a discrete cluster of abstract worldview premises finds continual expression over a wide range of material and artistic production. Western cultures view almost everything as lineal, as susceptible to being planned out (especially in a grid pattern), and as productive of certain ends. In contrast, Navajo see things as essentially cyclic and circular.

The Navajo weaver's concern is more with process than with end products (Worth — Adair 1972). The woven rug is the result of a long involved process which entails interaction between the sheep and the human herder, the shearer, the spinner of the yarn, and the weaver. In addition a number of plants are gathered during specific growing seasons. Hence there is interaction between the weaver, the animals, plants, and the annual cycle of seasons that is repeated over the lifetime of the weaver herself (Witherspoon 1981). Thus, repetition and redundancy of recurrent patterns suggest a commonality of form in which Navajo textiles map optic expressions of fundamental formal relationships.

The foregoing description of Navajo weaving and the Navajo world may be elaborated by recalling the concept of topology as discussed by Leach (1961). The same structural patterns appear in many areas of the Navajo world: in myth, in petroglyphs, in song, ritual, sand paintings, weaving, and even in their traditional hair buns. This scaling connects the microcosm to the macrocosm. The fundamental variable in topology is the degree of connectedness: there is a regularity of pattern among neighboring relationships. Topology is constructed and made public through *craftmaking* (Williams 1980: 47). The practice of craftmaking reproduces pattern and it has the capacity to transform pattern. Only in the history of craftmaking can one see the relationship between practice and pattern fully played out. Bourdieu's concept of "habitus" is appropriate here: pattern exists in and through its varying relationships with various kinds of actors (Ortner 1984: 149). Thus particular topologies of patterning are doubly practiced: they are both "lived in," as a public world of ordered forms, and "embodied" in the sense of existing as an enduring topology of dispositions that are stamped in and on actors' beings. These topologies are subsequently reproduced as an example of the relations between practice and patterns in an historical context.

Conclusion

Communication was accelerated through the incorporation of iconic forms in Navajo textiles to deflect the impact of powerful external influences which included merchant capitalism, missionary activity, government personnel, and educators. Although traders insisted that weavers place borders around their blankets to turn them into rugs which could be marketed off the reservation, the weavers resisted for more than a generation. But within twenty years of the traders' appearance on the reservation, color and pattern changed markedly in the textiles. Around the turn of the century the woven "eye dazzlers" were marketed as degenerative barbaric examples compared to textiles woven prior to the reservation period. Although the weavers were incorporating a wider color palette because traders had introduced aniline dyes, the rugs themselves contained multiple elaborations of iconic forms. But because the rugs were ripped from their context, no communication (to the buying public) occurred. The formerly communicative *form* became a utilitarian *thing* attractive to Western consumers.

Due to the gap separating the Navajo and Western worlds, most weaving produced by Navajo women during the last century is perceived by various professionals as lacking "authenticity" because of trader and market influences. In 1987, Witherspoon's monograph traced the relationship between textile production and Navajo worldview. Today some researchers, both anthropologists and historians who have worked with Navajo textiles for decades, disagree with his analysis. But Witherspoon's interpretive analysis reveals far more about Navajo society and culture than all the tabulating, classifying, and dating of Navajo artifacts combined. Yet adherence to a linguistic model as the basis of analysis confuses the *map* with the *territory* (Bateson 1988: 20). Although a very powerful explication of the Navajo worldview as expressed in weaving, the notion of symbol/meaning is conflated with signifier/signified and conjoined with the notion of cosmic activity. Weavers were compelled to make more elaborate maps of the territory of their symbolic universe as a whole. A map is a human interpretation and configuration of an ecological or cosmological phenomenon that is essentially a topological phenomenon. "Naming is always classifying and mapping is essentially the same as naming" (Bateson 1988b: 30). Semiotics seeks to extend scientific (analytic) procedures to symbolism. But semiotics is doing what science has already done. As Kenneth Burke stated (1967: 141), "science aims to evolve a vocabulary that gives the name and address of every event in the universe." Thus when symbols are treated isomorphically and taxonomically, they become "thing-like." There is a breakdown in understanding (hence communication) that leads to reductionism. Symbols become isolates when they are "de-coded" then reassembled in a gesture which passes as understanding. But recognition of *relationships* is fractured. Instead, according to Sperber, symbols are tacit knowledge, part of a typology of meta-categories that help map the territory, but they are *not* the territory. A semiotic analysis confuses the two levels of map and territory. Language depends primarily on nouns which seem to refer to things. When verbal taxonomies are created to categorize "things," the aesthetic dimension or realm is often destroyed or placed in an isolated category separate from practice (Williams 1980: 46). It is clear from Witherspoon's analysis that the Navajo have no equivalent to the Cartesian dualism that pervades Western thought. Their sense of an aesthetic unity with their environment, and the continual affirmation of the sacred via hózhó pervades Navajo thought and life.

In his article "Style, Grace and Information in Primitive Art" Bateson (1972) notes that any art object is "both itself internally patterned and itself part of a larger patterned universe — the culture or some part of it." This is an apt description of the location and function of Navajo weaving. For Bateson (1972: 131 – 132) the essence of communication is "the creation of redundancy, meaning, pattern predictability, information and the reduction of the randomness by restraint." This is precisely the role that weaving has played for the Navajo, especially during the last century. Through practice, through the creation of textiles, Navajo weavers continued to validate and perpetuate the Navajo worldview, and they continued to communicate their appreciation and affirmation of the sacred aesthetic dimension.

The recent emphasis on praxis in anthropology appears to reconcile somewhat the mind/body dualism. Because it never existed for the Navajo (or other aboriginal peoples), the damage wrought through its application is poignantly reflected in the following comment by Mali historian Amâdou Hampâte Ba:

> We live in a very curious age. The amazing development of science and technology goes hand in hand, contrary to all expectations, with a worsening of living conditions. Along with the conquest of space has come a sort of shrinking of our world, which has been reduced to its material and visible dimensions alone, whereas the traditional African craftsman, who has never moved from his little village, had the feeling of participating in a world of infinite dimensions and being linked with the whole of the living Universe (Amâdou Hampâte Ba 1976: 12).

The Navajo valiantly attempted to communicate, but the "message" went unacknowledged by traders who saw potential profits, consumers who desired bold, colorful, and primitive patterns, and an art world which saw only a functional rug woven on a primitive loom. But Navajo weavers continue nevertheless to reaffirm Navajo identity and continuity via praxis. The creation of woven patterns continually reaffirms Navajo cultural identity and maintenance of hózhó thus ensuring that the sacred permeates Navajo thought and life.

References

Amsden, Charles A.
    1975   *Navajo weaving: Its technique and history*. Salt Lake City, UT: Peregrine Smith.
Ba, Amâdou Hampâte
    1976   "African art, where the hand has ears," New York: *The UNICEF Courier*, February, 12.
Bateson, Gregory
    1988   *Mind and nature: A necessary unity*. Toronto: Bantam Books.
    1972   *Steps to an ecology of mind*. San Francisco: Chandler.
Bateson, Gregory — Mary Catherine
    1988   *Angels fear: Towards an epistemology of the sacred*. Toronto: Bantam Books.
Beck, Brenda
    1978   "The metaphor as a mediator between semantic and analogic modes of thought," *Current Anthropology* 19(1): 83–97.

Burke, Kenneth
  1967   *The philosophy of literary form: Studies in symbolic action.* 2nd ed.
          Baton Rouge: Louisiana State University Press.
Carpenter, Edmund
  1970   *They came what they beheld.* New York: Ballantine.
Fiske, John
  1982   *Introduction to communication studies.* New York: Routledge.
Gadamer, Hans G.
  1986   *The relevance of the beautiful and other essays.* Cambridge: Cambridge
          University Press.
Garry, Ann − Marilyn Pearsall (ed.)
  1989   *Women, knowledge, reality.* Boston: Unwin Hyman.
Harries-Jones, Peter
  1987   "Putting salt on the demon's tail," in: Greg Williams (ed.) 11: 4−6.
Hauser, Arnold
  1965   *Mannerism: The crisis of the Renaissance and the origin of modern
          art.* Vol. I. New York: Alfred A. Knopf.
James, Harold L.
  1976   *Posts and rugs: The story of Navajo rugs and their homes.* Globe, AZ:
          Southwest Parks and Monuments Association.
Kant, Immanuel
  1951   *Critique of judgement.* New York: Hafner Press.
Kent, Kate Peck
  1985   *Navajo weaving: Three centuries of change.* Santa Fe, NM: School of
          American Research.
Kristeller, Paul O.
  1951   "The modern system of the arts: A study in the history of aesthetics"
          (I), *Journal of the History of Ideas* 12: 496−527.
  1952   "The modern system of the arts: A study in the history of aesthetics"
          (II), *Journal of the History of Ideas* 13: 17−46.
Kubler, George
  1963   *The shape of time: Remarks on the history of things.* New Haven:
          Yale University Press.
Leach, Edmund
  1961   *Rethinking anthropology.* University of London: Athlone Press.
Ortner, Sherry
  1984   "Theory in anthropology since the sixties," *Comparative Studies in
          Society and History* 26(1): 126−166.
Parker, Rozsika − Griselda Pollock
  1981   *Old mistresses: Women, art, and ideology.* New York: Pantheon.
Pendleton, Mary
  1974   *Navajo and Hopi weaving techniques.* New York: Collier Macmillan.
Pepper, George
  1902   "The making of a Navajo blanket," *Everybody's Magazine*, (January):
          3−8.

Pericot-Garcia, Luis — John Galloway — Andreas Lommel
    1967   *Prehistoric and primitive art.* New York: Harry Abrams.
Pevsner, Nikolaus
    1940   *Academies of art, past, present and future.* Cambridge: Cambridge
            University Press.
Reichard, Gladys
    1939   *Dezba: Woman of the desert.* New York: Macmillan.
    [1971] [Reprint ed., Glorietta, NM: Rio Grande Press.]
    1936   *Navajo shepherd and weaver.* New York: J. J. Augustin.
    [1968] [Reprint ed., Glorietta, NM: Rio Grande Press.]
    1934   *Spider Woman.* New York: Macmillan.
    [1974] [Reprint ed., *Weaving a Navajo blanket.* New York: Dover
            Publications.]
Sohn-Rethel, Alfred
    1977   *Intellectual and manual labor: A critique of epistemology.* Atlantic
            Highlands, NJ: Humanities Press.
Sperber, Dan
    1975   *Rethinking symbolism.* London: Cambridge University Press.
Turner, Victor
    1967   *The forest of symbols: Aspects of Ndembu ritual.* Ithaca, NY: Cornell
            University Press.
Wheat, Joe Ben
    1976   "Navajo chiefs blankets," *Indian Art Magazine.*
Whitbeck, Caroline
    1989   "A different reality: Feminist ontology," in: Ann Garry — Marilyn
            Pearsall (eds.), 51 — 76.
Wilden, Tony
    1981   "Semiotics as praxis, strategy, and tactics," *Recherches Sémiotiques/
            Semiotic Inquiry* (RS/SI) 1: 1 — 33.
Williams, Greg (ed.)
    1987   *Continuing the conversation*: A newsletter in cybernetics.
Williams, Raymond
    1980   *Problems of materialism and culture.* London: Verso Press.
Witherspoon, Gary
    1974   "The central concepts of the Navajo world view," *Linguistics* 161:
            69 — 88.
    1977   *Language and art in the Navajo universe.* Ann Arbor: University of
            Michigan Press.
    1981   "Self-esteem and self-expression in Navajo weaving," *Plateau* 52:
            28 — 32.
    1987   *Navajo weaving: Art in its cultural context.* Flagstaff, AZ: Museum
            of Northern Arizona. Research paper 36.
Wolf, Eric
    1982   *Europe and the people without history.* Berkeley: University of Cali-
            fornia Press.

Worth, Sol — John Adair
   1972   *Through Navajo eyes: An explanation in film communication and anthropology.* Bloomington: Indiana University Press.
Yeo, Eileen — E. P. Thompson
   1971   *The unknown Mayhew.* New York: Pantheon.

What is a t-shirt?
Codes, chronotypes, and everyday objects

Betsy Cullum-Swan and Peter K. Manning

Introduction

Semiotics is the study of how signs convey meaning in everyday life, but not all signwork is immediate, visible, or even a noticeable aspect of social life.[1] It would appear that making visible the semiotic work of everyday objects requires an articulation of ethnography, or close cultural description, using the tools of semiotics. Ethnographic work should result in the explication of the underlying codes and principles that order surface phenomena. It should serve to clarify the polysemic nature of communication.

Since semiotics deals with differences in context that produce meaning, rather than the reality of "the world out there," it provides a rich vocabulary of terms and techniques for analysis of the codes and signs that constitute the reality of social relations. The principles that underlie how signs convey meaning within a system of relationships have to be extracted from the features of everyday life. The semiotic model, relying on the comparison of differences within a context, can be employed to isolate changes in the functions of signs, sign vehicles, paradigms and codes, and to analyze meanings.

Stability and continuity combined with requisite variety are fundamental features of communication. Signs are incomplete (Peirce 1931); fundamentally context-dependent and possess imminently multiple meanings. Context, or what is brought to the communicational situation, adumbrates the sign, and is shaped by equivocality and ambiguity in messages. Constitutive conventions firmly link the expression and related content to produce a sign. To accomplish stabilized communication, people depend heavily on institutional contexts and interpretative processes (Goffman 1959; Culler 1977).

But such stability is not simply a matter of interpersonal communication and experience. Personal communication and interaction are increasingly shaped by mass media produced imagery. Increasingly, media images and once-processed impressions replace personal experience with events, and floating signifiers (those without clear signifieds) or *simulacra* (Baudrillard 1988) abound. As *simulacra* or images are widely reproduced and reified, especially by the mass media, they become commodities and an unquestioned social reality. The media become the locus of the illusion of reality (Denzin 1986: 196). The "reality" to which such imagery refers is the reality created by imagery (other images), fraught with rich connotative, ideological, and mythological meanings (Barthes 1972), and the forms of *hyperreality* (signs about signs taken to be objective or universal opinion or truth) that media produce and reproduce. The point is that other images, rather than immediate personal experience or local knowledge of events, become the source of veridicality.

Objects are of course no less shaped and given reality than social relations. They are caught in the mesh of intersubjective reality amplified by the media. The analysis of communication, especially that about objects, will require more than the application of semiotics. It requires a fully explicated imaginative ethnography involving principles derived from semiotics (Eco 1979). Barthes (1983: 27), for example, suggests that once a system of relations is identified, one should use the "commutative test." This means that given an identified structure of relations, one alters an element and examines the social consequences. By examining alterations in elements of a structure in conjunction or separately, one can identify a general inventory of "... concomitant variations ... and consequently ... determine a certain number of commutative classes in the ensemble of a given structure" (Barthes 1983: 19−20). These variations in relations within a system may also be patterned chronologically as *chronotypes* (Bakhtin 1937).

Our analytic procedure requires careful description of a structure, fashion, the marketing of differences, its units, paradigms and codes. Fashion refers on the one hand to the physical and material world, and, on the other, to the symbolic world of the idea of difference and changes in dress. Semiotics provides a vocabulary: the vestimentary system (that describing clothes), the code(s) or rules that articulate instances of dress, paradigms or associational contexts that organize the meaning of units. Our topic is the garment called the "t-shirt." This label originated after World War Two and is currently in common use.

The t-shirt in the fashion system

Fashion is a dramatic example of the production of items for display and the display of these images for mass consumption. Fashion produces images to market and sell alterations in appearance; fashion is, as much as anything, the marketing of differences.[2] Fashion is itself a highly differentiated system.[3] Our interest is not in "high fashion" but "low fashion," and in explanations for the rapidly changing character of a banal object, the t-shirt. The t-shirt now plays a functional role in any ensemble of clothing, as well as in the fashion system itself.

The shirts worn now as underclothes or as outer garments in warm weather, sometimes called "t-shirts" (an iconic metaphoric name derived, presumably, from their shape), "vests," or "underwear," are rather banal everyday objects. From these humble utilitarian beginnings, the t-shirt has risen, at least metaphorically, to assume an important symbolic role. It has become one of the prime emblems or icons of modern life, encoded in changing codes, and carrying sign functions. It is a sign vehicle whose functions not only express selves, but the social and political fields in which it exists. What follows, unfortunately, is not a proper social history of the t-shirt. We rely on observations gathered on the streets of several university towns, in tourist areas and souvenir shops in Chinatown, in San Francisco, and the French Quarter of New Orleans. It should be noted that as a socio-semiotic analysis, unique, individual meanings of a shirt are not discussed. The fact that a person is attached to a shirt because it was once his brother's, father's, or boyfriend's, a gift from a loved one, or has rich associations with a past event, place or time, is important at the individual level. These features can be associated with shirts encoded in any of the following ways. We have no data on this (other than our own well-loved t-shirts).

The analysis proceeds as follows. The first task for a semiotic analysis of t-shirts is to identify the system and the fundamental *units* or syntagms (11 are identified) within the vestimentary code of that system. The second task is to sort out the five associative contexts or *paradigms* that organize the meaning of these units. The third task is to discuss the shirt using the seven *codes* that organize both units and paradigms. Discussion of the codes and examples thereof constitute the bulk of the paper. A concluding section speculates on the role of temporal change in codes and the salience of key elements or units in three chronotypes or eras.

Conceptual framework

The eleven units. At least eleven interchangeable elements (or syntagmatic units) are necessary for the semiotic production and consumption of a t-shirt. They appear to be related to the evolution of this shirt in North America from a home-made item worn beneath visible garments to a very complex signifying public garment. These units are: where the shirt is made; the materials used to make the shirt; the values expressed by the shirt, including both expressive and utilitarian values; where it is intended to be worn (public-setting vs. private wear, front vs. back stage); the cut of the shirt; the nature of its adornment; the color(s) of the shirt; what it represents or symbolizes publicly; the social roles or statuses it connotes; its association with other garments in a fashion system; and the nature of the reflexivity of the garment. Although this is not an exhaustive list of potential units, it captures many of the key aesthetic and semantic aspects of the shirt as a sign vehicle.

The paradigms. The units cluster together in a non-random fashion. They can be further organized into metaphoric or paradigmatic clusters of meaning. These make explicit certain themes in the "vertical organization" of meaning. Five paradigms set out the t-shirt's changing meaning: the technology used to produce the shirt (material, source, where the shirt was made); the functions or purposes (social values), both expressive and utilitarian, of the item; the primary setting(s) for use (setting, roles, and statuses claimed); style (cut, adornment, color, role in the fashion system); and the nature of the involvement of the self in the object (the self and representational themes). These metaphoric clusters also contain a set of metonymic relations. They offer clues to what patterns of presence or absence of units determine the overall configuration of the object. However, certain underlying principles or codes reveal the rules governing how shirts are perceived and used. The remainder of the paper outlines the patterning of these syntagms and paradigms by codes.

What is a t-shirt? Seven codes

A code is a set of principles that organizes the patterning of signs semantically and syntactically. Codes, encoding, and decoding are essential features of signwork (Guiraud 1975). At least seven non-exclusive codes encode the t-shirt as an object. By seeing the shirt as a function of preformed codes, one shifts attention from the shirt as an object to its perception and use. Let us list the relevant codes in order: the utilitarian code, the mass-produced manufactured code, the code of leisure (the t-shirt as a visible outer garment), the code of complex and fluid expressive signs, the code for problematic icons, the code of the t-shirt as a walking visual pun, and the t-shirt as a copy or double.

Code one: The t-shirt as a utilitarian undergarment

The "t-shirt" is a soft, plain, uncolored, sleeveless or short-sleeved garment, usually cotton, that was originally worn under another shirt, blouse, or heavier overgarment. Now called a "t-shirt," "vest," or "singlet," it was a useful and functional item of apparel unmarked with insignia, slogans, sayings, or emblems. It served the private and unseen purposes of protecting the wearer from the harsh, perhaps prickly, material of heavier outer garments such as sweaters or wool shirts, absorbing sweat, giving support to breasts, or simply conserving heat and permitting air to circulate around the body. Made to wear under heavy outer shirts, they were once called "undershirts." The degree to which these utilitarian functions were sex-differentiated remains arguable.[4] When it was "home made," the t-shirt, and the makers and wearers of the t-shirt, shared a value system, exchange values, and imagery governing the exchange.

Code two: The t-shirt as a manufactured item

Probably in the early part of this century, these undergarments became widely available, mass-produced manufactured items. They were and are sold in mail order catalogs and in department stores such as J. C. Penney; Sears, Roebuck, and Company; and Hudson's Bay. Although the upper and upper-middle classes continued to employ seamstresses and tailors, the middle classes shopped and bought underwear by mail or in shops. No longer were most undergarments individually home spun or made, nor were they hand tailored and sewn. Large companies, with their own brand names, "Jockey," "Fruit of the Loom," "Munsingwear," "Sears," or "J. C. Penney," manufactured and sold them. Competition arose as other companies began selling underwear. The t-shirt then was distinguished in part by labels, and to a lesser degree, by minute variations in cloth and style. Brand names and associated stylistic variations became bases (since the shirt itself was a simple and undistinguishable item of apparel) for competition, insidious advertising, and marketing. A commodity, it differentiated people by class and life style. The shirt became a distinctive unit in a system of monetary exchange, a commodity produced for sale.

Code three: The t-shirt as a visible outer garment

Perhaps in the early 1960s, t-shirts became visible outer garments. As visible items of dress, they served as status symbols that differentiated status and taste groups, even within social classes. T-shirts were previously unacceptable to the middle classes, because they were viewed as the leisure wear of the tired "working man at home," shown in the media stereotypically as white, soaked with sweat, stained and torn. The t-shirt as outer wear in the 1950s had additional and important stylistic or connotative meanings. As shown in movies and plays, e.g., Tennessee Williams's "A Streetcar Named Desire," it symbolized the raw passions of the unsocialized and proto-rebellious working classes. It signalled animal vitality. The modest, short-sleeved, t-shaped undershirt became more popular as an outergarment, while the "track jersey" style of sleeveless jersey with thin straps and a ribbed bodice was not worn as outer wear. It lost popularity although it reappeared later as a "tank top" style.

Changes in the composition of cloth and production technology also contributed to changes in the t-shirt's sign functions. Polyester and other artificial fibers, along with the introduction of "drip dry" cycles on clothes dryers, expanded the range of colors, styles, and textures of shirts, and increased their durability. In time, emblematic and multi-colored t-shirts made of new synthetic materials, and blends of these materials with cotton, also appeared.[5]

The mass production of undergarments to be worn as outergarments proceeded apace. Plain cotton shirts were now manufactured in primary colors, some with pockets which indicated they were to be worn in public and meant to hold something the wearer needed, such as a pen, a ticket, a map, or a package of cigarettes. The middle classes could now be seen wearing simple colored t-shirts for social occasions: barbecues, golfing, sailing or other weekend leisure activities.

Fashion began to affect t-shirt design. The shirts took on connotative signification that resonated in the social world of fashion. They became widely available mass-produced signs of identity, sign vehicles carrying a variety of signifiers whose referents were themselves and their wearer. They referred to other signifiers and various signifieds within the fashion code. They spoke the language of fashion.

Code four: The t-shirt as a representational sign vehicle

T-shirts became an assemblage of signs. They conveyed messages while residing in an "open text" (Eco 1986) or contained many messages that the reader or observer could interpret. A range of types of shirts, all communicating a variety of messages about the wearer, his or her experiences, attitude, or social status, appear in the post-1960s era. A connection remained between experience, role and status, and symbolization.

The code orders meaning by constructing the t-shirt as a mirror of social relationships. The t-shirt conveys representations that signal or communicate membership in a group, work place or collectivity. Consider how t-shirts now carry emblems, words or pictures (or all three) announcing various social identities or locations: a place (Virginia Beach, N. C., Oregon); a business (Mac's Bar, Gilley's − Pasadena, Texas); an institution (Harvard, MSU, Haslett High School); another form of group or collectivity (UAW Local 650, B-O-C engine assembly); a team (usually, in turn, sponsored by business, e.g., Gino's Tavern, East Lansing Plumbing Supply); a rock concert, tour or play ("Les Miserables," "Cats," "A Chorus Line" − also at times the name of a forthcoming album − "Joe Jackson's Night and Day Tour");[6] a valued commodity (Jaguar, Panasonic Speakers); or an axial ceremonial experience ("The Temple Family reunion, Hood River, 1979," or "I survived my son's [or daughter's] wedding") or just an experience ("Veni, Vedi, Visa − I came, I saw, I shopped"). Some cry out slogans ("Take a walk," "Save the whales" or "Free Nelson Mandela"). Others combine the announcement of a personal name and a team as in the football jerseys that display a name across the upper portion of the back and the team name and number on the front and back.

In spite of their ambiguity as a basis for a status or identity claim, the representations on these shirts are in Eco's (1979: 135) terms "under-coded." They stand in a synecdochical relationship (a part stands for the whole, the t-shirt stands the self of the person) to some important ostensive experience, social relationship, role, or status claimed explicitly or implicitly by the wearer. The message of the shirt is not only about the club, place, play or business, but about the wearer's status claim: "There is more to my self than what you see; here's a sample." The viewer is meant to assume that the wearer of an "Oregon" t-shirt with a waterfall on the front has been to Oregon in fact and that this experience, in turn, is significant in some way that the wearer wishes to announce (or to be asked about, as in the front license plates that ominously announce, "Let me tell you about my grandkids"). This turn toward validation from the other of a self or identity signals a transition into an extension of this code: a fully ironic reflexivity.

The messages or representations found on these shirts, in turn, yield yet another complex and non-exclusive sign function. With increased travel and affluence, and mail order catalogs selling souvenir items, one is no longer required to have been somewhere to make a claim to the experience. Once a shirt is seen, e.g., "Oxford University eights, Spring, 1991," many interpretative possibilities arise. One might have been merely briefly visiting a place (long enough to buy the shirt, to be sure), could have acquired it by mail, or been given it as a gift. It may have no connection whatever to the experience. Although the assumption remains for "souvenir" t-shirts that the wearer has been there, done it, worked there, or had a role in it, one could wear nevertheless a "Sorbonne" or "Cambridge" t-shirt without having been enrolled or visited either. T-shirts are disconnected from direct experience and no longer unambiguously communicate membership status.

Since validation of such ambiguous signs rests with the other, the degree of doubt and lurking equivocality of the t-shirt-based message are relevant to decoding the communication. The status claims of the wearer remain problematic. As Weber (1958) and C. Wright Mills (1960) noted, any claim to status if it is to be successful, must be legitimated and deferred to by an audience. It is impossible, on the basis of the t-shirt alone, to interpret with finality the wearer's claim(s). Any message of a t-shirt is equivocal and an audience may distrust the message(s). Could wearing this shirt be the manipulation of a status symbol? What is being claimed from whom by the wearer of such a t-shirt? In other words, the signs and sign vehicles convey ambiguous representational integrity and coherence. The diversity of the codes means that "readings" became more equivocal, and more likely to convey aesthetic or poetic meanings.

Code five: The t-shirt as a problematic icon

Undershirts, as they are commodified and exchanged in part for their image-creating value, no longer directly index experience, action, membership, institutional or social identity. They display signifiers with ambiguous signifieds. They may index experiences or statuses the wearer has not had or does not posses, statuses which are fantasized or imagined. Various forms of truth are reproduced and honored. Signifiers float and play on fictive relationships and social identities. T-shirts now speak to manufactured, copied, or fabricated identities. They joke about these identities; they reflect on the purely personal.

Here, one might consider how the t-shirt has become the quintessential modern icon. It states something about the wearer and something about the other. T-shirts are sold as commercial jokes, e.g., "My parents went to New Orleans, but all I got was this lousy shirt" (worn by a child). Shirts also display stylistic puns, interpersonal provocation and forms of self-mortification: "Old Fart," and a matching shirt reading "Old Fart's wife;" or "Baby under construction." Shirts contain paired reflexive identities "Why?" (for the putative child) and "Because I say so" (for the adult). Claims are made not to membership, but claims play on the absence of membership: "Stolen from (or property of) Alcatraz" or "MSU Athletic Department."

One sees floating epithets such as statements emblazoned on the front of shirts referring to a putative self or identity, usually vulgar, crude, attention-seeking or all three, e.g., "Kissing Instructor," "I don't have a drinking problem: I drink too much, I fall down, no problem," or "Not leavin til we're heavin." Some are more vague: "Shit happens." Some variations are combinations of the above: "Retired. My job is having fun." On an ancient harridan shopping in a local produce market: "I am Not Old. I am a Recycled Teenager."

Ambiguous status claims, displayed on a shirt, are made to membership in non-existent groups, e.g., "Michigan State Polo Club," "Drunken State University," "Naked Coed Lacrosse Team" (or basketball — "skins vs.

skins"), "Bedrock Varsity" (with pictures of characters from "The Flint-stones" cartoons on the front).

These modes of communication via a t-shirt in public express claims about what a person is not. This is surely a double negative: a dubious claim to membership in non-existent organizations. T-shirts may function to state longing and desire for status by association or a desire for the absent or unattained. These cloth icons retain some oblique relation to personal referents or are directly but contentiously self-referential. They may index political meanings, reference political ideologies, or have direct referential functions, but the relationship between the field of broader political activities and the person's claims is tenuous at best.

T-shirts are useful mini-billboards advertising products as well as displaying selves and identities. At some point, t-shirts to be worn as living advertising were sold or given away by companies such as beer manufacturers. This trend has increased in the last ten years. T-shirts (and hats worn as an integral part of the head) with emblems of the labels of beer on the front or back are sold as leisure wear: "Budweiser, the King of Beers;" "Corona-light-cervesa." Companies also now make clothes, t-shirts and other types of leisure wear bearing the names of the manufacturer, "Coca Cola," "Nike" or "Wilson," and sell them in department stores as mass produced ready-to-wear items of clothing. They are not defined by wearers as advertisements for the product, but as indicative of the status and income of the wearer, loyalty toward or trust in the trademark. They also announce an identity of sorts: I am a person (are you?) who drinks this sort of beer, or soft drink, or wears this brand of sunglasses.

Since wearing the clothing made by certain manufacturers connotes a life style, showing the proper label connotes taste, albeit simultaneously advertising the product. An example of this is the Benetton, Ralph Lauren, or Calvin Klein labels, worn or positioned on the garment by the manufacturers to insure that they are read. Thus, a small alligator, a little polo pony and rider (and their variants by large department store chains that copy them) are also significant. Not only do they symbolize the status that consuming expensive "designer" clothes conveys, but also status within the designer label world. An up-market label differentiates a t-shirt from those with the symbols of "down market" brands, such as the fox on a J. C. Penney sport shirt.[7]

To further complicate the question of reality and copies, copies of the jerseys of professional sports teams with names, insignia, and numbers were mass produced and became widely available. Sporting goods shops sold team jerseys to anyone, and the gray "sweatshirt," worn originally under football pads, or for team sports practice, was worn publicly by those not belonging on teams. Internal differentiation within the system of objects or commodities became increasingly important not only to the manufacturer, but also to the consumer and status-seeker.

Code six: The t-shirt as a walking pun

T-shirts, once solely undergarments, are now mass postmodern commodities in so far as they are intended to display their status as a desirable consumable. Figurative language creates *dramatis personae*; it connects self and substance. Seeing something in terms of something else can be accomplished semiotically, and once seen as something, the object can refer to itself in these very terms.

T-shirts are reflexive and even self-referential. The reflexivity of shirts (the reference to themselves as sign vehicles as well as carriers of other communicating signs) is another kind or level of sign function. It is captured best by the "poetic code" since the message or text refers to itself and to feelings (Jakobson 1970). Self-reflexive shirts playfully redefine their own slogans, make puns, or covertly or overtly dissemble. They communicate about other signs.

They may contain representational or iconic puns, like the sign on a t-shirt reading "This is a t-shirt," "Your name here," "Home sweet home" (showing the earth from a distant star) or the t-shirt for physicians that has a white coat, stethoscope, and tongue depressor painted on its front. Happy babies can now wear a "Happy Baby" t-shirt. Some t-shirts show rather complex puns such as the shirt with four illustrations of signing (four hands making letters in signing) labelled "Say it with signing" (a pun on "Say it with flowers" or "Say it with music"), or the t-shirt with a picture of two cows melting in a field, entitled "Salvador Dairy" (a visual and verbal pun on Salvador Dali's most famous picture, "The disintegration of the persistence of memory").

Emptiness, abstraction and non-referentiality are compounded to produce examples like the MIT t-shirt that reproduces Maxwell's equation (one basis for computing) or a shirt that says in Greek, "Sigma Phi Φ (Φ means "nothing" and stands for "omega," the last letter in the Greek alphabet). A t-shirt showing a cat walking along a fire escape was captioned "Cat Walk." One shirt's message, written in French, read (rough translation) "Here is the man who all the others love." Variants on the commercial message t-shirt, presumably playing on the theme of selling oneself, are seen, such as the shirt reading "This bud's for you" on the front, a picture of the Budweiser beer label on the back and "Michigan" printed in bold letters where "Budweiser" is meant to be. A parallel example is the shirt saying "Just do it" (a reference to Nike athletic shoes) and a play on it with the slogan "Just do me." Both of these examples are self-referential and intertextual (see below). Other visual puns are more serious such as the example of iconic mimesis [visual onomatopoeia is the term used by Steven Dubin (1990)] showing the outlines of Africa set out in black, green, and red using the words "Abolish Apartheid in South Africa." In Toronto, two punnish shirts were being offered for sale, one reading "nice dog" on the front and showing a snarling wolf on the back and another showing a piranha fish on the back and the label "vicious fish" on the front. Some t-shirts pun on deixis such as the t-shirt in a window in Ann Arbor saying "You are Here, Ann Arbor, Michigan," or "This side up."

Code seven: Copies and real copies

T-shirts are now massively reproduced and distributed. Copies are abundant, but some copies are seen as more real than others (Eco 1986, 1990). Baudrillard (1988: 145) writes, "A possible definition of the real is that for which it is possible to provide an equivalent representation." Copies can be distinguished (from others, if not from an original as in fine art) through various means.[8] One is through ostensive or putative definitions. For example, National Basketball Association (NBA) teams license companies to make, merchandise, and distribute "official copies" of their jerseys, hats, shorts, and jackets. The items carry a label: "Official NBA approved souvenir." These items are mass commodities that take meaning within a system of other undergarments. They are "real" when compared to the non-sanctioned official NBA souvenirs. They are also false in the sense that they are not the same coats, jerseys or uniforms produced by the same companies to be worn by the players. In an additional irony of form, basketball teams permit "baseball caps" to be produced and sold with the team name and logo on them even though basketball players do not wear baseball caps when they play professional games.[9]

T-shirts by the late 1980s attained a new, additional, iconic sign function. They then referred to and reproduced images found in other formats as well as on other t-shirts. They became self-referential reproductions of reproductions, or representations of representations (Uspenskij 1973). One can buy a shirt with the picture of a famous person on the front, a rock star, politician, composer or hero of some kind to someone, or with a picture of oneself generated by photography and computer graphics. The viewer sees simultaneously a double representation: the embodied person and a reproduced image of the person. Of course, one can custom-design a shirt to display and signal anything about anything and have it made up at a custom t-shirt shop.

Shirts signal intertextuality (the display of a mode of communicating in the context of another), and double-referentiality. Museums, such as the Dali Museum in St. Petersburg, sell t-shirts with Dali pictures on the front, a representation of a representation as surely as the t-shirts showing Bart Simpson, the television/cartoon character, screaming "Cool your jets, man!" Shirts are sold with reproductions of the photography of accomplished/well-known photographers in the center of the shirt, captioned with the title at the bottom and the photographer's name at the top.

Consider two t-shirts celebrating heroic victories. The University of Michigan won the championship of collegiate basketball in March, 1989, and shortly thereafter, a t-shirt was displayed in the window of an Ann Arbor shop that reproduced the front page from the *Ann Arbor News* showing the day's headlines, story about the game, and a nearly full page picture of the Michigan Star, Glen Rice, celebrating after the victory. The same sort of t-shirt was produced by a company sanctioned by the Detroit Pistons after they won their second NBA championship in a row in June of 1990. One t-shirt used the theme "Hammer time," a pun on a song by a rap group, "M. C. Hammer" (the title of the group in turn being a pun), and showed crossed hammers on the back of the shirt along with another pun, the caption "back to back." (When the Pistons were defeated in the 1991 play-offs by the Chicago Bulls, the "Threepeat" shirts were marked down from 18 to 9 dollars by the morning after the defeat.)

These shirts reproduce on their front or back newspaper photos originally printed following an event. Although the wearer could have attended the event (t-shirts were sold at the games and after the tournament ended), the shirt locates the person as one wearing a reproduction of a picture of an event. This intertextual display is a reproduction of a picture on a t-shirt reproduced in the thousands for sale. Perhaps it says: "Celebrate with me" or "Do you celebrate with me?" and displays an image to be validated.

Changes in code and chronotype

Maybe another way to examine changes in the meanings of the t-shirt, or semiosis, is to place the shirt in three representational eras or chronotypes, using the units listed above: early industrial, late industrial, and postmodern (Cf. Baudrillard 1988).

In the pre-industrial era the shirt is home made for a particular person from local materials (perhaps even grown nearby and woven in the home) and is worn under or with an outer garment and only worn openly in private or in the home or while at hard work. It has utility function while expressing labor and the work ethic. It is white or uncolored, unadorned, functional, worn for protection and/or insulation, and represents the person directly: it displays him or her as they display it. The signwork is direct and simple.

In the second period, the mass-produced era, beginning perhaps shortly after World War Two, the shirt is manufactured, woven and assembled in this country from materials grown in the United States or abroad in standardized sizes for any buyer. It is worn both publicly and privately. It can be worn alone as an outer garment and as such expresses mostly leisure pursuits. It is now colored and adorned, and can express various degrees of informality, depending on color, cut, and emblems. The cut is various and functional, but can be a representation of a sporting jersey. It is now worn in part to display a role, status, or an experience. The shirt, a sign vehicle, is one part of an ensemble chosen to create and sustain an ambiguous display. These shirts are multi-colored, multi-textured, adorned (usually), and signal many contexts. Their relationship to the self and experience becomes more tenuous and problematic, and this ambiguity is often amplified by the particular signs featured on the shirt.

In the current era, the postmodern, the shirt is made for anyone, and can be manufactured anywhere using a variety of materials of many textures and cuts. It functions variously and is context-dependent. It expresses mass informality: it is not an occasioned item of dress, but crosses social classes, gender identities, and social situations. It is worn as an item in the uniform of the mass consumer, but can be worn in virtually any setting. It carries iconic puns and displays hyperreality: t-shirts mimic other t-shirts. The postmodern shirt is something of an open text, a functional carrier of signs and signs about signs that variously signify social relations, the self or identity of a wearer and other t-shirts. The shirt floats with other *simulacra* in the sense that few social constraints govern its content or occasion. The shirts and their signs grasp at fragments of meaning and experience, pun on them, or signify what is not true for the wearer. It signals an image or tentative picture that may be validated by others, but the validation lacks intrinsic meaning.

Conclusion

The three eras summarized suggest global and general changes in the meanings of the t-shirt. The shirt as a sign vehicle has been modified physically and technologically. Changes in the sign functions of the t-shirt, as seen within the chronotypes, indicate shifts in modern sensibilities and technology: how the shirt was made, sewn, cut, and put together; modifications resulting from the introduction of public standards and aesthetics; and the relevance of the iconic code of fashion. As the technological paradigm alters the material capacity of the society to mass-produce shirts, social changes in function, in style, and in setting relevance of the wearing of the shirt occur. The self becomes increasingly lodged in public displays of claimed statuses, imagined positions, missing or desired feelings, and the ever-present absent consumable, other selves. In this sense, Barthes' commutative test would suggest that the paradigm of self-reflexivity contains the salient units illustrating these changes in the object. As these evolve, they signal changes in the other paradigms and their relationships to the system as well. The very idea of "fashion" arises when the shirt begins to manifest differences rather than similarities. The codes into which the t-shirt and its signs, material and visual, have been encoded have changed, as we have noted.

Modifications in the coding of the clothing reveal or indicate still other social changes. The first code distinguishes the t-shirt within the code of clothing. It had an idiosyncratic or personal kind of self-referential reality for the wearer at that time since the undergarment was a part of the person's clothes, made by the person or someone in the family for him or her. Self and clothes were physically, socially, and psychologically close. In the last three codes, connections between self and display are complex, mediated and problematic; the instantiations of the code are more open to multiple interpretations. The signs convey messages that are arbitrary, ironic, commodified, and perhaps even intertextual. The modern t-shirt is close to the person only physically. Shifts in the salience of units within the paradigms suggest that the postmodern perspective illuminates changes in sign functions. That is, style and self-reflexivity indicate the nature of the code and the salience of given signifying functions of the shirt.

Signs are fundamental to representation. Modifications in the sign functions of the t-shirt represent an evolution from the shirt as an empirically available physical reality to an interpretant. Questions of representation and misrepresentation arise naturally.[10] T-shirts now question the credibility of the viewer by presenting evocative, floating, adrift and elusive signifiers that are free from easy assumptions, conventions or social verification procedures. The drift of the shirt as sign vehicle involves changes from misrepresentation (where there may be some sense of contrast between reality and unreality) to dissimulation and dissembling, simulation and new forms of hyperreality. In the latter case, only the reproducible remains.

Changes in the vestimentary code suggest that a t-shirt is converted from a useful private undergarment to a publicly displayed physical sign vehicle carrying representations and representations of representations. Shirts increasingly communicate about the fashion system, its connotations, and about themselves. Shirts now mark claims and display fantasies about status honor and wishes for recognition. The features of t-shirts no longer merely mark differences within the code of clothing; they mark distinctions in the imagined — the fantastic world — and fashion's *simulacra*. These shirts publicly transmit messages about one's self, status, life style, and attitude(s) to life, as well as what one wishes to be known as. They display what one is *not*, and may call out for validation of one's absent desires.

Notes

1. Delivered in draft form at the conference "The Socio-semiotics of Objects: The Role of Artifacts in Social Symbolic Processes" convened at the University of Toronto, June 22–24, 1990. We thank Norman Denzin for his detailed written commentary given at the conference.

2. Three broad kinds of analysis of the changes found in low fashion might be considered. These are an analysis of the system of signs and codes represented by the clothes within the system of dress (the vestimentary code), and the language used to discuss these two elements (Barthes 1983); the technological aspects of clothing manufacture (of interest here only as they play an increasing role in the sign-carrying capacity of the garment); and the aesthetic language of fashion. This latter language is undeveloped in the case of the t-shirt. The focus here is on the first — it undertakes an analysis of the system of signs and codes and the related meaning entailed by these codes.

3. Three sorts of fashion exist. World-wide trends and marked changes characterize the esoteric yet familiar world of "high fashion," which involves designing original clothes for distribution to a select number of clients and outlets. It is associated with professional designers, especially Parisian designers. "Mass fashion," on the other hand, is a system for creating, distributing, and selling copies of designer clothes. A third system of fashion considered here is "vulgar" fashion, the fashion created by mass-produced copies of mass fashion, often a few years later.

4. Exploring the gender-based differences in underwear would require detailed analysis of the infrastructure of meaning of these items and would go well beyond the topic of this paper. However, the addition of other structural supports under cotton jerseys such as brassieres, corsets, slips, and the like appeared later. Simple undergarments such as the camisole worn by women were functionally very similar for everyday wear to the "t-shirt" worn by both men and women.

5. In the late 1960s, in a countertheme or movement to arts and crafts and to self-sufficiency, the t-shirt was personalized. It became again a craft item. Artisans of a kind, using tie-dying or batik technics, produced unique, individually made and stylized t-shirts. These manifested colorful, even "psychedelic," patterns. Soon batik shirts were mass produced, sold at rock concerts, and then commercially distributed and sold widely as items of "nostalgia."

6. The film "Dick Tracey," released in the summer of 1990, was promoted by giving away t-shirts to those who attended the openings of the film, much like runners in a ten kilometer race are given a t-shirt if they compete. This marketing technique, such as selling t-shirts at a rock concert with the dates of the concert listed on it, closely couples an experience and the representation.

7. "Designer" is a rather dubious term for mass-produced clothing that is not unique or limited in number. The connotations are rich, but the denotations of the word are derived from the work of dress designers who created clothing, either one of a kind or one of a handful, for sale to an elite clientele. Now it means simply that an expensive, mass-produced shirt, trousers, or sweater can be identified easily by a designer's name on it. Perhaps this is a special

kind of sign function in which commodity, sign, and ideology are sufficiently integral to suppress or overcome the (assumed) resistance to being an unpaid advertisement.

8. While in the past a definition of "art" was a unique object created by an artist or craftsperson, now the capacity to reproduce something is endless, and the point of origin, shifting and dubious. New mechanisms are required to sort out various versions of reality (Eco 1986) and to socially discriminate copies.

9. False eponymy is also possible. A few years ago, the National Football League sanctioned jerseys with the names of famous players on the back, so that one could make an obvious false claim (being Roger Staubaugh, for example, a famous quarterback at the time) with an officially sanctioned copy of his jersey. Such shirts do not state or claim an experience, a pattern of social relations or role while conveying a modicum of prestige by association within the system of fashion. It should be noted finally that young people who have been given the actual team jerseys or hats worn by famous professional players are, on the surface at least, no more likely to be granted status than the proud owner of an officially sanctioned item.

10. Norman Denzin, in his comment on this paper in the symposium at Toronto in which it was delivered, pointed out an important limitation of this paper. It does not address the meanings of metacoding of t-shirts within an ideological system such as a "race conflict" or "racial oppression." His comment drew on the ideologically organized iconography of the t-shirts shown in Spike Lee's movie, "Do the Right Thing."

References

Bakhtin, Mikhail
1981   *The dialogic imagination.* M. Holquist (ed.). Austin: University of Texas Press.
Barthes, Roland
1983   *The system of fashion.* New York: Hill and Wang.
Baudrillard, Jean
1988   *Selected writings.* Palo Alto: Stanford University Press.
Bourdieu, Pierre
1977   *Outline of a theory of practice.* Cambridge: Cambridge University Press.
Clifford, James
1986   "Introduction," in: James Clifford – George Marcus, 1–26.
Clifford, James – George Marcus (eds.)
1986   *Writing culture.* Berkeley: University of California Press.

Culler, Jonathan
    1977   *Structuralist poetics*. Ithaca: Cornell University Press.
Denzin, Norman
    1986   "Postmodern social theory," *Sociological Theory* 4: 194–204.
Dubin, Steven
    1990   "Visual Onomatopoeia," *Symbolic Interaction* 13(1): 185–216.
Eco, Umberto
    1979   *A theory of semiotics*. Bloomington: Indiana University Press.
    1986   *Travels in hyperreality*. New York: Harcourt, Brace and Jovanovich.
Guiraud, Pierre
    1975   *Semiology*. London: Routledge and Kegan.
Goffman, Erving
    1959   *The presentation of self in everyday life*. Garden City, NY: Doubleday
            Anchor.
Jakobson, Roman
    1970   "Closing statement," in: Thomas Sebeok (ed.), 350–377.
Mills, C. Wright
    1960   *The sociological imagination*. New York: Oxford University Press.
Peirce, Charles Sanders
    1931   *Collected papers*. Cambridge: Harvard University Press.
Rapport, Roy A.
    1971   "Ritual, sanctity, and cybernetics," *American Anthropologist* 73:
            59–76.
Sebeok, Thomas (ed.)
    1970   *Uses of language*. Cambridge, MA: MIT Press.
Uspenskij, Boris
    1973   *Poetics of composition*. Trans. V. Zavarin and S. Wittig. Berkeley:
            University of California Press.
Weber, Max
    1958   *From Max Weber*: Essays in sociology. H. H. Gerth – C. Wright
            Mills (eds.). New York: Oxford University Press.

Interpreted, circulating, interpreting:
The three dimensions of the clothing object

Peter Corrigan

Introduction

This paper aims to present briefly the three main dimensions of the clothing object. The first is probably the most familiar to us, and concerns the quality of the object as a public thing revealing the various social attributes carried by clothing in a given society, such as indication of occupation, class, gender, ethnicity, age group, specific social occasion, and so on. Clothing here is an object that may be interpreted by any competent member of society.[1] In this first dimension, then, clothing is "our" object. In the second dimension, clothing is not so much an object to be interpreted in the above manner, as an object to which things happen — and I mean quite concrete things, for here the object is to be treated principally as a brute piece of matter in the world. Now lots of things may happen to objects, but the peculiar interest here is in how the clothing object circulates and what, if anything, is sociologically interesting about this. This second dimension, as we will see, concerns the political economy of the clothing object. Clothing is no longer an open public thing, but the object of a very specific professional discourse — clothing here, then, is "my" object as someone exercising a particular brand of sociology. The third dimension is rather more difficult to grasp, for it concerns clothing not as a public object in the street but as an object in the private domain of specific persons — in the case I will be referring to later, the domain of the family: clothing here, then, is "their" object. As well as being an object to which things happen, clothing in this dimension also *provokes* things to happen and, to exaggerate a little, is not so much interpreted as interpreting. A given concrete item of clothing may, of course, partake of all three dimensions — indeed, it probably does. So let us now take a closer look at what is involved in each of the three dimensions.

Clothing as a public object

If we consider the historically dominant theoretical discourses about clothing — namely religious, political, sociological and semiotic accounts — we find that they are generally concerned with the first dimension of clothing: the public object. In particular, they stress the way in which dress translates — or, perhaps more interestingly, *mis*translates — the given social structure (including social conflicts within or about that structure) into the realm of appearances. In the Qur'an (24: 30−31), for example, clothing plays a specific role in gender construction, in the handling of sexuality and in the upholding of determinate notions of kinship and servitude. Women:

> should not display their beauty and ornaments except what (must ordinarily) appear thereof ... they should draw their veils over their bosoms and not display their beauty except to their husbands, their fathers, their husbands' fathers, their sons, their husbands' sons, their brothers or their brothers' sons, or their sisters' sons, or their women, or the slaves whom their right hands possess, or male servants free of physical needs, or small children who have no sense of the shame of sex (as quoted in Badawi 1982: 5−6).

In the Bible, we find that "the woman shall not wear that which pertaineth unto a man, neither shall a man put on a woman's garment: for all that do so are an abomination unto the Lord thy God" (Deuteronomy 22: 5). Clothing here has a double quality: on the one hand, there is supposed to be clothing appropriate to men and clothing appropriate to women, thereby illustrating the differences between them for anyone with eyes to see. But it follows from this that clothing that inherently distinguishes can also confuse: it can be manipulated and thereby mislead us about the nature of the world. The overcoming of this problem was a central concern of some later writers: clothed appearance should indicate relevant social attributes of the wearer, and indicate them unambiguously. In the third century of our era, for example, Bishop Cyprian (1932 [249 A. D.]) wrote a tract in which he urged virgins to ensure that their clothing would never cause them to be mistaken for prostitutes: "Let chaste and modest virgins shun the attire of the unchaste, the clothing of the immodest, the insignia of brothels, the adornments of harlots;" "Showy adornments and clothing and the allurements of beauty are not becoming in any except prostitutes and shameless women" (Cyprian 1932: 57, 55). So here we have the virgin-whore distinction as another simple example of the translation of attribute into appearance. A rather more frequent distinction was class: the late sixteenth century English Calvinist Philip Stubbes complained that it was becoming dangerously difficult to tell classes apart:

> I doubt not but it is lawfull for the nobilitie, the gentrie, and the magisterie to weare riche attire, euery one in their callyng. The nobility and gentrie to innoble, garnish, and set forth their birthes, dignities and estates. The magisterie to dignifie their callyngs, and to demonstrate the excellencie, the maiestie, and worthinesse of their offices and functions ... And as for priuate subiectes, it is not at any hande lawfull that they should weare silkes, veluets, satens, damaskes, gold, siluer, and what they list (though they be neuer so able to maintaine it), except they beyng in some kinde of office in the common wealth, doe vse it for the dignifiying and innoblyng of the same; or at the commaundment of their superintendent, or archpri-mate, for some speciall consideration or purpose. But now there is suche a confuse mingle mangle of apparell in Ailgna, and suche preposterous excesse thereof, as euery one is permitted to flaunt it out in what apparell he lusteth himself, or can get by any kinde of meanes. So that it is very hard to know who is noble, who is worshipfull, who is a gentleman, who is not; for you shal haue those which are neither of the nobilitie, gentilitie, nor yeomanrie, no, nor yet any magistrate or officer in the common wealthe, go daiely in silkes, veluettes, satens, damaskes, taffaties, and suche like; notwithstanding that they be bothe base by birthe, meane by estate, and seruile by callyng. And this I compte a greate confusion, and a generall disorder in a Christian common wealthe (Stubbes 1836 [1585]: 16−17; original spelling).

Thirty years later, Barnabee Rych (1614: 47) complained that it was difficult to know a prince from a peasant, "a Lord from a Lout, [and] a Lady from a Launderess." The vast numbers of sumptuary laws passed in medieval Europe (Baldwin 1926) were, of course, a directly political attempt to overcome this problem of social confusion arising from "il-legitimately" worn clothing. Clearly, the underlying assumption is that clothing *ought* to tell us about the social world − we read it as if it did, hence the danger of illegitimately arrogated apparel in a world of rigid class differences.

The fascination with the idea that social structure can be read straight from appearances is perhaps clearest in the case of the tradition of utopian writings stretching from Thomas More (1974 [1516]) to Etienne Cabet (1848) − and, I would submit, to a lot of later sociological work. Whether we find ourselves in Utopia, the City of the Sun, Christianopolis, Nova Solyma, Salentum, or Icaria, we are always able to read off the social attributes relevant to these societies − generally gender, occupation, age, marital status and rank − straight and unambiguously from an inspection of clothing. Table 1 shows the relevant social attributes that clothing was to indicate in some classical texts of the utopian literature. Cabet is perhaps the one who expresses this most clearly:

> Not only are the two sexes dressed differently, but within each of these categories the individual switches clothing frequently according to age and social condition, for the particularities of clothing indicate all the circumstances and positions of the members of society. Childhood and youth, the ages of puberty and majority, the condition of being married, single, widowed or remarried, the different professions and various functions — everything is indicated by clothing. Everyone sharing the same social condition wears the same *uniform*; but thousands of different uniforms match thousands of different conditions (Cabet 1848: 58, my translation).

Table 1. Utopian text and social attributes

	A	B	C	D	E	F	G	H	I
Gender	+	+	+	+				+	+
Ocupation	+	+	+				+		+
Age			+			+	+		+
Marital Status	+								+
Rank				+	+				
Season	+	+	+						

Key

Author:	Name of Utopia:
A: More 1974 [1516]	Utopia
B: Campanella 1981 [1602]	City of the sun
C: Andreae 1916 [1619	Christianopolis
D: Gott 1902 [1648]	Nova solyma
E: Fénelon 1832 [1699]	Salentum
d'Allais 1966 [1702]	-----
G: Morelly 1970[1755]	-----
H: Diderot 1966 [1796]	Tahiti
I: Cabet 1848	Icaria

In some ways, semiotic work can be seen as part of this tradition: Bogatyrev recognizes four basic costume types in Moravian Slovakia, namely everyday, holiday, ceremonial, and ritual costumes. Each of these possesses a finite number of functions drawn from practical, aesthetic, regionalistic, ceremonial, holiday, ritual, and nationalistic functions, and social status or class identification, a specific order of a number of these functions characterizing each type of costume (Bogatyrev 1971 [1937]: 43–44). Social status includes occupation, age, religious affiliation, and marital status. Costume indicates each of these through a combination of particular elements: "one item may have different functions, depending on which other items are combined with it" (Bogatyrev 1971 [1937]: 42). Other work on folk costume, such as Delaporte (1979) or Enninger's (1984) study of Old Amish dress, also assumes that the social structure is manifest in clothed appearance, although of course semioticians tell us a lot more about the mechanics of how this is achieved than any utopian writer. Marshall Sahlins' (1976) account of the American clothing system can also be seen in this light:

> By various objective features an item of apparel becomes appropriate for men or women, for night or for day, for "around the house" or "in public," for adult or adolescent. What is produced is, first, classes of time and place which index situations or activities; and, second, classes of status to which all persons are ascribed. These might be called "notional coordinates" of clothing, in the sense that they mark basic notions of time, place, and person as constituted in the cultural order. Hence what is reproduced in clothing is this classificatory scheme. Yet not simply that. Not simply the boundaries, the divisions, and subdivisions of, say, age-grades or social classes; by a specific symbolism of clothing differences, what is produced are the meaningful differences between these categories (Sahlins 1976: 181).

Sociological work on distinction also stresses clothing's quality as manifestation of the social structure. For Veblen (1899: 167), clothing indicated wealth: "expenditure on dress has this advantage ... that our apparel is always in evidence and affords an indication of our pecuniary standing to all observers at a first glance. It is also true that admitted expenditure for display is more obviously present, and is, perhaps, more universally practised in the matter of dress than in any other line of consumption." Goblot (1925: 3) maintains that there are always material signs distinguishing class membership and its concomitant advantages from those non-members who may not make a claim on these advantages. Distinction, indeed, was of special importance to the bourgeois class, and clothing was a particularly vital material sign (Goblot 1925: 71). Simmel (1957 [1904]) also treated dress as indicative of class belonging, and reintroduced the notion of class struggle in clothing: the clothing of an upper class is imitated by members of a lower class, so to preserve the distinction the upper class changes appearance again – hence Simmel's account of fashion change. Bourdieu's (1979) work, of course, is also squarely in this tradition, if rather more sophisticated. Subcultural theory (e.g., Brake 1985: 12; Clarke et al. 1976: 14) can also be situated in terms of the class and distinction concepts discussed above.

Approaches laying stress on agency rather than structure have tended to see clothing in terms of its role in the definition of the situation. Goffman, for example, maintains that clothing is one of those expressive embodied signs that "seem well designed to convey information about the actor's social attributes and about his conception of himself, and of the others present, and of the setting" (Goffman 1963: 34), and that "dress carries much of the burden of expressing orientation within the situation" (Goffman 1963: 213), while Linton (1936: 416) argues that "by indicating social status, clothing does much to facilitate the relations between individuals. It makes it possible for a stranger to determine at once the social category to which the wearer belongs and thus avoids acts or attitudes towards him which would be social errors." For Stone (1959: 4), "one of the chief functions of clothing is to facilitate and organize the encounters of strangers and casual acquaintances by making it possible for them to cast one another in social roles."

Now the point of the foregoing is to establish the status of clothing as a public object making manifest the salient categories of the public thing itself: society. The "publicness" of the object can be seen quite clearly in references to the usefulness of appearance in orientating the behavior of people who are strangers to each other. Indeed, clothing is one of the fundamental components of social solidarity: Goffman (1963: 35) argues that "the understanding of a common body idiom is one reason for calling an aggregate of individuals a society," while Sahlins (1976: 203) maintains that clothing makes possible "a cohesive society of perfect strangers." So, if we are at all competent members of our own societies we will be able to watch people walking down the street and we will be capable of reading off a great deal of socially useful information from a glance at their apparel. But there are certain things that we will not, by definition, be in a position to see: we will not see, for example, that the first person walking down Main Street is wearing a tie that was a birthday present from his daughter, or that the second is wearing her boyfriend's t-shirt, or that the third surreptitiously took that jacket from her sister's wardrobe that morning. So this brings us to the second dimension of the clothing object: its modes of circulation. The examples I just gave are imaginary ones to make a point, but let us see if we can describe the political economy of the clothing object in concrete cases, and draw some generalizable conclusions.

The political economy of clothing

The first indication that there might be something of sociological interest in the ways in which clothing circulated occurred to me when I was doing some preliminary work on wardrobe contents. Although many of the items had been purchased by their owners on the market, a significant proportion, ranging from a quarter to a third, were gifts — and not just from random sources, but overwhelmingly from family members or candidate family members such as girlfriends or boyfriends. So it began to appear that clothing was not simply part of the market economy, but also part of a kin-based economy operating on quite different principles (gift rather than commodity circulation). Consequently, I began to research the ways in which clothing circulated in families. A sample of six families in Dublin, Ireland, was interviewed in 1983–84. Respondents were asked to comment on the clothes worn in family photo albums and those in their actual wardrobes, and a more formal interview schedule was administered.

Seven different modes of clothing circulation were discovered, specific combinations of these modes characterising the relations of specific categories of family members. Mode A — the most frequent — was a gift purchased on the market; Mode B was a gift made by a family member; Mode C, a commodity made within the family; Mode D, the cast off; Mode E, borrowing; Mode F, stealing (i. e., taking an item on temporary loan without asking permission); and Mode G was self-purchased. The circulatory patterns are described in detail in Corrigan (1989a).

It was found that more types of items circulate in mode A than in any other mode, followed by modes F, D, E, and B. There is a single occurrence of mode C. Both mode A (the favored one) and mode F — which can, of course, be seen as a negative gift — have the highest penetration rates among actual items of clothing. Blouses, sweaters, scarves, shirts, and ties are the most frequently purchased gift objects. Sweaters, indeed, appear to be the most universal objects of circulation: they partake of all modes, being particularly frequent in A and F. The sweater, in sum, seems to be the basic unit of circulation in the family clothing economy. Although there is no clear evidence from the sample, this may be because such apparel is both less gender-marked than most other items of clothing and will cover a greater range of body sizes than almost any other garment. Almost "anyone" could wear a given sweater. Generally, gifts in all modes tended to flow from females to males (indeed, male attempts at gift giving tended to be frustrated by female candidate recipients), and certain modes seemed to define certain types of relations. For example, relations between brothers tended to involve little more than cast offs, mutual stealing (negative reciprocal gifts, if you prefer) was practically constitutive of the relations between teenage sisters, and the transition to self-purchasing marked the end of the mother's ability to give items of clothing to her daughters. The latter, in particular, was the source of some conflict between mother and teenage daughters. (For a fuller discussion of the issues raised here, see Corrigan 1989a.)

One of the interesting things about the political economy of clothing is that it seems to indicate a thriving economy based on kin and gift relations rather than on nonkin and commodity relations. It is as if a "primitive" economy were to be found at the private heart of advanced capitalism: pre-capitalist modes have not been stamped out, but have found a refuge in the family. Indeed, if we consume more and more objects, and consume them not as the isolated consumers of much economic theory but as subjects caught up in a kin-gift economy, then perhaps consumer capitalism will develop in some rather unexpected directions.

A second interesting, and rather more concrete, point about the political economy of the clothing object concerns the fact that it is very much a *woman's* economy. As David Cheal's (1988) study of gift exchange in Winnipeg shows, this generalization seems to be both cross-culturally valid and holds for items other than clothing. This helps us to understand some aspects at least of the mother/daughter conflict: if the clothing economy *is* a woman's economy, then each woman would seem to need to attain her own independent control over it — hence a daughter's refusal of a mother's gift of a garment. Mothers in this case seem to be forced to give money which, as the general equivalent of the commodity economy, can be used by the daughter to purchase whatever she likes. We can also look at mutual sisterly stealing from this angle: if teenage daughters have as their task the overcoming of the mother's unilateral control of the clothing economy, then they would seem to have a shared task — so their wardrobes can often be treated as one, and "stealing" seems a perfectly natural thing to do. The significance of the above for the general theory of the gift is discussed in detail in Corrigan (1989a).

These are the sorts of things we find, then, if we look at clothing as an object that circulates. I have, of course, excluded production and retail aspects from this analysis, and, in my particular sample, there was very little circulation outside the family. The shift from the first dimension to the second has brought us from what Goffman (1959) might call the "front stage" to the "back stage" of the clothing object. We have moved from looking at clothing as an object to be interpreted to an object to which things happen. But what happens if we look at the object as something that *provokes* things to happen, as something that interprets rather than is interpreted — is there anything sociologically interesting and generalizable to be found here? This brings us to the third dimension of the clothing object.

Clothing as interpreter

This section explores the sorts of things the clothing object provokes in a specific setting — namely the sample of families I have already mentioned. Now it is not clear how this might be done methodologically. My solution to this problem was to look for what might be called "clothing crises": when a particular item of clothing causes so many problems in a family that it begins to lay bare what might be called the *deep structure of the familial-sartorial world view*. The last section referred to mother/daughter conflict in the teenage years. In most of the sample, the conflict period took place before my fieldwork, and the mothers now accepted their daughters' independent behavior. In one case, however, an incident took place during my period in the field that undoubtedly merits the description "clothing crisis." A seventeen year old daughter was given money by her mother to buy clothes, went to the shops and returned with a dress — which she was promptly ordered by her mother, father, and brother to bring right back to the store and replace with something else. She complied. This clothing crisis, then, was also a crisis of the family. So why was this clothing object so unacceptable that it had to be ejected from the family? Of those who insisted on ejection, the mother's account of the incident was the most detailed, and I will briefly summarize the analysis here (the full version is in Corrigan 1989b). This showed that, in the case of girls, she divided clothed life into three stages: pre-thirteen, between thirteen and twenty-one, and post twenty-one. The earliest stage was characterised by the coincidence of mother and daughter sartorial theoreticity, to adapt a concept from McHugh (1970): in practical terms, this meant that the mother could buy clothing for daughters of this age group and be sure that it would not be rejected. The middle stage consisted of an eight year span of troublesome bodies that did not know how to relate to clothing in an appropriate way, while once past twenty-one the body became settled and its possessor attained the right to dress as she pleased: independent adult sartorial theoreticity. "Proper" teenagers, in the mother's opinion, recognize that their bodies are troublesome and dress to hide this problem (the "lumps and bumps" of the developing teenage female body, as she would put it) — her daughters, however, are not "proper" teenagers in this sense and are inexpert dressers because they do not know how to clothe their bodies properly. Further perusal of the mother's interview transcripts revealed repeated references to age, analysis of which indicated that "proper," or "expert," dressers of any age — not just teenagers — dress in clothing appropriate to their age. So for the mother, there is a structure at work articulating age, status of body, clothing type, and expertise/inexpertise.

Now it might be thought that this is all very interesting but perhaps limited to just this one person. Is aged discourse some peculiar idiolect? Indeed, talk about age had not struck me as being of any special significance during the course of the fieldwork. But closer inspection of the interview transcripts showed that all of the women in the sample seemed to have a version of age-based sartorial appropriateness. Age, indeed, seems to be a central social attribute of the clothing object relevant to the sample, and was to be found under such headings as weather and age, aging bodies, being dressed for the wrong age, aging clothes, fashion and age, children and age and, in an example I will briefly consider, troublesomely aged mother clothing (Corrigan 1988: 231 − 244). Not only do mothers have trouble with daughters who, in their view, dress inappropriately for their age, but daughters also have problems with mothers who are not, for them, clad in age-appropriate terms. The following interview was with the thirty-one year old Claire Sheehan:

4571   PC: What do you think of the way your mother dresses?
4572   CS: Heh heh heh heh my mother? Heh. Well sometimes she dresses very well. Ehm she tends to dress ((clears throat)) (0.6) maybe a bit young for her age.

***

4740   CS: She (mother) doesn't dress for her age, and that's what's wrong. That's her problem, she dresses the wrong clothes for the age.
4741   PC: Uhm
4742   CS: I don't think she should be dowdy and old, but ehm. She'd buy pants I'd buy and they don't suit her.
4743   PC: Yeh, eh somebody, I don't know who it was, said to me that ehm, your mother tried to dress in a style that's like *yours* particularly
4744   CS: She copies a lot of my clothes, yes.

4745   PC: What what what do you think of that? (1.8) It's you specifically
         she (   )
4746   CS: That's right, yeh. What do I think of that? I think she's childish
         and I still think my mother's very childish.

Claire Sheehan begins her assessment of her mother with nuanced appreciation: "sometimes she dresses very well" (4572). The hesitant criticism of "maybe a bit young for her age" (4572) becomes much less hesitant in the second passage, especially in 4740. Dressing "the wrong clothes for the age" becomes a real problem — for Claire rather than her mother, as the mother has elected *Claire*'s age-appropriate clothes as appropriate to herself. Not knowing one's aged sartorial place means that one does not know how to behave as a sartorial adult: "I think she's childish and I still think my mother's very childish" (4746).

Much of the central part of my work was concerned with mother/daughter conflict over clothing, but once mothers and daughters began to be compared more closely over the whole sample it slowly became clear that, in fact, there was a great deal of agreement on important sartorial matters. Appropriateness of clothing to age grade appears to be the almost universal measure of consensus among both daughters and mothers, with concern also shown for appropriateness to body. Those who did not follow this logic were considered *not to know how* to dress. Where, then, was the conflict? I suggest that it lay around the notion of sartorial theoreticity, but it was not simply a question of one side being sartorially theoretical and the other not. Adolescence may be called the *time of disputed theoreticity*. So we have a passage from: sartorially incompetent child − > disputed adolescent sartorial competence − > sartorially competent adult.

We can improve on this still further, however. McHugh (1970), from whom I borrowed the notion of theoreticity, combined theoreticity ("one knows what one is doing") and non-theoreticity ("one does not know what one is doing") with conventionality ("it might have been otherwise") and non-conventionality ("it could not have been otherwise"). We have discovered a period where these distinctions are open to dispute. This would also imply a period of *disputed conventionality*. A new summary is provided in Table 2.

Table 2 is obviously valid for the sample only — and then only from the point of view of the women in it. But the categories are probably generalizable: different social groups might place actors differently within the schema, and this could clearly be investigated in future work.

Despite conflict, then, there seems to be agreement between mothers and daughters on the general scheme of things. Mother/daughter conflict

Table 2. Sartorial theoreticity and conventionality

	Sartorially non-theoretical	*Sartorial theoreticity disputed*	*Sartorially theoretical*
Conventional	Not dressed according to age and body, e.g., "childish mother"	Age/body appropriate dressers "adults"	
Disputed conventionality		Teenage daughters vs. mothers	
Non-conventional	Children Males		[example: adults in occupational uniforms]

appears to be less over the content of this scheme than over the right to (recognized) independent control over it. Claire's problem with her mother, who dressed in similar clothes, illuminates this point from another angle. Sartorial adulthood may mean that mothers and daughter share the same general scheme in the end, but the fact that independent control is important means that there must be a difference somewhere: in this case, as the form (age appropriateness) is shared, the content should be different. But Claire's mother claims through her practice that the content is the same, thus forcing Claire to shift difference to form. As Claire is unlikely to give up her adult perspective that she is an age-adequate dresser, this can only mean that her mother is not: therefore she is "childish."

Conclusion

The third dimension of the clothing object brings us back, in a way, to the first: of the social attributes dear to the utopians and others, age seems to be not only of public interest, but operates at quite an intimate level, influencing family relationships. Forced ejection of the clothing object relates also to the second dimension, the political economy of the clothing object, as does accession to independent control of the clothing economy. The same item of clothing may be involved in all these dimensions. So are there more than three dimensions of the clothing object? Perhaps — but three will do to start.

Notes

1. The stress here is on "competent." Not all are equally "competent" faced with interpreting the clothing signs of the various social groups and subcultures to be found in contemporary societies. What is "overcoded" for one observer may be "undercoded" for another (Eco 1976: 129ff). Utopian and religious writings, as we will see below, attempted to overcome this problem through the elaboration of unambiguously coded clothing signs.

References

d'Allais, Denis Vairasse
   1966 [1702] "The economy and education of the Sevarambians," in: Frank
       E. Manuel — Fritzie P. Manuel (eds.), 49–57.
Andreae, Johann Valentin
   1916 [1619] *Christianopolis*. Trans. Felix Emil Held. New York: Oxford University Press.
Badawi, Jamal A.
   1982   *The Muslim women's dress according to the Qur'an and Sunnah.*
       London: Ta-Ha Publishers and Federation of Student Islamic Societies in U. K. and Eire.
Baldwin, Frances Elizabeth
   1926   *Sumptuary legislation and personal regulation in England.* Baltimore:
       Johns Hopkins.
Bogatyrev, Petr
   1971 [1937] *The functions of folk costume in Moravian Slovakia.* The Hague:
       Mouton.
Bourdieu, Pierre
   1979   *La distinction: Critique sociale du jugement.* Paris: Les éditions de
       Minuit.
Brake, Michael
   1985   *Comparative youth culture: The sociology of youth cultures in America,
       Britain and Canada.* London: Routledge and Kegan Paul.

Cabet, Etienne
1848   *Voyage en Icarie.* Paris: Bureau du Populaire.
Campanella, Tommasso
1981 [1602] *The city of the sun: A poetic dialogue.* Trans. Daniel J. Donno. Berkeley: University of California Press.
Cheal, David
1988   *The gift economy.* London: Routledge.
Clarke, John — Stuart Hall — Tony Jefferson — Brian Roberts
1976   "Subcultures, cultures and class: A theoretical overview," in: Stuart Hall — Tony Jefferson (eds.), 9 — 74.
Corrigan, Peter
1988   Backstage dressing: Clothing and the urban family, with special reference to mother-daughter relations. Unpublished Ph.D. dissertation, University of Dublin, Trinity College.
1989a   "Gender and the gift: The case of the family clothing economy," *Sociology* 23 (4): 513 — 534.
1989b   "Troublesome bodies and sartorial dopes: Motherly accounts of teenage daughter dress practices," *Semiotica* 77 (4): 393 — 413.
Cyprian, Saint
1932 [249 AD] *The dress of virgins* [*De habitu virginuum*]. Trans. Angela Elizabeth Keenan. Washington, D. C.: Catholic University of America.
Delaporte, Yves
1979   "Communication et signification dans les costumes populaires," *Semiotica* 26 (1 — 2): 65 — 79.
Diderot, Denis
1966 [1771] "Supplément au voyage dc Bougainville, ou dialogue entre A et B." Reprinted in: *Le Neveu de Rameau.* Paris: Livre de Poche.
Dreitzel, Hans Peter (ed.)
1970   *Recent sociology*, No. 2. New York: Macmillan.
Eco, Umberto
1976   *A theory of semiotics.* Bloomington: Indiana University Press.
Enninger, Werner
1984   "Inferencing social structure and social processes from nonverbal behavior," *American Journal of Semiotics* 3 (2): 77 — 96.
Fénelon, François de Salignac de la Mothc
1832 [1699] *Les aventures de Télémaque.* Reprinted Dublin: J. Cumming.
Goblot, Edmond
1925   *La barrière et le niveau: Etude sociologique sur la bourgeoisie française moderne.* Paris: Felix Alcan.
Goffman, Erving
1959   *The presentation of self in everyday life.* New York: Doubleday Anchor Books.
1963   *Behavior in public places.* London: Collier-Macmillan.

Gott, Samuel
1902 [1648] *Nova Solyma*. Walter Begley (ed.). London: John Murray.
Hall, Stuart — Tony Jefferson (eds.)
1976 *Resistance through rituals: Youth subcultures in post-war Britain*. London: Hutchinson.
Linton, Ralph
1936 *The study of man*. New York: D. Appleton-Century.
McHugh, Peter
1970 "A common-sense perception of deviance," in: Hans Peter Dreitzel (ed.), 151–180.
Manuel, Frank E. — Fritzie P. Manuel (eds.)
1966 *French utopias: An anthology of ideal societies*. New York: Schocken Books.
More, Thomas
1974 [1516] *Utopia*. Reprinted in his *Works*, Vol. 4. Edited by Edward Surtz — J. H. Hexter. New Haven, CT: Yale University Press.
Morelly
1970 [1755] *Code de la nature*. Paris: Editions Sociales.
Rych, Barnabee
1614 *The honestie of this age: Proouing by good circumstance that the world was neuer honest till now*. London: printed for T. A.
Sahlins, Marshall
1976 *Culture and practical reason*. Chicago: University of Chicago Press.
Simmel, Georg
1957 [1904] "Fashion," *American Journal of Sociology* 62 (6): 541–558.
Stone, Gregory P.
1959 Clothing and social relations: A study of appearance in the context of community life. Unpublished Ph.D. dissertation. University of Chicago.
Stubbes, Philip
1836 [1585] *The anatomie of abuses*. London: W. Pickering.
Veblen, Thorstein
1899 *The theory of the leisure class: An economic study in the evolution of institutions*. New York: The Macmillan Company.

Psychoanalytic jewels: The domestic drama of Dora and Freud

John O'Neill

The symbolic economy of jewels

From the earliest times, men and women have adorned themselves. They have done so not only to transcend the common necessities of life but to celebrate and to enhance life itself. Thus in India jewellery has always been used to mark the principal stages in the life of a Hindu (Dongerkery 1971). Twelve days after the birth of a child, at *namakarana*, the goldsmith puts a gold pin through the ear and curls it into a ring. A silk cord is tied around the child's waist and another, with a silver or gold pendant, is tied around the neck. The pendant is designed to ward off evil spirits, while the earring is thought to protect against nervous diseases. Similarly, the adornment of women was not merely cosmetic, as it might be today. Jewellery marked the stages in the life-cycle concerned especially with women's fertility but it was also the source of the property a woman brought to her marriage. Thus the *stridhana* functioned as both a love-token and as a token of exchangeability in marriage. For this reason the law of *stridhana* (woman's property) is an extremely complex part of Hindu law. It is noticeable that in the Hindu practice, it is customary to give the bride some very inexpensive jewellery of beads, shell, coral and ivory — perhaps to make all women equal in marriage, if not to make each woman the most precious jewel. Thus we might say that there has been a long cultural history in which a woman is regarded as the jewel she has/is, however such jewellery is acquired.

Jewellery is at once an ordinary object that has abounded throughout human history and an object of wonder, scarcity and holiness. A particular invention of the Egyptians — namely, funerary jewellery (Andrews 1990), made expressly for the journey from this life to the next, represents the extreme form of the desire of the wearer of jewellery and ornamentation to influence the power of nature and divinity that determine life and death, health and disease, fertility and barrenness. Thus the colors in Egyptian jewellery are more important than the semi-precious stones in it — green (new life, vegetation), blue (protective night sky, joy), red (blood, power). As such, jewellery partakes in that double perspective of the sacred and the profane through which human beings mark their species in both its limits and its excesses. Very little is to be gained from spelling out the endless codings of these two dimensions of human artifacts which rule in every field of food, fashion, utensils, architecture, as much as in ornamentation. What must be noticed is that the human body is not simply the bearer, producer and consumer of its artifacts but is itself produced, consumed, transported, enjoyed, feared, worshipped and reviled to heightened degrees depending upon its use of ornaments, potions and prosthetics of every kind. Jewellery exerts a continuing fascination because of its closeness to the body, to its chances in love, its hopes of fertility and our ruses of possession and dispossession.

Bodies, gifts, and exchanges

The Dora case is perhaps the purloined jewel of psychoanalysis, having occasioned as much discussion as Poe's famous letter (Freud 1980). There can be little doubt that we are left with a continuing riddle that challenges equally our scientific and literary intelligence — and this is likewise the hallmark of Freud's case histories. The Dora "case" contains a secret that is hidden everywhere — on the body, in language, in relationships, in dreams, in boxes, in jewellery, in portraits. Everything discloses Dora's sexual secret but for Freud's scientific modesty and artistry. Or so it would seem but for Freud's own self-revelations in a story that — as in other case histories — entraps him. Here I propose to trace the semiotic strategies employed by Freud to explore what he calls "a wonderful sexual geography" where times and places are displaced upon the body which in turn displaces its relations to other bodies in households that are the theater of a young girl's loves and losses. Since Freud's treatment of Dora has not satisfied recent feminist critics, I shall look at how Hélène Cixous recreates the Dora drama — but with specific reference to her use of the symbolism of the pearl ear drops longed for by Dora's mother but not given by her father. Here I think that Cixous creates a text of violence by violating the text in a way that conscripts Dora for feminist purposes but without any privilege over Freud's inscription of her case for psychoanalysis.

> I am aware that — in this town, at least — there are many physicians who (revolting though it may seem) choose to read a case history of this kind not as a contribution to the psychopathology of neuroses, but as a *roman à clef* designed for their private delectation. I can assure readers of this species that every case history which I may have occasion to publish in the future will be secured against their perspicacity by similar guarantees of secrecy, even though this resolution is bound to put quite extraordinary restrictions upon my choice of material (Freud 1980: 36).

From the very start, the Dora case upsets its own pretense of neutral reportage as a "fragment of an analysis of a case of hysteria." Freud's effort to keep the lid on what he may have suspected to be a Pandora's box is doubly revealed in the dating of the publication (1901 and 1905, with a later postscript 1924) and in the substitute name (Dora) of the patient whom many believe to have been a forced gift (sacrifice) to psychoanalysis. The name he gave to conceal his patient (Dora, i. e., gift) repeats Freud's expropriation of her confidence required by the scientific publication of the case history. Moreover, despite Freud's initial withholding of the case, and his careful prefaced concerns, the Dora case clearly gets away from Freud and the domestic circle which conspired to place Dora in his hands. By the same token, the text of the case history reveals a struggle between the artist and the scientist in Freud, each trying to give shape to the entanglement of lives, where power, secrecy and sexuality provide the fortunate occasion for psychoanalysis to demonstrate its mastery of misfortune.

At age eight, Dora had developed severe dyspnoea. She caught the usual childhood diseases — from her brother who had milder attacks than she experienced. Freud notices her emphasis upon this connection and refers us to a later interpretation regarding his hypothesis of shared masturbatory behavior with her older brother. Alternatively, Freud might have considered the analogy with Dora's mother contracting from her father an illness which lies at the base of Dora's constitution, as he himself had remarked. This hypothesis would lead directly into the semiotics of the gift exchanges in Dora's domestic economy where the women are not only exchanged but receive in exchange the bad seed of the father's sins. Freud's medicalization of the syphilitic symptoms — tabies, hives, dyspnoea — rather than employ the direct sexual terminology where appropriate, or direct usage, like "hard breathing" goes a long way to mystify himself and his readers in exchange for indulging his image as a physician. From twelve years onwards, Dora suffered from nervous coughing — tussis nervosa — with a loss of voice (aphonia). She had received medical treatment for these problems but this had only inspired her derision and renunciation of doctors. Yet Freud risks an alliance with the medical profession − at least a terminological, Latin alliance − when in fact he meant to triumph over their methodological failures with his own psychoanalytic method.

Here, then, a dramatic entrance. A beautiful woman, who can hardly bare to live, is driven desperate by her father whom she loves, and delivered over to another man, Freud, who is also old enough to be her father, and who will only give her back her life in exchange for the secret she is determined to take to the grave rather than release. Since there is a limit to the reader's capacity for bizarre detail, I propose to introduce a device to allow us to grasp the intricate threads woven into the case history. I propose to redescribe Freud's narrative in terms of a *method of triangulation* in which the primal triangle is historically repeated in later familial triads which determine and are themselves determined (*nachträglich*) by the recollection of the primal triad. While her father had been recovering from tuberculosis in a small provincial town (B), he and his wife had become intimate friends with a couple − Herr and Frau K. The latter had, in fact, nursed Dora's father during his long illness while Herr K. spent time talking with Dora, making her occasional gifts. Dora, in turn, was "almost a mother" to their children. In Figure 1 we may already observe a double triad which seeks a third triad to resolve the family dynamics into which Dora has been drawn both complicitly and reluctantly along the lines of affection and disaffection.

The implicit logic of these relationships came to a head when Dora refused to stay longer than her father on a visit to the K's. A little after,

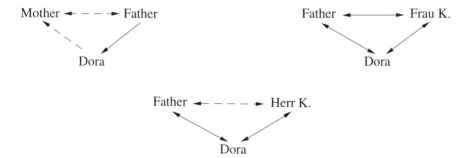

Figure 1. Triangulation of family relationships. Broken lines of disaffection, solid lines of affection.

she gave her mother the excuse that Herr K. had made her a proposal while on one of their walks by the lake. Having insisted that her father be informed by her mother, Herr K. was called to account by her father and uncle. However, Herr K. denied any seductive intention on his part and accused Dora of being over-interested in sexual matters, arousing herself while at the lake with such reading matter as Mantagezza's *Physiology of Love*. Her father, rather than break off with the K's, as Dora beseeched him, sided with Herr K's accusation that Dora was engaged in sexual fantasy. At the same time, he invoked his unwillingness to cause Frau K. pain by charging her husband with immorality, even though he held no very high opinion of him. Dora's father then implored Freud to try to bring her to reason lest she destroy the one bit of affection left to himself and Frau K.

> We are just two poor wretches who give one another what comfort we can by an exchange of friendly sympathy. You already know that I get nothing out of my own wife (Freud 1980: 57).

Freud observes that Dora's father vacillates between ascribing her behavior to an obstinacy inherited from him and to her mother's behavior as the source of everyone's craziness. Here, we note that the fateful remark to the effect that he "got nothing" out of his wife will be heard again by Dora in a remark about his wife made to a servant dismissed by Herr K. Whether or not her father's usage is wholly sexual is arguable in so far as he claims to Freud that his health hardly permitted anything "wrong" in his relation with Frau K. What is clear, however, is that Dora's mother is given no sympathetic treatment and at this stage is, so to speak, out of the game.

Freud remarks that he had difficulty in getting Dora to focus upon Herr K. whom she had put out of her mind, whereas his thoughts were preoccupied with her father with whom she was angry because he still maintained relations with Herr K. and, as she was convinced, was involved in a "common love-affair" with Frau K. Dora noticed everything that confirmed her own suspicion but never got any satisfactory answers from either her mother or her father whom she considered a liar. Thus, unlike her mother, she did not believe his story that he was beholden to Frau K. for talking him out of a suicide (Freud reminds us of Dora's similar attempt) and when he and Frau K. each moved their bedroom to rent rooms across from each other in a hotel suite shared by the two families, Dora was appalled at their openness. This continued in her father's daily appointments with Frau K., once they returned to town, despite everyone's comments and even Herr K.'s complaints to Dora's mother. As well, her father had plainly made gifts to Frau K. — not the least of which seems to have been the recovery of her health and liveliness. The relation between the couple finally shifted from the town of (B) to Vienna where the two families continued to be united so that her father no longer had to go off to (B) where his coughing fits were so marvellously calmed due to the fortunate circumstance of Frau K.'s similar retreats. In the midst of these events, Herr K. sent flowers to Dora everyday for a year and made her valuable presents while spending as much of his time with her as possible. Yet Dora's parents did not suspect anything that marked his behavior as "love-making."

Here Freud entertains the possibility that Dora's reproaches with respect to her father were exaggerated, if not a further displacement of her own self-reproach in view of her possible compliance with a re-triangulation of the family relationship, i. e., the *exchange of women*.

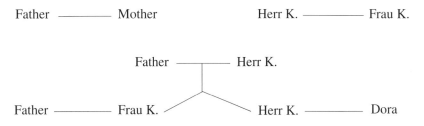

Figure 2. Triangulation of the exchange of women.

This sexual economy is simultaneously mediated by an *exchange of gifts* through which Dora's father and Herr K. recognize their appropriation of each other's women. To receive a gift is to be exchanged in this economy, Dora's mother does not exchange because she has withdrawn her sexual favors. By the same token, she from whom the male "gets nothing" is perceived by them to be the cause of everyone else's search for happiness. However, so far from spoiling the game, Dora's mother is in fact the "spoil" (the "*Schmuck*") of the game in which Dora is in turn a spoil (a "jewel"). This is because Dora's mother first receives the bad gift of her husband's syphilitic seed from which she can never cleanse herself or her household. So far from remaining beneath the level of psychoanalysis, Dora's mother is "out" because her obsessional behavior constitutes a *meta-comment* upon the rotten state of things around her while refusing any of the petty alliances set-up to accommodate the father.

It emerges that Dora's own compliance with her father's affair had continued even though she had been told about it by her last governess, a spinster whose wide-reading Freud had considered largely responsible for Dora's own tastes. Moreover, this governess had also urged Dora's mother not to tolerate her husband's relation to Frau K. Dora's reaction was to insist upon the dismissal of the governess whom she detected to be in love with her father and therefore deceiving Dora about the affection she thought they enjoyed between them. We now see another structure of *exchange and betrayal* in Figure 3.

Figure 3. Triangulation of exchange and betrayal.

In this case, Dora no less than her governess is in love with a married man and, although no one else is deceived, both women hide their love behind their love of children, if not for one another.

In the *domestic economy of the mind*, as Freud so marvellously puts it, there are unconscious motives for holding a family member to ransom through illness. In Dora's case, her bitterness at her father's dismissal of the lake scene with Herr K. as a fantasy undoubtedly lay at the root of things. But Freud postpones the solution to this riddle until he has reached the analysis of the second of Dora's two dreams. At this stage, Dora's constant coughing which accompanied her complaints about her father required attention, i. e., a search for the *sexual situation* which first aroused it. The clue came from an expression she used when insisting that Frau K. only loved her father because he was a "man of means" (*ein vermögender Mann*).

A jewel-case

We have now to consider the first of Dora's two dreams. Interestingly enough, Freud reports that Dora shared in the interpretation of the dream, having had some previous training, although he does not say with whom she had worked:

> Here is the dream as related by Dora: "A house was on fire. My father was standing beside my bed and woke me up. I dressed quickly. Mother wanted to stop and save her jewel-case; but Father said: 'I refuse to let myself and my two children be burnt for the sake of your jewel-case.' We hurried downstairs, and as soon as I was outside I woke up" (Freud 1980: 99).

Freud begins by asking for the first occasion of the dream. In response, Dora remembers that she had the dream three nights while at the lake where the scene with Herr K. had taken place, in addition to a few recent repetitions in Vienna. Freud then prompts her to take the dream bit by bit, anyway it comes. Dora reveals a recent quarrel between her mother and father over her locking the dining room at night because this also closed off her brother's room. This distressed her father because, as he said "something might happen in the night so that it might be necessary to leave the room." Dora recalls that after a siesta at the lake she suddenly awoke to find Herr K. standing beside her bed — just as she had seen her father in the dream. She became guarded with Herr K. and got a key for the bedroom door from Frau K. The next day she dressed with the door locked but the key had already disappeared when she looked for it in the afternoon. Bringing together the mention of a key in this incident and in the quarrel between Dora's parents, Freud drops the following colloquialism into a footnote as though it were anything less than the very key to the kingdom of psychoanalysis.

> I suspected, though I did not as yet say so to Dora, that she had seized upon this element on account of a symbolic meaning which it possessed. "*Zimmer*" ["room"] in dreams stands very frequently for "*Frauenzimmer*" [a slightly derogatory word for "woman;" literally, "women's apartments"]. The question whether a woman is "open" or "shut" can naturally not be a matter of indifference. It is well known, too, what sort of "key" effects the opening in such a case (Freud 1980: 102).

Freud's remark at this juncture has occasioned considerable feminist comment. Quite apart from the political issues involved, it may be said that this textual remark errs on the salacious side since medical propriety would preclude such speculation except by someone willing to risk degrading himself while trying to disparage a woman, let alone a young unmarried girl. All Freud needed to do was to speculate on the key to the two situations which may be compared in Figure 4.

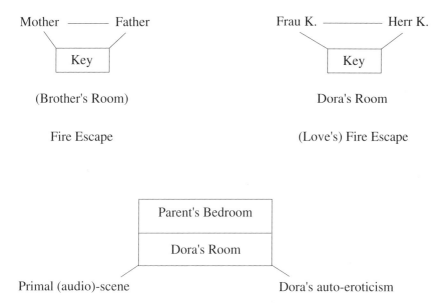

Figure 4. Triangulation of the primal (audio)-scene and Dora's auto-eroticism.

Here I have triangulated the two scenes with the primal scene in order to capture the domestic lay-out, or topography, of the dream sequence that Freud traces in terms of the metaphor of a "key" (*Schlüssel*). The benefit of my device is that it contributes to our understanding of Freud's construct of a *sexual geography* at work not only *on* the body (in displacements of symptomatology) but also *between* bodies, rooms and settings at a distance – yet both temporally and spatially co-present in the unconscious. I am not, however, seeking to abstract the semiotics of this sexual geography from the constitutive splitting (*Spaltung*) of the intra-subjective self in its inter-subjective experience of language and society. My device of triangulation is merely a graphic technic for re-minding ourselves of this very psychic structure just as the oedipus legend is a narrative device for achieving the same effect.

Freud resumes the dream interpretation by asking Dora about the jewel-case her mother wanted to save from the burning house. She related an argument over a gift of pearl drop earrings which her mother would have liked rather than the bracelet her father preferred to give her. Freud surmises that Dora hoped to get the bracelet her mother had rejected in line with his hypothesis that Dora wished to take the place in her father's affection that her mother had refused. He then turns Dora's attention to the jewel *case* her mother was trying to save which prompts her to recall that she had received a very expensive case from Herr K. just before the dream. There follows an exchange that has attracted a great deal of feminist comment:

> Then a return-present would have been very appropriate. Perhaps you do not know that "jewel-case" (*Schmuckkästchen*) is a favorite expression for the same thing that you alluded to not long ago by means of the reticule you were wearing — for the female genitals, I mean.
> I knew *you* would say that (Freud 1980: 105).

Freud is not put off. He proceeds to invert or to change the value of all the signs in Dora's account. By placing her mother at the center of the dream, he argues that Dora was as willing to take her mother's place with her father as she now is to take Frau K.'s place with Herr K. but wants her father to save her from her own fires just as he once saved his little daughter. Moreover, he adds, Dora is tempted now to drop Freud because the treatment was her father's idea, referring now to Dora's anger at being sacrificed rather than saved by her father.

It turns out that Dora blamed her father for her illness not only because of the way she felt he had sacrificed her love for him to his affair with Frau K. but also because she knew he had syphilis and had infected her mother and herself with bad health. Freud, too, believed that the offspring of "luetics," as he calls them, were disposed to neurosis. Yet he persists in treating the line of complaint by Dora and her mother as a "*self*-accusation," much of it due to her early masturbation. He convinced himself of this even more on observing the "symptomatic" act of Dora playing with her reticule (purse, "pussy") during a session on Freud's sofa. He then pronounces his great generalization upon how the analyst can count upon each of us to leak our secrets:

> There is a great deal of symbolism of this kind in life, but as a rule we pass it by without heeding it. When I set myself the task of bringing to light what human beings keep hidden within them, not by the compelling power of hypnosis, but by observing what they say and what they show, I thought the task was a harder one than it really is. He that has eyes to see and ears to hear may convince himself that no mortal can keep a secret. If his lips are silent, he chatters with his finger-tips; betrayal oozes out of him at every pore. And thus the task of making conscious the most hidden recesses of the mind is one which it is quite possible to accomplish (Freud 1980: 114).

An economy of pollution

With everything drawn together in this way, Freud declares the clinical picture "complete and without a flaw." Yet the master cannot resist a further *supplement* to account for Dora's substitution of "dyspnoea" (coughing) for bed-wetting. The answer comes from the proximity of the parental bedroom to Dora's room and her interpretation of her father's heavy breathing as the sound of "something sexual." Identifying her father's sexual exertion with her own masturbatory exertions, Dora "inherited" an asthmatic cough. Similarly, she had switched the vaginal discharge (leucorrhoea) from which she and her mother suffered to her throat, complaining of catarrah. In turn, this provided for her fantasy of the *fellatio* between Frau K. and her impotent father, and perhaps what Herr K. would require of her too.

Freud's triumph, however theatrical, deprives him of understanding the father's bad gift — the contaminated seed that had polluted his family, driving off his wife into an obsession with cleanliness and distorting his daughter's conception of her future sexuality. Freud does not consider how the "luetic" penis drives everyone's sexuality away from genital intercourse. The polluted phallus contaminates its own domestic economy, determining every relationship of gift, counter-gift and refusal. Because he gives insufficient attention to this *economy of pollution*, Freud can only treat it historically, i. e., in terms of the aetiology of hysteria traced to early masturbation as the determinant of either "abandonment to sexuality" in the pervert, or of "repudiation of sexuality" and illness and neurosis in Dora's case. Even when Freud gets close to the central clue, he loses its significance by attributing it to Dora's precocious sexual knowledge:

> Dora knew that there was a kind of getting wet involved in sexual intercourse, and that during the act of copulation the man presented the woman with something liquid *in the form of drops*. She also knew that the danger lay precisely in that, and that it was her business to protect her genitals from being moistened (Freud 1980: 128).

The avoidance of "pollution" in Dora's family was due to the fact of her father's venereal disease and not to her mother's dullness or her frigidity. Freud remarks that Dora "seemed to understand that her mother's mania for cleanliness was a reaction against this dirtying." Returning to her mother's rejection of the husband's gift of a bracelet, he points out the significance of her preference for a gift of pearl drop earrings. They symbolize the pure white drops or seeds that she had wanted to enter her (box) as a young married woman. Freud failed to see that the mother had been sadly fooled (*Schmuck*) by the gift and so he misses Dora's smart-refusal of the game in which he too was "fooled" into taking the father's side against his daughter whom he remains convinced − via another "switchword" − was still burning for Herr K. on whom he had displaced his own desire for a kiss from Dora:

> "Mother's jewel-case" was therefore introduced in two places in the dream; and this element replaced all mention of Dora's infinite jealousy, of the drops (that is, of the sexual wetness), of being dirtied by the discharge, and, on the other hand, of her present thoughts connected with the temptation − the thoughts which were urging her to reciprocate the man's love, and which depicted the sexual situation (alike desirable and menacing) that lay before her. The element of "jewel-case" was more than any other a product of condensation and displacement, and a compromise between contrary mental currents. The multiplicity of its origin − both from infantile and contemporary sources − is no doubt pointed to by its double appearance in the content of the dream (Freud 1980: 130).

Thus Freud's science-fiction casts Dora on a cliff where either way she turns disaster must befall her. If she runs backwards, she will be sacrificed by the father she loves. If she moves forward to be caught in the arms of Herr K., she will embrace her father's ally in an exchange of power and sexuality whose coinage is women and their ruin. But that is another woman's story: another pearl.

Dora had a second dream on which Freud could only work with her for two hours before he was given notice − rather like the fortnight's notice given by Dora to her governess once she had cooled towards her. Freud seems somewhat razzled and notes that he cannot recall the exact order of analysis and so he takes his thoughts as they come. A connecting thread in the material is given by its internal reference to pictures. Thus the mention of a strange town with a monument in one of its squares could be traced to a picture album sent to Dora by a young engineer whose acquaintance she had in the provinces. It was kept in a box for which she had to ask her mother just as her father had to ask her for the key to the sideboard (chest, box) where his brandy was kept − without which he could not sleep (since he and his wife no longer "slept" together). Dora's dream of wandering around town was also connected with her acting as a guide to her cousin who had just visited Vienna. This visit had reminded her of her own visit to the picture gallery in Dresden where, all alone, she had stood "two hours" before the Sistine

Madonna "rapt in silent admiration." Except for tying the nymphs in the background of the portrait to the lake scene, Freud ignores any analysis of the Madonna. Instead, he pursues the switch between "station" and "box." Noticing Dora's adoption of a male attitude, he insists on her remaining concerned with copulation, both desiring and not feeling free enough for it until her father was dead, as the dream content showed. Thus there is a line between the *Bahnhof* and the *Friedhof* in as much as she would only enjoy intercourse once her father enjoyed the peace of the grave:

> At this point a certain suspicion of mine became a certainty. The use of "*Bahnhof*" ["station;" literally, "railway-court." Moreover, a "station" is used for purposes of "*verkehr*" ("traffic," "intercourse," "sexual intercourse"): this affords the psychological wrapping in many cases of railway phobia] and "*Friedhof*" ["cemetery;" literally, "peace-court"] to represent the female genitals was striking enough in itself, but it also served to direct my awakened curiosity to the similarly formed "*Vorhof*" ["vestibulum;" literally, "fore-court"] — an anatomical term for a particular region of the female genitals. This might have been no more than a misleading joke. But now, with the addition of "nymphs" visible in the background of a "thick wood," no further doubts could be entertained. *Here was a symbolic geography of sex!* "Nymphae" [in German the same word, "*Nymphen*," represents both "nymphs" and "nymphae"], as is known to physicians though not to laymen (and even by the former the term is not very commonly used), is the name given to the labia minora, which lie in the background of the "thick wood" of the pubic hair. But any one who employed such technical names as "vestibulum" and "nymphae" must have derived his knowledge from books, and not from popular ones either, but from anatomical text-books or from an encyclopedia — the common refuge of youth when it is devoured by sexual curiosity. If this interpretation were correct, therefore, there lay concealed behind the first situation in the dream a phantasy of defloration, the phantasy of a man seeking to force an entrance into the female genitals (Freud 1980: 139–140).

Freud's conclusions impressed Dora enough to induce her to add a second ending to the dream. Upon hearing of her father's death "she went calmly to her room and began reading a big book that lay on her writing table." Freud continues to probe into her reading books for the source of her hysterical symptoms — in particular gastric pains and appendicitis. But it is the remark where she pictures herself going up the stairs that leads him to discover that she had developed a limp after her appendicitis and for this reason avoided stairs. Curiously enough, Freud refrains from oedipalizing Dora's limp! Instead, this "true hysterical symptom" (*perityphilitis*) which bore no organic connection, is made to "fit in better with *the secret and possibly sexual meaning of the clinical picture.*" It then transpired that the timing of Dora's appendicitis was nine months after the lake scene and therefore represented a *fantasy of childbirth.* Rather than connect this fantasy to the portrait of the Madonna, to explore the fantasy of the Virgin Mother as an escape which she and her Mother had sought from the polluted sexual economy to which they had been sacrificed, Freud races on to conclude that Dora's limp is a self-punishment for her unconscious wish for defloration by Herr K. — "and Dora disputed the fact no longer." Yet there is a supplementary note. In it, Freud inverts the hierarchy of Dora's association with the portrait of the "Madonna." Firstly, both were adored; secondly, she was motherly to Herr K.'s children; and lastly, she had a child though she was still a girl. In addition, young girls were attracted to the idea of the "Madonna" to relieve their feelings of sexual guilt. Freud specifically ignores the idea of virgin birth, i. e., of immaculate (unstained, unpolluted) conception. He never considers that Dora's reading might have derived from a fascination with an alternative economy of birth — the fantasy of parthogenesis — opposed to the heterosexual economy in which she was to be swapped.

Portrait of Dora with jewels

At several points we have remarked upon aspects of the Dora case which produce an equivocation that feminist critics have explored. The question is, are we dealing with a portrait *of* Dora as the passive object of description, or with a portrait *by* Dora, in as much as her own values and beliefs might have resisted Freud's medicalized and patriarchal viewpoint upon her hysteria. This equivocation riddles the French expression "*Portrait de Dora*" in which Dora is both the material and the form, active and passive, of the picture we have of her. But, even in English, the act of portrayal is never very far from that of betrayal and is never free from the question of justice that divides the artist and the client as viewer. What is true of art in this case is especially true of the literary portrait and the question of Freud's betrayal of his subjects in the case histories will occupy us throughout our study (See also the treatment of fidelity in O'Neill 1982). It is therefore tempting to feminist critics to enter this problematic with the argument that they are in a better position to avoid Dora's expropriation — to restore her name, her values and her struggle to the woman's movement and to fight against patriarchy. Once we begin to see Dora as a fighter, rather than as a minor hysteric whom Freud did his best to render exciting by his own standards of erotic literature, we shall have the true portrait of Dora. I propose now to consider Hélène Cixous's (1983) short and powerful representation of the Dora case in her theater-theory piece, "Portrait of Dora." The play skilfully takes on the temporality and texture of the case history, its dreams and symptomatology, with Freud caught in his own plot. Unfortunately, all I can comment upon is the text of the play in certain "key" places. My intent is to show where Cixous's portrait supplements the case-history with two remarkable fantasies with respect to Dora's relation to Herr and to Frau K., as well as to remark upon a curious re-circulation of the pearl drops longed for by Dora's mother.

The play opens with the lake scene, with Dora "half threatening, half begging": "If you dare kiss me, I'll slap you" (Cixous 1983: 2). Freud wants to know all about it — or rather, wants to know all about what Dora knew all about. Well enough. Yet, what could a young girl know? Everyone in the trio — Father, Herr K., Frau K., — protests that she is "still a child" to be treated like a child. But is she an innocent child, already compliant with the game of deception going on around her? Does not her sexual curiosity betray her? Her protests are perhaps not so much against the game — but against "getting nothing out of it," if she loses, like her mother or like the governess. It is a dangerous but exciting game, behind doors, the key missing, what if...

> Dora: ... if I don't enter, I die, if I entered, if I wanted to see Herr K. but if papa saw me, but I don't want to see him, but if papa saw me see him, he would kill me, I could see him once. It would be the last time. Then... (Cixous 1983: 4).

Dora is caught in a game where she would rather die than be "it" — or die if she is not, at least she would be in the game. But it is a deadly game. It would kill her father if he saw her playing it. And it would kill her if he saw her and did save her because he had already sacrificed her to Herr K. whose flowers would mark her virgin grave:

> Dora: The unsaid, lost, in the body, in between the bodies.
> No need to open it. It's always opened. I can open. Don't open. That man had beautiful teeth, *like pearls on a bracelet*. I can open just slightly. And why wouldn't you open? That which is opened can be unopened. What happened can have not happened (emphasis added) (Cixous 1983: 7).

It will be revealed that Dora's mother had always wanted pearl drop
earrings from her husband and not the bracelet which he offered her and
that she said he might as well give to "someone else" — Frau K., although
Dora hoped to get it. Cixous, however, fantasizes a pearl *bracelet* erasing
the mother's desire and displacing it through Dora upon Herr K.'s pearly
teeth about to sink into Dora's throat but for the knife with which she
slits Herr K.'s throat, according to the law:

> Dora (voice sometimes clear, sometimes drowsy):
> *Waiting wouldn't have helped.* We could have waited, if I had wanted to.
> *I saw him in a dream.* He was mild-mannered, had a pleasing appearance,
> would not stop staring at me. *But it was not him. Is this him now, behind
> the door? I don't know.* I open the door halfway. There's a man in the
> darkness. I can't see his head. He bends down. I understand his motives.
> I shut the door, lock *the latch.* I don't doubt he'll force the door open.
> He's pushing against the latch. *I feel his erection. He's leaning against the
> door. Too late. He's going to force the door open.* He has already opened it.
> I can't close it. The door is pushed open. I push against the door. I gather
> my strength up against the left side of the door. I smell smoke. *How simple
> and deadly everything is. It's Him or Me.* In the darkness I am dark. The
> fictitious flesh that pushes at the door disgusts me. *I must kill. It's a law.*
> It's a key. The one must kill the other who kills the one who wants to kill
> who wants to be killed? *I want to kill him. He knows that. He wants to kill
> me. I know that* (emphasis in original) (Cixous 1983: 7−8).

Cixous's supplement obeys the *lex talionis*, to be sure. But it involves a
fantasy of revenge too terrible for the Dora child. Herr K. is sacrificed
in a ritual slaughter and bloodshed that reverses Dora's defloration,
opening the phallus, closing the hymen. Cixous introduces a founding
rite of feminism whose dramatic excess — conventionally placed off-stage
— risks sacrificing Dora to a sacred struggle quite beyond her vision.
Certainly, Cixous manages thereby to raise the dramatic level of Dora's
irritable throat, whereas Freud had been concerned not to bore his readers
with the story of a minor hysteria. But her version of Dora's capacity
for revenge is rendered far more physical through the fantasy than the
slap or her suicide note or even Herr K.'s accidental death would justify.
But the greatest textual violence lies in the fantasy of extricating Dora
from the web of love and deception which she inhabits like everyone else
to the bitter end. Cixous's determination to depict Dora as an actor able
to cut the knot is marked by a curious indifference to Dora's mother
whose desire to be removed from the unpolluted sexual economy in which
she suffers is expressed not only in her tedious housewife psychosis but
in her wish for a gift of pure seed — the white pearl drop earrings.

Cixous, however, assigns the pearl a place anywhere but where the mother's protest can be located. We have seen that she imagines Dora seeing Herr K.'s teeth like pearls set in a bracelet and she has her telling Freud that Frau K. told her that her pearls looked better on Dora than herself. Again, Dora dreams of Frau K.:

> Dora: Always in white. Milky white veils. Crêpe de Chine. I saw *HER*. The whiteness of her body, especially her back. A very soft luster; *pearly* (emphasis added) (Cixous 1983: 10).

And as she stands in adoration of the Madonna, Cixous has Dora say (recall Herr K.'s teeth):

> Dora: It was *The Sistine Madonna*, I stood, alone, immersed. In the painting. Two hours. In her aura. A very gentle smile. You cannot see her teeth. Only a *pearly* glimmer, between her lips (emphasis added) (Cixous 1983: 11).

Then, somewhat later (Cixous 1983: 14), in a series of exchanges with Freud seeking to establish with whom Dora wishes to be alone, with Frau K. as she imagined, or with Herr K. as he believed − Cixous has Dora dream that Herr K. rejected her:

> Dora: ... then he said these words: "I'm taking back my *pearls*!" He did say that, and then: "I gave you the key to the box; I'm taking it back." What use was it to cry? In the midst of such absurd words? And I said: yes, yes − as if I wanted to die. But what key?
> Herr K.: What key?
> Freud: What box? (emphasis added) (Cixous 1983: 14).

Having displaced her mother's pearls onto Frau K., as one source of Dora's gift, and on to Herr K., as another source of Dora's gift, Cixous loses the key to the case. The "return gift" can only be violent, murderous and revengeful within the heterosexual economy so long as the transcendental fantasy contained in the mother's wish and the Madonna's plenitude is ignored. In part, this occurs because Dora herself projects this transcendent fantasy upon Frau K.'s adorable white body:

> Dora: Her way of looking at herself. Of loving herself. Of not suffering. Of not looking at me. Of looking at me, so calmly. With that smile (Cixous: 1983: 12).

Dora's homosexuality, however, cannot turn against the heterosexual economy in which she is exchanged because she has already internalized the division of the sexes in its reversed love:

> Dora: She's an intelligent woman, superior to the men who surround her, and adorably beautiful! ... How white your back is! and your skin! How I love you!
> (*Murmur and very light brush of a kiss.*)
> Can I? ... and also here, just above.
> You cannot imagine how I love you: if I were a man, I would marry you, I would carry you away and I would marry you, I would know just how to please you (Cixous 1983: 12).

Cixous allows Dora to dream of an omnipotent Frau K., full of everything that women know how to do ... "make jam, make love, put on make-up, bake pastries, *adopt* (sic.) babies, cook meat, dress a bird." But Dora remembers these things only through her grandmother, not her mother − hence the elision of birth and her consequent indecision between the male and female parts which she can resolve only as Frau K.'s man. For her part, Frau K. does not want to be transfigured by Dora. Like the mother, and the governess, and Dora herself − she loves a man, she loves difference and disfiguration: she is full of the fall:

> Frau K.: You are always so serious, my little one: too serious. Be careful. You must know what life is all about. Do you know enough about life? *You cannot be a madonna.* You are too handsome, little one (emphasis added) (Cixous 1983: 29).

It is a rare man or woman who can abandon love's game whatever its injuries. Only Dora's mother seems to have withdrawn from the love market in which husbands, wives, children, and servants are swapped openly or secretly to recover losses and to assuage wounds that no doctor can heal. This is a hard game for children to learn, even though their (sexual) curiosity draws them to it, and repeats the game down the ages. Only a tough child will imagine he or she can play/not play the game better than the old ones:

> Frau K's voice: They all take their guns. They shower Dora with thousands of *pearls* to show she's stronger than all of them combined. They prove this amidst a cloud of smoke.
> When the smoke clears, we see Dora's ghost, the strongest of them all gathering thousands of these small *pearls* in her apron, which she then releases over an opened attaché case. That's in case they might be short of ammunition (emphasis added) (Cixous: 1983: 26).

(*Exeunt omnes*) Dora stands alone, ghostly, stroking a pearl-handled pistol, still smoking. Cixous, too, has bought Freud's shibboleth, firing where there was only smoke. Killing where there was only love. Exchanging Dora for her new sisters.

References

Andrews, Carol
1990   *Ancient Egyptian jewellery*. London: British Museum Publications.
Cixous, Hélène
1983   "Portrait of Dora," *Diacritics* 13(1), 2–32.
Dongerkery, Kamala S.
1971   *Jewellery and personal adornment in India*. New Delhi: Indian Council for Cultural Relation.
Freud, Sigmund
1980   *Case histories*, I. Harmondsworth: Penguin Books.
O'Neill, John
1982   *Essaying Montaigne: Studies in the Renaissance institution of writing and reading*. London: Routledge and Kegan Paul.

Subject Index

Name Index